Dismembered Policing
in Postwar Berlin

Dismembered Policing in Postwar Berlin

The Limits of Four-Power Government

Mark Fenemore

BLOOMSBURY ACADEMIC
LONDON • NEW YORK • OXFORD • NEW DELHI • SYDNEY

BLOOMSBURY ACADEMIC
Bloomsbury Publishing Plc
50 Bedford Square, London, WC1B 3DP, UK
1385 Broadway, New York, NY 10018, USA
29 Earlsfort Terrace, Dublin 2, Ireland

BLOOMSBURY, BLOOMSBURY ACADEMIC and the Diana logo are trademarks of Bloomsbury Publishing Plc

First published in Great Britain 2023
Paperback edition published 2024

Copyright © Mark Fenemore 2023

Mark Fenemore has asserted their right under the Copyright, Designs and Patents Act, 1988, to be identified as Editor of this work.

Cover image: Female uniformed police officers in training attempting resuscitation 1946 © E.O. Krueger / Bundesarchiv
Cover texture: © Nick Iliasov / Unsplash

Bloomsbury Publishing Plc does not have any control over, or responsibility for, any third-party websites referred to or in this book. All internet addresses given in this book were correct at the time of going to press. The author and publisher regret any inconvenience caused if addresses have changed or sites have ceased to exist, but can accept no responsibility for any such changes.

Every effort has been made to trace the copyright holders and obtain permission to reproduce the copyright material. Please do get in touch with any enquiries or any information relating to such material or the rights holder. We would be pleased to rectify any omissions in subsequent editions of this publication should they be drawn to our attention.

A catalogue record for this book is available from the British Library.

A catalog record for this book is available from the Library of Congress.

ISBN: HB: 978-1-3503-3416-8
PB: 978-1-3503-3417-5
ePDF: 978-1-3503-3418-2
eBook: 978-1-3503-3419-9

Typeset by Deanta Global Publishing Services, Chennai, India

To find out more about our authors and books visit www.bloomsbury.com and sign up for our newsletters.

To survivors of trauma, not least those who inhabited Greater Berlin in the period 1945–9.

Contents

List of illustrations	viii
Acknowledgements	ix
List of abbreviations	xi
Introduction: Mentalities as revealed by the history of policing	1

Part I Policing the messy, painful aftermath of defeat. The special conditions and circumstances of policing a post-conflict city, occupied by foreign troops

1	Year zero/zero hour	21
2	Restoring order: Rebuilding the police	40
3	Allied occupation itself a source of crime	61
4	The non-crime of interracial sex	82

Part II Cutting the Gordian knot of overlapping, entangled jurisdictions. The policing implications of ripping a town in two in the opening battles of the 'cold war'

5	Initial cooperation and attempts at four-power government	103
6	The splitting of the police, 1948	123
7	Policing public order without East-West cooperation	142
8	The Soviet Blockade and Allied Airlift	164

Part III Cases of continued cross-border crime amid divided policing. Stopping cross-border crime sprees in their tracks, despite limits on police cooperation

9	Cross-border capers: The Gladow Gang	185
10	The 'charming murderess': Elisabeth Kusian	205
Conclusion		224
Bibliography		237
Index		247

Illustrations

Figures

1	*Frischer Wind*, 1.10.1947	65
2	*Frischer Wind*, 1.11.1948	145
3	*Frischer Wind*, 1.9.1948	149
4	*Frischer Wind*, 15.5.1948	186

Tables

1	Crime Statistics, 1911–47	22
2	Reasons for Women Leaving Police Service, 1947	50
3	Crimes That the WKP (Female Detective Police) Dealt with in the Period 1 December 1946 to 9 April 1947	52
4	Official Black and White Offence (including Venereal Disease) Rates among US Troops in Occupied Germany, 1945–6	84

Acknowledgements

I would particularly like to thank Caroline Brooke, Simon Potter, Kathryn Hurlock, Damian Mac con Uladh, Josie McLellan, Anthony McElligott, Patrick Major and David Meeres for moral support, reading drafts, sparking thoughts or otherwise improving this project. Back in the 1990s, no doubt channelling Jeremy Bentham, Mary Fulbrook, Mark Hewitson and the inimitable Martin Swales helped to form my approach.

I would also like to thank the British Academy, the University of Limerick and the John W. Kluge Center at the Library of Congress for providing generous financial assistance that enabled my research.

I appreciate too the helpful staff of the UK and US National Archives, the *Bundesarchiv, les Archives Diplomatiques*, the *Landesarchiv* Berlin, the Berlin Police Museum and the Federal Commissioner for the Records of the State Security Service. In the latter agency, Herr Dickow was especially helpful. The British Military Government (Berlin) Newspaper Cuttings Archive spans the period 1946–81 and is held at the University of Nottingham. Ta, Ducks!

'Love takes off the masks that we fear we cannot live without and know we cannot live within', James Baldwin wrote in his 1963 novel *The Fire Next Time*. This project would probably not have come into being if John ('Jack') Lea had not sparked an inchoate but unwavering love of history in me at the age of eleven. After his National Service in the Royal Corps of Signals, stationed in Germany and possibly in Berlin, Jack read history at Exeter College. When I encountered him in mid-1980s Lancaster, he had been head of history at the Royal Grammar School there for over twenty years. For Jack, education occurred as much outside as in the classroom. As well as editing the school magazine, he ran both the Chess and the Stamp Club. I did not know it at the time, but he was also an amateur thespian, appearing in *Tartuffe* and *The Madness of George III*. At the tender age of seventeen, I was let loose on the recently united, but still bullet-scarred, city of Berlin, encouraged to experience and explore it fully (albeit possessing only pidgin German), thanks to a grant he disbursed.

LRGS was a school in which forceful personalities abounded as teachers: when he was not terrorizing us with a toy squeaky-hammer or a sawn-off golf club, Brian ('Bas') Salmon loudly proclaimed that it was completely normal to be a bisexual. Stylishly dressed classicist 'Doc' Synge regaled us with semi-pornographic quizzes that put the 'copro' into coprophilia. Puce-faced, quick to anger 'RET' Turner combined an appreciation of romantic French literature with an unusual, but unquenchable, attachment to Birmingham ('We unquestionably possess Europe's largest library and more canals than Venice'). Although he had a sense of the dramatic, Jack was less showy or extrovert: with his combover, forever-creased brown suit and nicotine-stained hands, he seemed worse for wear. The yellow came from the Woodbines that he could be seen puffing in all weathers, at break time, as his hair blew vertical.

What I loved were his tangents, which steadily grew longer and more immersive as we got older. He would start off talking about Cardinal Richelieu and end up back on the still-ruined streets of cold-war Berlin. To my ears, his tales were as intriguing and revealing as those of (a not yet existing) Bernie Gunther. The hate-filled contempt of a Prussian tram conductor at the sight of him, in uniform, alongside a German girlfriend had seared itself into his memory. Jack (or, in reality, John) died in 2016, aged eighty, having led a full and interesting life. My recollections of his stories are too hazy to include in a work of history. Writing this, I realized that he was probably in Germany between 1954 and 1956 (unless the British Army deployed ten-year-olds). Nevertheless, his experiences there were an essential component of the man that he became.

It takes a global village to educate a Modern European historian. Thanks to my old pals Angela Brock, Anita Winkler, Torsten Halsey, Vladimir Orlov, Joey Molenda, Ulrike Ehret, Phil Blood, Nick Terry, Olena Yatsunska, Nicholas St. Hill and Guy Thomas for keeping me sane. I am grateful to licentious Leipzigers Sascha and Ulrike, as usual, for inspiring me and keeping me on my toes. Closer to home, love to Samia, Tariq and Luka for taking my mind off the machinations and assorted body parts.

In their artistry and originality, always pursued with subtlety and grace, Keimoy and Kyra remain exemplars. While naïve humanists like me ponder the meaning of existence, as expressed in the peculiar features and functioning of the world, scientists and innovators like them just get on with improving it.

As Professor Ann Phoenix, of my disruptive, always provoking and challenging alma mater, argues: 'When Black Lives Matter, All Lives Will Matter'.

Abbreviations

AWOL	Absent without Leave
BMW	*Bayerische Motoren Werke* (Bavarian Motor Works)
BstU	Federal Commission for the Records of the State Security Services of the GDR (*Bundesbeauftragte für die Unterlagen des Staatssicherheitsdienstes der ehemaligen DDR*)
CARE	Cooperative for American Remittances to Europe
CDU	*Christlich Demokratische Union Deutschlands* (Christian Democratic Union of Germany)
CIA	Central Intelligence Agency
CID	Criminal Investigation Division, US Military Government
DPs	Displaced Persons
EAC	European Advisory Committee
FDJ	Free German Youth
GASAG	*Berliner Gaswerke Aktiengesellschaft* (Berlin Gas Works Corporation)
GIs	'Government-Issue' US infantry soldiers, phrase attributed to cartoonist Dave Breger
HO	*Handelsorganisation* (East German 'Trading Organization' retail chain)
JCS	Joint Chiefs of Staff
KPD	*Kommunistische Partei Deutschlands* (Communist Party of Germany)
LDP	*Liberal-Demokratische Partei* (Liberal Democratic Party)
MPs	Military Police(men)
NAACP	National Association for the Advancement of Colored People
NAAFI	British Navy, Army and Air Force Institutes (food and retail outlets)
NKVD	People's Commissariat for Internal Affairs
NSDAP	*Nationalsozialistische Deutsche Arbeiterpartei* (National Socialist German Workers' Party)
NSRB	*Nationalsozialistischer Rechtswahrerbund* (National Socialist Association of Legal Professionals)
OMGUS	Office of Military Government, United States
POWs	Prisoners of War

PX	American Post Exchange (store selling produce on a military base)
RIAS	Radio in the American Sector
SA	*Sturmabteilung* (Paramilitary Nazi stormtroopers)
SED	*Sozialistische Einheitspartei Deutschlands* (Socialist Unity Party of Germany)
SHAEF	Supreme Headquarters Allied Expeditionary Force
SPD	*Sozialdemokratische Partei Deutschlands* (Social Democratic Party of Germany)
SS	*Schutzstaffel* (Protection Squads)
UNRRA	United Nations Relief and Rehabilitation Administration
USSR	Union of Soviet Socialist Republics
VVN	*Vereinigung der Verfolgten des Naziregimes/Bund der Antifaschistinnen und Antifaschisten* (Association of Persecutees of the Nazi Regime/Federation of Antifascists)
WSP	*Weibliche Schutzpolizei* (Female Uniformed Police)

Introduction

Mentalities as revealed by the history of policing

As the war in Europe came to an end, the autopsy room in the *Hannoversche Straße* had been thoroughly looted. Pillaging most of the equipment, the raiders had left only the corpses. Without working air-conditioning, the bodies began to putrefy. Ominously, rats could be heard scurrying about in the morgue cellars. Berlin's foremost autopsist coped with the stench of an overflowing mortuary, using cigarettes and perfume-soaked handkerchiefs. While he dissected, swallows flew in through the shattered windows, in search of maggots. Conducting autopsies without running water, soap or climatization was challenging, to say the least. Suicide victims, mainly women and children, began to pile up. They lay alongside murder victims, some of whom had been partially hacked to pieces. In his words, it was a veritable 'kaleidoscope of horror'.[1]

As this book will show, many people thought that artificially dividing the defeated, prostrate city (into international sectors) made it a breeding ground for crime. In this sense, dismembered corpses were an expected, if unnatural, consequence (and by-product) of artificially dividing (and geopolitically 'dismembering') the city. For a long time, large parts of the city appeared as prone, and devoid of life, as the bodies on the slab. Nevertheless, despite assisting in its dismemberment in July 1945, the Western Allies began nursing their half of the city back to health. In the spring of 1945, the devastated, bullet-scarred, partially flattened city of Berlin stood at the crossroads of an exhausted and freshly carved-up Europe.[2] As well as waves of German refugees from the East, there were significant numbers of recently released foreign Prisoners of War (POWs) and Displaced Persons (DPs) passing through. The Soviet victory and sole occupation of the city had been marked by a collapse of law and order. The arrival of the other three occupation armies, in the summer of 1945, partially ended the period of fear and anarchy, but complicated the situation of governance, with significant implications for policing. Each occupation government brought with it its own working methods, preoccupations, culture and ideology. This book assesses postwar Berlin from the perspective of four-power government, particularly in relation to policing.

Ruined Berlin represented the intersection of multiple alternative narratives. The fragmented, war-ravaged surface concealed a complex, ambivalent history.[3] Taking account of the differing viewpoints of the various actors, the book approaches Berlin from multiple perspectives. Historians tend to pick a side before studying the Allied occupation of Berlin. Although the French Sector is no longer entirely neglected, accounts of Soviet and American actions predominate.[4] We currently lack an in-depth study of the British Sector or an examination of how the various sectors interacted.

While most studies of occupied Berlin concentrate on one of the four Allies, this one focuses on the stances and interactions of all four Military Governments, as well as the two rival and increasingly hostile police forces.[5] The files of the occupation governments themselves constituted the main sources for this international, multi-archival approach. In addition, we have memoirs, local police reports, newspaper clippings and newsreel films. Occupation historian Susan L. Carruthers stresses the role intimate eyewitness accounts, in her case soldiers' letters, can play in reconstructing postwar (and cold war) mentalities.[6] Police self-understandings are as important as issues of personnel, equipment and technical proficiency.

This book explores the crucial role played by the Allies in influencing the culture and operation of the German police in the four-power, post-conflict city. As such, it has relevance beyond the history of postwar Germany. In the last hundred years, similar issues have arisen in the policing of divided cities like Jerusalem, Belfast, Shanghai, Danzig and Trieste. Many of these were also 'post-conflict cities', with implications for how they could be policed. Although Alice Hills cited Berlin, along with Vienna, as a key example of such a city, with regard to policing reforms, nobody has studied either city thoroughly using this theoretical lens.[7] Was Berlin sui generis, an incomparably exceptional case, or did it behave similarly to other cities emerging from the violence of war?

Although there are several excellent studies of the Allied occupation of Germany and the onset of the cold war, this is the first to see the breakdown of four-power cooperation through the perspective of policing. Such an approach allows the study of wider, fundamental questions concerning the relationship between crime-fighting and civic governance (or domination). This allows a reassessment of what it meant to live in (and to be) a city under foreign occupation. For many Berliners, order and policing were synonymous; post-1945, they suffered a shortage of both. Even when a city is not in crisis, the police are at the forefront of dealing with emergencies involving citizens. Through cooperation and understanding, they can seek to resolve problems affecting the community. Ideally, policing is about providing security and reassurance, as well as arresting criminals. In some regimes, the relationship of domination (or *Herrschaft*), based on violence, is more transparent and/or legitimate than in others. We do not need to witness a policeman kneeling on someone's neck for several minutes, until the life drains from their body, to know that policing can also be an illegitimate expression of cruelty and disregard for life.[8] With revolution underway in his homeland, German historian and social theorist Max Weber agreed with the (Soviet) People's Commissar for Foreign Affairs and Brest-Litovsk, Leon Trotsky, that 'Every state is founded on violence'.[9] Whether between or within states, politics (and policing) were (and are) about obtaining, defending, distributing and, only occasionally, about relinquishing power. Weber defined *Herrschaft* in terms of an ability to enforce one's own will, despite opposition and antagonism. In the physical form of policemen and women, the state demands obedience, claiming them to be 'the bearers of legitimate power' (commonly expressed through unchallenged violence).[10]

For *New York Times* correspondent Drew Middleton, postwar Berlin combined the ambiance of a garrison town, a ramshackle mining camp and the setting for tales of espionage and skulduggery.[11] In the thirty-six months following the defeat, there was plenty of violence but precious little order. Post-1945, Greater Berlin created a unique urban container, bottling up and influencing local inhabitants. Together, Berliners and their occupiers coexisted, interacted and cooperated against the ruined backdrop. Nevertheless, misunderstandings and frictions could occur, often expressed through ferocious words and physical violence. In postwar Berlin, the wielding of legitimate authority was complicated by foreign occupation, aimed at transforming the German people, by re-educating them (to 'civilization' and democracy) after National Socialist tyranny and genocide.[12] At the end of the period, rival police forces faced each other across the geopolitical chasm of a dismembered, ripped apart city. Continuing crime and disruptions to law and order were also expressions of an absent sovereignty, with profound implications for hegemony as well as for administrative mastery.[13] The new police agencies played a very important role in putting the city back on its feet. However, as a fledgling force made up of individuals, many of whom lacked policing experience, it faced overwhelming obstacles, challenging the uniformed profession's ability to cooperate and capacity to exercise *Herrschaft*. The example of policing in postwar Berlin thus makes it possible to address wider questions concerning the history of mentalities.[14] Against a backdrop of distrust and propaganda point scoring, the ideological and geopolitical field of force, represented by that pressurized container, could heighten the emotions, experienced by Berliners, until they reached a fever pitch.

Occupier-occupied relationships went much further (and deeper) than abstract discussions about lofty principles in stuffy *Kommandatura* meetings (the four-power body tasked with governing the city). Berlin was a centre not just for geopolitical tension, but also for intimate, personal-political (or biopolitical) entanglements between the rulers and the ruled.[15] Imbalances of power could thus be experienced personally and privately 'between the sheets', as well as publicly and violently in the streets. This gives an alternative perspective on dominance, mastery and control. Examining policing in cold-war Berlin thus complicates our notions of complicity, consent, control and 'crisis'. As well as a technological modus operandus, or means of attacking a problem, policing is also a performance of ideology, self-conception and gender.[16] In Berlin, as in the American Zone, ugly expressions of racial prejudice often jarred with official espousals of freedom and democracy. The gender and racial aspects of the occupation alter our understanding of relations of power, hierarchy and hegemony.[17] This book focuses on the beliefs, values and mentalities that influenced crime and policing in postwar and early cold-war Berlin. Such an approach combines micro-historical close-ups, in the form of case studies, and wider, more panoramic tracking shots. Viewing the city in this way makes it possible to shift the lens of examination and scrutiny from the important and eminent actors at the apex to the human beings at the bottom of the pyramid of power and privilege. The shift in perspective and approach makes it possible to reconceive and reassess the cold war, as fought in Berlin.[18]

This approach sees mentalities as expressed principally through behaviour rather than through discourse. On its own, but particularly when it is deployed on behalf of ideology, violence can have semantic force. It is possible to recast policing during the early cold war as a specific set of practices, outlooks, modi operandi, performances and experiences. If the proof of the pudding is in the eating, the policing of criminal (and criminalized) behaviour provides a more persuasive indicator of mentality than words on their own.[19] As a consequence, the focus of this book is as much on the concrete mechanisms of surveillance and control, as expressed by the policemen facing one another across the invisible border, as on vistas of division, as expressed through discourse. As such, concrete behaviour can provide us with alternative, non-discursive socio-historical transcripts. Currently, the literature divides over whether to see entanglements as principally or predominantly geopolitical (often expressed socio-economically through cross-border smuggling or the black market) or intimate and sexual (in other words 'biopolitical').[20] Of course, the black market was intimately connected to sex. Acting as protectors conveyed notions of gender as well as reflecting a hierarchical understanding of patron-client, ruler-ruled, Allied-German relationships. Such imbroglios affected perceptions of legitimacy and public confidence in authority as well as complicating law enforcement. The occupiers' attempts at radically altering the German political system – together with education, culture and mentalities – cannot be seen as separate from the 'sexual politics' engendered by the occupation. Blatant moral failings could only demoralize the people they were supposed to be re-educating.

Clash of cultures in the 'goldfish bowl' of postwar Berlin

In examining the history of the four victorious powers, and of their neighbouring sectors, it would be easy to fall into national stereotypes: loud and brash Americans; stiff-upper-lipped Englishmen; preening, peacock-like Frenchmen; and sly, cunning Russians (and Germans). This was, after all, how contemporaries tended to talk about one another when not lapsing into clear racism.

> A large part of the Red Army is derived from races which have only recently come in touch with what we think of as civilisation. Many of them – the Asiatic ones – have in their blood a tradition of cruel and ruthless warfare. And, in fact, they have been fighting against the Germans a cruel and ruthless war. . . . It is unfortunate that British soldiers can talk to the Germans but not to the Russians. It is unfortunate that these varied races in Russian uniform tend to emphasise the racial kinship of the British and Germans.[21]

Having been subjected to years of propaganda, orchestrated by Joseph Goebbels, Germans were conditioned to see the non-European Soviet troops in their streets as 'mongoloid-animalistic' and particularly savage.[22] However, on arrival in Hitler's defeated capital, British and American troops quickly picked up similar prejudices. With notions of pride overlapping with, and bleeding into, experiences of shame, the clash of cultures in postwar Berlin was referred to very often in racial terms. Having followed the reversals of fortunes between 1940 and 1945, Western Europeans commonly had a clear hierarchy (or league table) of cultured and uncultured races. It is nevertheless jarring to read, in a work of contemporary history, that 'the French, for all their Negro troops and the stories of their degeneration, were a cultured race'.[23]

Although the racial understandings have gone out of fashion, a certain amount of the one-upmanship remains.

In embracing their role as occupying powers, the representatives of the four nations balanced their requirement to act as protectors for the Berliners with their wider responsibility, as guardians of democratization and denazification, to humanity as a whole. In large part, the occupation of Berlin was a matter of prestige for the Western Allies. Franco-German historian Dorothea Führe sees evidence of a general neglect for the French Sector, on the part of historians of the cold war.[24] Latecomers in arriving in Berlin, the French were keenly disappointed at only receiving two fairly tatty and down-at-heel boroughs, on the northern fringes of the city.[25] These were parts of the British Sector that the haughty 'Anglo-Saxons' no longer wanted. The French authorities correctly took their allocation of such marginal districts as a slight, symbolic of France's postwar weakness and humiliating loss of stature.[26] This was a far cry from the last time French forces had occupied Berlin, 140 years earlier. In October 1806, Napoleon had celebrated his victory with a parade down *Unter den Linden*. Not content with humiliating their enemy, with pomp and ceremony, the French had stripped the Prussian capital of its prized possessions. These included the quadriga from the magnificent but subjugated Brandenburg Gate, which Napoleon had boxed up and sent to Paris.

The French keenly felt the snub at not being invited to the Potsdam Conference (17 July to 2 August 1945). It has been suggested that in 1945, having been granted scraps from the table of the mighty, the French found it hard to inhabit the role of magnanimous victor convincingly. Although immediately stigmatized as 'second-class victors', by sceptical Berliners, they sought to act as if they were still important and powerful.[27] In December 1944, the French diplomat René Massigli had fondly imagined that France would occupy the centre of Berlin, the cultural and strategic heart of the city. It was natural for him to imagine the Gendarmenmarkt, Französische Straße and Pariser Platz would thrive in French hands.[28] In this context, the French considered it a humiliation to be given such unimportant and culturally barren districts. Reinickendorf and Wedding lacked theatres, opera houses, museums and publishers of note. Their seemingly benighted inhabitants could have little need for universities or libraries worthy of the name.[29] The French never stopped coveting the greener grass of the other sectors. Although their military men believed that they had just helped to win the war, this was not a view shared by the other Allies.[30]

Even without hubristic displays of pomp and envy, running and policing a major city on a four-power basis was a challenging undertaking, fraught with potential for misunderstandings. The American (Deputy) Military Governor, Lucius D. Clay, saw Berlin as a precedent and model for international cooperation at the fledgling United Nations. In spite of initial optimism and goodwill, however, partnership proved difficult. The requirement for translation into three languages made meetings glacially slow moving. With such wide differences in culture and ideology, achieving unanimity was frequently difficult if not impossible. Each power had a veto and could use it to stymie four-power government. The *Kommandatura*'s responsibilities were so wide-ranging that it lacked clear demarcations and boundaries.

The cultural differences between the occupiers were real enough, but they tended to get filtered through national stereotypes. This was possibly the first time that representatives of the different nations had tried to work with each other so closely, since the Versailles peace negotiations of 1919. While attempting to get along, contrasting outlooks and methodologies overlapped with differences in personality and character. The French repeatedly referred to the 'phlegmatism' displayed by the 'Anglo-Saxons' (lumping together both the British and the Americans, as if they were indistinguishable). For his part, Maxwell D. Taylor, US Commandant from 1949 to 1951, praised his French counterpart, General Jean Ganeval, as 'a most reasonable, intelligent man', who generally eschewed the propensity for creating needless difficulties that French officials usually displayed.[31] The foremost US soldier-diplomat, General Clay, was initially more reticent, arguing that it was impossible to get the smallest smidgeon of support, even moral, from the French.[32] By contrast, Clay found Marshal Vasily Sokolovsky a pleasant and intelligent interlocutor. The American knew no other person who could quote the Bible so accurately. A deeply cultured man, he was particularly fond of the novels of Jane Austen.[33]

The British and American Military Governors, who in 1948 galvanized the united response to Soviet aggression, shared a certain introversion and aloofness. General Clay referred to Sir Brian Robertson (Military Governor of the British Zone and later High Commissioner to the Federal Republic) as 'typical of what we have come to expect from the regular British officer – well groomed, poised, reserved almost to the point of stiffness'. In the difficult days of 1948, he proved a splendid and dependable ally. Nevertheless, despite all they had in common, the West Point graduate found it difficult to break through his ally's seemingly impervious 'outward reserve'.[34] Robertson was too reticent (or diplomatic) to say what he really thought of Clay. He did, however, reveal that 'The Englishman likes the role of proconsul, and indeed he is good at it; we have had much experience as a race'. Echoing the Roman lyric poet Horace, he insisted that the Western Allies had ruled justly, firm in their enlightened purpose. They had refused to be swayed by the multitude of voices, clamouring for them to take hasty but wrong decisions, nor by the looming presence of a menacing tyrant.[35]

Robertson accredited the Western Allies' success in Germany to what he saw as 'the innate decency and Christian charity of the Anglo-Saxon peoples'.[36] He also believed that if the Military Governors concentrated on the job at hand then the principles would resolve themselves.[37] Many Germans had the feeling that the unflappable, but steely, British officers were treating them like an unruly 'Indian mountain tribe'. The old colonial elite was doing everything in its power to turn its new subjects into loyal and obedient vassals. In Berlin, the Allies often expressed 'quasi-imperialist' perceptions and mentalities in relation to their German subjects. For one American observer, 'really open-minded Britishers were rare'. The Soviets may have offended British notions of sportsmanship and fair play, but the British in turn alienated the other Allies with their blatantly patronizing attitudes, notably towards the Soviets. For his part, the extrovert and outspoken (not to say irascible or foot-in-mouth) American Deputy Commandant, Colonel Frank L. Howley, described the Soviets as 'thick-skinned and impervious to sarcasm'. Nevertheless, by taking their behaviour personally, he allowed them to get under his own skin.[38] Despite worsening relations, the British tended to underplay how serious the situation was. As an Air Commodore confided to his boss's wife, Lady Tedder: 'Our Russians, particularly General Alexandrov, who went to the opera with us, are being naughty and exasperating, but in the air we have their measure and there is nothing they can do.'³⁹

There was a strong urge to infantilize the Soviets, thereby underestimating their skills and abilities, not least in byzantine manoeuvring.⁴⁰ Still smarting from their experience in 1940, the French wondered how the Soviets could have defeated the Germans with such ragtag, undisciplined troops. Ordinary British soldiers came to Berlin expecting to get on famously with the Russians, but their actual actions and behaviour caused surprise, then disillusionment and ultimately disgust.⁴¹ Jokes about the Soviets' supposed lack of toilet training reinforced notions of racial and cultural superiority, on the part of both the Western Allies and defeated Berliners.⁴² In the clash of civilizations that was postwar Berlin, the Soviet side was widely seen as poor, backward and simple; their men as childish, dangerous and stupid. Although there was plenty of competition and conflict amid the rubble, servicemen could also find unexpected affinities. Despite his guff about Slavs and Teutons, occupier-turned-historian Michael Balfour liked what he called 'the natural Russian, inquisitive, garrulous, introspective and jovial, serenely indifferent to the passage of time'.⁴³ Philadelphian author William Gardner Smith recounts:

> We visited the British often because they liked 'you brown Americans'. . . . The Russians often were like little children and they did crazy things. . . . But they were friendly to the American Negroes, offering us vodka and pounding us hard on the back when they greeted us on the street.⁴⁴

Some Allied soldiers preferred the company of pleasant, interesting and intelligent Germans to time wasted with slow-witted and uncongenial fellow countrymen. In the first years after the war, Allied soldiers, Military Government employees and civilians moved easily between the four sectors, taking in the sights, sounds, smells and experiences. 'We could go anywhere we wanted to in Berlin.'⁴⁵ For them, living in the postwar city was like a paid holiday, but with four different foreign cultures and cuisines to taste. The defeated capital may have offered more rubble than palm trees, but it nevertheless represented a playground, with a wide range of seedy bars and exotic nightclubs open all night.

The palimpsest city

What defines a city? What shapes its character, its personality, its ethos? Is it defined by its people or vice versa? The influx of tens of thousands of foreigners – many not speaking the language, some still teenagers, who all lived according to their own laws – did alter the dynamic. While, for the Allies, Berlin was something of an exotic playground, for the Berliners, in May–August 1945, life had been reduced to bare survival. The consequences were not immediately apparent, but the Soviets' actions on taking Berlin rapidly transformed the Red Army (in the eyes of Berliners and, eventually, of the Western Allies) from heroes to villains. Even after the other Allies arrived, desperation, violence and disease stalked the ruins. Large areas of the city seemed like an empty, obliterated husk. The Allies remarked on the fact that the Berliners wandering the streets seemed dazed rather than defiant; hunger was omnipresent and insatiable. Many Berliners had been perpetrators in or bystanders to Nazi crimes, but after the Battle of Berlin, they came to see themselves as survivors and victims. Heaping their contempt on foreign DPs, some of them Jewish survivors, they quickly began to see themselves as the injured parties, in a corrupt black-market economy that existed with the knowledge and connivance of Allied troops.

The Western Allies went into Berlin determined to cooperate with the Soviets and to remain aloof from the Germans. Anti-fraternization orders required them to express disdain and distrust even when they had to work with German local officials and experts. Having seen the horrors of the Concentration Camps, the Allies went into Berlin expecting to treat the Germans harshly. They assumed that nearly all Berliners were corrupt and tainted former Nazis. At first, ordinary occupation soldiers expressed overt hostility and wrath towards the Germans they encountered. They told each other that these defeated and dejected souls deserved their misfortune. Such an attitude made it permissible to exploit them sexually and to prey on their weakness.

The present in 1945 was built on layers of the past.[46] As well as Berlin's recent role, as capital of the Third Reich, it was also the repository of memories about Weimar freedoms and excesses. Something of Berlin's reputation as a sinful city had survived national socialism. As the historian of sexuality and vice, Jennifer V. Evans, argues: 'Relished by teen gangs, frequented by rent boys, and sought out by prostitutes, Berlin's ruined bunkers and bomb cellars served as emblems of the chaos and lawlessness of defeat.'[47] In traversing the city, foreigners and Berliners carried expectations, whetted by stories about sensuous, Weimar-era Berlin. As well as preaching high-sounding virtues, like democracy and freedom, the occupiers also wanted to get 'down and dirty' with the Berliners, exchanging bodily fluids for food. The inequity and vicissitudes of such a relationship are one of the themes of this book. For their part, when they arrived, American wives had few qualms about exploiting German desperation, in order to swap food and cigarettes for valuable heirlooms. While the rank-and-file went out into the black market, officers' spouses let it come to them. Pedlars sold porcelain and silverware door-to-door.

Those who have lived among them will know that it is rare for Berliners to be speechless, or to hold back with criticism. The citizens of this once-great city became all too familiar with the quirks and idiosyncrasies of their foreign occupiers. In the goldfish bowl of the four-sector city, the Allies judged each other just as the Berliners judged them. Various correspondents asserted that the defeated Germans cynically spread oral propaganda about their occupiers:

> The Russians are dirty, they eat with their hands. . . . The Americans have no manners, they always talk in a loud voice. . . . All Russian women look dowdy, they have no [fashion] sense. . . . All American women are empty-headed, they don't care for anything except money and clothes.[48]

When the Allies came together to govern defeated Berlin, they illustrated the huge disparities that existed in wealth and organizational structure between them. To

Germans, the Americans, with their excess of tinned goods, appeared nonchalant and impossibly wealthy, apparently 'bored with the monotony of Europe'. Soviet soldiers, meanwhile, supposedly gawped, wide-eyed in wonder, at the luxuries of western living standards, but smelled of the cowshed.[49] As well as new sights, sounds and smells, the occupation of Berlin created a novel emotional landscape, reflective of differences of mentality.

The unique experiment in four-power government

As well as offering temptations to travellers, Berlin offered a unique experiment in four-power government. As cold-war historian Hope Harrison argues, the cold war 'began and ended in Germany', but decisions in Moscow and Washington also played an important role in creating the new era of hostility and tension.[50] At times, Berlin lagged behind; at other times, it acted to accelerate and heighten the ideological fissure.[51] During the period 1945–9, Berlin became the arena in which the cold war was waged on an everyday basis 'in microcosm'. Even before World War Two had ended, Prime Minister Winston Churchill had begun highlighting what he saw as Soviet bad faith since the Yalta Conference. Foreseeing the difficulties, which would arise if the Soviets were allowed to take Berlin single-handedly, Churchill had wanted British and American troops to capture the capital before the Soviets. However, he failed to persuade Supreme Commander, General Dwight Eisenhower, to alter his battle plan.[52] As the Soviets cemented their hold over Eastern Europe, Churchill began to talk privately of an 'Iron Curtain' descending across Europe. If the Berlin genesis of the cold war can be disputed, the modes of war of nerves and brinkmanship certainly originated in Berlin.

Two major sticking points for East-West cooperation were the issue of reparations and the forced merger, in the Soviet Zone, of the Communist and Social Democratic parties (KPD and SPD). The Soviets and the French desperately needed reparations, in order to rebuild their shattered, war-torn economies. The British and Americans had made promises to their Allies in relation to reparations but wanted to wait until their zones were again economically viable before releasing payments. The French and the Soviets thought that reparations should precede unification while the British and Americans came to believe the reverse: central political and economic control were essential for recovery. They saw no reason why they should provide food and resources from their own stocks to the West Germans so that they could pay reparations to the Soviets.

With hindsight, it would be easy to see the cold war as inevitable. In the first weeks of the occupation, American troops had shot and killed Soviet soldiers in Berlin. The Allies had also arrested what they termed 'NKVD snatch squads' (agents of the People's Commissariat for Internal Affairs) in their sectors. Looking back, western observers tended to see early Soviet actions as deliberate and pre-emptive. Siting important institutions in their own Sector, while continuing to squat at strategic points in the others, showed considerable power-political foresight. The arrival of the Ulbricht Group (a Communist provisional government led by future East German dictator Walter Ulbricht), while fighting was continuing around Hitler's bunker, showed that the Soviets had thought carefully about securing their power in the defeated city. From the start, their representatives were perspicacious and farsighted as well as peremptory and unpredictable. They would have been happy to accept local democracy if the population had been willing to vote Communist. However, although the Soviets could be wilful and arbitrary in their dealings with the Berliners, so too, to a lesser extent, could the other Allies in the first years after the war.

Despite obstructionism, all four powers did make genuine attempts at cooperation in the first two years of the occupation. Fear and distrust of the Soviets, because of their role in committing mass rapes and disappearing Berlin citizens, were important but were nevertheless tinged with grudging respect. Without Soviet sacrifices, Germany would probably not have been defeated so quickly and so comprehensively. The Treptow Memorial, on top of a mass grave, was an object of veneration not just for the Soviets. Even with the onset of the cold war, the Western Allies may have condemned the Soviets and their East German underlings day-in-day-out, but they retained some residual, grudging respect for the Red Army as Allies and fellow victors in World War Two. Although the cold war destroyed most of the spirit of four-power obligations, the Western Allies saw it as opportune to preserve some of their shared duties. Despite increasing hostility and venom, from 1948 onwards, the four Allies continued to guard the old and expensive Spandau Prison complex together. This arrangement ended only when the last prisoner, Rudolf Hess, committed suicide in August 1987.[53] Although West Berlin was increasingly drawn into West Germany's orbit, the Allies refused to allow the city to join the Federal Republic as a component federated *Land*. Even after abandoning their radio station in Charlottenburg, in July 1956, Soviet guards continued to police their war memorial (as an important Soviet quasi-enclave in the British Sector) into the early 1990s. These continued institutional obligations and jurisdictional entanglements express the messiness of the postwar Berlin situation.[54]

Methodology: History of mentalities

The police constituted both a political instrument and the organization tasked with solving crimes. This book is the first to address both functions in the difficult postwar period, 1945–50. It explores how (geo)political division was imposed on the city, encouraging rather than fundamentally altering the behaviour of the criminals. As such, it is, in part, a history of (cold war) mentalities as well as of law and order. In developing this approach, the research was most influenced by Robert Darnton's ethnographic microhistory and Alf Lüdtke's everyday-history approach.[55] Anthropologist Clifford Geertz influenced both practitioners of 'history from below'.[56]

Along with Berlin-based German historians Burghard Ciesla, Michael Lemke and Thomas Lindenberger, Reading University's Patrick Major and the North Americans Paul Steege and Jennifer V. Evans pioneered an everyday approach stressing how porous, ambivalent and entangled cold-war identities were.[57] Their focus is on Berliner outlooks and identities rather than on the melting pot of cultures and perspectives. Using multiple archives (in Berlin but also in Paris, Washington and London), it is possible to identify and assess a range of specific cold-war 'mentalities'. The political scientist who coined the terms 'biopolitics' and 'geopolitics' argued that 'The ideal state must be a nation-state', structured outwardly 'so that the nation does not spill over its borders into other states, and inwardly so that no other nations spill over their borders into it'.[58] Even with the onset of the cold war, Berlin remained ethnically and linguistically homogenous. As systems of meaning, capitalism and communism tended to act like oil and water. Nevertheless, in terms of human behaviour, the 'East' of the city bled into 'West', like an invasive watercolour, and vice versa. Each side saw the other as alien and trespassing. Oftentimes, the juxtaposition of the hostile systems created a liminal, 'betwixt and between' space, neither outrightly at war nor fully at peace, which robbed the geopolitical power actors of authority and purchase.[59] This book shares Steege's focus on the specific 'set of meanings and practices' created by the city's peculiar 'liminal state', but goes beyond the policing of smuggling to assess the political and psychological dimensions of division and how they impacted on crime and policing. Where Berliners got their precious (and deeply appreciated) coal, potatoes or milk during the Blockade was important, but it was one aspect among several.

Although fragile, malleable and often obscured, 'mentalities matter'. They give geopolitical boundaries concrete form. Borderland anthropologist Daphne Berdahl focused on 'walls in the head' before and after 1961.[60] Such work provides an example of how to approach the layered borderscape with equanimity and curiosity. Separately, Thomas Lindenberger and Richard Bessel approached the operation and functions of the East German police, in an effort to discover more about East German social history.[61] Without the crucial local (political and social) context, the cold war, as fought in Berlin, is cut off (like a dismembered body part) from its actual meaning and import. This book starts from the premise: What if we write the postwar/cold-war history of Berlin from the perspective of local actors? Ultimately, the goal of this book is to apply an approach developed by the Marxist historian E. P. Thompson. His aim of writing 'history from below' can be applied to the field of postwar and cold-war studies in Berlin.[62] In the early 1960s, Thompson and his French counterparts pioneered histories, focused on the 'lived experiences' of ordinary people, rather than of the high and the mighty. Such an approach puts ordinary people – with their foibles, weaknesses and (both serious and petty) crimes – centre stage.

Microhistory is better able to capture the ambiguities and multiple contradictions represented by pseudo-protests in the early cold war not to mention the cross-border disposal of bodies. German *Alltagsgeschichte* (the history of everyday life) and Franco-Italian *microstoria* (microhistory) are competing lodestars in seeking to elucidate non-Marxist experiences of the oppressed. Teasing out the connections between the micro and the macro, the everyday version of microhistory provides a valuable set of conceptual tools. Anthropologically informed everyday history, of the sort pioneered in the study of the Third Reich, provides a useful guide. Exploring the 'lived experiences' of ordinary Berliners and their occupiers allows historians to situate their actions in the 'concrete webs of social relations'. While, in part, rejecting Marxist conceptions and ideological baggage, the history of everyday life sought 'to awaken a feeling of *Betroffenheit*', or historical empathy, for the disadvantaged and the marginalized.[63] Cultural anthropology has unquestionably enriched our understanding of people in the past by shifting the focus from top-down social structures to (potentially bottom-up) everyday practices.⁶⁴ Gilbert Ryle came up with the concept of 'thick description', later popularized by Clifford Geertz, for finding our feet as outsider observers (and connecting) with a strange, foreign people. The insight they both drew from the term is less about description than about perception: 'A statesman signing his surname to a peace-treaty is doing much more than inscribe the seven letters of his surname.'⁶⁵ Everyday history gives us both close-ups and panning shots. At times, other people's behaviour can be strange, alien and irregular: 'Doing ethnography is like trying to read (in the sense of "construct a reading of") a manuscript – foreign, faded, full of ellipses, incoherencies, suspicious emendations and tendentious commentaries.'⁶⁶ Actors produce behaviour that is symbolic, even if that is not their explicit intention.

Immersing oneself, like a detective, allows the possibility of microscopic analysis. Thanks to reading real detective reports, the researcher can know the colour of the victim's tie, the shape of the kitchen knife used to cut up his body and the social relationships of the shared flat in which he was dismembered. Some historians like to imagine that they are actual detectives.⁶⁷ Yet these analogies say more about our romantic fantasy than about reality: 'I slam the car door, light a cigarette and look over the façade of the building with my coat collar turned up.' Seeing himself reflected in a shop window, veteran everyday-anthropological historian Lutz Niethammer could only laugh at 'the splendid detective-film pose' he had assumed.⁶⁸ Like detectives, historians seek to elucidate the systematic within the episodic.⁶⁹ The hidden secret of historical research is that they rely not just on laboriously assembled evidence but also on intuition or gut feeling. Some suggest that there are parallels between the way historians approach cold cases and how detectives read a crime scene. We attempt to understand societies in the past, by interpreting and deciphering clues. Nevertheless, historians have different standards of proof and evidence to police investigators and lawyers.⁷⁰ Like crime-fiction writers, historians are also interested in story and plot, dropping important clues to the reader. Nevertheless, there is an 'uncanny valley' feeling about the blurring of fact and fiction. The historian of the Third Reich Raul Hilberg found novelist Robert Harris's mixture of an authentic document with invented quotations deeply disturbing.⁷¹

History from below is, in part, about giving voice to the voiceless. Citizens do not sink much lower than when they have been killed, dismembered and scattered in the ruins of a devastated city. Within narratives of global one-upmanship, waged by mutually exclusive, would-be messianic powers, there is space for examining otherwise voiceless subaltern groups. By exploring how people in the past tried to live their lives, their concrete behaviour reveals cultural and temporal shifts in psychology and mentalities. Although hunger, necessity and trauma were important, in creating propitious circumstances for crimes of violence to develop, the stimulus for criminal actions was also often unfulfilled longings and yearnings.

Chapter breakdown

This book examines the policing of Berlin from Germany's defeat in May 1945 through to 1950, focusing particularly on the onset of cold-war division in 1947–8. The intervening period saw a novel attempt to govern Berlin mutually (and internationally) by means of the Allied *Kommandatura*. Its Public Safety Committee, together with the individual sector commandants and the Berlin City Executive (or *Magistrat*), all competed to reform and direct the re-established police force.[72] As such, the city was an unparalleled experiment first in four-power government and then in cold war. Part I focuses on the impact of Germany's defeat on the policing of Berlin, in other words, how it was governed as a post-conflict city. Referring to the period, remembered by Berliners as one of utter lawlessness, it asks what the implications of defeat were for law and order.

Policing played an important role in the development of misunderstandings and tensions that ultimately found expression as the 'cold war'.[73] Part II examines the attempt to make four-power government work both in the *Kommandatura* and outside on the streets. Using two case studies of cross-border crime, Part III explores the implications of division for everyday detective work and policing. It demonstrates that by rendering coordinated police action – and mutual assistance in cross-border investigations – more difficult, the open (but divisive) border between the eastern and western sectors created opportunities for criminals to exploit. In 1949–50, the wounds of the city and its people were still fresh.[74] Along with desperate hunger and deprivation, the anomalous situation of a city divided (or dismembered) into four sectors – some of them mutually hostile – encouraged renewed crime waves.

Notes

1 Waldemar Weimann, *Diagnose Mord: Die Memoiren eines Gerichtsmediziners* (Bayreuth: Hestia, 1964), 275–6.
2 Sylvia Conradt und Kirsten Heckmann-Janz, *Reichstrümmerstadt: Leben in Berlin 1945–1961* (Darmstadt: Luchterhand, 1987).
3 Jennifer V. Evans, 'Life Among the Ruins. Sex, Space and Subculture in Zero Hour Berlin', in *Berlin Divided City, 1945–1989*, ed. Philip Broadbent and Sabine Hake (New York: Berghahn, 2010), 20.
4 Norman Naimark, *Russians in Germany: A History of the Soviet Zone of Occupation, 1945-1949* (Cambridge, MA: Belknap Press of Harvard University Press, 1995). William Stivers and Donald A. Carter, *The City Becomes a Symbol: The U.S. Army in the Occupation of Berlin, 1945-1949* (Washington, DC: Center of Military History, United States Army, 2017). Dorothea Führe, 'Der Vergessene Sektor. Die französische Besatzungsmacht in Reinickendorf und im Wedding', in *Sterben für Berlin? Die Berliner Krisen 1948: 1958*, ed. Burghard Ciesla, Michael Lemke and Thomas Lindenberger (Berlin: Metropol, 1999). Dorothea Führe, *Die Französische Besatzungspolitik in Berlin von 1945 bis 1949: Déprussianisation und Décentralisation* (Berlin: Weißensee-Verlag, 2001).
5 In the absence of memoirs, Jones carried out interviews with veterans. He was particularly interested in differences between Anglo-American and Continental conceptions of policing and how these impacted on the resurrected force. Eugene Gilbert Jones, 'The Allied Reconstruction of the Berlin Police, 1945-1948', PhD, University of California, San Diego, 1986, xx, 6, 179. Since his excellent thesis, the rebuilding of Berlin's police force has attracted little attention in German or English.

6 Susan L. Carruthers, *The Good Occupation: American Soldiers and the Hazards of Peace* (Cambridge, MA: Harvard University Press, 2016), 14.
7 Alice Hills, *Policing Post-Conflict Cities* (London: Zed, 2009).
8 Nevertheless, the video of George Floyd's murder was incontrovertible evidence of that. 'How George Floyd Was Killed in Police Custody', *New York Times*, 24 January 2022.
9 Weber gave the talk on 28 January 1919 in Munich. Max Weber, 'Politik als Beruf', in *Geistige Arbeit als Beruf. Vier Vorträge vor dem Freistudentischen Bund* (Munich: Duncker and Humblot, 1919), 4. *The Monopoly of Violence*, directed by David Dufresne (France 2020). Even today, those in power continue to present the police as paragons of virtue, almost like 'latter-day saints'. Robert Reiner, *The Politics of the Police* (Brighton: Wheatsheaf, 1985), xii.
10 Weber, 'Politik als Beruf', 4.
11 Drew Middleton, *Where Has Last July Gone? Memoirs* (New York: Quadrangle, 1973), 148.
12 Both Berlin and Vienna possessed police forces tainted with violence and repression. Lindsay K. MacNeill, 'Professionalism and Brutality: The Viennese Police and the Public in Extraordinary Times, 1918–1955', PhD, American University, Washington, DC, 2020, 341, 347.
13 Stuart Hall et al., *Policing the Crisis: Mugging, the State and Law and Order*, 2nd edn. (Basingstoke: Palgrave Macmillan, 2013), 206, 211, 214.
14 Patrick H. Hutton, 'The History of Mentalities: The New Map of Cultural History', *History and Theory* 20, no. 3 (1981): 237–59.
15 The idea of bio- and geopolitics being connected came from conservative Swedish political scientist Rudolf Kjellén, who coined both terms. Rudolf Kjellén, *Die politischen Probleme des Weltkrieges* (Leipzig: B.G. Teubner, 1916), 46. Such ideas were appropriated by Adolf Hitler in the form of *Lebensraum*. Michel Foucault reappropriated the term, disconnecting it from its Nazi baggage and seeing it as the juxtaposition of 'the permitted and the prohibited', in the form of the 'veridiction of desire'. 17 January 1979, Michel Foucault, *The Birth of Biopolitics: Lectures at the Collège de France, 1978-79*, ed. Michel Senellart (Basingstoke: Palgrave Macmillan, 2008), 35. My use of the concepts of biopolitics and biopolitical differ slightly from theirs.
16 Klaus Weinhauer, *Schutzpolizei in der Bundesrepublik: zwischen Bürgerkrieg und innerer Sicherheit: Die turbulenten sechziger Jahre* (Paderborn: Ferdinand Schöningh, 2003).
17 Hall et al., *Policing the Crisis*, 201.
18 Cf. Mark Fenemore, *Fighting the Cold War in Post-Blockade, Pre-Wall Berlin: Behind Enemy Lines* (London: Routledge, 2019), 13.
19 In both Berlin and Vienna, these were part of the contested legacy of national socialism. MacNeill, 'Professionalism and Brutality', 347–8.
20 Atina Grossmann, *Jews, Germans and Allies: Close Encounters in Occupied Germany* (Princeton, NJ: Princeton University Press, 2009). Jennifer V. Evans, *Life Among the Ruins: Cityscape and Sexuality in Cold War Berlin* (Basingstoke: Palgrave Macmillan, 2011). Paul Steege, *Black Market, Cold War: Everyday Life in Berlin, 1946–1949* (Cambridge: Cambridge University Press, 2007).
21 Alexander Clifford, 'Shots and Suspicion Split the Rulers of Berlin', *Daily Mail*, 6 November 1945. Michael Balfour, himself an occupation officer and ex-psychological-warrior, repeated this argument that the Soviet troops were 'no more Russian than Gurkhas are English'. He quoted an unnamed Soviet source as

saying, 'The Red Army perished on the battlefields of 1941 and 1942. These are the hordes of Asia whom we have whipped to war'. Michael Balfour, *West Germany: A Contemporary History* (London: Croom Helm, 1982), 111.
22 See Schöneberg resident, Franz Göll's, diary entry from 3 May 1945 in Peter Fritzsche, *The Turbulent World of Franz Göll: An Ordinary Berliner Writes the Twentieth Century* (Cambridge, MA: Harvard University Press, 2011), 180–1.
23 Michael Balfour and John Mair, *Four-Power Control in Germany and Austria, 1945–1946* (London: Oxford University Press, 1956), 58.
24 Führe, 'Der Vergessene Sektor', 79.
25 Patrick Major, *Behind the Berlin Wall: East Germany and the Frontiers of Power* (Oxford: Oxford University Press, 2010), 26.
26 Führe, *Die Französische Besatzungspolitik*, 242–3.
27 Wolfgang Schivelbusch, *In a Cold Crater: Cultural and Intellectual Life in Berlin, 1945-1948*, trans. Kelly Barry (Berkeley, CA: University of California Press, 1998), 30. Cf. Führe, *Die Französische Besatzungspolitik*, 5.
28 K. H. Adler, 'Selling France to the French: The French Zone of Occupation in Western Germany, 1945-1955', *Contemporary European History* 21, no. 4 (2012): 577–8.
29 Schivelbusch, *In a Cold Crater*, 30.
30 Wilfried Loth, 'Die französische Deutschlandspolitik und die Anfänge des Ost-West-Konflikts', in *France-Allemagne 1944-1947*, ed. Klaus Manfrass and Jean-Pierre Rioux (Paris: Institut d'histoire du temps present, 1990), 85.
31 He, nevertheless, doubted Ganeval had a 'particularly brilliant military record', given France's showing in World War Two. Interview with Maxwell D. Taylor, 14 May 1981, Landesarchiv Berlin, B Rep. 037, Nr. 96, 6.
32 Jean Edward Smith (ed.), *The Papers of Lucius D. Clay. Germany, 1945-1949* (Bloomington, IN: Indiana University Press, 1974), 2, 704.
33 Jean Edward Smith, *Lucius D. Clay: An American Life* (New York: H. Holt, 1990), 262.
34 Lucius D. Clay, *Decision in Germany* (Westport, CT: Greenwood, 1970), 106. For his part, SPD politician, Dr Otto Suhr, praised Robertson's 'chivalry and impartiality'. 'Berlin Tribute to Sir Brian Robertson', *Manchester Guardian*, 16 June 1950.
35 Robertson suggested that the ode was particularly appropriate to the Control Commission in Germany. *British Zone Review* 1, no. 8 (1946): 2, as cited by Christopher Knowles, 'Winning the Peace: The British in Occupied Germany, 1945-1948', PhD, Kings College, London, 2014, 43.
36 Lord Robertson of Oakridge, 'A Miracle? Potsdam – Western Germany 1965', *International Affairs* 41, no. 3 (1965): 407, 409.
37 F. J. Leishman for Foreign Office, 16 June 1947, C8122, UK National Archives, FO 371/64457 as cited by Stivers and Carter, *The City Becomes a Symbol*, 197.
38 Frank L. Howley, *Berlin Command* (New York: G. P. Putnam's Sons, 1950), 98.
39 Air Commodore R. H. White to Lady Tedder as cited by Richard Reeves, *Daring Young Men: The Heroism and Triumph of the Berlin Airlift, June 1948-May 1949* (New York: Simon and Schuster, 2010), 34. The original letter from 9 June 1948 is displayed in the Allied Museum Berlin.
40 Gordon Harrington talked of their 'strange mixture of savagery and childishness'. Gordon Harrington, 'How Berlin Looks', *The Spectator*, 27 July 1945, 77.
41 Richard Brett-Smith, *Berlin '45: The Grey City* (London: Macmillan, 1966), 54.
42 Steege, *Black Market*, 25.
43 Balfour and Mair, *Four-Power Control*, 47–8.
44 William Gardner Smith, *Last of the Conquerors* (London: Victor Gollancz, 1949), 58.

45 'A Lot of Pleasure in Berlin' – Interview with Lawrence Johnson', http://www.aacvr-germany.org/ (accessed 1 May 2013).
46 MacNeill, 'Professionalism and Brutality', 341–3.
47 Evans, 'Life Among the Ruins', 12.
48 Ernest Borneman, 'Back to Berlin: The Diary of a Native's Return', *Harper's Magazine*, August 1948, 66.
49 Erich Kuby, *The Russians and Berlin, 1945*, trans. Arnold J. Pomerans (London: Heinemann 1968), 209, 212.
50 Hope Harrison, 'Berlin and the Cold War Struggle over Germany', in *The Routledge Handbook of the Cold War*, ed. Artemy M. Kalinovsky and Craig Daigle (London: Routledge, 2014), 56.
51 David E. Barclay, 'Division of the Spoils: Berlin as Symbol and as Prize', in *Cold War Berlin: Confrontations, Cultures, and Identities*, ed. Scott H. Krause, Stefanie Eisenhuth and Konrad H. Jarausch (London: Bloomsbury, 2021), 33. Cf. Carolyn Eisenberg, *Drawing the Line: The American Decision to Divide Germany, 1944–1949* (Cambridge: Cambridge University Press, 1996).
52 Schivelbusch, *In a Cold Crater*, 9–10.
53 Within weeks, the British had begun demolishing the prison complex so that it would not become a shrine to one of the last Nazi war criminals. 'No Respite for Spandau', *Times*, 19 August 1987.
54 Fenemore, *Fighting the Cold War*, part one. The Allies departed in 1993.
55 Robert Darnton, *The Great Cat Massacre* (London: Penguin, 1991). Alf Lüdtke, *The History of Everyday Life: Reconstructing Historical Experiences and Ways of Life* (Princeton, NJ: Princeton University Press, 1995).
56 Clifford Geertz, 'Thick Description: Toward an Interpretive Theory of Culture', in *The Interpretation of Cultures* (New York: Basic Books, 1973), 3–30.
57 Ciesla, Lemke, and Lindenberger (eds), *Sterben für Berlin*? Major, *Behind the Berlin Wall*. Evans, *Life Among the Ruins*.
58 Kjellén, *Die politischen Probleme*, 46.
59 Steege, *Black Market*, 12, 293.
60 Daphne Berdahl, *Where the World Ended: Re-unification and Identity in the German Borderland* (Berkeley, CA: University of California Press, 1999).
61 Thomas Lindenberger, *Volkspolizei: Herrschaftspraxis und öffentliche Ordnung im SED-Staat, 1952–1968* (Cologne: Böhlau, 2003). Richard Bessel, 'Policing in East Germany in the wake of the Second World War', *Crime, History and Societies* 7, no. 2 (2003): 5–21.
62 E. P. Thompson, 'History from Below', *The Times Literary Supplement*, 7 April 1966, 279–80. As early as 1932, *Annales* founder Lucien Febvre had argued that history written from below, focused on the masses at the bottom, rather than on the stars (*vedettes*) at the top of the pyramid, would be more interesting and revealing.
63 Brad S. Gregory, 'Is Small Beautiful? Microhistory and the History of Everyday Life', *History and Theory* 38, no. 1 (1999): 100–4.
64 Before introducing his ideas to an American audience, Lüdtke explored the possibilities of historical anthropology in the journal *Historische Anthropologie*.
65 'The Thinking of Thoughts: What Is "Le Penseur" Doing?', in *The Thinking of Thoughts*, ed. Gilbert Ryle (Saskatoon: University of Saskatchewan, 1968), 20.
66 Geertz, 'Thick Description', 22.
67 After the war, Philip Kerr's hardboiled detective, Bernie Gunther, could not make the trip home 'to his beloved Berlin'. Too many people knew him there and a good

number of them wanted him dead. So he wandered between the Côte d'Azur and West Germany. Jane Kramer, 'The Third Reich's Good Cop: Philip Kerr's Bernie Gunther Solves Crimes for Nazi Germany. Why Do We Like Him So Much?', *New Yorker*, 3 July 2017.
68 Lutz Niethammer, *Ego-Histoire? Und andere Erinnerungs-Versuche* (Vienna: Böhlau, 2002), 12.
69 Gregory, 'Is Small Beautiful?', 102.
70 Achim Saupe, *Der Historiker as Detektiv – der Detektiv als Historiker: Historik, Kriminalistik und der Nationalsozialismus als Kriminalroman* (Bielefeld: transcript, 2009), 46, 51. Lothar Kettenacker, 'Der Historiker in der Rolle des Kriminalkommissars', *Süddeutsche Zeitung*, 6 November 2006. Carlo Ginzburg, *The Judge and the Historian*, trans. Antony Shugaar (London: Verso, 1999).
71 Saupe, *Der Historiker as Detektiv*, 319.
72 Jones, 'The Allied Reconstruction of the Berlin Police', 85.
73 Fenemore, *Fighting the Cold War*.
74 Karen E. Till, 'Wounded Cities: Memory-work and a Place-based Ethics of Care', *Political Geography* 31, no. 1 (2012): 3–14.

Part I

Policing the messy, painful aftermath of defeat. The special conditions and circumstances of policing a post-conflict city, occupied by foreign troops

1

Year zero/zero hour

Berliners commonly referred to the catastrophic collapse of order that occurred in their city immediately following the death throes of Hitler's Third Reich as zero hour. In the final, agonizing hours of defeat, the crimes committed by Nazi henchmen began to merge with those perpetrated by Soviet soldiers, German civilians and released forced labourers. In April–May 1945, the clock literally stopped; the German war effort shuddered to a halt and the nation collapsed into chaos and anarchy.[1] Then, slowly and painfully, the survivors began their lives again from scratch. Their minds were not wiped clean; not all of them deserved a fresh start. However, although damaged and dazed, they began to re-establish life in the city.

The Battle for Berlin

Hitler's refusal to consider surrender meant that Nazi Germany would only be defeated by a bitter house-to-house conflict, amid the ruins of an already devastated city. In late April 1945, the noose tightened. Faced with unrelenting shelling, Berliners retreated to the cellars. The once proud master race was reduced to a rat-like existence. Forced into proximity, neighbours and strangers grew to rely on each other but also to hate one another.[2] There were heartbreaking accounts of lost children found wandering without parents in the ruins.[3] Determined to defend every floor of every house, SS men hanged people from lamp posts for trying to desert. Some policemen were tasked with burning records; many others were killed in the fighting or in rescue work. The Police Presidium building on Alexanderplatz was almost completely destroyed in one of the last bombing raids. With it went a large part of the criminal records, fingerprint databases and 'rogues' galleries'. The Soviets sent anyone they captured, who was wearing a uniform, eastwards into captivity. As well as members of the SS, *Wehrmacht* and *Volkssturm,* the column of dejected captives also included police, firemen, railway guards and tram conductors.

Disorder following defeat

In the regime's death throes, horror followed horror with little respite. Then suddenly, on 30 April 1945, Hitler committed suicide in the bunker and it was all over. Germany had ceased to be governed weeks before; there was no longer any functioning administration. In the absence of policemen, little effective policing occurred. Some foreign forced labourers sought revenge for all the abuse and humiliations they had suffered. Kuby estimated that as many as 800,000 'foreign workers' (forced and POWs) remained in the Berlin area; however, this figure seems incredible.[4] A minority significantly exacerbated the breakdown of law and order, by embarking on an orgy of looting, drunken rape and murder. The war had greatly increased the reservoir of hard, dangerous, desperate men who were willing to turn to crime in the stark conditions of postwar Germany. This included a roving band of Spaniards, dubbed the 'romantic robbers'. Having narrowly escaped execution, they had somehow managed to gain release, thanks to indiscriminate Soviet clemency.[5] The sudden collapse of the Nazi dictatorship removed effective policing at the very moment that crime was increasing exponentially. The streets were littered with firearms and body parts as well as debris. Insufficient rations encouraged blackmarket trading, using looted property. Caught between necessity and opportunity, the normal inhibitions, in relation to unlawful activity, were fatally eroded. Young people, in particular, were seen as 'running wild', without the usual normative curbs to constrain them.[6] It is difficult to get accurate crime figures for the period April–September 1945. Nevertheless, in July 1945, the authorities recorded 123 murders, 598 attacks on women, 1,483 robberies and 5,500 black-market arrests. Several German policemen were shot while trying to hinder looting.[7] Table 1 suggests that robberies peaked in the postwar years.

With legally obtainable food insufficient to support life, the population had little choice but to engage with the black market. There, unrepentant Nazis rubbed shoulders with desperate refugees together with Soviet soldiers. The chaos and destruction wrought by war encouraged crime, while at the same time seriously impeding police attempts to prevent it. Bomb damage made apartments difficult to secure. Unless they possessed a working telephone, victims of night-time burglaries could not report the crime until the curfew was lifted the next day. Nevertheless, contrary to expectations, the occupation did not encounter serious resistance.[8] Apart from sporadic assassinations of Soviet officers, the expected insurgency and *Werewolf* actions did not materialize. In terms of public order, the dazed Berliners were remarkably quiescent; most of the problems were caused by renegade Soviet troops.

Table 1 Crime Statistics, 1911–47

	1911–13	1922–4	1946	1947
Murder, attempted murder and manslaughter	152	350	351	172
Infanticide	14	15	15	11
Robbery, looting	271	799	3,012	1,358
Bodily injury	5,439	4,328	2,327	1,469

'Kriminalität und Polizei in Berlin', *Die Volkspolizei. Zeitschrift für das Gesamte Polizeiwesen* Nr. 4 (June 1948), Landesarchiv Berlin, C REP 120, Nr. 3249.

Mass rapes

In the days and weeks after the end of the fighting, Soviet officers proved unwilling or unable to control their men. Captured field post indicates the mood of the troops who descended on the city: 'Our revenge is just fine. Fire for fire, blood for blood, death for death.'[9] Lev Kopelev received a prison sentence of twenty-five years for protecting German civilians against his fellow soldiers. He recorded his commanding officer, Colonel Zabashtansky, urging the troops to do what they wanted and to 'Hammer away!' Creating such fear that the victims' great-grandchildren would remember and be afraid was the desired effect. He encouraged his troops to 'kill the little Fritzes in the heat of the moment', until his troops were thoroughly sick of massacring and raping.[10]

The result of this widespread desire for revenge was mass indiscipline, drunkenness, thefts and mass rapes.[11] Berliners remember the terror they felt in April–June 1945 as Soviet soldiers swept the cellars, taking watches ('*Uri, Uri*') and picking female victims ('*Frau komm*').[12] Ordinary citizens entered an excruciating, never-ending nightmare, in which the few, remaining German men were unable to offer any protection. Survivors bitterly stress their timorousness and willingness to trade women's immediate safety for their own.[13] Far from defending women, men often told them to submit to their fate. An anonymous journalist provides a detailed account of the terror-filled ordeal. She remembers her countrymen telling her not to resist so that she would not get them into trouble.[14] However, the horror of being unable to protect their wives and children naturally weighed heavily on ordinary men and to suggest otherwise is to downplay their suffering. Soviet soldiers often raped their victims repeatedly, while forcing other family members to watch.[15] Their inability to intervene, to defend their loved ones, was the worst experience of these men's lives. Some courageous policemen were arrested by the Soviets, and sentenced to an uncertain fate, for trying to prevent rapes.

In recording the horrors, contemporaries agreed that no woman was safe: not Antifascists, not victims of Nazism, not hospital patients, nurses or even nuns.[16] The rapists considered any woman still alive in Berlin, regardless of her age or physical appearance, as fair game. Above all, the survivors stress the unpredictability. The same Soviet soldiers, who were abusing them night after night, could suddenly and unexpectedly show kindness to the sick or injured. Some raped with an air of embarrassment; some wanted to impress their fellow soldiers; a few demonstrated absolute hatred and sadism; most were inebriated.[17] They justified their behaviour by saying that on the road to Berlin they had seen too many horrors wrought by retreating German troops. Gang raping women in front of their children was particularly callous but not uncommon.

Some of the rapists expressed a disconcerting nonchalance about their crimes. They felt perfectly entitled to rape the conquered like this was the most normal thing in the world. Soviet historian Dan Healey argues that in the Russian countryside violence, misogyny and lack of consent often dominated heterosexual interactions.[18] US journalist Cornelius Ryan suggests that it was not necessarily the front-line fighters who did the most damage. Rather, it was the reserve troops who were most aggressive, in seeking to subjugate the women conquered by braver men.[19] For Germans, already traumatized by incessant bombing and weakened by hunger, the nightmare went on night after night, for weeks on end. Women were vulnerable in the cellars, but also when they went out to look for bread or water. Going to the building's communal lavatory became an unprecedented act of heroism. Few dared to perform the trip alone. However, in the accounts of the inescapable, endemic rapes, real trauma is mixed with undiluted Nazi racism. Victims assumed that it must have been those that they found physically repulsive, the 'Mongolians', who had raped them. Even though there were very few genuine Asian troops in Berlin, incessant Nazi propaganda had taught German civilians to assume that they would be overrun by a 'primitive Asian horde', so that was what they saw.[20]

Survivors had to endure sexually transmitted diseases as well as physical injuries. In the event of pregnancy, many were desperate to get abortions. As the victims of a horrific but taboo crime, they felt ashamed and tainted. Even if witnessed, there was virtually no chance of bringing the perpetrators to justice in the summer of 1945. There was no functional police to report crimes to or which could investigate. Although the Soviet authorities quickly encouraged newspaper printing, none could report on the major crime wave or warn civilians to take precautions. Nevertheless, there was an overwhelming sense of collective suffering. At the time, it was clear that the rapists were not just hurting an individual, they were punishing the German people as a whole. As historian Antony Beevor argues, rape in war is a 'collective experience'.[21] There is no question that the rapes were committed deliberately in order to humiliate the Germans.[22] There were rumours that a minority of Berliners took the message and killed themselves. 'Honour lost, all lost' were the words of one horrified, bewildered father. For a daughter subjected to twelve rapes, he could only offer a rope. In the circumstances, there were no words he could find to keep her alive.[23]

Nevertheless, even in the midst of this unprecedented torment, women developed strategies to survive. A common trick was to try to make themselves look old and ugly in order to avoid rape. They wore male clothing and smeared themselves with dirt or faecal matter. They masked their bitter resignation to an inescapable fate with pragmatic cynicism and the blackest of gallows humour.[24] For the anonymous journalist, prostituting oneself to a protector, with access to food and shelter, made more sense than remaining cold, hungry and at the mercy of the rabble. In her mind, she had 'to find a single wolf' to escape the pack. She would attach herself to an officer – 'as high-ranking as possible, a commandant, a general, whatever I can manage' – in order to carry on surviving.[25] Some women simply gave up: in July, a 35-year-old housewife reported herself to the police for the murder of one daughter and the attempted murder of the other. Raped by five Soviet soldiers, she wanted only to end it all. Having cut her own and her one-year-old daughter's wrists, she ordered the older daughter to do the same. Although aged only eleven, she manifested a stubborn determination to carry on living. While able to prevent her mother from killing herself, the baby was already drowned. Recognizing the extent of this family's desperation, the judge set her free.[26]

Norman Naimark has studied the rapes, using both German and Soviet sources. He argues that historians will probably never know exactly how many German women were raped by Red Army soldiers.[27] Mayor Ferdinand Friedensburg reckoned that as many as half of all women aged between sixteen and sixty had been raped.[28] Journalist Ruth Andreas-Friedrich comes up with a similar figure, based on her contacts at the Charité hospital. In the waiting room, she recalled faces expressing utter bewilderment and despair. Their eyes revealed how terribly weighed down they were by the cruel burden fate had imposed on them.[29] They had been forced to pay the price of retribution for Nazi crimes. Nevertheless, the rapes also served to emphasize German victimhood and to deflect attention away from complicity.[30] For this reason, the Western Allies were often initially reluctant to give the rumours credence. Many soldiers went into Berlin convinced that suffering would provide the Germans with a salutary lesson in civilized behaviour. Those among the victors, who heard the stories, rationalized that, given the suffering of the Soviet people during the German invasion, a certain amount of anger and desire for revenge was to be expected. They dismissed tales of brutality as the natural sort of thing Nazis would say. For *Le Monde* journalist, Pierre Frédérix, the stories recounting 'rape and pillage' constituted the main topic of conversation between Germans and their occupiers. Suggesting that such tales of horror were coloured by Nazi propaganda, he argued that it was difficult to know where reality ended and the psychosis began.[31] Nevertheless, over time, Allied soldiers came to identify with the suffering of the women of Berlin and to see the Soviets as characteristically cruel and vindictive.

The callous indifference of the Soviet High Command to the rapes increased the sense of grievance and injury. Lieutenant-General Vasily Sokolovsky supposedly told journalist Alexander Werth, in a 5 June interview, that it was natural for 'nasty things' to happen at the end of a racial war of annihilation. The fan of Jane Austen suggested that the 'master-race (*Herrenvolk*)' women had it coming. His major concern was not injury to German pride but the horrendous 'spread of clap' among his own troops.[32] Soviet figures of authority tended to excuse and dismiss the actions of their men as a natural response to the flush of victory. The Soviet-licensed newspaper *Tägliche Rundschau* was trolling its German readers when it referred to the 'chivalrous behaviour' demonstrated by the Red Army towards the civilian population.[33] The journalist Rudolf Herrnstadt was one of the German Communists who accompanied the Red Army into Berlin. Writing about it later, he referred to 'the muck of history' clinging to the invaders' boots. Recognizing that the soldiers were inflamed and, in parts, brutalized, he stressed that it was war that coarsened people.[34] His fellow Communist, Hermann Matern, privately admitted that it would now be almost impossible for the party to win German women over to its cause.[35]

While some Antifascists tried to understand and explain what the Soviets had done, others could only despair at their behaviour. Robert Bialek was an Antifascist resister and later the police chief of Dresden. His world collapsed when two ordinary Soviet soldiers raped his wife and subjected his sister to an attempted rape. Through their brutish actions, they had demoralized him in a way that no Nazi tortures had succeeded in doing.[36] Another Berliner, a Social Democrat who had been ready to welcome the Red Army as liberators, found that their indiscriminate violence broke his heart: their coarse actions sullied 'all the beautiful phrases'. No German would ever believe the propaganda now. The attacks, many in broad daylight, totally destroyed the confidence of many workers in anything akin to communism.[37] Behind closed doors, German Communist leaders complained that the actions of Soviet troops – continuing to dismantle factories and to extract reparations from current production as well as the rapes and the robberies – were doing them no favours.[38] If Stalin had genuinely desired to win over the German people, then the actions of his troops went completely against this aim. The brutality of Soviet conduct seemed to prove the veracity of Nazi propaganda. For his part, the Soviet dictator viewed his troops as letting off steam. Equally perversely, he saw any protests by members of the Ulbricht delegation as besmirching the honour of the Red Army.[39] The sense of fear and animosity, created by such insensate, misdirected fury, was to last for decades, fatally tainting the Communist project.

Without scrutiny from the Western Allies, this vacuum of power lasted the best part of two months. The very force responsible for creating fear and disorder, by raping and stealing from the Germans in the areas under their control, was also responsible for policing. Rationing no longer worked; with the food supply broken down, the main priority of the population was to get some, any food. The image of desperate crowds 'hacking chunks of meat' from dead horses, reproduced in Rossellini's *Germany, Year Zero*, had a place in reality.[40] The sight of female Berliners, up to their elbows in blood, suggested desperation but also primal ruthlessness in response to precariousness. The Soviets did not limit their search for material reparations to the eastern sector. They ensured that about 70 per cent of the industrial capacity of West Berlin, not destroyed by the war, was dismantled and shipped over the border.[41] The electrical industry was particularly hard hit; the Soviets carted off a whole modern power plant they found in what became the British Sector. In addition, Soviet forces took most of the buses, streetcars and (overhead) *S-Bahn* trains. Although of questionable value to the Soviet economy, with much material dismantled by non-experts and left to rust in rail sidings, this wrecking denuded the western sectors of valuable machinery. When they arrived, the Western Allies viewed this deliberate stripping of the city of resources as an unfriendly act akin to looting. Anything of real value had been taken. When the British finally reached their Sector, they were surprised to find that the Soviets had taken everything, down to individual light bulbs, door handles and taps.[42] The later British Commandant, Major-General Otway Herbert, referred to the Soviet dismantling as 'systematic looting'.[43] One prime target was the atomic reactor at the Max Planck Institute. Some suggest that its 'uranium oxide stocks' were the real reason Stalin was so desperate to be the first to Berlin.[44]

Soviet pre-emptive political reorganization

With Germany defeated and the other Allies hundreds of miles away, the Soviets began systematically reconstructing life in the city according to their own ideas of correct governance and societal development. By taking the capital before the other Allies could get there, Stalin had unquestionably taken possession of the city. Following twelve years of dictatorship, and months of intense suffering, what little was left of city government had crumbled away to nothing. On 17 May 1945, the Soviets appointed a City Executive (*Magistrat*) for Berlin. It was no accident that nine out of the sixteen members of this organ of the city government were Communists. Although the Soviet-appointed Mayor was not a party man, his Deputy Karl Maron was the real power behind the throne. By July 1945, when the Western Allies arrived, the Soviets had been able to stack the deck of cards in their favour. Walter Ulbricht and other leading German Communists had arrived by plane as early as 30 April, the day Hitler committed suicide.[45] Before his untimely motorcycle accident, Soviet commander Nikolai Berzarin ensured that key strategic positions in the police were securely in Communist hands.[46] He was particularly effective in ensuring that any 'rebuilding of the police' in the city would be undertaken by loyal Communists. As the youngest member of the Ulbricht Group, Wolfgang Leonhard recalled that surviving exile leader's main idea for political organization was subterfuge: 'It's quite clear – it's got to look democratic, but we must have everything in our control.'[47] The permitted parties all pursued 'Antifascist' politics along Soviet lines, giving the Communists a head start. As early as 21 May 1945, *Berliner Zeitung* began publication, with the subtitle 'Organ of the Red Army'. It was edited by Soviet officers, resistance fighters and members of the Communist Party of Germany (KPD).

Negotiating the Western Allies' entry to Berlin

Despite being the product of long hours of intense discussion, the actual details for the division of Berlin into sectors, and Germany into zones, were somewhat sketchy and haphazard. One envisaged solution had been to divide Germany into four zones that would radiate out of Berlin 'like the spokes of a wheel'.[48] James W. Riddleberger, of the American State Department, did suggest dividing Germany into three, wedge-like segments centred on Berlin. Nevertheless, this 'cartographically clear' and, in some ways, 'geometrically elegant' solution failed to find favour. It was judged too utopian and abstract, ignoring physical features like rivers and other obstacles.[49] Although keen to demonstrate international cooperation, negotiators insisted that the zones required defensive boundaries. At a micro-level, the geopolitical wedges would have led to roads and houses being cut at odd angles, with one stretch of tarmac or part of a bedroom in one jurisdiction and the rest in another. A winding road, for example, would have crossed repeatedly in and out of different sectors.

The solution found for dividing up Vienna shows that the situation in Berlin could have been even more complex and difficult. The British Sector of Vienna had a Soviet enclave in the middle of it. In addition to four sectors for the victorious Allies, the centre of Vienna, referred to by the Allies as 'Bezirk I', had been declared an international zone. Here, all the Allied Powers were supposed to act in concert, jointly providing security and control. Each nation took it in turns to garrison the International Sector, on a month-by-month rotation basis, which coincided with chairmanship of the Inter-Allied Council. As a consequence, law and order in the Austrian capital became the permanent shared responsibility of all of the Allied Powers, acting in unison and in concert. Joint patrols were known as 'Four Men in a Jeep' operations.[50] They manifested the difficulties of policemen with different cultures and languages working together in a confined space. Despite occasionally pulling pistols on one another to decide which police station they should take suspects to, they were said to have developed a strong esprit de corps.[51]

Despite long and complex negotiations, the Western Allies went into Berlin without clear and unequivocal guarantees on supply and access. With Germany defeated and war in Europe over, Marshal Georgy Zhukov unexpectedly made Allied entry to Berlin conditional on British and American forces vacating the territory they currently occupied in what was to be the Soviet Zone. It had taken the British Foreign Office from January 1944 to May 1945 to realize that they had gifted Stalin far more territory than he had ever expected to get. Realizing the unexpected largesse that had been handed to his Soviet counterpart (who now controlled nearly all of Central and Eastern Europe), British Prime Minister Winston Churchill furiously tried to back-pedal on the British and American withdrawal. Recognizing the strategic value of capturing Berlin, he desperately tried to get a meeting of the big three prior to ordering any departure of Allied troops from Soviet Zone territory.[52] Arguing that Stalin's bad faith in relation to Poland (and other breaches of the shared understanding at Yalta) justified a rethink of the commitments made, he questioned why Britain and America should observe Yalta to the letter while Stalin systematically breached every agreement on Polish democracy with impunity. Churchill increasingly came to see conformity to the agreements, by withdrawing from the Soviet Zone without reaching agreement on such sticky issues, as a defeat. Despite being very rude and undiplomatic to the Soviet Foreign Minister Vyacheslav Molotov, President Harry Truman did not believe that the US or Britain could renege on their commitments, to withdraw from the Soviet Zone. This was, after all, what Roosevelt and Churchill had agreed to after long-drawn-out consideration and careful, detailed discussions.

If Truman had supported Churchill in using the huge preponderance of Allied troops in Germany to alter the status quo, then the deadlock between the West and the Soviet Union would have become an open rift much sooner. Privately, Churchill was already talking about an Iron Curtain, which had fallen across Europe.[53] He commissioned 'Operation Unthinkable', which assessed the possible outcome of an attack by British and American troops on Soviet forces stationed in East Germany.[54] In the end, Churchill was thwarted by Truman's reluctance to abandon the agreements reached at Yalta and was forced to leave the Potsdam Conference because the British public had voted in a Labour government. By this point, the Western Allies were exhausted by war and had little appetite to renegotiate the occupation of Germany from the beginning.

Arrival of the Western Allies

At the beginning of July 1945, the Soviets 'grudgingly' admitted the Western Allies into Berlin, nearly three months after their own arrival.[55] Stalin had stalled Churchill by arguing that his senior military men had to return to Moscow for the spectacular victory parade. Also citing problems with clearing mines, in the ruined German capital, he was probably simply gaining time for his troops to complete their extraction of plant and machinery. Entry to Berlin was conditional on prompt and complete Allied withdrawal from the Soviet Zone. Colonel Frank Howley had tried several times to lead a reconnaissance party to the American Sector but kept getting turned back when he reached Potsdam. Then suddenly, on June 30, he was ordered to abandon all his plans and move his troops to Berlin post-haste. Having kept them out, the Soviets suddenly insisted that they immediately move to Berlin. Howley had come to see the fertile territory of Saxony and Thuringia as more attractive and valuable than a heap of spoliated rubble in Berlin.

American troops and Military Government personnel moved quickly to meet the three-day deadline imposed by the Soviets. When Howley arrived in Berlin with his troops, he did what came naturally to an American military man: he drew his vehicles into a protective circle, as if they were covered wagons on the prairie rather than in the Grunewald. Having posted guards, he felt confident that 'Not a Russian, not a German could have interfered with us'.[56] Military historians Stivers and Carter describe Howley as 'inveterately belligerent'. But even he had a soft spot for the Soviets in the beginning. Seeing Soviet troops as 'hard bargaining, hard playing, hard drinking, hard bodied, and hard headed', Howley was ready for a spot of roughhousing. 'If you are soft, you'd better stay away from them. If you are competent, informed, fair and "fearless", you'll get along fine.'[57] Often the mingling turned to quibbling and fighting; competitive drinking enjoyed by American and Soviet troops often ended in good-natured brawling. Military Police consequently played an important role in the advanced guard. The few courageous German uniformed police (*Schupos*) initially saluted their new masters but then were banned from doing so.[58] The rubble-strewn battleground of Berlin presented an apocalyptic vista and an olfactory as well as a visual assault; everywhere there was the stench of death. Foreign observers stressed how dirty and dishevelled the surviving Berliners looked.[59] Nevertheless, male arrivals were pleased to see German girls dressed in summer frocks. They seemed to emerge 'trim as butterflies', as if by magic, from 'dingy, rubble-covered cellars'.[60]

The population of the western sectors expressed thanks that they were being occupied by the British and Americans. With relief, they asked, 'Why did you not come sooner?' The questions they fired at their latest occupiers suggested an immediate affinity and sense of protection. 'Were we British? *Gott sei dank*. And were we going to stay? *Gott sei dank*.'[61] Nevertheless, the Western Allies were determined to be strict with the German population. Shaking hands with them was *verboten*; relations were supposed to be formal, unequal and stiff. According to *Le Monde* journalist, Frédérix, the Brandenburg Gate had become the 'crossing point between two worlds': in the East, peasant smocks and horses predominated; in the West, the Allies stood out with their short jackets and jeeps. His own survey of Berliners, chosen at random in the street, suggested that eight or nine out of ten preferred the Americans to the Soviets. Englishmen, Canadians or Belgians were equally popular: the main thing was that they were Westerners. Alluding to the rapes, he suggested that if the French had taken Berlin using 'our Moroccan troops' then they too would have been branded criminal.[62] Berliners quickly compared notes on their new occupiers. Despite Frédérix's hopes, the French were initially despised and feared in equal measure. To bolster their spirits, the British had the tricolour flown from the Victory Column (*Siegessäule*) monument, which had been erected to celebrate Prussia's victory over France in 1871.[63] Thus the flag representing everything that was glorious and heroic about France flew from the very symbol of Prussian militarism.

Berliners supposedly liked the British 'polite bearing' but found them tough and 'matter-of-fact'.[64] Determined to sweep up the chaos left by the Soviets, the Anglo-American occupiers viewed the Germans with aloof coldness. The sights that greeted Western troops when they arrived in Berlin were red flags flying everywhere, including over the Brandenburg Gate, and placards proclaiming Stalin's words that The Hitlers may come and go, 'but the German state and the German people would endure.'[65] Both before and after the arrival of the Western Allies, Soviet propaganda showed no distinction between the eastern and western sectors. They treated both as the prize, won solely through their own, heroic efforts. Despite it being outside their Sector, the Soviets had control of the radio facilities, located in the British Sector, and refused to share them with the other Allies. This seemed unnecessarily selfish and irksome, but all subsequent attempts to change this stance proved futile.[66]

Pride and celebration were mixed with some *Schadenfreude*, in seeing how the mighty had fallen. The new governors marked their presence with military parades and flag ceremonies; wherever possible, they destroyed Nazi symbols. If the other Allies had misgivings about the Soviets, they were initially at pains not to show this to the Germans. When told about Soviet behaviour, some of the Western Allies at first refused to believe what their Allies had done. They assumed that the Berliners were exaggerating or deliberately blackening the Soviets in order to win sympathy and to divide the victors.[67] German contemporaries recalled their faces turning to ice. 'Our Allies, their cold look says, and it makes us fall respectfully silent.'[68] When they did believe what the Berliners were telling them, then they often sought to justify these actions because of what the Soviet forces had suffered in their thousand-mile march through territory devastated by the German army. In this justification, the soldiers who had committed rape had been influenced by the tortures and murders inflicted on the Soviet people. Over time, though, they came to believe the worst: the Western Allies began to identify with the people of Berlin against the Soviets. Even their greatest supporters felt that the Berliners went out of their way to exploit the tacit alliances created by such empathy.[69]

The Soviets had not allocated the British any accommodation, so they were initially forced to sleep, like sardines, in overcrowded tents. Despite the fact that the Soviets showed no sign of withdrawing from the British Sector, Brigadier O. M. Wales encouraged his men not to be affronted. He insisted that they should not misinterpret this as an expression of mistrust or suspicion on the part of their Soviet Allies. Rather, it was an expression of their 'extremely high standard of security'. Although 'rather unexpected', his men should accept the unusual circumstances 'with good grace' and without displays of ill temper or loss of dignity.[70] The biggest impact of the other Allies' arrival was felt in relation to public safety. When the Americans arrived in their Sector, on 2 July 1945, they were surprised to find that there were still sizeable numbers of Soviet soldiers residing in their territory without any discernible control. They tended to hide during daylight only to venture out at night in search of food and drink. The British Deputy Military Governor, Robert Hinde, was equally surprised to find Soviet troops carrying on as if they were still the Military Government of his Sector.[71] The Western Allies struggled to assert their authority on their sectors because of Soviet intransigence and refusal to cooperate. Soviet soldiers tore down proclamations put up by the American authorities. In addition to a surfeit of 'absent without leave' (AWOL) Soviet troops, the Western Allies were surprised to learn that their Soviet hosts expected them to provide the 1,600,000 Germans in their sectors with food and fuel. All their occupation plans had been based on the Soviets continuing to provision the whole city. While some celebrated the Soviet achievement in keeping Berliners fed, others argued that they were already on the edge of starvation.[72] It was a bit rich for the Soviets to impoverish the whole of Berlin and then expect the Western Allies to feed the population, who no longer had any tangible means of support.

The overwhelming desire of the British and American commanders was to restore law and order to their sectors. First and foremost, this meant removing Soviet soldiers from the territory they controlled and finding a way to keep them out. CIA historian Donald P. Steury stresses the lawless, Wild-West aspects of the early occupation. Careering through the streets in jeeps provided by lend lease, Soviet troops were ready to use violence in their search for 'booty and liquor'. While some were intent on robbery and murder, others sought to carry out illegal arrests.[73] There was an impasse for over a week, during which Soviet officials claimed that they had received no orders to leave the western sectors. Getting frustrated, Colonel Howley had signs put up declaring that the border districts of Kreuzberg and Neukölln now belonged to the American Sector.[74] By nine o'clock in the morning, Howley's forces set about raising the American flag in each borough. By posting ordinances, setting up summary Military Government Courts and handing out orders to the local mayors, they established their authority and determination to govern.[75] General Lucius D. Clay, Deputy to General Dwight D. Eisenhower as Military Governor, remembered a rush of protest, but suggested that the late-sleeping Soviets had been caught on the hop. The American occupiers had learned that fait accompli was the best way to 'obtain Russian consent'.[76] Nevertheless, the Soviets did not officially leave the American Sector until 12 July. As late as 16 July, Soviet troops continued to occupy eleven buildings in Zehlendorf. The American Military Government reported continued looting and plundering in this district at the heart of their Sector.[77] Into late July, Soviet and American armed guards faced each other at a strip of disputed territory in northern Kreuzberg.[78]

Through into August 1945, there were repeated reports of misconduct in the American Sector by Soviet troops. American officials accused Soviet soldiery of all sorts of looting and general highway robbery. Soviet soldiers still seemed unashamed to take possessions from German civilians in broad daylight, seeing it as their portion of dismantling and reparations. More seriously, on 6 August, the American governors caught 'NKVD police', disguised in civilian clothes, apparently in the act of 'snatching' German civilians.[79] In particular, the other Allies were shocked and appalled by the nonchalance with which Red Army soldiers continued to go about raping German citizens.[80] While some Allied observers tried to dismiss the horror stories as hysterical exaggeration and propaganda, those who directly witnessed Soviet aggressions were disgusted by them. As news spread of Soviet depredations, there was a swift deterioration of relations.[81] In their determination to restore law and order to their Sector, American troops were quite prepared to use deadly force. In the first weeks of the occupation, they shot over a dozen Soviet soldiers who resisted arrest. Howley suggested that nothing less could be expected of the tank boys of the Second Armored

Division. As fine soldiers, it was impossible to 'expect them to stand by and watch women being raped and kids frightened out of a year's growth'. Soviet soldiers who pulled a gun on them could expect Americans to shoot to kill.[82] His aide, Colonel John Maginnis, recounted similar Wild-West scenes: in Schöneberg, German police alerted American MPs (Military Policemen) to an attempted rape by two Soviets. The altercation 'ended in a shooting contest'. According to Maginnis, Captain Charles Bond 'went along to see the fun and almost got himself killed'. The Americans managed to subdue the Soviets, but only after one of the MPs received a bullet wound in the thigh.[83]

Different notions of lawful use of firearms became an early bone of contention in the four-power city. Philharmonic conductor and resistance hero Leo Borchard was an early victim. An American sentry shot up the car of British Colonel Thomas Creighton in which Borchard was travelling. Believing that the Soviets responded only to force, Howley admitted that the Americans tended to 'shoot first and ask questions later'. In his view, the British preferred to beat 'the hell out of' Soviet soldiers (enough to knock out their front teeth). The Soviets understood and greatly preferred this method. They found shooting excessive and undignified.[84] The Berliners heard about the shoot-outs and hoped the situation would benefit them. Possibly in light of this, the Allies organized international, joint Military Police patrols.[85] At night, Soviet Military Policemen rode along with their opposite numbers from the US, British and French Sectors. The goal was to reduce misunderstandings and international incidents. They once again proclaimed themselves eager to demonstrate their sincerity in trying to make quadripartite government work. Despite problems of language and communication, these efforts began to produce results. However, off-duty Red Army soldiers continued routinely to carry submachine guns and carbines with them. Even at the peak of quiescence, bursts of gunfire could be heard sporadically throughout the night.

Years into the occupation, the Allies still had to deal with a plague of Soviet deserters, drunks, renegades and desperadoes. As the future American Commandant put it, the Red Army soldiers had been free to rape and loot at will for two months. Even after the other Allies' arrival, they continued to make forays into the American Sector. Given the levels of crime being perpetrated by armed Soviet soldiers, the Military Policemen had a huge task ahead of them. As the head of the US Military Government put it, 'Soldiers, guns and liquor' was a highly explosive combination. Night clubs and other sleazy dives were not propitious for law and order.[86] In public, the Western Allies tended to play down their doubts and concerns about the Soviets for fear of being manipulated by the 'cunning Germans', who were already striving to estrange and antagonize the Allies.[87] Berliners did gleefully recount the nightly shoot-outs between the Americans and the Soviets and the fact that the Allied soldiers failed to salute one another. 'They don't seem to like each other, our Allied occupation powers.'[88]

Restoring order amid the chaos

Although arbitrary and, in parts, highly destructive, the Soviets had also done 'much of the heavy lifting' when it came to 'restoring basic services' in the city.[89] There was, at first, no functioning administration, news or postal service. Berliners tried to get in touch with family and friends, who had been bombed out, by leaving little notes for one another or chalking messages on the ruins where they used to live. In the absence of public transport, it could take a whole day to cross the city on foot. Maintaining communications between the different districts and the centre was very difficult. Without motor ambulances, transporting the sick and the dead could only be accomplished by hand stretcher or by handcart. Dead bodies littered the canals and lakes or lay stinking under bomb debris. Amid the chaos of defeat, through accidents, suicides or foul play, bodies continued to accumulate at the morgue.[90]

Journalist Egon Bahr sees all the Allies as haughty and disinterested in their German subjects. The subjugated population only learned the decisions made in the Allied Control Council once they had been decided. There was no pretence of consultation.[91] Hostility to the Germans persisted long after the armistice. Colonel Howley earned the sobriquet of 'Beast of Berlin', even in American newspapers, when he declared that the only reason the Allies brought food into Berlin was because they did not want the rotting corpses of German civilians to infect their troops.[92] For Howley, there were only gradations of 'bad' as far as the Germans went. He was inclined to treat the vanquished roughly. He later acknowledged, 'Perhaps I had been unnecessarily blunt in saying so, but I had come to Berlin with the idea that the Germans were our enemies.'[93] Clay admits that Howley, who had been an advertising executive in civilian life, was not always diplomatic or timely in his language, but his actions helped to put Berlin back on its feet. He marvelled at his subordinate's energy and courage in facing the huge obstacles and challenges.[94]

One of the largest sources of suffering was the continual arrival of refugees during 1945. Approximately 6,000 homeless Germans a day came in by train from the East. The Allied response was to give them one hot meal and then to ship them on. Each train contained several dead bodies. Because they carried contagious diseases, they constituted a grave health problem.[95] Gradually, Howley and his men brought order to the chaos and helped to relieve human suffering. While the Americans under his command attacked the problems with immense energy and optimism, in spite of their scale, the French tended to succumb to depression, disheartened by the atrocious working conditions and stymied by the scale of the unpropitious conditions.[96] Conditions were such in 1945 that workmen, employed to repair Allied offices, fainted from hunger and exhaustion.[97] The old and the very young were the first to perish because of malnutrition. Out of every twenty babies, born in the United States Sector in July 1945, nineteen died.[98] Mothers were forced to use newspaper sheets instead of nappies; soap for even the most basic hygiene was unavailable.

To the shock of total defeat was added the psychological damage caused by the harsh conditions of survival amid a ruined landscape of abandoned and destroyed infrastructure. Their previous lives were distant memories: the past was destroyed or tainted; the future was uncertain. People lived in the present, which was one long, unending struggle for survival. Those who were lucky enough to have a roof over their head lacked electricity, drinking water or gas. Like the transport system, hospitals had largely ceased to function. Because the population was so weak from hunger, epidemic diseases like dysentery and typhoid easily took hold.[99] Berliners were dying at four times the prewar rate.[100] Afterwards, occupation soldier Richard Brett-Smith wrote that it was merciful that the expected famine and epidemic failed to materialize. Though many died, the calamity was less severe than expected.[101] For their part, Berliners remembered the harsh winter when all they had to make do with was a few frozen potatoes and no coal.

Conclusion

Having encouraged the Soviets to advance on Berlin, the Western Allies got cold feet about what might happen if their comrades controlled large parts of Eastern Europe and took the German capital on their own. Nevertheless, the messy handover of power – with Roosevelt dying and Churchill losing the general election, together with the accumulated exhaustion of having just won a long and devastating war – meant that the British and Americans were unprepared to negotiate a different, more restrictive deal with Stalin. Truman could hardly sacrifice years of diplomacy because of one telegram from a disgruntled ally.

In 1945, defeated, prostrate Germany had a surfeit of disorder and confusion, heightened by the aftereffects of Allied area bombing. Large parts of the city were in ruins and acted as breeding grounds for crime and disease. During the sole Soviet occupation, Red Army soldiers had wrought terrible revenge on the defeated German civilians. Berliners had to fend for themselves in a situation of extreme scarcity and lack of government. At first, new arrivals to Berlin hoped that the rumours and stories they were hearing were regrettable isolated cases, but over time they realized that the stories of retribution were true.[102] Gangs of Displaced Persons sought revenge on the Germans who had persecuted and humiliated them. Despite the ongoing depredations and nightly attacks on the civilian population, the Soviets sought to re-establish a police force. On their arrival in Berlin, the Western Allies were surprised to learn that the Soviets had allowed German political parties to reform. This move stemmed less from an abstract or principled commitment to democracy than as a means of establishing and securing Soviet hegemony.

The difficult law-and-order situation was not so much remedied as complicated by the arrival of the three Western Allies. Even when the other Allies took possession of their sectors, they had difficulties convincing Soviet officials that they were no longer in charge. Outstaying their welcome at the victory party, stubborn Soviet soldiers had to be nudged and cajoled into leaving West Berlin. Soviet officials happily remained where they were and countermanded orders issued by the British and Americans. The Western Allies initially emphasized the Soviets' sacrifices in defeating the Nazis, but increasingly came to decry their cruelty during the taking of Berlin. Faced with lack of cooperation, combined with overt hostility and interference on the Soviets' part, the Americans responded forcefully to attacks on the women in their Sector. They succeeded in dampening the continued lawless activity, by Soviet troops, by using lethal violence. Howley linked the shoot-first tendency to America's experiences in the Wild West.[103]

Despite the aggression and violence shown by their soldiery to the defeated population of Berlin, Soviet administrators were prepared to use German collaborators

– especially Communists – from the very beginning of their occupation. The other Allies were continually on the back foot in relation to a resolute and determined Soviet steamroller. Notwithstanding disagreements, the victorious powers resolved to govern Berlin together by means of the *Kommandatura* (or four-power local governing body). While some at the top expressed misgivings, those at the bottom, tasked with everyday cooperation, sought to put disputes with their Allies down to misunderstandings. In the desperate weeks and months after the defeat, hunger, disease and violence stalked the ruins. Normal life often seemed an impossible dream. Careers were cut short; people were adrift in extraordinary circumstances, from which there was little relief. If cities come close to living organisms, Berlin was very close to death in the summer of 1945.[104] Policing expert Richard Bessel argues that we tend to associate Germans with order and discipline. Nevertheless, at the end of World War Two, Berlin experienced a catastrophic collapse of lawfulness.[105] The next chapter explains how order was gradually reimposed through the everyday actions of policemen and women. For ordinary people, what dominated their lives was the struggle to obtain food, fuel and shelter. With armed gangs of former slave labourers seeking revenge on a population that had ignored their existence and suffering for so long, security was another luxury they could no longer afford. One ordinary Berliner summed up his mood on 11 July 1945: 'Rubble, hunger, shards and poverty' – that was all that remained of his beloved Berlin. He desperately wished he could shut his eyes and banish the sight of the ruined city forever.[106]

Notes

1. Although it was a caesura, 1945 was not a *tabula rasa*. Richard Overy, 'Interwar, War, Postwar: Was There a Zero Hour in 1945?' in *The Oxford Handbook of Postwar European History*, ed. Dan Stone (Oxford: Oxford University Press, 2012), 63–4. Cf. Ian Buruma, *Year Zero: A History of 1945* (New York: Penguin Press, 2013).
2. Erich Kuby, *The Russians and Berlin, 1945*, trans. Arnold J. Pomerans (London: Heinemann 1968), 92, 143.
3. Krim. Insp. M III: 'Tätigkeitsbericht vom 4.6.-9.6.1945', 9 June 1945, Landesarchiv Berlin, C Rep 303–9, Nr. 249, 207f.
4. Kuby, *The Russians and Berlin, 1945*, 40, 237.
5. Eugene Gilbert Jones, 'The Allied Reconstruction of the Berlin Police, 1945-1948', PhD, University of California, San Diego, 1986, 147.
6. Richard Bessel, 'Establishing Order in Post-war Eastern Germany', *Past and Present* 210, Supplement 6 (2011): 140.
7. '123 Murders in July', *Manchester Guardian*, 27 August 1945.
8. SHAEF, *Handbook for Military Government in Germany: Prior to Defeat or Surrender*, December 1944, paragraph 457.
9. As cited by Catherine Merridale, 'Culture, Ideology and Combat in the Red Army, 1939-45', *Journal of Contemporary History* 41, no. 2 (2006): 319.
10. Lev Kopelev, *To Be Preserved Forever* (Philadelphia, PA: Lippincott, 1977), 52–3.
11. Norman Naimark, *Russians in Germany: A History of the Soviet Zone of Occupation, 1945-1949* (Cambridge, MA: Belknap Press of Harvard University Press, 1995),

69–140; Richard Bessel, *Germany 1945: From War to Peace* (London: Harper Collins, 2009), 116–18; Atina Grossmann, 'A Question of Silence: The Rape of German Women by Occupation Soldiers', in *West Germany Under Construction: Politics, Society and Culture in the Adenauer Era*, ed. Robert G. Moeller (Ann Arbor: University of Michigan Press, 1997), 33–52.
12 Frank L. Howley, *Berlin Command* (New York: G. P. Putnam's Sons, 1950), 66.
13 Hsu-Ming Teo, 'The Continuum of Sexual Violence in Occupied Germany, 1945-49', *Women's History Review* 5, no. 2 (1996): 208. Cf. Franz Göll's diary entry from 3 May 1945 in Peter Fritzsche, *The Turbulent World of Franz Göll: An Ordinary Berliner Writes the Twentieth Century* (Cambridge, MA: Harvard University Press, 2011), 180–1.
14 Anonyma as cited by Kuby, *The Russians and Berlin, 1945*, 156, 277–8.
15 Ruth Andreas-Friedrich, *Battleground Berlin: Diaries 1945-1948*, trans. Anna Boerresen (New York: Paragon, 1990), 15.
16 Naimark, *Russians in Germany*, 116–17, 81.
17 Ferdinand Friedensburg, *Es ging um Deutschlands Einheit: Rückschau eines Berliners auf die Jahre nach 1945* (West Berlin: Haude and Spenersche, 1971), 22, 24. Cf. Margret Boveri, *Tage des Überlebens: Berlin 1945* (Munich: R. Piper, 1968), 119.
18 Dan Healey, 'Comrades, Queers, and "Oddballs": Sodomy, Masculinity, and Gendered Violence in Leningrad Province of the 1950s', *Journal of the History of Sexuality* 21, no. 3 (2012): 521.
19 Cornelius Ryan, *The Last Battle* (London: Collins, 1966), 382.
20 Frau J. as cited by Kuby, *The Russians and Berlin*, 273, 266. Antony Beevor argues that witnessing 'campfires in their streets', together with 'shaggy Cossack ponies and even camels', Berliners managed to convince themselves that their city had been occupied by Mongol hordes. He suggests that Goebbels's propaganda heightened the impression that Soviet occupying troops were of Central Asian origin, even though photographic evidence proves that this was not the case. Antony Beevor, *Berlin: The Downfall 1945* (London: Penguin, 2002), 418.
21 Antony Beevor, 'Introduction' to Anonyma, *A Woman in Berlin*, trans. Philip Boehm (London: Virago, 2005), 11. The book first appeared in English as *A Woman in Berlin*, trans. James Stern (New York: Harcourt Brace, 1954) and was first published in Germany in 1959.
22 Bessel, *Germany 1945*, 116.
23 Andreas-Friedrich, *Battleground Berlin*, 16–17.
24 Boveri, *Tage des Überlebens*, 157. Beevor, 'Introduction', 6, 11.
25 Anonyma, *A Woman in Berlin*, 85.
26 K.J. M III: 'Tätigkeitsbericht vom 20.-26.7.1945', 27 July 1945, Landesarchiv Berlin, C Rep 303-09, Nr. 249, 212.
27 Naimark, *Russians in Germany*, 132–3.
28 Friedensburg, *Es ging um Deutschlands Einheit*, 23.
29 Andreas-Friedrich, *Battleground Berlin*, 84.
30 Paul Steege, 'Ordinary Violence on an Extraordinary Stage. Incidents on the Sector Border in Postwar Berlin', in *Performances of Violence*, ed. Austin Sarat, Carleen Basler and Thomas L. Dumm (Amherst, MA: University of Massachusetts Press, 2011), 150.
31 Pierre Frédérix, 'Dans Berlin en Ruines L'Est et L'Ouest se sont rencontrés', *Le Monde*, 20 July 1945.
32 Alexander Werth, *Russia at War* (New York: Dutton, 1964), 984.

33 'Ein Monat nach der Kapitulation', *Tägliche Rundschau*, 8 June 1945.
34 Rudolf Herrnstadt, 'Über die Russen und über uns', *Neues Deutschland*, 19 November 1948.
35 Naimark, *Russians in Germany*, 120.
36 Stewart Thompson and Robert Bialek, *The Bialek Affair* (London: Allan Wingate, 1955), 31–3.
37 Gerhard Keiderling, '"Als Befreier unsere Herzen zerbrachen". Zu den Übergriffe der Sowjetarmee in Berlin 1945', *Deutschland Archiv* 28, no. 1 (1995): 237.
38 David E. Murphy, Sergei A. Kondrashev and George Bailey, *Battleground Berlin: CIA vs: KGB in the Cold War* (New Haven, CT: Yale University Press, 1997), 401, 404.
39 Wolfgang Leonhard, *Child of the Revolution*, trans. C. M. Woodhouse (Cologne: Kiepenhauer and Witsch, 1979), 365.
40 *Germany, Year Zero*, directed by Roberto Rossellini (Italy, 1948).
41 T. H. Elkins and B. Hofmeister, *Berlin: The Spatial Structure of a Divided City* (London: Methuen, 1988), 37.
42 Richard Brett-Smith, *Berlin '45: The Grey City* (London: Macmillan, 1966), 48.
43 Major-General E. O. Herbert, 'The Cold War in Berlin', *Journal of the Royal United Service Insitution* XCIV, no. 574 (1949): 165–6.
44 Neal Ascherson. 'Hitler's Teeth. Berlin: The Downfall, 1945 by Antony Beevor, April 2002', *London Review of Books* 24, no. 23 (2002): 15–16.
45 Robert Spencer, 'The Berlin Dilemma', in *The Shaping of Postwar Germany*, ed. Edgar McInnis, Richard Hiscocks and Robert Spencer (New York: Frederick A. Praeger, 1960), 105.
46 'Public Safety, July 1945 to 31 August 1949', 1, US National Archives, RG260, 390/48/27/2, Box 893. A similar strategy was pursued in Vienna. Lindsay K. MacNeill, 'Professionalism and Brutality: The Viennese Police and the Public in Extraordinary Times, 1918-1955', PhD, American University, Washington, DC, 2020, 366. Jochen Staadt, 'Die Berliner Polizei in der "Stunde Null"', in *Feindwärts der Mauer: Das Ministerium für Staatssicherheit und die West-Berliner Polizei*, ed. Klaus Schroeder and Jochen Staadt (Frankfurt am Main: Peter Lang, 2014), 22.
47 Leonhard, *Child of the Revolution*, 303.
48 Eric Morris, *Blockade: Berlin and the Cold War* (London: Hamish Hamilton, 1973), 42.
49 Wolfgang Schivelbusch, *In a Cold Crater: Cultural and Intellectual Life in Berlin, 1945–1948*, trans. Kelly Barry (Berkeley, CA: University of California Press, 1998), 8.
50 Robert L. Gunnarsson, *American Military Police in Europe* (Jefferson, AL: McFarland, 2011), 168–9. A film was produced, *Four in a Jeep*, directed by Leopold Lindtberg and Elizabeth Montagu (Switzerland, 1951).
51 'Men of Four Nations Keep Vienna's Peace', *Sydney Morning Herald*, 25 March 1952.
52 Winston S. Churchill, *The Second World War, vol. 6, Triumph and Tragedy* (London: Cassell, 1954), 520, 581, 523.
53 Ibid., 498–9.
54 'Operation Unthinkable', https://archive.org/details/OperationUnthinkable/page/n19/mode/2up (accessed 20 April 2020).
55 The first British scouting party arrived on 1 July 1945. 'Russians Escort Our Spearhead to Berlin', *Daily Mail*, 2 July 1945.
56 Howley, *Berlin Command*, 44.
57 *US Army Military Government Report* (4 January–4 July 1946), 8.
58 Frédérix, 'Dans Berlin en Ruines'.

59 Renée Bédarida, 'Une Française à Berlin en 1945', in *France-Allemagne 1944-1947*, ed. Klaus Manfrass and Jean-Pierre Rioux (Paris: Institut d'histoire du temps present, 1990), 149.
60 Brigadier C. E. Ryan, 'The Kommandatura's Debut', *Journal of the Royal United Service Institution* 96, no. 582 (1951): 267.
61 Gordon Harrington, 'How Berlin Looks', *The Spectator*, 27 July 1945, 77.
62 Frédérix, 'Dans Berlin en Ruines'.
63 William Murray, *Germany Today* (Pathe, 1947).
64 Keiderling, 'Als Befreier unsere Herzen zerbrachen', 238.
65 Michael Derenburg, *Streifzüge durch vier RIAS-Jahrzehnte: Anfänge und Wandlungen eines Rundfunksenders* (Berlin: Presse- und Informationsamt des Landes Berlin, 1986), 6.
66 'The Berlin Radio Station, Intelligence Notes', October 1946, Landesarchiv Berlin, F Rep. 037, Acc. 3971, Nr. 240.
67 Michael Balfour and John Mair, *Four-Power Control in Germany and Austria, 1945-1946* (London: Oxford University Press, 1956), 76.
68 Andreas-Friedrich, *Battleground Berlin*, 75–6.
69 Brett-Smith, *Berlin '45*, 161.
70 'No Billets for Our Troops in Berlin', *Daily Mail*, 7 July 1945.
71 'British in Berlin', *Times*, 9 July 1945.
72 Howley, *Berlin Command*, 8.
73 Donald P. Steury (ed.), *On the Front Lines of the Cold War: Documents on the Intelligence War in Berlin, 1946 to 1961* (Washington, DC: CIA History Staff, Center for the Study of Intelligence, 1999), 1.
74 Howley, *Berlin Command*, 49.
75 Earl F. Ziemke, *The U.S. Army in the Occupation of Germany, 1944-1946* (Washington, DC: Center of Military History, United States Army, 1975), 303.
76 Lucius D. Clay, *Decision in Germany* (Westport, CT: Greenwood, 1970), 31.
77 'U.S. Sector Military Government of Berlin', 18 July 1945, Landesarchiv Berlin, F Rep. 037, Acc. 3971, Nr. 247.
78 'U.S. Sector Military Government of Berlin', 24 July 1945, Landesarchiv Berlin, F Rep. 037, Acc. 3971, Nr. 247.
79 Major General John J. Maginnis, *Military Government Journal: Normandy to Berlin* (Amherst, MA: University of Massachusetts Press, 1971), 282. The NKVD was the People's Commissariat for Internal Affairs or secret police.
80 'Rapport de Gendarmerie de Wedding sur des actes de violence commis par un officier de l'armee Russe sur une fillette de 10 ans', Wedding, 18 August 1945, Archives Diplomatiques, GMFB 1/1102.
81 Brett-Smith, *Berlin '45*, 156.
82 Howley, *Berlin Command*, 68.
83 Maginnis, *Military Government Journal*, 294.
84 Howley, *Berlin Command*, 71.
85 Andreas-Friedrich, *Battleground Berlin*, 75. Howley complains that the Soviets used this as an opportunity to spy on the western sectors. Howley, *Berlin Command*, 72.
86 Clay, *Decision in Germany*, 137.
87 'Argument in Berlin', *Daily Mail*, 9 July 1945.
88 Andreas-Friedrich, *Battleground Berlin*, 75–6.

89 William Stivers and Donald A. Carter, *The City Becomes a Symbol: the U.S. Army in the Occupation of Berlin, 1945-1949* (Washington, DC: Center of Military History, United States Army, 2017), 68.
90 Waldemar Weimann, *Diagnose Mord: Die Memoiren eines Gerichtsmediziners* (Bayreuth: Hestia, 1964), 6.
91 Egon Bahr, *Zu meiner Zeit* (Munich: K. Blessing, 1996), 40.
92 'Foreign News: New Commander', *Time Magazine*, 15 August 1949.
93 Howley, *Berlin Command*, 87.
94 Clay, *Decision in Germany*, 32.
95 'U.S. Sector Military Government of Berlin', 19 July 1945, Landesarchiv Berlin, F Rep. 037, Acc. 3971, Nr. 247.
96 Bédarida, 'Une Française à Berlin en 1945', 150.
97 Clay, *Decision in Germany*, 31.
98 Spencer, 'The Berlin Dilemma', 105.
99 'Berlin Fear of Typhoid', *Daily Mail*, 23 July 1945.
100 Alec Cairncross, *A Country to Play With* (Gerrards Cross: Colin Smythe, 1987), 35.
101 Brett-Smith, *Berlin '45*, 109.
102 Leonhard, *Child of the Revolution*, 296.
103 Howley, *Berlin Command*, 39.
104 Curt Riess, *The Berlin Story* (London: Frederick Muller, 1953), 9.
105 Bessel, 'Establishing Order in Post-war Eastern Germany', 139.
106 Karl Deutmann diary, http://www.hdg.de/lemo/forum/kollektives_gedaechtnis/010/index.html (accessed 27 April 2014).

2

Restoring order

Rebuilding the police

Policing cities that have recently been at war poses special, often seemingly intractable, problems.¹ In Berlin, an effective police force was necessary not only to fight crime but also to forestall sabotage by concealed, unrepentant Nazis. The Western Allies saw a reformed and denazified police force as essential to their efforts at democratization. Before 1945, Berlin's position, as capital of Nazi Germany, had turned the police force into the most 'thoroughly nazified' branch of the German administration. Reforming the legal and judicial system was a fundamental component of democratic re-establishment. Nevertheless, the bombed city presented important obstacles to rebuilding an effective police body.² In the chaos of zero hour, a combination of Soviet arrests and Allied bombing had destroyed what remained of police authority and effectiveness. As the previous chapter showed, most policing personnel had been scattered asunder or taken prisoner. A direct hit on the police headquarters (known to Bernie Gunther simply as the 'Alex') destroyed many of the criminal records. The hastily recruited replacements had to operate without a command structure or proper equipment.

By far the most important task facing the Soviets in May 1945 was the reforming of the police. On 19 May 1945, as sole occupiers, the Soviets re-established the Police Presidium for Greater Berlin, under the leadership of 35-year-old Paul Markgraf. Its new headquarters was at the Linienstraße in East Berlin. The governor of Berlin, Nikolai Berzarin, issued an official order on 25 May.³ Although proclaiming them as Antifascists, the Soviets were ready to recycle some former Nazis and sympathizers if they had useful skills. Police President Markgraf was a former *Wehrmacht* Captain, who had been captured by the Soviets at Stalingrad. He had a long and relatively distinguished military career, having served in the *Wehrmacht* from 1931 to 1943.⁴ He had personally received the Knight's Cross (*Ritterkreuz*), the highest award for bravery in the Third Reich, from Hitler himself.⁵ Once captured, however, he became disillusioned with Hitler's leadership and involved himself in the 'Free Germany' movement. He was personally taught in the Antifa School by the exiled German Communist leaders Wilhelm Pieck, Hermann Matern and Walter Ulbricht.⁶ Before the war's end, Markgraf had assisted the Soviets by making propaganda broadcasts on Radio Moscow. As a consequence, the Gestapo had begun investigating his family at home in Germany.⁷ The Soviets chose him for Berlin's most important policing job after he completed an essay 'What I Would Do if I Was appointed Berlin Police President'.[8] Markgraf did not officially belong to any party in 1945 but later joined the Socialist Unity Party of Germany (SED). Before he took up his new post, the Soviets hastily promoted him to the rank of colonel.

As Markgraf's second-in-command, the Soviets appointed Dr Johannes Stumm. Stumm described Markgraf as 'pretty helpless' despite his police-colonel's uniform. As a military man, he had little concept of how to organize an effective, peacetime police force. Stumm disparagingly remarked that one could expect little from someone whose professional training was as a baker.[9] For his part, Markgraf remembered being faced with utter chaos. The Police Presidium was in ruins; most police stations were empty or levelled. Ignoring Stumm, he did not initially possess a single competent police officer. He knew how to order people about but had little grasp of the details of concrete policing. From a loyal officer under Hitler, Markgraf transformed himself into a totally loyal policeman under Stalin.[10] Journalist and pioneer of psychological warfare Curt Riess argued that, as their appointment of Markgraf showed, the Soviets had no deep-rooted concerns about employing former Nazis. 'If they needed a Nazi, they put him to work for them.'[11]

As an experienced professional, Stumm cannot have been happy about having to play second fiddle to Markgraf. Of all the leading personalities, Stumm was the most experienced and capable. He had been one of the youngest Detective Superintendents in Prussia during the Weimar Republic, before being forced out of police service by the Nazis.[12] In cracking down hard on Nazi demonstrations in the period 1928–33, he had done nothing to endear himself to the new rulers. His successor as Police President in the 1970s and 1980s, Klaus Hübner, praises the courage with which he stood up for his democratic beliefs at this time.[13] By returning to the police in the summer of 1945, Stumm hoped to avoid difficulties with the Soviet authorities. Volunteering his services to the occupiers seemed the best way of escaping 'an unknown fate' at the hands of the alien victors.[14] As a competent and seasoned police administrator, he was aghast at what he saw in 1945. In his new role, as Vice-President, he managed to employ several fellow SPD members as his underlings, notably Dr Hans-Georg Urban.[15] Dismissing ardent Nazis made sense, even if it left behind organizational problems. Nevertheless, Patrick Wagner describes the development of policing after 1945 as a new beginning with little in the way of 'repentance or remorse (*Neubeginn ohne Reue*)'.[16] Along traditional lines, the police force was divided into three sections: the uniformed police, the detective squads and the administrative police.

Stumm also ensured that the police administration was reformed on the model which had existed in the Weimar Republic. This ensured that, despite extensive denazification, the organization's structure, outlook and approach remained little changed from its historical roots. He could not, however, prevent the Soviets from getting rid of the policeman's special civil-servant status. In the view of the foremost historian of police reform, this move 'fundamentally altered' the status of police officials in the defeated capital.[17] From the beginning, Markgraf used his position to appoint Communists to police posts and to 'disappear' people who fell afoul of the Soviets. Markgraf said that he was particularly interested in employing policemen who had professional experience but who had opposed the Nazis.[18] As the Stasi later put it, to be recruited, the applicants had to prove their 'Antifascist outlook'.[19] As far as possible, he ensured that ardent Communists were appointed to leading positions. Within two months, Markgraf had 16,222 men at his disposal. It was unfeasible, in the difficult immediate postwar conditions, to check the previous political backgrounds of all recruits. They had to fill in questionnaires, but these could not be checked adequately. This allowed criminals as well as Nazis to slip through the cracks.[20]

When the Western Allies arrived at the beginning of July, *The Times* proudly proclaimed that henceforth the 900,000 Germans of the British Sector would live 'under British law'.[21] The Military Police stepped into the gap left by inadequate German policing.[22] Nevertheless, the Allies pledged to manage policing on a combined, citywide basis. There would be one police force covering the whole city, but the policemen would be responsible to the commandant of their particular sector. This arrangement generally worked satisfactorily, but it was no guarantee of policemen's safety. The police in Charlottenburg reported back to their Police President, Markgraf, that the first thing the British Major asked was how the Soviets had treated the population in the interim.[23] As early as autumn 1945, British officers were complaining of the Soviet-appointed policemen's lack of interest in capturing criminals. Both petty and serious crimes were rampant, and policemen, too, could be tempted to plunder. In particular, the new, hastily recruited, appointees lacked training as detectives. To the other Allies' evident surprise, the Soviets seemed unconcerned about the seemingly endless waves of larceny and robbery. For the British Military Police (MPs), they were more concerned about grabbing political suspects. In pursuit of 'Nazi mischief-makers', they showed no concern for the sector boundaries, entering the British Sector to remove people at will.[24]

In the summer of 1945, justice was swift but not necessarily fair. The Americans tried 8,000 Berliners in their courts, according to Allied occupation law. Selling alcohol to American troops was an offence against Allied occupation rules but not against German law. One German received six months in prison for unlawfully obtaining six meagre cans from the US commissary. Stivers and Carter see this as a benign form of dictatorship, although those Germans who faced execution for their crimes may have begged to differ.[25] Colonel Howley writes that the US authorities provided the policemen in their Sector with small cards. Printed in both English and German, they just had the words 'rape', 'theft' and 'murder' together with a few basic phrases. The idea was that these would help communication between German policemen and American MPs in an emergency.[26] The recreation of a rehabilitated police force played a hugely important symbolic role in the restoration of order to postwar Berlin. Visible police patrols reinforced a sense that order was returning.

The case of Karl Heinrich, head of the uniformed police

Expressing a Stalinist outlook that was unfamiliar to their western counterparts, the Soviets continued to influence personnel decisions in arbitrary ways. Karl Heinrich was one of the first West Berlin policemen to disappear without trace. He was a reminder of the persistence, in certain Communist quarters, of an antipathy towards the police, as an enemy of 'the people'. Prior to 1933, he had been a senior policeman but had been dismissed by the Nazis for political unreliability.[27] Afterwards, Heinrich spent seven years (1935–42) in various Nazi prisons and Concentration Camps. After the war, the Soviets appointed him commander of the uniformed police (*Kommandeur der Schutzpolizei*) in Berlin. Police President Markgraf called him to a meeting in East Berlin, on 2 August 1945, after which he was never seen again.[28] The Soviets later claimed that Heinrich had been guilty of secretly collaborating with the Gestapo.[29] They accused him of a range of anti-democratic and 'counter-revolutionary offences'. Jochen Staadt argues that Heinrich was hated by the Nazis and Communists alike for his actions during the last days of the Weimar Republic. Joseph Goebbels had dubbed him 'Truncheon Heinrich', a phrase that also appeared in Communist propaganda.[30] Fred Loll, a former Communist, had been appointed Police Inspector for Neukölln, in the American Sector. When he attended a meeting in the Presidium in the early summer of 1945, he asked if his new commander was the same person as 'Truncheon Heinrich'. He connected him to police brutality in suppressing a Communist demonstration in 1929. Markgraf and Berzarin encouraged Loll to bring any evidence he had against Heinrich to them. Both Heinrich and his accuser had been incarcerated in Brandenburg Prison during the Third Reich.[31] Other Communist former prisoners came forward to accuse Heinrich of having shown excessive zeal in his role as barracks elder. They accused him of informing on fellow inmates and of hitting them with a rubber truncheon.[32]

The precise accusation in 1945 was that Heinrich had illegally possessed a pistol and had taken part in the 'Bloody May' suppression of a Communist demonstration in 1929.[33] However, Heinrich had also tried to get the British to sack unsuitable police recruits. Some alleged that he was gathering material, implicating senior Communists in the police, not least Erich Mielke.[34] The *Social Democrat* newspaper contrasted the fate of Heinrich, an upstanding defender of socialism and democracy, with that of Markgraf, who before his capture had willingly and loyally served Hitler. Markgraf said that he had asked the Soviets several times what happened to Heinrich but was told that it was a Soviet, not a German, matter.[35] Two years after his disappearance, the East Berlin newspaper *Berliner Zeitung* published a letter Heinrich had supposedly written to Hitler in October 1944. It stated that he wished to take part in the momentous struggle for his people's existence. Nevertheless, the *Social Democrat* newspaper dismissed this as a forgery.[36] Given what had happened to Heinrich, Stumm became wary of the Soviets and took other policemen to every meeting in Karlshorst, in an attempt to prevent himself from being arrested like Heinrich. He remembered having to watch his every step. The Soviets were quick to regret having taken him back. He recounted reluctantly becoming a key character in a tense political thriller.[37]

Communist domination of the newly formed police

Markgraf's appointment was of crucial importance in establishing Communist power throughout Berlin. Stumm later complained of Soviet interference, Communist spying and frequent disappearances.[38] The Soviet intelligence agency, the NKVD, played an important but sketchy role in the reconstruction of the police. The Soviets gave several leading positions to former political prisoners, who had recently been released from Brandenburg Prison. German Communists, who had managed to survive Hitler's repression, found it hard to take certain orders, even when they came from the Red Army.[39] In the first flush of victory over Nazism, they were keen to hang out red flags and other KPD symbols. Some armed themselves, ready to construct revolutionary barricades. Some saw the bourgeoisie, rather than the Nazis, as their main enemy.[40] Recently released Communists in Charlottenburg, for example, were initially reluctant to take orders from a former *Wehrmacht* officer. They warned Markgraf that they would arrest him, if he dared to set foot in Charlottenburg.[41] One KPD veteran, Heinrich Fomferra, resented having to work with ex-Nazi 'slime-people'. It seemed cruel and unjust of the Soviets to force those persecuted by the Nazis to work with such people.[42]

Expertise and professional skills were in short supply in 1945. Finding suitably qualified and politically reliable recruits was extremely difficult. The Soviets banned former National Socialist German Workers' Party (NSDAP) members and career soldiers (Markgraf excepted) from joining but, lacking usable records, this ban was difficult to enforce. In the chaos of defeat, hundreds of Nazis, criminals and other unreliable elements were able to infiltrate the fledgling police force. The postwar confusion made it difficult to check their names against criminal and other records. Pretending to be former Concentration-Camp inmates was a way of getting access to police salaries and ration cards. At the height of cynicism, Gestapo and SS men tried to join the police under the pretence of being Antifascists.[43] Stumm later claimed that many of his police recruits were 'old lags from Brandenburg Prison'. Somehow they had managed to convince the Soviets that they were actually political detainees.[44] Fred Loll records how he recruited as many Communists ('our comrades') as possible. Nevertheless, a few '33ers' (policemen dismissed by the Nazis) were necessary to teach them basic policing.[45] Many policemen active in the Third Reich eventually managed to return to policing, first in the Federal Republic and then in West Berlin. Claiming professionalism and continued commitment to legality, they often insisted that they had been absorbed into the SS or the Gestapo against their will. They could continue to fight gypsies and vagrants, asocials and career criminals using similar techniques and perspectives to those deployed in the Third Reich.[46] From 1959, a number of these policemen were put on trial for offences, including war crimes and genocide, they had committed during the Third Reich.[47]

The new police could establish rudimentary criminal investigation departments as early as June 1945. Their focus was on the most serious crimes: murders committed by unknown perpetrators; missing persons; the identification of bodies; deadly accidents, including hit-and-runs; arson; sex offences, involving women and children; incest, rape, sadism; homosexuality and blackmail of homosexuals; procuring, pimping and abortion; and the spreading of pornography. The vice squad treated male and female prostitution as distinct crimes, requiring different specialists. By the beginning of 1946, Berlin had established an unenviable reputation for itself as the world's foremost crime capital.[48] 'Incidents involving Russians', the combating of VD (venereal disease) and the black market constituted key initial issues facing the police. The authorities recorded an unprecedented number of murders, suicides and thefts, together with sex crimes. For many German citizens, the problems caused by defeat – whether administrative chaos, hunger or the total collapse of the central German state – seemed insurmountable. There was a strong desire for normalcy, but it was hampered by the continued spike in criminality. Food scarcity and economic distress were seen as the causes of most crimes. Nevertheless, the Berlin population was said to be overjoyed at being able to converse with policemen 'in their own language, without losing their watches in the process'.[49] Ordinary Berliners recorded the hope and sense of safety inspired by once again seeing policemen on the streets.[50]

Gangs of orphaned young Germans joined together to fend for themselves. Children, in particular, were quicker and smaller and thereby more difficult to catch. Roaming the streets, boys aged ten to twelve relished their independence. They adapted to the circumstances of hungry mothers and absent fathers by rapidly becoming streetwise survivors. Historian Paul Steege argues that young people were often more adept black-market traders than adults.[51] They created their own hierarchies and moral norms and made whole areas of the city unsafe after dark.[52] Around one-third of such teenagers were supposed to have been infected with venereal diseases. Experts debated what to do with these criminally inclined youths.

Most of the police recruits were thrown into patrolling without any training, let alone medical or academic tests. Few of the recruits had any previous experience of policing. For those with a clean record and good physical health, however, policing as a career was suddenly open to them.[53] In spite of their inexperience and lack of training, they were thrown straight into police work and learned on the job. Their new line of work was risky: more than fifty officers were killed in the first years after the war.[54] The hungry, makeshift policemen tried their best to prevent the worst. Unarmed and poorly equipped, they lacked nearly everything – whether buildings, working equipment, motorized transportation, weapons, means of communications or records – necessary for effective policing. The police not only lacked vehicles and office equipment; even paper was in short supply. At first, the hastily recruited and inexperienced police volunteers did not even have suitable uniforms. Although in theory supposed to wear pre-1933 uniforms, policemen were just one element in a long list of people in desperate need of clothing. Often the only thing indicating that the new recruits were policemen was a white armband with 'German Police' written in German and Russian.[55] In 1945, their main tasks included finding missing persons, searching for weapons and defusing and destroying old munitions.[56]

Later, policemen wore whatever they could find, so that a colourful confusion of assorted styles reigned.[57] Policemen who looked like scarecrows were bad for authority. Dyeing former *Wehrmacht* uniforms proved ineffective. 'Whenever it rained or snowed, our policemen looked like tigers – the dye ran down them in broad stripes.'[58] Nevertheless, by December 1945, the police were sufficiently smartly dressed, for their changing of the guard at the Town Hall, to remind one contemporary of the 'finest days of Prussian drill'. Despite French efforts at deprussianization, there was little evidence that the force had been freed from such a yoke. Professionalism was important both to the Allies and to the German population, but their understandings of what it meant differed markedly. The Mayor, Dr Arthur Werner, stated that he did not think that the public would take umbrage at such a noble and uplifting display of order and discipline.[59] The Allies only issued recruits with wooden truncheons in September 1945.[60] Before then, every crook in the city knew that the police were completely defenceless. With large quantities of weapons and ammunition in circulation, the 'chair legs', provided by the British, were of little use in dealing with heavily armed gangs.[61] Armed bandits were outgunning the poorly armed police. However, the British and French dragged their feet on equipping patrols with pistols.

Detectives insisted that they needed to be able to carry pistols in all four sectors. However, in July 1945, the Americans arrested five detectives, for carrying sidearms, and brought them before a Military Tribunal.[62] Even police chief Markgraf found himself the victim of a carjacking, after being forced to hand over his service revolver to American MPs at the border.[63] The rules of occupation forbade all German policemen from interfering with or apprehending Allied soldiers; this was the sole responsibility of Allied MPs. In the early days of the occupation, lightly armed 'cavalry scout cars' patrolled the city, on the lookout for black-market traders and smugglers.[64] Adding to the confusion, there were criminal gangs and Displaced Persons (DPs) wearing cast-off Soviet and American uniforms.[65] Initially, none of the Allies placed much faith in the German police force. The Western Allies stuck to their policy of keeping the Germans at arm's length (symbolized by a refusal to shake hands with Germans or to allow them to salute them) even after they realized that the Soviets had no such qualms. However, little by little, they were able to transfer responsibility for public order and security to the German policemen under their command.[66]

The Allies established a rudimentary police school in Spandau in November 1945; however, it could do little to help the situation.[67] The first cohort passed out in December 1945. They had received first aid and weapons training, in addition to learning about Allied regulations. In their post-Potsdam push for demilitarization, the Allies were determined that there should be no 'Sergeant-Major atmosphere (*Feldwebelton*)' in the training institutions. They were anxious to stress the civilian, democratic character of the new police, in contrast to its recent misuse by the Nazis.[68] Contemporary reports and memoirs suggest that the new recruits were completely overwhelmed by the level of criminal activity and chaos they faced. Often, they could only record that a crime had been committed, without being able to intervene.[69] Secret intelligence reports record Berliners blaming the high rates of petty crime on leniency. The 'democratized' police were less willing to infringe citizens' rights, even when those involved were clearly criminals. Given the degree to which the population was suffering, not least because of crime, they felt that criminals deserved to be inconvenienced by cold jails.[70] Much of the city's infrastructure had been damaged, either by the aerial bombing or by the house-to-house fighting. It took months to get telephone exchanges and public transport working again. Getting streetlamps lit in the evenings was an important achievement in the crime-fighting endeavour, accomplished in the British and American Sectors in March 1946.[71] The French, like the Soviet Sector, remained gloomy and crime-ridden.

Policemen only received 160 Reichsmarks a month but were given the best ration category.[72] As a consequence, people joined the police for the food, clothing and shelter it could offer, rather than a genuine desire to help their fellow citizens. Consequently, many recruits only saw their police membership as temporary until conditions improved. Nevertheless, it took sturdy and stout-hearted people to earn their living this way rather than by trading cigarettes.[73] An American, who worked closely with the police at this time, said that many of them were old, 'emaciated, indifferent and totally unprepared' for police duty.[74] They worked fourteen to sixteen hours a day, often patrolling outside in all weathers. They had to write their reports by hand because there were no typewriters or ribbons. Without cars or vans, they had to ferry prisoners to and from court using crowded public transport. There was no other way of transporting serious criminals, even if they were guilty of triple murder.[75] Literacy was a strong advantage for budding detectives; arguably the police needed people who could sift through evidence as well as daredevils.[76] In the 1940s as in the 1920s and 1930s, the police headquarters was conveniently located next to the main criminal district. Policemen did not have to go far to meet their touts in the seedy bars around Alexanderplatz.[77] Communicating with the police stations was difficult because of the lack of telephone and wireless communication. In many stations, registration index files lay strewn on the floor of windowless rooms; the telephones had been ripped out of the walls. The remaining furniture had been smashed to pieces.[78] Nevertheless, the reopening of police stations was a cause for muted optimism and even celebration. On its own, this had an important symbolic and psychological impact.

The recruits endured long hours and poor working conditions for relatively low pay; consequently, there was a great deal of turnover of staff.[79] Four thousand people had left the police by the end of 1945. Seventy-five per cent of the original complement were no longer policemen by the middle of 1946. Contemporaries referred to this huge flow of people in and then out of the organization with the phrase 'Everyone should try being a policeman at least once'. Criminals seemed inexorably drawn to police service, like flies to a cowpat, keen to take advantage of the chaos. Even non-criminal officers were subject to enormous temptation to profit from the disarray, not least by exploiting the scarcity of food amid a roaring black market. The belief that the police took the confiscated goods for themselves was widespread.[80] The Linienstraße headquarters resembled a 'bubbling cauldron': people came and went; policemen made arrests only to be arrested themselves or simply disappeared.[81] Where possible, the postwar *Volkspolizei* continued to use criminal albums created in the 1930s.

Compared to Vienna, the Berlin police force was relatively well purged of Nazis in the immediate postwar period. Nevertheless, there too was a desperate need for expertise and knowhow.[82] As Heinrich had complained before disappearing: the haste with which the police force had been reconstructed meant that large numbers of 'untrained, inept and even criminal elements' had managed to infiltrate it.[83] Twenty-three per cent of the dismissals of policemen in 1947 were for criminal behaviour.[84] Some criminals had joined the police because they thought that it would protect them from arrest. Adding to the confusion, there were a number of 'phony detectives' using stolen warrant cards to commit crimes.[85] The American Public Safety Branch viewed a significant number of high-ranking officers as 'unqualified' and unsuited for their positions but could not persuade the Soviets to dismiss them.[86] The need to replace so many personnel meant that denazification remained a continual problem and a strain on Allied Public Safety departments.[87]

According to eastern statistics, which should be taken with caution, the detective squads consisted of:

17 per cent of old civil servants in the Soviet Sector
43 per cent in the American Sector
45 per cent in the British Sector
23 per cent in the French Sector.[88]

These figures suggest that the Anglo-Americans preferred experience while the French and Soviets retained Antifascists longer.

Recruitment of policewomen

As well as the many men, a few brave women plucked up the courage to join the Berlin police. The British and Soviets were particularly keen on their appointment, but the British nevertheless insisted on employing them on an inferior basis.[89] The *Kommandatura*'s Public Safety Sub-Committee agreed to appoint women to the uniformed police on 23 April 1946. The police authorities now looked for young women, aged between twenty-three and thirty. As well as adequate education, they needed to possess relevant life experience. Previous professional experience, especially in the fields of 'social work, nursing, teaching, customer service or the civil service', was crucial. In addition to a flawless reputation, candidates needed to be over 1.6 metres tall, be 'physically well constituted' and to possess good eyesight. They should know how to swim and be ready to be tested on their courage and agility. Former Nazis need not apply.[90]

The training would not be easy for them: few women were expected to cope with abstract logic or dry paragraphs from legal texts.[91] Newsreels showed girls in shorts grappling with each other and grabbing each other by the hair, at the police training school, while uniformed male policemen looked on and laughed. Recruits received necessary training in self-defence and judo. After just six weeks of training, those who passed the tests were ready for practical service. The first batch of uniformed policewomen were assigned to the inner-city police stations in August 1946. The Allies divided the initial eighty uniformed recruits equally between the four sectors.[92] By March 1947, there were 353 of them.[93] Once trained and put on the streets, their main tasks involved searching female detainees and taking charge of children and juveniles.[94] The new female beat members began patrolling in the company of male officers. The first uniforms for both men and women were dyed labour service uniforms. Women were expected to make full use of their female tact and capacity for empathy. Often this was more effective than the standard 'rough male justice'.[95] Soppily, *Neues Deutschland* declared that they would soon capture 'the hearts of Berliners'; the *Telegraf* called them Berlin's fearsome amazons.[96] Male Berliners demonstrated a certain amount of respect for their determination. They seemed to be holding their own.

The press showed an inordinate interest in the 'pretty' uniforms that the female recruits would wear and described them in meticulous detail. Helping to free Berlin of dubious characters required 'neat and tidy' pigeon-blue uniforms, altering the street scene substantially.⁹⁷ The *Tagesspiegel* foresaw a struggle between rule violators and 'heart breakers'. These courageous young women were no longer 'guardians of the stove'; instead, they protected law and order. Fitting the sexist, patronizing tone, their three-month probation was described as an 'engagement period'.⁹⁸ Nevertheless, despite positive press coverage, they continued to face opposition from within the higher ranks of the police. One internal report declared that women were both unpredictable and unusable. Training them was simply 'not worth the effort'. It concluded that women were like flowers: if they were not constantly cared for and looked after, then they tended to wilt.⁹⁹ There were still 219 uniformed policewomen in the western sectors in 1950. But, by September 1953, there were only 115 left.¹⁰⁰

In coping with the manifold pressures and tensions generated by everyday policing, ordinary patrolmen tend to fall back on themselves. Everyday policing practice is strongly shaped by the prevailing 'police culture'. Each police precinct develops its own specific values, norms and meaning-giving perspectives. Policing historian Robert Reiner also refers to this insulated mentality as 'craft rules' or 'cop culture'. Others see such a rank-and-file modus operandus as a 'canteen culture' that is impervious to change. Often it manages to frustrate managerial strategies and policies, not least externally imposed reforms. Values, attitudes and behaviours are shaped more by the realities of the situation they face and peer pressure than by pressure from on high. Criminologists focus on the organization's assumptions and behavioural norms, as reflected in the specific requirements of beat patrolling. Training is designed to 'strip away', or divest, individuals of their 'personal characteristics' and to reform them with the organization's values and ethos. However, the harshness of the conditions they encounter creates something of a 'reality shock'. Reinforced by the 'war stories' that the veterans recount, an alternative, informal teaching or socialization takes place. There is a rapid shift in perceptions and attitudes: recruits become more cynical and pessimistic; they lose any residual idealism or naivety. Their sense of mission and desire to impact on society become blunted. Working every day with people they perceive as the dregs of society – marginal people they call 'the basic form of life in the jungle conditions of the bad areas' – they can end up with a warped view of society, based on a strong sense of it being 'us against them'.¹⁰¹ Professional suspiciousness, when combined with isolation, tends to reinforce a sense of 'internal solidarity' and a feeling of 'us against the world'.¹⁰² In their interactions with the public, patrolmen and women are constantly reading how people react towards their uniform, whether they look 'rattled'. This suspiciousness, which they require to do their job, easily leads to cynicism about politics and other reform measures.

There is a strong pressure to internalize the prevailing culture. Faced with a vociferous and threatening macho culture, fresh policemen and women are wise to keep their opinions and impressions to themselves. Often the peer group is more influential on values and norms than management or community expectations. Policemen can gang up on each other as well as on criminals and members of the public who annoy them by 'talking back'.¹⁰³ To survive in the precinct and on the streets, both policemen and women must develop a thick, hardened skin. Police officers rely on one another in potentially very dangerous situations. The dangers of street policing make bonds with fellow officers especially important. Officers expect their comrades demonstratively to 'pull their weight', by defending and backing up their fellow officers. Police employees monitor one another for signs of egotism or disloyalty. They are conditioned to read aloofness in one another as a threat. People who rock the boat or who go against the prevailing norms can be ostracized in such circumstances. It is easy for policemen to become insular. Feeling besieged from all angles, they pull up the drawbridge and become an even tighter community. Faced by outside threats, they close ranks; to go against the culture is not just to invite critique but runs the risk of losing vital opportunities for support. To fit in and maintain support, they have to turn a blind eye to infractions, abuses and mistakes.[104] In part, police authority is based on tone of voice and body language. But belonging is also demonstrated and maintained through banter and in-jokes. As Hills argues, indigenous police cultures are notoriously impervious and 'resistant to change'. Berlin supports Hills's contention that the imposition of women officers, particularly when only motivated by outside scrutiny and intervention, tends not to alter the prevailing mindset or 'canteen culture'.[105]

The same senior policemen who stood up to the spread of Communist influence in the police also resisted the employment of women in important positions. *Schupo* chief, Hans Kanig, argued that women should be employed solely as typists and be paid at the level of a cleaning lady.[106] Although hostile to Kanig, in terms of office politics, Dr Stumm agreed that women were simply psychologically incapable of police service.[107] For their part, the police recruits denied that they were only good for looking after women and children.[108] They resented being dubbed a sort of '*Blitzmädel*' (the term for uniformed *Wehrmacht* assistants). 'We are all war widows, who have to look after children.' In comparison to the women trading their virtue for a few cigarettes, they were proud of their duty and sacrifice. They suggested that the newspapers might like to write negatively about such women instead.[109] Up to 17 March 1947, forty-four members of the Women *Schutzpolizei* left or had to leave police service (Table 2).

Policewomen continued to play an important, but undervalued, role in policing Berlin. Twenty-six-year-old Fräulein Eva T. was the first uniformed Police Sergeant in the British Sector. The male interviewer was taken with her mixture of feminine charm combined with conscientiousness and discipline. Nevertheless, she did not have the power to give orders to her male colleagues.[110] In 1952, the police high command

Table 2 Reasons for Women Leaving Police Service, 1947

Unfit for police service	17 police women
Of their own accord	16
Unfitness for further service	4
Removed from service for important reasons	5
By order of the Military Government	1
Deceased	1
Total	44

Public Safety Committee: 'Berlin's Women Schutzpolizei' (19.3.1947), Landesarchiv Berlin, C Rep 303-09, Nr. 73, 203.

made the momentous decision to allow its policewomen to wear make-up and nylons while on duty.¹¹¹ Patrol women in Neukölln complained that they continued to receive sexist comments from their colleagues. Male policemen said women were unsuited for the work and fell ill more frequently. Female recruits protested that it was the lack of adequate underwear and shoes that made policewomen ill. They said that their health would be much better if they were allowed to wear trousers.¹¹² Retrospectively, the decision to appoint Female Uniformed Police (*Weibliche Schutzpolizei*, WSP), who were quickly dubbed 'wasps', was presented as a popular move. Many were single mothers with several children to support. In the western sectors, recruitment of women was only a stopgap measure; the police stopped recruiting women in 1950, after the breakdown of four-power relations. Following a cold-war hiatus, the West Berlin force only began recruiting women for uniformed service again in 1978.¹¹³ Throughout the early period, the police hierarchy considered women police more as social workers, with a special welfare role, than as equal colleagues.¹¹⁴ Nevertheless, when the police were armed (in January 1946), they too carried pistols as well as their truncheons.¹¹⁵

Female detectives

Twenty-two female detectives were serving in April 1946. Only four of them were fully qualified employees; the others attended training in addition to their daytime duties. Led by a 22-year-old ardent Communist, they were mainly responsible for the questioning of women and female adolescents. They also inspected cinemas and theatres, bars and other places of amusement. The women detectives complained about the conditions they were working under. The strains were immense, and the risk of illness was high, particularly because of inadequate clothing, footwear and sanitation. Often, they had to take part in night-time raids. The women were responsible for accompanying children to and from the main children's home. Questioning and transporting girls, who were 'covered from head to toe in syphilitic rashes, as well as lice-ridden children and young people with gonorrhoea', was particularly dangerous because of the continued lack of soap. The adults they had to search following black-market raids were often 'equally as revolting' (Table 3).¹¹⁶

As a sign of the importance of equal rights in East Berlin, the Soviets closed a separate women's investigation department and transferred the female detectives to mixed departments.¹¹⁷ The American Sector was the first to decentralize its female detectives. After the fact, they judged the appointment of women to the district police stations to have been very expedient. The female police were praised for their work in rounding up stray kids and getting them back into school.¹¹⁸ Nevertheless, they needed to be quicker in catching the young ruffians, who stole ration cards and then disappeared either into the ruins or their homes.¹¹⁹ Over time, the female detectives got to know all the regular young prostitutes and their madams, so that it was difficult to feign innocence and to continue lying about what they were up to. Although hunger explained why many girls started to sell their bodies, prostitution was seen as stemming from a craving for pleasure together with a reluctance to do honest work. Otherwise inoffensive fifteen-year-olds wanted to possess watches, mechanical pencils, nail care

Table 3 Crimes That the WKP (Female Detective Police) Dealt with in the Period 1 December 1946 to 9 April 1947

	Children under the age of 14	Young people under 18
Petty larceny	52	28
Grand larceny	10	7
Bodily injury	1	2
Fraud	1	–
Document forgery	–	1
Embezzlement	–	2
Damage to property	1	1
Stealing by finding	2	–
Unauthorized possession of weapons	1	–
Threats	10	26
Refusal to work	–	1

K. K. Schöneberg, W.K.P: Bericht (Schöneberg, den 10. April 1947), Landesarchiv Berlin, C Rep 303-09, Nr. 249, 25.

and toiletry sets like their classmates. They paid for these through sex, often with Allied servicemen.

Dangerous work

In postwar Berlin, policing could literally resemble a minefield. Because police stations were used to stockpile and safeguard munitions found in the rubble, the danger of explosion was all too real. Several major accidents occurred, one of them caused by a young recruit joking around with a live hand grenade.[120] He accidentally pulled the pin and then in a panic threw it back on the pile of munitions. The other policemen in the courtyard had time to get to safety before the whole lot of munitions (estimated at over a hundred tons) went off. Two were nevertheless killed and over a hundred people were injured, some very seriously. As a former soldier, he was supposed to know better; he got a year and three months in prison.[121] The *Telegraf* suggested that people who dealt every day with explosives began not to see their danger.[122] In all, fifty-two policemen were killed making safe munitions in the first months of the occupation.[123]

As the previous and subsequent chapters will demonstrate, the down-on-its-luck megalopolis developed a reputation for crime and corruption, tinged with vice. The black market further eroded notions of law and order already undermined by Nazism and war. The presence of large numbers of single soldiers encouraged iniquity as well as power imbalance. According to the *Daily Mail*, because the city lacked proper 'unified control' it became a haven for criminals. The British tabloid summarized the remaining refugees and POWs as 'ne'er-do-wells ... all the imaginable thugs and rascals' that, like parasites, attached themselves to the prone body 'of a once flourishing community'.[124] The initial lawlessness encouraged ongoing deprivation and violence. However, the introduction of rapid-response 'flying squads' and improved communications did improve the situation somewhat.[125]

Displaced Persons and the black market

The black market had been a major problem since before the end of the war. In the dark halls of Friedrichstrasse station, young lads and girls, but also adults, murmured the prices for chocolate, American cigarettes, candy, nylon stockings or coffee.[126] The waiting rooms were home not just to black-market traders but to a motley crew of beggars, vagrants and whores. They responded to attempts to move them on with violence and hoots of derision. After a successful razzia, they were back in the same waiting room two hours later, laughing at the station management and at the toothless police.[127] Contemporaries condemned the black market for thwarting legitimate trade. The major racketeers grew fat by exploiting the needy.

In the immediate postwar years, DPs dominated the black market in Berlin. Many of them had been forced labourers or Concentration-Camp inmates before Nazi rule collapsed.[128] After 1945, they lived in United Nations Relief and Rehabilitation Administration (UNRRA) camps and were not allowed to do normal work.[129] Given their experiences prior to German defeat, in any case, the DPs disliked the idea of working for Germans. The idea of requiring such liberated forced labourers to work among their former slavemasters was abhorrent to them and to the Allies. Nevertheless, this separation tended to create alternative systems, which were difficult for outside authorities to control and police. With Berliners ready to trade their valuables and precious metals for food, made available by the Allies, the DPs were in a relatively privileged position as middlemen.[130] The DP camps operated like miniature cities. As well as barber and shoe-repair shops, theatres, recreational facilities and churches, they possessed their own governing bodies. These administered the internal affairs of the camp relatively efficiently, but also allowed them to function as states within the state, with their own rules and omerta.[131]

About 6,000–7,000 Polish Jews lived in the Mariendorf and Schlachtensee-Düppel camps in the American Sector. For their part, Berliners denounced these camps as 'hotbeds of criminal activity', peopled and policed by foreign delinquents.[132] As well as Jews, there were stateless men and women from Soviet-controlled territories.[133] Given that they were made up of no fewer than forty different nationalities, they were difficult to organize and to police. Some female DPs engaged in prostitution.[134] In March 1946, German police in Stuttgart shot and killed a Jewish DP. The victim of the shooting had survived Auschwitz and Mauthausen and only just been reunited with his family.[135] Subsequently, the Allies banned German police from entering the camps armed or without Military Police supervision.

In the words of *Der Spiegel*, after 1945, Berlin became an 'El Dorado of shady characters of the demimonde and underworld'. Four-power Berlin acted as a haven for all sorts of stateless individuals and foreigners.[136] On no account were they willing to enter the Soviet Sector: 'I stay in American Sector. I not go in Soviet Sector!' Attempts to arrest them led crowds to form, which insulted and threatened the police, in broken

German.¹³⁷ The DPs, who had been uprooted and had suffered terribly under the Third Reich, saw all German officials as criminals.¹³⁸ Guilty Germans continued to stigmatize them as unruly lawbreakers and intrusive, invasive foreigners, rather than as victims of national socialism. Although, to some extent, nearly everyone participated in the black market (including policemen), Berliners sought to hold the foreigners solely responsible for this evil.¹³⁹ Historian Laura Hilton challenges the notion that DPs were principally responsible for black-market trading. She argues that German involvement in illicit trading was far greater in terms both of numbers and of proportions than either DPs or Allied troops.¹⁴⁰ Nevertheless, the myth of postwar Jewish victimization of Germans was widespread and affected some Allied perceptions and actions.¹⁴¹ For the East Berlin press, foreign black marketeers were parasitic nuisances who should be energetically dealt with by the police. They saw the 'gold and silver men' of Potsdamer Platz as extremely pushy, despite their broken German. 'You know the faces. For months, it's the same ones. Only the police seem unable to recognize them.'¹⁴²

Remnants of Nazi racism mingled with Communist prejudices against DPs who refused to be repatriated to the Soviet Union and other Eastern Bloc countries. A concerned citizen wrote to his local Mayor, condemning DP women who used their prams as cover. They did not seem ashamed to neglect their housework. The phrase 'parasites on the racial body (*Parasiten am Volkskörper*)' and the desire for harsh action was reminiscent of Nazi racism. For Herr D., the very least the authorities could do was to force them to perform labour.¹⁴³ Clearly there was a residue of antisemitism in this kind of language. Another Berliner went so far as to accuse the police of being in cahoots with the black-market traders.¹⁴⁴ Black marketeers of all stripes tried to bribe policemen to turn a blind eye to their activities. Razzias could involve the arrest and processing of as many as 16,000 people. There had been 165 of these mass arrests by June 1946.¹⁴⁵

Conclusion

The chaos of defeat was the antithesis of Germany's famous order and discipline but did not compare to the damage wrought by a civil war. It was an enormous struggle to contain the forces of disorder, but German policemen and women took on this difficult task. Hastily recruited, inexperienced volunteers lacked nearly everything necessary for their work. The recruits – most of whom had no relevant experience – were sent out to police the ruined streets with only rudimentary equipment, understanding and ability. Tired and hungry volunteers paced the streets, with only a flimsy armband to show that they were policemen. On-the-job learning was crucial: policemen and policewomen gained their most important skills and knowhow from their more experienced colleagues. Their bravery and self-sacrifice meant that a difficult and dangerous situation did not become worse.

Creating an effective police force was a crucial part of restoring law and order to the city. Although it was a key early priority, there were limits on how far the occupation authorities could identify former National Socialists to prevent them from serving. The chapter takes account of the *Kommandatura* decision to recruit and employ women as patrol officers. Despite sexist opposition from the police hierarchy, they played a crucial role in helping the population to survive. With their help, the police force became the thin blue line between order and chaos. They braved the elements in threadbare, ill-assorted uniforms and inadequate footwear, determined to keep the people of Berlin safe. In the first year after the war, as well as those killed by munitions, seventeen policemen were killed on duty and a further eighty suffered serious injuries. Many of the recruits were incompetent or politically 'undesirable'; some were hardened criminals. There was a high turnover as people joined and left the police service, depending on the wider economic and food situation. The Berlin police had few resources to fight the crime wave; they lacked nearly everything. Although the police fought to re-establish order, their efforts were often undermined by the continued presence of Allied troops, who were immune to prosecution by German courts. Despite the valiant efforts of the police, the very dire economic and food situation in Berlin cast a long shadow. In the extremely difficult postwar conditions, nearly everyone engaged in some kind of illicit trading. Nevertheless, most would have been law abiding 'under normal conditions'.[146] Although tasked with eliminating it, policemen could also be found trading on the black market or misappropriating confiscated goods. Although hunger was an important factor, not all crimes were economically motivated. There were cases of kidnappings of children, back-street abortions, illicit sexual relations with minors and exhibitionism.[147]

Notes

1 Alice Hills, *Policing Post-Conflict Cities* (London: Zed, 2009).
2 Eugene Gilbert Jones, 'The Allied Reconstruction of the Berlin Police, 1945-1948', PhD, University of California, San Diego, 1986, 66.
3 Norbert Steinborn and Hilmar Krüger, *Die Berliner Polizei 1945 bis 1992: von der Militärreserve im Kalten Krieg auf dem Weg zur bürgernahen Polizei?* (Berlin: Arno Spitz, 1993), 3. Befehl des Militärkommandanten der Stadt Berlin (25 May 1945), Landesarchiv Berlin, C Rep 303-09, Nr. 20. Oberst Markgraf: 'Wir packen mit an, Ordnung schaffen', 25 May 1945, C Rep 303-09, Nr. 1.
4 Stefan Winckler, 'Ein Markgraf als williger Vollstrecker des Totalitarismus. Die Biographie des deutschen Berufsoldaten Paul H. Markgraf (SED) unter besonderer Berücksichtigung seiner Amtszeit als Berliner Polizeipräsident 1945-48/49', in *Die DDR – Analysen eines aufgegebenen Staates*, ed. Heiner Timmermann (Berlin: Duncker and Humblot, 2001), 343–56.
5 'La Situation à Berlin', no date, ca. 1948, Archives Diplomatiques, GMFB 1/214. The article in *Völkische Beobachter*, 10 January 1943, was helpfully reproduced by the *Telegraf*, 2 January 1947.
6 Jochen Staadt, 'Die Berliner Polizei in der "Stunde Null"', in *Feindwärts der Mauer: Das Ministerium für Staatssicherheit und die West-Berliner Polizei*, ed. Klaus Schroeder and Jochen Staadt (Frankfurt am Main: Peter Lang, 2014), 20. Cf. Peter Rhode, 'Lebensbild des Genossen Oberst der VP a.D. Paul Markgraf', Diplomarbeit, 1988, 3, Police Museum, Paul Markgraf File.
7 Federal Commission for the Records of the States Security Services of the GDR (*Bundesbeauftragte für die Unterlagen des Staatssicherheitsdienstes der ehemaligen DDR*), BStU MfS AP 8203/65.

8. Jones, 'The Allied Reconstruction', 80–1.
9. Erich Kuby, *The Russians and Berlin, 1945*, trans. Arnold J. Pomerans (London: Heinemann 1968), 309.
10. Winckler, 'Ein Markgraf als williger Vollstrecker des Totalitarismus'.
11. Curt Riess, *The Berlin Story* (London: Frederick Muller, 1953), 45.
12. Steinborn and Krüger, *Die Berliner Polizei*, 50.
13. Klaus Hübner, *Einsatz: Erinnerungen des Berliner Polizeipräsidenten 1969–1987* (Berlin: Jaron, 1997), 320–1.
14. Jones, 'The Allied Reconstruction', 82.
15. Steinborn and Krüger, *Die Berliner Polizei*, 44.
16. Patrick Wagner, *Hitlers Kriminalisten: die deutsche Kriminalpolizei und der Nationalsozialismus zwischen 1920 und 1960* (Munich: C. H. Beck, 2002), 149.
17. Jones, 'The Allied Reconstruction', 32, 43, 82, 93, 132.
18. Der Polizeipräsident an die Alliierter Stadtkommandantur, Public Safety Committee, 11 March 1946, Landesarchiv Berlin, C Rep 303-09, Nr. 58, 14f.
19. 'Vergangenheit und Entwicklung der westberliner Polizei'. Berlin, den 12 April 1962, BStU MfS AS 306/80, Band 2, 3f.
20. 'Public Safety July 1945 to 31 August 1949', 1, US National Archives, RG260, box 893.
21. 'British Decoration for Russian Generals', *Times*, 13 July 1945.
22. Their motorcycle patrols played an important role in policing traffic violations, mostly by Allied vehicles.
23. 'Übernahme d. Pol. Inspektion Charlottenburg durch die Engländer', 21 July 1945, Landesarchiv Berlin, C Rep 303-09, Nr. 1.
24. George Bilainkin, 'The Allies in Berlin', *Contemporary Review* 168 (1945): 346.
25. William Stivers and Donald A. Carter, *The City Becomes a Symbol: The U.S. Army in the Occupation of Berlin, 1945–1949* (Washington, DC: Center of Military History, United States Army, 2017), 109.
26. Frank L. Howley, *Berlin Command* (New York: G. P. Putnam's Sons, 1950), 70.
27. 'Der Fall Karl Heinrich', *Der Sozialdemokrat*, 5 June 1947. 'German Held by Russians. Official's Anti-Nazi Record', *Times*, 16 June 1947.
28. 'Ein Kämpfer für die Freiheit. Karl Heinrich, der 1. Kommandeur der Berliner Schutzpolizei nach dem Kriege', *Berliner Polizei* 10, no. 9 (1962).
29. Jones, 'The Allied Reconstruction', 112. Cf. 'Wußte das Markgraf?', *Der Sozialdemokrat*, 24 June 1947.
30. Staadt, 'Die Berliner Polizei in der "Stunde Null"', 48–9.
31. Genosse Fred Loll, 'Diskussionsauszüge zur "Geschichte der Deutschen Volkspolizei"', Police Museum, Paul Markgraf File.
32. 'Sowjetische Untersuchungsakte Karl Heinrich', Privatarchiv Peter Erler. Reproduced in Police Museum, Karl Heinrich File. SPD prisoners had a very different story to tell of Heinrich's behaviour. 'Eine Antwort, aber keine Klärung', *Tagesspiegel*, 19 June 1947.
33. Staadt, 'Die Berliner Polizei in der "Stunde Null"', 50.
34. Forschungsgruppe für Berliner Nachkriegsgeschichte: Bericht über den ersten Kommandeur der Berliner Schutzpolizei nach 1945 Major Karl Heinrich', Berlin-Dahlem, 14 November 1956. Police Museum, Karl Heinrich File.
35. 'Markgrafs Antwort', *Der Sozialdemokrat*, 18 June 1947.
36. '"... Ein unermüdlicher Kämpfer ..." es fragt sich nur, gegen wen. Der Fall des Polizeimajors Heinrich', *Berliner Zeitung*, 27 June 1947. 'Das ist zuviel!', *Der Sozialdemokrat*, 27 June 1947.

37 Riess, *The Berlin Story*, 59.
38 Staadt, 'Die Berliner Polizei in der "Stunde Null"', 30.
39 Genosse Fred Loll.
40 Norman Naimark, *Russians in Germany: A History of the Soviet Zone of Occupation, 1945–1949* (Cambridge, MA: Belknap Press of Harvard University Press, 1995), 270.
41 Staadt, 'Die Berliner Polizei in der "Stunde Null"', 30–1.
42 Naimark, *Russians in Germany*, 43–4.
43 Rhode, 'Lebensbild des Genossen . . . Paul Markgraf', 13.
44 Kuby, *The Russians and Berlin, 1945*, 308.
45 Genosse Fred Loll.
46 Wagner, *Hitlers Kriminalisten*, 155, 169, 185. On the West Berlin police's obligation to take such men back as a result of the 131 cover law, see Mark Fenemore, *Fighting the Cold War in Post-Blockade, Pre-Wall Berlin: Behind Enemy Lines* (London: Routledge, 2019), 93.
47 Wagner, *Hitlers Kriminalisten*, 183.
48 Lieutenant-Colonel W. Byford-Jones, *Berlin Twilight* (London: Hutchinson, 1947), 150.
49 'Vom Knüppel zum Funkwagen. Ganoven, Markgraf und RAD-Uniformen – Die Wandlung der Berliner Polizei seit 1945', *nacht-depesche*, 7/9 May 1955.
50 Karl Deutmann diary, http://www.hdg.de/lemo/forum/kollektives_gedaechtnis/011/index.html (accessed 27 April 2014).
51 Paul Steege, *Black Market, Cold War: Everyday Life in Berlin, 1946–1949* (Cambridge: Cambridge University Press, 2007), 121.
52 Jennifer V. Evans, *Life among the Ruins: Cityscape and Sexuality in Cold War Berlin* (Basingstoke: Palgrave Macmillan, 2011), 40, 69–71.
53 Newsreels show the police racing each other in the Olympic swimming pool while wearing their uniforms. *Welt im Film* 119/1947, 5 September 1947.
54 Riess, *Berlin Story*, 107.
55 Willi Neumann cited in Hans-Werner Hamacher, *Polizei 1945 – ein neuer Anfang*, 2nd edn. (Hilden: Verlag Deutsche Polizeiliteratur, 1989), 217, 270.
56 Jones, 'The Allied Reconstruction', 144. Cf. Staadt, 'Die Berliner Polizei in der "Stunde Null"', 28.
57 'Vom Knüppel zum Funkwagen'.
58 Dr Stumm as cited by Kuby, *The Russians and Berlin, 1945*, 310.
59 Walther Jirak (KPD later SED), '34. Magistratssitzung vom 10. Dezember 1945', LAB (STA), Rep. 100, Nr. 764, Bl. 40-45 reproduced in *Die Sitzungsprotokolle des Magistrats der Stadt Berlin 1945/46*, ed. Dieter Hanauske (Berlin: Arno Spitz, 1995), vol. 1.
60 Jones, 'The Allied Reconstruction', 148.
61 Steinborn and Krüger, *Die Berliner Polizei*, 13.
62 Präsidium der Volkspolizei (ed.), *Zeittafel zur Geschichte der Volkspolizei Berlin 1945-1961* (East Berlin: Präsidium der Volkspolizei, 1985).
63 Alec Cairncross, *A Country to Play With* (Gerrards Cross: Colin Smythe, 1987), 44.
64 US Command Berlin and US Army Berlin, *The Story of The Berlin Brigade* (Military History Branch pamphlet, 1981), 11.
65 Steinborn and Krüger, *Die Berliner Polizei*, 19. Cf. Jones, 'The Allied Reconstruction', 135.
66 Richard Bessel, 'Establishing Order in Post-war Eastern Germany', *Past and Present* 210 (2011): 146.

67 Hamacher, *Polizei 1945 – ein neuer Anfang*, 152.
68 Staadt, 'Die Berliner Polizei in der "Stunde Null"', 53. This contrasted with later developments. Fenemore, *Fighting*, chs 4 and 5. Even before the creation of the *Bereitschaftspolizei* (or Bepo), however, there was some residue of military style that continued to shape leadership style and bearing.
69 Hamacher, *Polizei 1945 – ein neuer Anfang*, 67.
70 'Secret, Headquarters Berlin Command, OMGUS, Combined Intelligence Summary No. 6', 5–11 December 1946, US National Archives, RG 260, Box 903.
71 US Command Berlin and US Army Berlin, *The Story of The Berlin Brigade*, 12.
72 Hamacher, *Polizei 1945 – ein neuer Anfang*, 128.
73 Oberregierungsrat Dr. Horst speaking at the 'Großkundgebung der Berliner Polizei', *Die Berliner Polizei* 2, no. 7 (1950): 124.
74 Correspondence cited by Jones, 'The Allied Reconstruction', 139.
75 Helmut Starke, Berlin, cited in Hamacher, *Polizei 1945 – ein neuer Anfang*, 259.
76 Wolfgang Mittmann, *Gladow-Bande: Die Revolverhelden von Berlin* (Berlin: Das Neue Berlin, 2003), 18, 107, 119.
77 Byford-Jones, *Berlin Twilight*, 151.
78 'Vom Knüppel zum Funkwagen'.
79 Bessel, 'Establishing Order in Post-war Eastern Germany', 149.
80 Steinborn and Krüger, *Die Berliner Polizei*, 21.
81 'Woher Polizisten nehmen?', *Spandauer Volksblatt*, 8 May 1955.
82 Lindsay K. MacNeill, 'Professionalism and Brutality: The Viennese Police and the Public in Extraordinary Times, 1918-1955', PhD, American University, Washington, DC, 2020.
83 Jones, 'The Allied Reconstruction', 87–8.
84 Steinborn and Krüger, *Die Berliner Polizei*, 10.
85 Jones, 'The Allied Reconstruction', 147.
86 'Weekly Intelligence Report No. 1', 16, 3–9 October 1947, US National Archives, RG260, 390/48/27/3, Box 903.
87 It is possible that denazification persisted longer in Berlin than in Vienna. MacNeill, 'Professionalism and Brutality', 366.
88 'Kriminalität und Polizei in Berlin', *Die Volkspolizei: Zeitschrift für das Gesamte Polizeiwesen* no. 4 (June 1948), Landesarchiv Berlin, C Rep 120, Nr. 3249. Unfortunately 'old civil servants' is not defined, but it probably means policemen who served before 1933.
89 Steinborn and Krüger, *Die Berliner Polizei*, 30, 158. Cf. Jones, 'The Allied Reconstruction', 142. The East Germans were subsequently very proud of their women police officers.
90 Der Polizeipräsident in Berlin, 'Bestimmung', 23 April 1946, Landesarchiv Berlin, C Rep 303–09, Nr. 73, 8.
91 'Weibliche Schutzpolizei', *Nachtexpress*, 15 July 1946.
92 'Frauen in Uniform', *Der Tagesspiegel*, 23 August 1946.
93 Public Safety Committee: 'Berlin's Women Schutzpolizei', 19 March 1947, Landesarchiv Berlin, C Rep 303-09, Nr. 73, 202f.
94 'Directives concerning the female police', 23 April 1946, Landesarchiv Berlin, C Rep 303–09, Nr. 73, 22f.
95 '"Fräulein Wachtmeister". Berlin erhält "Mädchen in Uniform"', *Deutsche Volkszeitung*, 10 May 1946. The reference to the 1931 film about lesbian schoolgirls cannot have been accidental.

96 'Weibliche Schutzpolizei in Berlin', *Neues Deutschland*, 22 May 1946. 'Berlins Amazonen', *Telegraf*, 22 May 1946.
97 *Tägliche Rundschau*, 24 May 1946.
98 *Der Tagesspiegel*, 31 October 1946.
99 Anonymous report as cited by Ursula Nienhaus, '"Für strenge Dienstzucht ungeeignete Objekte..." Weibliche Polizei in Berlin 1945-1952', in *Nachkriegspolizei: Sicherheit und Ordnung in Ost- und Westdeutschland, 1945–1969*, ed. Gerhard Fürmetz, Herbert Reinke and Klaus Weinhauer (Hamburg: Ergebnisse Verlag, 2001), 142.
100 'Präsidialabteilung an den Leiter der Präsidialbabteilung Dr Urban: Einstellungen und Entlassungen in der Zeit vom 1.7.1949 bis 1.3.1950', 3 April 1950, Landesarchiv Berlin, E Rep 200-25, Nr. 157-158. 'Die letzte Wespe geht', *Deutsche Polizei* 12 (1986).
101 Reiner nevertheless argues that there are 'distinctions between types of "them" (as well as of "us")'. Robert Reiner, *The Politics of the Police* (Brighton: Wheatsheaf, 1985), 93–4.
102 Michael P. Banton, *The Policeman in the Community* (London: Tavistock, 1964), 107.
103 Ibid., 117, 150–1, 184.
104 Janet Chan, 'Changing Police Culture', *British Journal of Criminology* 36, no. 1 (1996): 109–34, 111. Nevertheless, their understanding of themselves – as having a mission to aid their fellow citizens – can paradoxically make them more resistant to reform than if their goal was simply self-serving and concupiscent. Reiner, *The Politics of the Police*, 89.
105 Hills, *Policing Post-Conflict Cities*, 85, 211.
106 Nienhaus, 'Für strenge Dienstzucht ungeeignet', 144.
107 Steinborn and Krüger, *Die Berliner Polizei*, 158. Cf. *Nürnberger Nachrichten*, 30 June 1951, Landesarchiv Berlin, Rep. 200, Acc. 2549, Nr. 152.
108 'Mädchen in Uniform sind ernst zu nehmen. Mit den Polizistinnen vom Alexanderplatz auf dem Dienstweg', *Tägliche Rundschau*, 13 September 1946.
109 'Für die Ehre unserer weiblichen Polizei', *Nachtexpreß*, 1 April 1947.
110 'Die erste Frau als Polizeioffizier. Neueinrichtung der Schutzpolizei. Betreuung der weiblichen Beamten durch Unterinspektorinnen', *Der Sozialdemokrat*, 15 June 1948.
111 'West Berlin Policewomen', *New York Times*, 17 November 1952.
112 'Schutzpolizistinnen wollen Hosen', *Tägliche Rundschau*, 7 October 1947.
113 'Die letzte Wespe geht'.
114 Klaus Weinhauer, *Schutzpolizei in der Bundesrepublik: Zwischen Bürgerkrieg und Innerer Sicherheit* (Paderborn: Ferdinand Schöningh, 2003), 102.
115 BK/O (46) 35 v. 12.1.1946. Nienhaus, 'Für strenge Dienstzucht ungeeignete Objekte...', 140. 'Mädchen mit Pistole', *Telegraf*, 22 June 1948.
116 Krim.-Inspektion M III: 'Überbelastung und gesundheitliche Gefährdung der W.K.P.', 27 April 1946, Landesarchiv Berlin, C Rep 303-09, Nr. 249, 19f.
117 Präsidium der Volkspolizei (ed.), *Zetttafel*.
118 K.J.M.III: 'Bericht', 16 May 1947, Landesarchiv Berlin, C Rep 303-09, Nr. 249, 27.
119 Weibl. Kriminalpolizei Steglitz/Zehlendorf: 'Bericht', Steglitz, den 10. April 1947, Landesarchiv Berlin, C Rep 303-09, Nr. 249, 26.
120 'L'explosion du siège de la police de Berlin serait accidentelle', *Le Monde*, 25 July 1947.
121 'Explosion am Alex vor Gericht. 100 Tonnen Blindgänger in die Luft geflogen', *Telegraf*, 18 August 1946.
122 'Leichtsinnigkeit verursachte Explosion', *Telegraf*, 25 July 1947.
123 'Vom Knüppel zum Funkwagen'.

124 Paul Bretherton, 'There's chic again in Berlin's ruins', *Daily Mail*, 6 November 1947.
125 Jones, 'The Allied Reconstruction', 149.
126 'Treffpunkt der Bahnhofsschieber', *Berliner Zeitung*, 18 October 1947. Cf. Gewerbeaussendienst, Gadstelle Mitte: Schwarzhandel am Bahnhof Friedrichstr. 31 December 1947, Landesarchiv Berlin, B Rep 020, Nr. 7091.
127 Mitropa: Schwarzhandel im Bahnhof Friedrichstraße, 15 January1948, Landesarchiv Berlin, B Rep 020, Nr. 7091.
128 Gerhard Fürmetz, Herbert Reinke and Klaus Weinhauer, 'Nachkriegspolizei in Deutschland. Doppelte Polizeigeschichte 1945-1969', in *Nachkriegspolizei*, 17.
129 'Hier sind die schwarzen Märkte', *Vorwärts*, 3 December 1947.
130 'Herr Huber hilft', *Der Spiegel*, 27 February 1952, 9.
131 Berlin Command, OMGUS: 'History of Activities', 1 November 1946-30 June 1947, 84. US National Archives, 390/50/23/3, BOX 19, 143.
132 Steege, *Black Market*, 27.
133 Atina Grossmann, 'Home and Displacement in a City of Bordercrossers. Jews in Berlin 1945-1948', in *Unlikely History: The Changing German-Jewish Symbiosis, 1945-2000*, ed. Leslie Morris and Jack Zipes (New York: Palgrave, 2002), 74.
134 Lucius D. Clay, *Decision in Germany* (Westport, CT: Greenwood, 1970), 232, 234.
135 Atina Grossmann, 'Grams, Calories, and Food: Languages of Victimization, Entitlement and Human Rights in Occupied Germany, 1945-1949', *Central European History* 44, no. 1 (2011): 136-7.
136 'Herr Huber Hilft'.
137 'Goldschieber wollen nicht aus dem amerikanischen Sektor heraus', *Tägliche Rundschau*, 28 November 1947.
138 'Pflieger, Hauptabteilung Preisüberwachung', 26 November 1947, Landesarchiv Berlin, B Rep 020, Nr. 7091.
139 Steege, *Black Market*, 58-9, 295. Jones argues that police involvement 'was largely limited to the first few months of the occupation'. Jones, 'The Allied Reconstruction', note 47, 90/211.
140 Laura J. Hilton, 'The Black Market in History and Memory: German Perceptions of Victimhood from 1945 to 1948', *German History* 28, no. 4 (2010): 490.
141 Fürmetz, Reinke and Weinhauer, 'Nachkriegspolizei in Deutschland', 17. Grossmann, 'Grams, Calories, and Food', 136-7.
142 'Rund um den Potsdamer Platz. Schwarzhandel ganz offiziell', *Montags Echo*, 12 January 1948.
143 Letter from Max D. to Herrn. stellv. Oberbürgermeister Dr Acker, 30 December 1947, Landesarchiv Berlin, B Rep 020, Nr. 7091.
144 'Dr Knacke an das Polizeipräsidium Berlin, Linienstr', 26 January 1948, Landesarchiv Berlin, B Rep 020, Nr. 7091.
145 Steinborn and Krüger, *Die Berliner Polizei*, 20-1.
146 'Weekly Intelligence Report No. 1', 18.
147 K. K. Schöneberg, W.K.P: Bericht (Schöneberg, 10 April 1947), Landesarchiv Berlin, C Rep 303-09, Nr. 249, 25.

3

Allied occupation itself a source of crime

Relief at the end of sole Soviet occupation was tempered by dismay that the black market – with large quantities of currency but a shortage of food – continued.[1] In the immediate days after their arrival in Berlin in July 1945, achieving sovereign control of the area they occupied was of paramount importance to the Western Allies. As the US Public Safety Branch argued, establishing and maintaining law and order in the area it occupied constituted 'the first responsibility' of any occupying power.[2] Nevertheless, lawlessness characterized the western sectors of Berlin, even after the Soviets had been persuaded to leave.[3] Faced with a major crime wave, and with large numbers of illegal arms in circulation, the Allied forces armed their troops.[4] Captain D., a British veteran of the North African campaign, prepared for a night on the town by stashing a pistol and a hand grenade, much to the delight of his fellow revellers.[5] Even for occupation troops, the city remained a violent and potentially dangerous environment. When armed British and Soviet troops got drunk together, an altercation could easily lead to shots being fired.[6] As General Clay put it, 'Soldiers, just out of combat, carrying arms and meeting with the soldiers of three other nations in a conquered city with a destroyed economy, provided the ingredients for an explosive mixture.'[7]

Journalist Ruth Andreas-Friedrich prophetically remarked: 'Our conquerors will lose the game not though war, but through their behaviour in peace.'[8] Although they developed a reputation for disorderly conduct, the Soviets were not the only ones to commit sexual assaults or to discharge their weapons in the street when drunk.[9] Allied soldiers and employees of Military Government were exempt from German law and could only be arrested by Allied Military Police and tried in military courts.[10] Because German police were not allowed to charge them with crimes, Allied soldiers often saw themselves as above the law. Any attempts by the local police to control their behaviour quickly brought reminders of who had defeated whom in World War Two. Humiliating the local police was a widespread sport. In August 1945, American soldiers attacked a policeman in the Tiergarten and played kickabout with his *Tschako* (the distinctive police helmet).[11] In the 'goldfish bowl' atmosphere of postwar Berlin, each occupying army was on public display, not only to the other occupiers but to the civilian population of Berlin. They judged each occupier according to their own, established notions of civilization and decorum by assessing their visible orderliness and discipline.

Although in part guarantors of their security, often Berliners required protection from their protectors. The Military Police docket contained frequent incidences of drunk and disorderly conduct in the immediate postwar period, when drinks were free for Allied servicemen. As the occupation became more established, they also recorded cases of sexual assault and domestic disputes between GIs ('Government-Issue' ordinary US infantrymen) and German women.[12] Reports abounded of occupation soldiers (from all nations) looting, beating up civilians and committing sexual assaults. As in other occupied territories, so too in Germany, ordinary soldiers swung between loathing and loving the Germans under their command. Disgust commonly 'comingled with desire'.[13] Stivers and Carter insist that the offenses committed by American troops tended to be sporadic rather than endemic.[14] Nevertheless, US military forces tried to suppress these problems from the very first weeks of their occupation.

At the peak of the occupation, there were just 850 Military Policemen to keep a garrison of 30,000 men in check. The unruly violence was not confined to Germans. One female US Army employee complained of having to fend off drunks all day long: 'Twice already I was almost raped.'[15] An intelligence report from July 1946 estimated that the crime rate in Berlin was nearly thirteen times the rate for the Military District of Washington.[16] The pervasive violence threatened to tarnish Allied legitimacy. The notion that the Western Allies were in Berlin to protect them must have seemed like a bitter irony to the parents of a four-year-old boy abused and infected with venereal disease.[17] As far as the Allies were concerned, policing was tricky and brittle. Throughout the 1940s and 1950s, Allied troops in Berlin were required, on numerous occasions, to handle highly delicate situations, commonly involving Soviet troops, with immense geopolitical implications. One minute an official could be issuing commendations for bravery; the next, he could find himself charged with a crime. For example, the head of the British Military Police in Berlin, Major P. D. Witty, was subsequently cashiered for committing an indecent assault on a German female.[18]

The conditions when the Americans first arrived in Berlin

As General Lucius D. Clay remembered, the city American military leaders found in July 1945 contained numerous combat soldiers, representing the other Allied nations, with little in the way of law or order.[19] The city was heavily bombed out; there was a shortage of intact housing. On arriving in the city, the first thing American troops did was to requisition the best housing in their Sector for themselves.[20] Many Germans saw the requisitions of housing and furniture as little more than a legalized form of theft. The way American combat troops accomplished this task was often unnecessarily cruel and brutal. Without a shared language to communicate in, the previous occupants were simply forced out of their homes at the barrel of a gun. The combat troops who took Berlin over in 1945 did not put a great deal of emphasis on the human rights of the German civilians they encountered. The Americans came as conquerors to what they perceived as enemy territory. They remembered the sacrifices and losses that had been necessary to defeat the Nazi regime. They were aware of the horrific scenes that had greeted Allied troops when they had liberated the Concentration Camps. As one US Colonel put it, the combat troops often had the attitude that Germans were dirt under their feet.[21] Although the rapes committed by Soviet troops get most coverage, there were rapists among the ranks of all the occupying forces. The difference was in terms of scale and degree.[22] In Berlin, there were reports of the Eighty-Second Airborne Division carrying out plundering, theft and molestation of women. They even extended their depredations to Kleinmachnow in Soviet territory.[23]

Nevertheless, from the perspective of US Criminal Investigation Division (CID) chief Orazio R. Carlucci, the problem was German women throwing themselves at ordinary GIs. In his eyes, these were women who deliberately and aggressively sought out Allied soldiers for sex.[24] A common view (then and now) was that the economic/food situation was so dire that Allied troops did not need to rape. If German women could be bought for packets of cigarettes, force was not necessary.[25] US military historian Earl Ziemke is equally dismissive of accusations of rape involving American personnel. In a city plagued by starvation, rape was 'unnecessarily strenuous'.[26] In Berlin, in the first months of the occupation, the ongoing threat of sexual violence from the Soviets made it advantageous for women to seek out a powerful protector, preferably in one of the western sectors. Without apology, the anonymous Berlin journalist transformed herself from passive victim of rape to an active fraternizer. For her and others, sex with an occupier was a conscious survival strategy. The situation of German women was complex and ambivalent. For some, liberation from Nazism was also sexually liberating. For German teenagers, foreign soldiers appeared exciting and different. Girlfriends willingly embraced the foreign culture, picking up scraps of slang and adopting aspects of a new, attractive, live-fast lifestyle.[27] The moral compass was swinging so wildly that even 'good girls' aspired to be officers' mistresses.

US intelligence operative and whistle-blower Francis P. Miller claimed that girls used informal bulletin boards, on trees and walls, to offer their bodies in exchange for food and shelter.[28] Even the profoundest love matches between occupation soldiers and German women involved a cost-benefit analysis and quid pro quos. His head swimming, the occupation soldier could nevertheless forget that he was paying for the 'love' he received. With their wives and girlfriends stuck at home, soldiers also wanted to 'sow their wild oats'. In Berlin, amid copious 'indiscriminate drinking', a general debauchery ensued. Soldiers let off steam and celebrated 'Victory in Europe'. The former Chief Historian of the US occupation argued that every rank 'from generals down to privates' sought sex with Germans females. He also stated that some Americans became so involved in dalliances that they became 'sex maniacs'.[29] After such a vicious war, there was a strong appetite for vice – for the 'erotic games, drug parties and aphrodisiac shows', which were believed to be going on just under the surface of postwar Berlin.[30]

The fraternization ban

Celebration that the war was over was mixed up with hostility and barely concealed contempt for the defeated, supine Germans. General Dwight D. Eisenhower's instructions to the Joint Chiefs of Staff (JCS 1067) clearly stated that Germany would be considered 'a defeated enemy nation' rather than liberated territory. He advised his soldiers and administrators to be firm and aloof. Fraternization between the occupiers and German officials or civilians was strongly discouraged.[31] The ban was both on grounds of health and of military security. So-called Kraut-lovers were initially disciplined. The policy aimed at protecting Allied soldiers while punishing the Germans. However, many felt that its inflexibility and insensitivity went against common sense. A senior officer did not think that it would aid in democratizing the Germans.[32] In their first encounters, the occupiers did not seek to hide their hostility and disdain for such a people.[33]

Although the fraternization ban covered all friendly interactions, it was interpreted by GIs, and by everyone else, as a ban on sex.[34] Fraternization quickly became the euphemism for sexual intercourse in Germany. Many GIs wanted to humiliate the Germans by having sex with their women. Consequently, early on, many officers found the fraternization ban impossible to enforce. According to a questionnaire, in November 1945, as many as 54 per cent of US troops surveyed admitted to having interacted with German girls in some form during the fraternization ban.[35] Taking pleasure in breaching a rule they viewed as idiotic, they felt they should be rewarded for their sacrifices. The American authorities fended off attempts to identify servicemen who had had sex with Germans. They argued that there was no obligation for soldiers to register their paternity.[36] In the *New York Times*, GIs sang the praises of European women, much to the annoyance of their ex-sweethearts, who had slaved away in the American war factories at home. Theodore Singer marvelled at the 'all-out bootlicking' attitude of *Fräuleins* in Germany, which he contrasted sharply with the snooty attitude of French 'mademoiselles'.[37] A phrase which did the rounds was 'The German soldier fought for six years, the German woman only for five minutes!'[38] Field Marshall Bernard Montgomery suggested that German girls were deliberately performing striptease, to undermine the effectiveness of his fraternization ban. His chaps were 'putting up a good show' in the face of tantalizingly revealing clothing on the part of the ex-members of the League of German Girls.[39] Others argued that German women were learning English, as an extra-curricular activity, in bed.

Holding the Deputy Military Governor responsible for the moral failings of his soldiers, journalists largely blamed General Clay for allowing military discipline to disintegrate. He argued that only 'the lowest type of girl, the tramp' would meet with US soldiers in dark alleys.[40] Nevertheless, officers in Berlin noted the ease with which they could strike up friendships and liaisons with German women. Given half a chance, German girls were throwing themselves at the occupiers; this was a strange experience for many callow recruits.[41] A Lieutenant Colonel attributed the opportunities for sex to 'lack of food on the part of the Germans'.[42] Nevertheless, with hindsight, many Germans (male and female) remembered the excitement and attraction they experienced, as young people, when first encountering dashing, but casual, American troops. British, French and Canadians were different and, in their way, of interest, but the Americans had a confidence and swagger that was irresistible. These were well-fed, fit young men, brimming with vim as well as with chocolate and cigarettes. They had easy access to rides together with tradable commodities like nylons and records (Figure 1).

As one American officer admitted, after the victory, US Army discipline in the European Theatre collapsed.[43] Indiscipline and low morale was, in part, reflected in VD rates. Such circumstances created ideal conditions for the spread of what *Stars*

Figure 1 'Where did you get those beautiful stockings?'
'I traded them.'
'For what?'
'Why do you always ask such stupid questions?'

Drawn by Viktor Friese (1909–69), *Frischer Wind*, 1.10.1947.

and Stripes dubbed 'Jerry's deadliest V weapon'.[44] Sexually transmitted diseases became the principal health problem among US troops during the year 1946.[45] Army doctors found VD infections in all ranks, from Colonels to Second Lieutenants. A combination of alcohol and a reservoir of easily available women helped to spread it. The familiar community structures – of church, neighbourhood and family – that usually provided support, stability and restraint, were lacking.[46] After the horrors of war, Berlin was a paid vacation for many occupation soldiers. The combination of cheap schnapps and friendly *Fräuleins* proved irresistible.[47] Magazine articles routinely presented Berlin as a city of casual vice and moral corruption. It was highly dangerous to let eighteen- or nineteen-year-olds, in uniform, loose on a city, without adequate supervision, together with an almost limitless supply of cash. Their uniforms and positions of relative power put them on a par with Clark Gable, Gregory Peck or Cary Grant.[48] Black-market activity and sexual promiscuity were the norm. Alleging police collusion in illegal trading, the *Manchester Guardian* stated that Berlin had become a completely amoral city of sin.[49] Having left the city, one GI compared it to an insane asylum, where the abnormal had become normal and the warders had ceased to exercise control.[50] As General Clay put it, beautiful women abounded while food, soap and everyday necessities were in short supply. The effect of the disparity was to make German women looser and less discriminating.[51] Clay had more faith in currency reform solving the problem, than in draconian attempts to punish or to morally persuade his troops.

Behaviour of other nations' occupation troops

US journalist Raymond Daniell observed that the Americans were 'a noisy race: We advertise our sins'.[52] However, they were far from alone in experiencing moral lapses. All the occupying powers saw a collapse in discipline and morale after the victory. While Soviet soldiers made no secret of their black marketing and fraternizing, G-2 intelligence officer Colonel Thomas J. Betts suggested that the British were much more circumspect. Instead of getting drunk in the streets, they did their drinking in private. The Glaswegian economist Alec Cairncross, who was resident in Berlin in 1945–6, supported the argument that British troops were generally more circumspect in relation to women and property. The discipline of British troops in Berlin held up, and they generally expressed intelligence and good humour in their dealings with the Germans.[53] Asked what the key difference between the Americans and the other Allies was, Betts replied that he thought it was gasoline. British troops did not have easy access to trucks or jeeps. Generally, they were more discreet because their misbehaviour was less ostentatious or geographically far-ranging. If an American Mess Sergeant required a few pounds of coffee, he was encouraged to drive 20 miles in order to get it. Looking over the sector boundary, Betts was less convinced of French propriety, but saw looting as the chief French sin.[54]

Resistance veteran Renée Bédarida admitted that there were a fair number of 'adventurers and profiteers' among those who volunteered to serve in the French Military Government in Berlin.[55] The French authorities were aware of the danger of indiscipline and plundering by their troops. Some French occupiers seem to have volunteered to serve in Germany, in order to compensate themselves for the German occupation of France.[56] They resented the fact that former Nazis appeared to get better rations (in terms of bread and meat) than the people back home in France.[57] Some newspaper reports suggested that British and French soldiers were deserting and disappearing into the Berlin underground.[58] Berliners agreed that it was the French soldiery which was most in need of reprimand.⁵⁹ The French authorities recognized the importance of discipline and fairness on the part of their troops but struggled to control them. There were numerous incidents of misbehaviour on public transport and reports of attacks on civilians by French troops. A determination to be severe and harsh, in exercising law and order, made routine instances of maladministration worse, through fits of pique. There were reports of occasional canings and humiliations of German civilians, together with routine intimidation of local elected officials. While many French troops behaved badly, it was a serious crime for Germans to insult a French soldier or a Military Policeman.

Bédarida expressed anger and frustration at what she perceived as the Germans' stubborn refusal to accept any responsibility for Nazi crimes.⁶⁰ The chief analyst of the French occupation of Berlin, Dorothea Führe, asks whether these incidents should be seen as isolated expressions of revenge, by individual commanders, or a deliberate expression of occupation policy. When he tried to document violent French military actions, the authorities beat up SPD local politician and Acting Mayor of Reinickendorf, Franz Neumann. Neumann described himself as twice being a victim of arbitrary violence: 'once by the fascists and once by the French'.⁶¹ French low self-esteem combined with a desire for revenge and Germanophobia to create a potent cocktail of ill-concealed hatred. The working-class residents of Wedding were far from obsequious and tended to greet the arrival of French officers and *gendarmes* with a chorus of whistling. The French complained that German officials showed them a similar lack of respect. The latter complained of unnecessary military interference in civilian matters. In the early days of the occupation, someone (probably a Soviet soldier) fired shots in the vicinity of a French officer. A French Military Policeman (*Gendarme*) demanded that the German police find the culprit pronto. To encourage compliance, he told the hapless German police official that if the report was not on his desk in forty-eight hours, he would have him shot.⁶² Diarist Margret Boveri suggested that the inhabitants of each sector always assumed that their own particular foreign occupier was the worst, fondly imagining that their neighbours had it better. While they viewed the French as malicious and malevolent, the Berliners also appreciated their generosity in promoting cultural reconstruction, which was its own form of succour.⁶³

The roaring black market

With '*Fräuleins*', who could be bought for packs of cigarettes or bars of chocolate, there was a general temptation to engage in black-market activities.⁶⁴ At least one American General is supposed to have looted and engaged in illegal trading.⁶⁵ British Military Governor Sir Brian Robertson admitted that for all the ranks, the temptations offered by the illicit were considerable.⁶⁶ The severe economic dislocation in Germany led people to engage in criminal activities that they would never have dreamed of considering in other circumstances. When they reached central Berlin, the Western Allies found that Soviet forces were already doing a roaring trade in everything from coffee to watches. Howley suggested that the Soviet authorities had printed excess Allied Military Marks so that their soldiers could buy watches, rather than stealing them directly from the Germans.⁶⁷ By rendering the currency worthless, the Soviet authorities implicitly encouraged a barter economy. Several years of back pay for Red Army men had left them with suitcases full of bills. They were desperate to convert their worthless cash into cameras, clothing and watches that would have value and prestige at home.⁶⁸ They had to spend the money as soon as possible or risk losing it when they were abruptly sent home.

Although Howley claimed that it was Soviet backwardness which caused the black market, it did not take long for Americans to join in. Soviet soldiers' insatiable demand for American watches greatly inflated their value: a single watch could fetch $5,000. It did not take an above-average sense of business acumen to realize that, if watches could be brought in from the United States, then they would sell for many times their value. Ordinary GIs realized that huge profits could be made by providing the Soviets with the goods they craved. The Allies possessed large quantities of rare and hence high-value, tradable commodities, such as tobacco, chocolate and gasoline. US soldiers could easily convert a carton of cigarettes, purchased for $2, into $160. While Allied troops traded on the black market for fun, diversion and profit, the Germans had no choice but to trade their valuables and heirlooms because people who were desperately hungry would pay any price.

The basic fact was that a bar of chocolate, bought for five cents in the PX (American Post Exchange, equivalent to the British NAAFI), was worth five dollars on the black market. Every American soldier with access to PX rations became a virtual millionaire. The average German worker had to labour for a week to earn the equivalent of one black-market cigarette.⁶⁹ This made ordinary occupation soldiers inordinately rich. Cigarettes could easily be converted into cinecameras or binoculars. Soldiers frequently made more money than they knew what to do with.⁷⁰ The morality of these transactions was dubious to say the least. Unofficially, American troops were keeping Germans alive with Army food supplies but were profiting from the process. By exploiting the situation of near starvation, soldiers could enjoy sexual favours. The presence in any country of large numbers of unaccompanied members of foreign armed forces is liable to encourage prostitution, especially when they were of high-school age. Barely out of adolescence and keen for adventure, American troops were lonesome and thousands of miles from home. In 1942, author Philip Wylie had invented the term 'momism', when he predicted that 'a hysteria of homesickness' would soon engulf the US Army. Overly mollycoddled and insufficiently virile, he believed that these callow recruits would soon disgrace their service and homeland.⁷¹ In Berlin, the young GIs were subject to unceasing peer pressure and all manner of temptations.

Black-market trading was a compensation for boredom, homesickness and other dissatisfactions. Although technically illegal, the ban was difficult to police. The rubble created a warren for traders to escape into. The German police did not have authority to arrest Allied servicemen.⁷² Irving L. Janis was a soldier in Berlin, who went on to become a psychologist. He argued that most of his fellow servicemen had participated in the black market. 'Exchanging a few candy bars for a Leica camera' was not seen as exceptional. They were openly using the profits to buy sex. Getting a sexual partner was as easy and straightforward as going to a crowded public place and holding up a can of corned beef or spam. Janis subsequently used his observations of American GIs' behaviour as the basis for theoretical ideas about 'group dynamics'. He argued that the men inured themselves to feelings of guilt by competing with arguments for why German civilians 'deserved' to be treated badly. Contrary to the claims of Military Government officials, he argued that it was combat veterans who engaged in the most exploitative conduct. They felt that they had served their country and expressed resentment about not being sent back to the United States sooner.[73] For his part, former Second Lieutenant Henry Elkin ascribed hostility to the GIs' lack of self-esteem. The 'Government Issue' dog-tags around their necks undermined their individuality and geniality, reducing them to identical and standardized items of mass-production, akin to their clothing and rations.[74]

Although some observers saw British troops as better behaved, His Majesty George VI's venereologists were less certain about circumspection on the part of their troops. Flush with cigarettes, callow recruits lacked the safety and control exercised by their parents and home communities. In Berlin, temptations were much greater than anything at home. All sorts of nefarious influences could lead them astray. A Brigadier of the Royal Army Medical Corps argued that such milksops could apply their desire for 'motherly love and affection' to ladies of easy virtue.[75] Many Berlin girls did fall into 'semi prostitution', exchanging sex for food or cigarettes. Byford-Jones gave the view of the ordinary Tommy: that the girls of Berlin would 'take any treatment' and still treat their foreign suitor 'like a king'. Back home in Blighty, 'a lass wouldn't look at a threepenny bar of chocolate'. For these girls, however, it was 'like they were being offered the moon'. Although taking advantage of deprivation was widespread, some of the more perspicacious occupiers noticed that these were not really 'good time girls'. They did not look ill or malnourished in the club or on the street, but when they were alone with them, soldiers noticed that they were missing their periods. Lack of nourishment caused them to scratch their bodies; they suffered from dry skin because of a lack of fat in their diet. The glands under their arms swelled and their faces became puffy.[76]

There was something ineffably sordid about partying in a city suffering malnutrition and still reeking of death. Some saw fraternization as encouraging racism and antisemitism, with German-American couples bringing out the worst in each other. Sexual relations between the Western Allies and Germans were indisputably connected to notions of power and submission.[77] The amount of power they possessed over vulnerable young women made some of these men feel sick to the stomach with guilt. One described a German girlfriend by saying, 'She was just like my slave.'[78] When fraternization went wrong, it could lead to violence. Occupation soldiers were prone to jealous rages as well as drunken violence. The film *A Foreign Affair* brought the sexual excesses and black-market activities of postwar Berlin to a wider international audience.[79] In the form of Marlene Dietrich, it presented German women as highly seductive but ultimately corrupting. She sang: 'To, you, for your K-Ration, compassion and maybe an inkling, a twinkling of real sympathy. I'm selling out, take all I've got, ambitions, convictions, the works!'[80] At the end of the film, even the prim and morally upstanding Congresswoman from Iowa gets seduced by the lasciviousness and sensual pleasures of the corrupt city. Having arrived strait-laced and censorious, she all too rapidly loses sight of her mission to help clean up Berlin. Contemporaries sought to present German women, who solicited American soldiers, as expressing Nazi doctrines, which they associated with looseness and depravity.

Colonel Miller's accusations

On 14 August 1946, Colonel Francis P. Miller appeared before the US Senate's Special Committee to Investigate the National Defense Program. He made several accusations about misconduct and wrongdoings by representatives of the US Office of Military Government (OMGUS) in Germany.[81] Miller was a committed Christian and a disgruntled intelligence officer.[82] He had played an important role in preparations for the invasion of Normandy on D Day by placing agents behind enemy lines. After the war, he was attached to OMGUS headquarters in Berlin. In this capacity, he argued that intelligence opportunities in Berlin and throughout Germany were being squandered. Under General Clay's leadership, OMGUS was underestimating the Soviets, who were emerging as America's main enemy. Miller told the Senate Committee that the Soviet Union constituted the most 'formidable force in the world' faced by the United States. He stressed the intelligence and commitment to their cause of his Soviet spook counterparts.[83] Miller compared the situation in Berlin in the summer of 1946 to that of France after World War One or to US unpreparedness prior to Pearl Harbour. He charged that, in common with some 'older regular officers', Clay failed to understand intelligence. Harming the mission, he was utterly disinterested in it.[84] As a result, the Military Government was on the brink of a major disaster or catastrophe.

Colonel Miller had sought, on several occasions, to complain about illegal activities and moral failings, on the part of officers stationed in Berlin, but each time he had been rebuffed and told to report his concerns to his senior officers. Unfortunately, the people he was told to complain to happened to be the same powerful people he wanted to complain about. In his memoirs, Miller accused Clay of being indifferent to the psychological and moral wellbeing of the young troops under his command.[85] Miller recounted that he had tried to organize an unofficial investigation into the activities of administrative director General James B. Edmunds but was told to stop by General Clay. In front of the Senate Special Committee, Miller accused several officers under Clay's command of openly profiting from and exploiting the black market. He claimed that far more money was going out of Berlin than was coming in. A coterie of officers was sacrificing the national interest to pad their own pockets. He accused American officers of acting like pigs, shoving each other aside to get their fill at the 'delicious trough'.[86]

One of Miller's more sensational claims was that black troops were running amok in Germany (see Chapter 4). Their white officers were scared to discipline or control them. Lack of support from senior officers was leading to paralysis and an absence of effective control. He recounted the story of an officer he had met on the boat home. The officer said that his troops had not only killed one another, but one had thrown a live hand grenade at him. Miller told the Committee, 'I am sorry, Senator, if I am sober, but that is the story and the commanding generals there are absolutely terrified to touch it because of the repercussion here.' Overall, Clay came across in Miller's testimony as detached and distracted from important issues.

Counterarguments

Several investigators were sent to Europe, tasked by the Committee with investigating Miller's claims. Their investigations revealed that Clay was, indeed, strongly opposed to using secret-police agents. His priority was policing, not espionage. Miller's ambitious plans for a centralized intelligence agency, operating out of Berlin, had got lost in the command structure because they lacked an influential backer. He had expected to be made Director of Intelligence and to be allowed to build up a huge postwar intelligence organization. As a result, when his plans came to nothing, he was bitterly aggrieved.[87] Clay was preoccupied with governing American-occupied Germany and had little interest in covert intelligence on his Allies. Given all the practical problems of overseeing Berlin's administration – not least keeping the population fed during a terrible winter – intelligence was not a high priority in 1946.

It is true that Clay was much more interested in surveys revealing what ordinary Germans were thinking than in cloak-and-dagger shenanigans.[88] Consequently, he failed to exploit the chaos of the immediate postwar period, in order to infiltrate agents into the Communist-controlled areas. Instead, he initially put all his emphasis on establishing a relationship of trust with the Soviets.[89] Dr Walter L. Dorn was an agent for the Office of Strategic Services before advising Clay on denazification. He thought that this aversion to secrecy expressed Clay's innate democratic feeling. A democrat to the core of his being, Dorn felt that Clay represented more of a civilian outlook in Berlin than a great number of civilians at home.[90] Clay possessed a horror against using 'undercover agents' for the purposes of Military Government. In his memoirs, Clay restated his opposition to 'spying' on other people's private lives. He expressly ordered his Criminal Investigation Division to cease spying on the officers in his command. 'I said it was no one's business who visited their quarters or who spent the night with them.'[91] What the Germans needed was education in democracy, Clay believed, not a re-run of authoritarian government and Gestapo methods. He categorically did not want his Military Government to function using 'secret-police' mechanisms.[92]

As far as black-market activity and lecherous living in Berlin were concerned, several of the people who were interviewed mentioned Edmunds, Clay's director of administrative services. Colonel Miller was convinced that General Edmunds was engaging in illicit affairs with multiple German *Fräuleins*. He was also allowing his subordinates to profit from the black market.[93] When he came back to the United States, Edmunds brought no fewer than twenty-two packing cases full of belongings. Questioned about their contents, he said that he imagined that they contained 'figurines and the china' that his wife had picked up in the barter mart or at the Post Exchange. He suggested that this was the common pastime of American women in Berlin.[94] Upon his return to the United States, he received a reprimand for improbity and excesses of 'moral turpitude'.[95] Clay does seem to have placed too much trust in his right-hand man and to have delegated too much authority to him. It was unfortunate that when Miller had come to Clay with complaints, Clay had handed the dossier over to Edmunds, without looking at it, and simply told him to 'clean it up'.[96]

Nearly all of those interviewed by the investigators, tasked with assessing Miller's claims, admitted that the situation in Berlin had been a tremendous mess for at least the first six months of the occupation. Clay later wrote that it had been a 'period of unavoidable confusion'. His officers accused one another of loose and luxurious living. Some were too cruel towards the Germans; others too soft. A number felt that not enough was being done to remove Nazis from positions of influence. He was forced to concede that many of these charges 'had some basis in fact'.[97] The American garrison was isolated and thrown back on themselves. They were operating in a fishbowl, surrounded not just by perspicacious German civilians, but by the soldiers and administrators of the other occupying powers. The black market had had a terribly corrupting influence on everyone living in the city and not just on local teenagers. But Clay believed that bringing over the dependents had calmed and balanced out the situation. It provided much-needed stability and restored the troops' moral kilter.[98] At the same time, however, life in Germany for American dependents was sold in terms of its sumptuousness and comfort.

Bringing officers' wives over from the United States (beginning in early 1946) considerably reduced the excesses of lecherous living but led to a spike in black-market activities. Occupation wives proved no slouches 'when it came to getting something for next to nothing'. Indeed, many contemporary observers suggested that they represented the worst black marketeers that ever existed. As well as Meissen and other fine porcelain, US personnel and their wives sought jewellery, furs and cameras.[99] The arrival of US dependents in the European Theatre led to a return to normality, marked by a sharp decline in violent crimes committed by US personnel. American servicemen were less tempted by vice. It was just black marketing that failed to diminish. New arrivals wanted to keep up with the Joneses by fitting out a nice home. The hairstylists, manicurists, seamstresses and furriers of the Nazi elite now pampered American wives and secretaries instead. For those with access to scarce and otherwise exorbitant luxuries, Berlin was an incredibly cheap paradise. The Chief Editor of the Intelligence Control Division of the Military Government, Arthur D. Kahn, was shocked by the situation he found in Berlin. In March 1946, the black market had become so 'socially acceptable' that it formed the main topic of conversation at dinner parties. Every high official knew the 'prices of china, silk, jewellery, *objets d'art*, etc.' in packs of cigarettes. Most American occupiers were receiving cartons of cigarettes by mail and trading them for luxury items. The scale of everyday corruption was so great that 'even the most moral and conscientious people broke down and little by little became involved'.[100]

George F. Kennan, the diplomat who had warned President Harry Truman about Joseph Stalin's intentions, in February 1946, was equally worried that the Americans were losing sight of their mission in Berlin. He was horrified by the spectacle of the American elite using the ruins of a shattered country to camp in luxury.[101] Clay's chief solution was to arrange for a barter mart, to allow exchanges of goods to take place in a more controlled and less blatantly harmful way.[102] What was moral in a country under foreign occupation was difficult to establish. Conscious of the difficult security situation, exacerbated by the disparities of wealth between occupiers and occupied, Colonel Howley issued American civilians and their dependents with pistols. Should it become necessary, he wanted American wives to be in a position to 'shoot to kill'. Children, too, should be able to use guns if necessary.[103] Fitting his 'shoot first and ask questions later' approach in 1945, he was clearly unconcerned about the dangers of American wives and children shooting innocent, unarmed Germans. The pecking order of power and privilege could not have been clearer.

Problems of General Clay's administration

General Clay does seem to have been a bit detached and disinterested in the nitty-gritty of some of his underlings' behaviour.[104] Intelligence operatives wrote that 'General Clay, to us as to all, is aloof and Olympian'.[105] One of his officers suggested that Clay was too bogged down in the detail to grasp the true size of the problems that his Military Government faced.[106] He does not seem to have been overly concerned by the minutiae of what went on at ground level. Clay delegated the everyday administration tasks too much to Edmunds; his trust in his junior officer was probably misplaced. As the mission changed from administering a defeated enemy to trying to win friends in the developing tensions with the Soviet Union, many American officers found it difficult to trust the Germans. From the start, Clay was convinced of the need to re-educate the Germans in democracy.[107] Edmunds, meanwhile, continued to see them as enemies: 'A Kraut is a Kraut as far as I am concerned.'[108]

For Clay and his advisers, Miller's accusations came as a bolt out of the blue. Dorn remembers Clay coming into his office, after a long day, and saying, 'This is really extraordinary. This is the reward one gets for working day and night, never taking a holiday, attending to duty and doing one's very best.'[109] If the leaked inquiry detailed problems of his administration, Clay nevertheless came out of the investigation with his dignity largely intact. His chief of staff, Walter Bedell Smith, allegedly said that General Eisenhower had been recalled from Germany because President Truman had realized that the job of Military Governor would 'ruin any man's reputation', no matter how good he or it was.[110] There were some accusations that Clay had himself profited from the black market in Berlin. In particular, he was charged with using his personal plane to transport expensive art works. However, these allegations were never substantiated. As CID chief Carlucci put it: 'We didn't get very far with it. We were too busy at the time with shootings and assaults and trying to keep the GI's from killing one another and we really didn't have the time to go into the investigation as we wanted to.'[111] He nevertheless believed that General Clay lacked information about what was going on in his command.

If Clay appeared a bit standoffish, Miller came across as petty and spiteful. He had the air of a 'puritanical crusader', who was extremely narrow-minded and rigid in his morals.[112] His Berlin contemporaries remember him as the laughingstock of the officers' mess, for bawling out men and women for singing a slightly bawdy song. Colonel John C. McCawley said that Miller would have made an excellent Women's Christian

Temperance Union member.[113] Aside from condemning the extra-curricular activities of his fellow officers, Miller fiercely resented not being made head of an expanded intelligence agency in Berlin. His vendetta against Clay's administrators appeared to have resulted from Edmunds having his car impounded. Miller had ostentatiously been lugged around in an unregistered vehicle, driven by a DP in a chauffeur's uniform.[114] They took the car away from him because he did not have permission to possess one. They later thought that this was what had made him so enraged.

Miller was quick to accuse people he had run-ins with of immoral and dishonest conduct. However, the evidence for his accusations seemed to consist merely of gossip and hearsay.[115] He had no concrete evidence; he did not possess a smoking gun. In his testimony, he recounted seeing a Lieutenant General with 'six Fräuleins' in the back of his car. However, the investigators countered that this was nothing more than a blank wall. 'We don't know who the Lieutenant General is, we don't know who the six women are that are purported to be in the car, and we don't know what the General said [about] why they were there.'[116] Miller had sought an audience with the highest court of legislators in the land and had presented a series of exaggerations based on the flimsiest of evidence. His willingness to recount tittle-tattle did not give a very good impression of the quality of postwar intelligence operatives. Although nothing was said about his racism, his imputation that the high-ranking officers, who had helped to win World War Two, were 'terrified' of dealing with racial matters provoked scorn and indignation. The investigators concluded that, although he had high ideals and impeccable character, he had indulged in a 'frenzy of over-all vituperations'. By implication, at least, these had 'impugned the character and integrity' of people Colonel Miller barely knew.[117] Miller went on to run for Governor and later Senator of Virginia. In his memoirs, he blamed the lack of foresight regarding the building of the Berlin Wall as the result of General Clay's failure to give support to American intelligence activities in postwar Berlin. This failure to establish an efficacious intelligence network, operating in both East and West Berlin, was a glaring omission.[118]

Conclusion

Although presented as a source of guidance and concern, from the beginning, Allied occupation was itself a source of misbehaviour and crime. When they arrived in July 1945, the Western Allies only slowly came round to the view that they were liberators and not conquerors. They went into Berlin determined to cooperate with the Soviets and to remain aloof from the Germans. Assuming that nearly all Berliners were corrupt and tainted former Nazis, their behaviour was often tactless and unnecessarily harsh. The Allies compounded the dire housing situation by commandeering the best accommodation for themselves and their men. The shift from combat to occupation mode presented fresh challenges for military leaders. Much drunkenness occurred as soldiers from all the occupying armies celebrated their victory and the fact that they had survived the war unscathed. There was a heavy turnover of troops, with the combat units giving way to spotty teenagers. The latter had less reason to be proud of themselves but nevertheless saw themselves as conquerors.

The Americans blamed the Soviets for starting the crazy and destabilizing blackmarket situation, but GIs soon became fully involved in both small- and large-scale racketeering. The Germans desperately needed food, and the Soviets were obsessed with watches. Fortunes could be made by swapping cigarettes and food for items of value. Low-ranking Americans, with access to abundant resources, could become virtual millionaires overnight. Every time they were forced to trade a family heirloom for a few cigarettes or some potatoes, Germans were reminded that they were the losers and the Allies were the victors.[119] Nevertheless, however obtained, small amounts of food (whether milk powder or Canadian flour) made the difference between life and death for the very young and very old.

The juxtaposition of German desperation against Allied plenty ensured that the occupiers were in a position of extreme power. Many of the soldiers serving as occupiers exploited that position to gain material advantages and sexual favours. By day, the Military Governments of the occupiers sought to restore order to the city, by reaching agreements in *Kommandatura* meetings. However, by night, other occupation soldiers undermined their good work by drinking, whoring and stealing. While each Allied power sought to highlight the positive features of its own mode of government, designed to assist in the re-education of the Germans under its command, the exciting personal adventures ensured that the occupation experience was much less laudable and edifying. Looking back, Clay argued that the black market was the 'one thing' that had sullied his occupation government's record 'here and at home'.[120] Ordinary soldiers could convert supplies of food – whether coffee, chocolate or eggs – into objects of value – cameras, antique porcelain together with wads of dollars. For some Allied soldiers, the moral compass was spinning so wildly that they even asked the newly arrived chaplain if he wanted to trade his watch. The presence of so many young men, far away from home, alongside desperate, bored teenage girls, created a sexual economy despite initial bans on fraternization. Ordinary occupation soldiers with cans of K-rations or bully beef could barter them for sexual favours. The troops of the Western Allies wanted sex but generally they were prepared to engage in 'sales talk', and to pay a few cigarettes, to get it.[121]

The knowledge that girls were selling their virtue for a brace of chocolate bars was very damaging for German notions of honour. Soviet-controlled Radio Berlin later condemned this 'shameless exploitation' of German poverty. It was hunger that turned young women into Allied soldiers' prostitutes, ready to infect themselves with 'American syphilis' for the price of a bar of chocolate or 'a few Camels!'[122] Sex did not necessarily equate to love. Anti-German sentiments were still strong. Trying to dissuade an underling from marrying a German, a British officer stated that he would rather he 'married a wog'.[123] Initially, the military authorities viewed the desire of Allied soldiers, to settle down and marry their German popsies, as a major problem.[124] Sometimes, drink and jealousy led to violence against their sexual partners. Some soldiers did not just want to possess; they also wanted to subjugate and humiliate. Sadism mixed with self-righteous vengefulness, in a dangerous combination. They intended such intercourse to degrade and cause pain to the defeated. Accusations of female licentiousness and willingness to be defiled served to drown out and repress real cases of sexual violence. Having raped, Allied soldiers would toss a pack of cigarettes or a bar of chocolate at the victim, acting as if they were paying a prostitute.[125] Instinctively, many victims remained silent about what had happened, knowing that they would not be believed. Protection from the protectors was difficult because Allied Military Governments could have cases quietly dropped. So little was expected of the French that, when they behaved correctly, it was an unexpected relief. Berliners were more upset about unruly American behaviour.[126] Bad behaviour threatened to make a mockery of US attempts to export democracy to Germany.

Bringing over the dependents helped to stabilize the situation but brought its own spike in black-market trading. The Americans liked to think that only the Soviets were responsible for the black market, but successive waves of American occupiers and their dependents were quite as involved in bleeding the Germans dry. For journalist Curt Riess, the occupiers lived as if Berlin was the finest and most prestigious city in the world, not a heap of stinking rubble.[127] Continued misery was increasingly seen as an obstacle to improved Allied morale, as well as an impediment to common decency and to law and order.

Notes

1. Malte Zierenberg, *Berlin's Black Market, 1939-1950* (New York: Palgrave Macmillan, 2015).
2. 'Report of Public Safety Branch for the period 1 January 1947 through 30 June 1948', US National Archives, RG260, box 893.
3. Jennifer V. Evans, 'Protection from the Protector: Court-Martial Cases and the Lawlessness of Occupation in American-Controlled Berlin, 1945-1948', in *GIs and Germans: The Social, Economic, Cultural and Political History of the American Military Presence*, ed. Detlef Junker and Thomas W. Maulucci (New York: Cambridge University Press, 2013).
4. 'British Will Go Armed in Berlin', *Daily Mail*, 20 December 1945.
5. Richard Brett-Smith, *Berlin '45: The Grey City* (London: Macmillan, 1966), 104.
6. 'Russians began Red Room Riot', *Daily Mail*, 9 August 1946.
7. Lucius D. Clay, *Decision in Germany* (Westport, CT: Greenwood, 1970), 114–15.
8. Ruth Andreas-Friedrich, *Battleground Berlin: Diaries, 1945–1948*, trans. Anna Boerresen (New York: Paragon House, 1990), 56.
9. 'Incidents with US Personnel', 1 December 1947–26 April 1948, US National Archives, RG260, box 893.
10. C. D. Lush, 'The Relationship between Berlin and the Federal Republic of Germany', *The International and Comparative Law Quarterly* 14, no. 3 (1965): 779.
11. Jochen Staadt, 'Die Berliner Polizei in der "Stunde Null"', in *Feindwärts der Mauer: Das Ministerium für Staatssicherheit und die West-Berliner Polizei*, ed. Klaus Schroeder and Jochen Staadt (Frankfurt am Main: Peter Lang, 2014), 57.
12. Evans, 'Protection from the Protector', 214.
13. Susan L. Carruthers, *The Good Occupation: American Soldiers and the Hazards of Peace* (Cambridge, MA: Harvard University Press, 2016), 13.
14. William Stivers and Donald A. Carter, *The City Becomes a Symbol: the U.S. Army in the Occupation of Berlin, 1945-1949* (Washington, DC: Center of Military History, United States Army, 2017), 141.

15 William Stivers, 'Victors and Vanquished: Americans as Occupiers in Berlin, 1945-1949', in *Armed Diplomacy: Two Centuries of American Campaigning*, ed. US Army Training and Doctrine Command and Combat Studies Institute (Fort Leavenworth, KS: Combat Studies Institute Press, 2003), 159.
16 Stivers and Carter, *The City Becomes a Symbol*, 123.
17 'Sittlichkeitsdelikt an 4jähriges Kind', Landesarchiv Berlin, B Rep. 303/9, No. 84 as cited by Jennifer V. Evans, *Life among the Ruins: Cityscape and Sexuality in Cold War Berlin* (Basingstoke: Palgrave Macmillan, 2011), 76–7.
18 'Sentence Commuted', *Times*, 15 December 1954.
19 Testimony of Lieutenant General Lucius D. Clay, USA, taken at Berlin, on 22 October 1946. This and subsequent testimonies can be found in RG 159, Boxes 34-35, US National Archives. Several overlapping investigations explored Allied comportment and involvement in criminality in postwar Berlin. These were an undercover investigation by Colonel Charles G. Dodge, commissioned by General McNarney; a second investigation by Colonel Perry L. Baldwin, IGD, Headquarters, USFET, commissioned by General Clay; the investigation conducted by Brigadier General Elliot D. Cooke [hereafter known as the 'Cooke Report']. and the Mead Committee investigation headed by George Meader, Chief Counsel of the United States Senate Special Committee [henceforth 'Meader Report'].
20 Testimony of Colonel John C. McCawley, taken at Berlin, 17 October 1946.
21 Ibid.
22 Miriam Gebhardt, *Als die Soldaten kamen: die Vergewaltigung deutscher Frauen am Ende des Zweiten Weltkriegs* (Munich: Deutsche Verlags-Anstalt, 2015).
23 RG 260, US National Archives: Rpt of Opns, HQ, Berlin District, and 1st Abn Div, U.S. Army, 8 May–31 Dec 1945, as cited by Stivers and Carter, *The City Becomes a Symbol*, 122.
24 Testimony of Mr O. R. Carlucci taken at Frankfurt, 8 October 1946, by Cooke.
25 Judy Barden, 'Candy Bar Romance – Women of Germany', in *This Is Germany: A Report on Post War Germany by 21 Newspaper Correspondents*, ed. Arthur Settel (New York: William Sloane, 1950), 165.
26 Earl F. Ziemke, *The U.S. Army in the Occupation of Germany, 1944-1946* (Washington, DC: Center of Military History, United States Army, 1975), 304.
27 Erika M. Hoerning, *Zwischen den Fronten: Berliner Grenzgänger und Grenzhändler 1948-1961* (Cologne: Böhlau, 1992), 23.
28 Francis P. Miller, *Man from the Valley: Memoirs of a 20th-Century Virginian* (Chapel Hill, NC: University of North Carolina Press, 1971), 128.
29 Harold Zink, *The United States in Germany, 1944-1955* (Princeton, NJ: D. Van Nostrand, 1957), 137, 85.
30 Brett-Smith, *Berlin '45*, 104–5.
31 Franklin M. Davis, Jr., *Came as a Conqueror: The United States Army's Occupation of Germany, 1945-1949* (New York: Macmillan, 1967), 136.
32 Drew Middleton, 'Officers Oppose Fraternizing Ban. Americans and British Assert Order is Unworkable and Damaging to Discipline', *New York Times*, 25 June 1945.
33 Norman Naimark, *Russians in Germany: A History of the Soviet Zone of Occupation, 1945-1949* (Cambridge, MA and London: Belknap Press of Harvard University Press, 1995), 1, 5.
34 Percy Knauth, 'Fraternization: The Word Takes on a Brand-New Meaning in Germany', *Life*, 2 July 1945, 26.

35 'What the American Soldier in Germany says about Germany and the Germans', *The American Soldier in Germany*, November 1945, as cited by Margaret L. Geis and George J. Gray, *The Relations of Occupation Personnel with the Civil Population, 1946–1948* (Karlsruhe: Historical Division, European Command, 1951), 9.
36 Bruno Schrep, 'Kinder der Schande', *Spiegel*, 10 July 1995, 58.
37 Theodore Singer, Letter to the Editor, *New York Times*, 5 January 1946.
38 To add insult to injury, this was supposedly told to a German by an African-American soldier.
39 'German Staff to be Kept in Exile', *New York Times*, 22 June 1945. On the impressions and images presented of German women's dissoluteness, see Evans, 'Protection from the Protector', note 33, 226.
40 Clay, *Decision in Germany*, 62.
41 Middleton, 'Officers Oppose Fraternizing Ban'.
42 Further testimony of Lt Col P. V. Kiehl, MC, Berlin 18 October 1946.
43 Testimony of Col. G. Bryan Conrad, GSC, taken at Washington DC, on 25 September 1946 by Brig Gen Elliot D. Cooke, U.S. Army.
44 'Jerry's Deadliest V Weapon: VD', *Stars and Stripes*, 18 October 1944.
45 Berlin Command, OMGUS: 'History of Activities', 1 November 1946–30 June 1947, 84. US National Archives, 390/50/23/3, BOX 19, 93.
46 Geis and Gray, *The Relations of Occupation Personnel*, 36, 39.
47 Drew Middleton, 'U.S. Prestige Drops After GI Protests', *New York Times*, 13 January 1946.
48 Cary Grant makes a fetching war bride in *I Was A Male War Bride*, directed by Howard Hawks (USA, 1949).
49 'Light and Shadow in Berlin. Mental and Physical Isolation', *Manchester Guardian*, 18 August 1947.
50 Walter Slatoff, 'GI Morals in Germany', *New Republic* 114, no. 19 (1946): 686.
51 Testimony of Lieutenant General Lucius D. Clay.
52 'Unforeseen Problems Face us in Germany', *New York Times*, 30 September 1945.
53 Alec Cairncross, *A Country to Play With* (Gerrards Cross: Colin Smythe, 1987), 45.
54 Testimony of Col Thomas J. Betts, Washington DC, 25 September 1946, by Cooke.
55 Renée Bédarida, 'Une Française à Berlin en 1945', in *France-Allemagne 1944-1947*, ed. Klaus Manfrass and Jean-Pierre Rioux (Paris: Institut d'histoire du temps present, 1990), 150–1.
56 Dorothea Führe, *Die Französische Besatzungspolitik in Berlin von 1945 bis 1949: Déprussianisation und Décentralisation* (Berlin: Weißensee-Verlag, 2001), 26, 259.
57 Bédarida, 'Une Française à Berlin en 1945', 149. Cf. 'Comment Berlin est-il ravitaillé?', [no date, ca. 1945], Archives Diplomatiques, GMFB 1/866.
58 'Bekämpfung von Unrühen & Bandenunwesens', (1945–47), Landesarchiv Berlin, Präsidium der Volkspolizei Berlin, STA Rep. 303/9, Nr. 80.
59 Gerhard Keiderling, '"Als Befreier unsere Herzen zerbrachen". Zu den Übergriffe der Sowjetarmee in Berlin 1945', *Deutschland Archiv* 28, no. 1 (1995): 238.
60 Bédarida, 'Une Française à Berlin en 1945', 151.
61 Führe, *Die Französische Besatzungspolitik in Berlin*, 255–7.
62 Ibid., 237, 242, 250, 254.
63 Margret Boveri, *Tage des Überlebens: Berlin 1945* (Munich: R. Piper, 1968), 219.
64 Testimony of Col Thomas J. Betts. Cf. Walter H. Waggoner, 'House Report Criticizes Military on Occupation Policy in Germany, Charges "Vast Majority" of Troops Took Part in Black Market', *New York Times*, 3 January 1947.

65 Office of the Chief of Military History, Margaret L. Geis, Dorothy Russell and W. H. Maehl, *Morale and Discipline in the European Command, 1945-1949* (Karlsruhe: Historical Division, 1951), 44.
66 Lord Robertson of Oakridge, 'A Miracle? Potsdam – Western Germany 1965', *International Affairs* 41, no. 3 (1965): 406.
67 Frank L. Howley, *Berlin Command* (New York: Putnam, 1950), 90.
68 'Black Markets Boom in Berlin. Red Army men are biggest buyers', *Life*, 10 September 1945.
69 Naimark, *Russians in Germany*, 173.
70 Lieutenant-Colonel W. Byford-Jones, *Berlin Twilight* (London: Hutchinson, 1947), 35.
71 Philip Wylie, *Hearst's International Combined with Cosmopolitan* 120, no. 6 (1946): 26–7, 154–6.
72 'Berlin police trap big Black Market', *Daily Mail*, 24 July 1945.
73 Irving L. Janis, 'Group Identification Under Conditions of External Danger', in *Group Dynamics: Research and Theory*, ed. Dorwin Cartwright and Alvin Zander, 3rd edn. (New York: Harper and Row, 1968), 89.
74 Henry Elkin, 'Aggressive and Erotic Tendencies in Army Life', *American Journal of Sociology* 51, no. 5 (1946): 408.
75 T. E. Osmond, 'Venereal Diseases in Peace and War with Some Reminiscences of the Last Forty Years', *British Journal of Venereal Diseases* 25, no. 3 (1949): 113.
76 Byford-Jones, *Berlin Twilight*, 28–9.
77 Evans, 'Protection from the Protector', 215–16.
78 Byford-Jones, *Berlin Twilight*, 37.
79 Percy Knauth, 'Marlene Dietrich Steals the Show in an Uproarious Hollywood Version of Low Life in Postwar Berlin', *Life*, 9 June 1948, 59.
80 *A Foreign Affair*, directed by Billy Wilder (Paramount, 1948).
81 Kevin C. Ruffner, 'The Black Market in Postwar Berlin. Colonel Miller and an Army Scandal', *Prologue: Quarterly of the National Archives and Records Administration* 34, no. 3 (2002): 171–85.
82 During World War Two, he had worked for the Office of Strategic Services as a civilian before being commissioned a Lieutenant Colonel, on 7 June 1943.
83 'Cooke Report'.
84 Ruffner, 'The Black Market in Postwar Berlin'.
85 Miller, *Man from the Valley*, 130.
86 Ruffner, 'The Black Market in Postwar Berlin'.
87 Testimony of Brigadier General Robert A. McClure, USA, taken at Berlin on 19 October 1946. Instead of a thousand intelligence officers, he only had twenty five.
88 Testimony of Lieutenant General Lucius D. Clay. In October 1945, the Information Control Division Branch created a research team overtly employing German surveyors who were 'trained in Gallup techniques'. Stivers, 'Victors and Vanquished', 159.
89 Testimony of Colonel Harry G. Sheen, Cav, taken at Washington DC, on 21 September 1946.
90 Testimony of Dr Walter L. Dorn, taken at Berlin, 18 October 1946.
91 Jean Edward Smith, *Lucius D. Clay: An American's Life* (New York: Henry Holt, 1990), 333.
92 Testimony of Lieutenant General Lucius D. Clay.
93 'Cooke Report'.

94 Testimony of Colonel James B. Edmunds, GSC, taken at Washington DC, on 19 December 1946 by Brig Gen Elliot D. Cooke, USA, and Colonel James H. Day, IGD.
95 'Meader Report', 40.
96 Testimony of Brig Gen Edwin L. Sibert, taken at Boston, Mass. on 24 September 1946 by Brig Gen Elliot D. Cooke, IGD.
97 Clay, *Decision in Germany*, 63-4. In publishing Clay's papers, Jean Edward Smith omitted those detailing 'personal peccadilloes by members of military government'. Jean Edward Smith (ed.), *The Papers of General Lucius D. Clay: Germany 1945-1949* (Bloomington, IN: Indiana University Press, 1974), xxvi.
98 Smith, *Lucius D. Clay*, 325. Nascent CIA operatives agreed. 'Report on Berlin Operations Base, 8 April 1948', in *On the Front Lines of the Cold War: Documents on the Intelligence War in Berlin, 1946 to 1961*, ed. Donald P. Steury (Washington, DC: CIA History Staff, Center for the Study of Intelligence, 1999), 16.
99 Geis and Gray, *The Relations of Occupation Personnel*, 46.
100 Arthur D. Kahn, *Betrayal: Our Occupation of Germany* (Brooklyn: Beacon, 1950), 95-6.
101 George F. Kennan, *Memoirs 1925-1950* (Boston: Little Brown, 1967), 428.
102 On the 'Barter Mart Experiment', see Geis, Russell and Maehl, *Morale and Discipline in the European Command*, 43f. Davis claims that the barter market was Mrs Clay's idea. Davis, *Came as a Conqueror*, 155.
103 'Guns for Americans in Berlin', *Manchester Guardian*, 31 July 1946.
104 Jean Edward Smith describes him as 'Aloof, austere and basically a very shy man', but one who 'did not suffer fools gladly'. Smith (ed.), *Papers of General Lucius D. Clay*, xxxi–xxxii.
105 'Report on Berlin Operations Base', 43.
106 Testimony of Mr Kenneth D. Johnson, taken at Washington DC on 30 September 1946.
107 Nevertheless, as late as June 1946, Clay was still insisting that American military officials remain distant from Germans and on no account to 'entertain' them. Stivers, 'Victors and Vanquished', 165.
108 Testimony of Mr Kenneth D. Johnson.
109 Testimony of Dr Walter L. Dorn.
110 Lyford Moore, 'The Man in the Goldfish Bowl', in *This Is Germany: A Report on Post War Germany by 21 Newspaper Correspondents*, ed. Arthur Settel (New York: William Sloane, 1950), 27.
111 Testimony of Mr O. R. Carlucci.
112 'Cooke Report'.
113 McCawley Testimony.
114 Edmunds also tried to take possession of the CIA's motor pool. 'Report on Berlin Operations Base', 81.
115 Miller's further testimony 'indicated that he did not possess the data to support his charges'. Geis, Russell and Maehl, *Morale and Discipline in the European Command*, 46.
116 Further Testimony of Colonel Francis P. Miller, GSC, taken at Washington DC on 19 September 1946.
117 'Cooke Report'.
118 Miller, *Man from the Valley*, 132, 197.
119 Testimony of Mr O. R. Carlucci.
120 Geis and Gray, *The Relations of Occupation Personnel*, 44.
121 Byford-Jones, *Berlin Twilight*, 30.

122 Probably broadcast by Wilhelm Girnus, as cited by W. Phillips Davison, *The Berlin Blockade: A Study in Cold War Politics* (Princeton, NJ: Princeton University Press, 1958), 259.
123 Christopher Knowles, 'Winning the Peace: The British in Occupied Germany, 1945–1948', PhD, Kings College, London, 2014, 226.
124 Geis and Gray, *The Relations of Occupation Personnel*, 20.
125 Gebhardt, *Als die Soldaten kamen*.
126 Michael Balfour and John Mair, *Four-Power Control in Germany and Austria, 1945-1946* (London: Oxford University Press, 1956), 58.
127 Curt Riess, *The Berlin Story* (London: Frederick Muller, 1953), 66.

4

The non-crime of interracial sex

One of Colonel Miller's most explosive and controversial claims was that black troops in Germany were running amok. In particular, he sought to bring to attention German fears about race mixing.[1] In part, such anxiety reflected German prejudices against black troops, which had existed since the French occupation of the Ruhr in the 1920s. Then, Germans contemptuously referred to their military occupiers as 'coloured Frenchmen' and the 'black shame'. In part, the French authorities had aimed to impress African troops by demonstrating how low the fearsome and mighty Germans had sunk.[2] The reversal of racial hierarchies led Germans in occupied areas to feel that they had unjustly been subjugated and enslaved.[3] Nazi propaganda endlessly repeated these concepts in connection with the so-called 'Rhineland bastards', mixed-race children fathered by non-white colonial troops.[4] They insisted that such children were 'living proof' of an injurious attempt to pollute and defile the Aryan race.[5]

The Nazis had founded their claims to racial superiority on condemnation of race mixing and had used both legal and extra-legal measures to prevent it (including arbitrary imprisonment and sterilization). Adolf Hitler argued that popular press evocations of black lawyers, teachers, pastors and musicians constituted a deliberate attempt, by the Jews, to preach racial equality, in order to undermine the German race.[6] On 23 May 1940, *Wehrmacht* propaganda units on the ground in France sought propaganda photographs juxtaposing German soldiers who were Aryan and 'particularly good-looking' with especially 'bestial-looking Senegalese Negroes'. For Nazi racists, such 'sharp racial contrasts' were of crucial importance.[7] Such photographs also found their way into ordinary soldiers' albums. Though small enough a minority to fall through the cracks of Nazi 'racial justice', mixed-race adolescents would probably ultimately have shared the fate of Jews and gypsies in the death camps. Although horrified by what they had encountered when they liberated the camps and further concerned by what they had learned about the Holocaust at Nuremberg, the Western Allies also recognized that they would have to tread carefully in relation to German racial prejudices. 'What Berliner did not think with horror of the propaganda at the time of the occupation of the Rhineland with its evil rumours, when the first Negroes entered Berlin?'[8]

Black troops recognized that Berlin had been the setting for Nazi race baiting, where people like them had been compared to 'semi-apes'.[9] Even after the defeat of Nazi Germany, notions of *Rassenschande* (racial defilement) lingered on in people's minds. Nazi propaganda had warned that coming with the American army were rapacious '*Neger*'.[10] Although most of the relationships after the armistice were consensual, notions of a deliberate desire to cause 'black shame', through miscegenation, persisted. On entering Berlin, in July 1945, the French had brought some non-white, colonial troops with them. They recorded that German officials had expressed 'visible satisfaction' that, although these North African troops had paraded on 14 July 1945, at least they had not included 'negro elements'.[11] Pernicious Nazi racism was clearly far from banished from defeated Germany. Both the French and the Germans remembered the 'black shame' of the 1920s. The Germans were not alone in assuming that black troops had a propensity to commit rapes of white women. Historian Mary Louise Roberts has made a detailed survey of the case files of rapes, supposedly committed by African-American soldiers in France after the liberation. She not only shows how individual black soldiers could falsely be accused of rape but how little the US military authorities were concerned to convict the right men. Both the French and the US authorities shared a 'set of racist attitudes' that could easily prove deadly. In meting out justice, they used harsh deterrents (like the death penalty) out of a fear that the situation was running out of control.[12] Racist white officers, convinced of the natural propensity of 'negroes to rape', carried out summary justice, based on the flimsiest of evidence. Historians of American military race relations suggest that we can in no way be sure that the men executed were the perpetrators or, in some cases, that rapes had actually been committed.

The Military Police (MPs) could charge African-American GIs with rape, even when the French or German women involved insisted that 'their relationships were consensual'.[13] In this sense, the arrest rate could reflect the resentment felt by all-white ('all-cracker') MP units at interracial fraternization, rather than a reality of sexual violence. The National Association for the Advancement of Colored People (NAACP) argued that disproportionate charging reflected endemic institutional racism.[14] Although Roberts demonstrates weaknesses in investigation and justice, she also points to the problems caused by American troops, in trying to negotiate for sex with foreigners, whose language they did not speak or understand. In a racially charged atmosphere, consensual relationships could easily be reclassed as rape. In one case, a white American officer took his German girlfriend up and down the ranks, encouraging her to identify a black soldier as her rapist.[15]

Before the Senate Committee, Colonel Miller had begun by saying that, as a white Southerner, he was unlikely to be believed, because of the prejudices that white Southerners had to live with. Nevertheless, he described the conduct of the black troops stationed in Germany as 'one of the most disgraceful episodes' in America's long history. 'For generations to come', the German people would remember 'what undisciplined, uncontrolled Negro troops have done to them'.[16] He implied that black troops were raping and pillaging in Germany, but the most serious incident he mentioned involved consensual sex with German women. He complained of the camp followers or whores who followed black units. He saw it as abhorrent that black troops were appealing to German women, by tempting them with American uniforms and Army rations. When the German police arrested the women, who he said were living in the woods, he claimed that the black troops had freed them, killing four German policemen.[17] On questioning, however, it appeared that Miller had little reliable information to go on. His comments on race relations were as erroneous, distorted and based on hearsay as his comments on officers' misbehaviour. He had some general claims that discipline had lapsed compared to the situation thirty years previously, but he could not name concrete instances or the officers who were afraid to control their black troops.

The first set of investigators, sent to Germany to explore Miller's claims, found that while coloured troops had higher rates of venereal disease, violent incidents and motor accidents, the courts-martial rates were also much higher for black troops.[18] Although they concluded that the behaviour of black troops was worse than that of white GIs, they could not ascertain a collapse in overall discipline, because white officers were still disciplining and punishing their men. Senate investigator George Meader claimed that War Department records demonstrated that the behaviour of black troops in Germany was 'no credit to the negro race'. Nevertheless, he did not believe that solving the problem should result in unfavourable reactions on the part of 'any intelligent negro leaders'.[19] Historian of race Heide Fehrenbach counters this clearly racist viewpoint by arguing that there is no question that black American troops could succumb to 'indiscipline and disease'. Rather, what is important to recognize is that in recording and assessing African-American misbehaviour, white American officials had a particularly negative view of undisciplined black masculinity. They routinely assumed that black troops would be sexually aggressive or unsoldierly.[20] In other words, African Americans faced a racist military justice system that disproportionately punished and executed them for infractions that would be viewed as less grave if committed by whites. It judged them guilty of crimes because of their race, whether they had committed them or not. The failings of black troops were blamed on the intrinsic inferiority of their race, without taking into account other factors. Fifty-five out of the seventy American soldiers, executed for crimes in the European Theatre, were black.[21] Where there was reluctance to discipline the men, this was blamed on black officers. Spurred on by letters from African-American soldiers complaining of overly harsh and unjust treatment, the NAACP launched an investigation into the 'racist assumptions and practices' that underlay a non-colour-blind system of military justice.[22] They found that black troops did violently defend their white girlfriends from MP raids. They pointed out, however, that white troops did not need to fear similar interventions.[23] Officers tended to see white troops' dalliances as a normal part of occupation while condemning similar behaviour on the part of blacks (Table 4).[24]

Table 4 Official Black and White Offence (including Venereal Disease) Rates among US Troops in Occupied Germany, 1945–6

	Rate per thousand	
	White	'Coloured'
Venereal disease	143	724
Incidents (altercations, fights, etc.)	4.84	6.45
Accidents (motor vehicle)	1.00	1.88
Courts-martial	1,137	3,477

War Dept, Special Staff, Office of the Inspector General: Inquiry regarding certain phases of the Army's Administration of the United States Zone of Occupied Germany (21 November 1946).

An intelligence survey from 1948 described the Criminal Investigation Division (CID) of the Berlin district as a 'hard-boiled outfit', run by tough, big-city cops. It contrasted sharply with the much more genteel atmosphere of the Public Safety Branch. Acting in some respects 'as a law unto itself', CID carved a path through 'the lush lawlessness' of the ruined city 'with gusto and abandon'. Its commander, Orazio R. Carlucci, was a former private detective who acted partly as General Clay's personal bodyguard and partly as a detective, combating occupation-related crime.[25] Born in Montclair, New Jersey, Carlucci compared his latter tasks to policing a big, complex city like Newark. He said that he had been watching black troops for three and a half years in Sardinia, Italy, North Africa, Marseille and Berlin. Asked what the situation was relating to 'coloured troops in Berlin', he argued that there were too few of them to cause much in the way of trouble. He agreed that, in the past, there had been 'quite a lot of trouble with them', in relation to 'rapes, assaults and shootings'. Asked if their officers had been afraid of them, he believed that, in some cases, this had been the case and that it had resulted in lax discipline. His remedy had been to get most of them out of the city. Although he partially supported Miller's argument, he nevertheless stated that, in his view, the coloured soldiers were only acting normally. 'I could probably stay here an hour and try to explain what I mean.'[26] The questioner said, 'I think I know what you mean. . .', but did not elaborate. It was no secret that the effects of racial prejudice were highly corrosive. These could have a major negative impact on discipline and behaviour. The worse black troops were treated, the worse they could be expected to behave. It is possible this was what Carlucci was getting at, but, unfortunately, we will never know.

The wounds of segregation

Although most parts of the American high command remained committed to continuing segregation within the military, some officers were beginning to see that it was causing tremendous harm. In 1948, President Harry S. Truman issued Executive Order 9981, which called for the military to provide equal treatment and opportunity, regardless of race, initiating a far-reaching policy of desegregation. Truman recognized that treating African Americans as second-class soldiers, as well as second-class citizens, was damaging their morale. The US War Department nevertheless initially sought to blame the black press for the low morale of black troops.[27] Racial discrimination went against the ideals of freedom and democracy for which they had supposedly been fighting. There were clear contradictions for the American military in attempting to eradicate the remnants of German racial supremacist ideology, at the same time as upholding what amounted to an American system of command based on racial segregation.[28] Continued hostility and blatant discrimination by racist Military Policemen could lead to a smouldering rage, which could spill over into violent insubordination and potent 'racial flare-ups'.[29] It made no sense to deploy a segregated army to put an end to Nazi racism. Why had black troops been fighting for democracy abroad when they could not get it at home?[30] Why had their fellow soldiers sacrificed their lives for continued humiliation, lynching and terror? In 1946, the obstacles (legal, administrative and social) which stood in the way of desegregation seemed insurmountable.[31] The military that occupied Germany was every bit as segregated as it was in the Deep South. Few contemporary American observers dared to voice opposition to racial policy, despite its clearly damaging effects. Eyewitness and sociologist E. T. Hall writes that the upper echelons in the military failed to lay down clear policies on how to treat black soldiers. The subject was seen as too hot a potato and few officers wanted to jeopardize their careers by sticking their necks out.[32]

General Joseph McNarney, US Military Governor in Germany, had stated that it would take over a hundred years before black troops had attained 'parity with white Americans'.[33] As well as cultural and educational problems, he saw black troops as inherently inferior. Nevertheless, he also blamed their defensiveness and irresponsibility on the way white America had handled them post-emancipation.[34] Despite his obvious reservations, he agreed to create black MP units. For his part, Major General Ernest Harmon, the commander of the US Constabulary in Germany, informed his all-white troops that sending coloured soldiers to the European Theatre had been one of America's stupidest mistakes. Now the 'Niggers' (he had no hesitation in using the word) were a much bigger problem to the military administration than the Germans.[35] Other military commanders agreed that there were too many unskilled black troops in Germany.

In part, the American military authorities brought African-American soldiers to Berlin in order to promote their particular notion of democracy. However, the army that the Americans took to Germany was a Jim Crow army, still characterized by ugly racial segregation. Mess halls, barracks and bars all had to be kept strictly separate. While this was customary for Americans, Europeans (even including Germans, who had been schooled in racism) found it strange and unwholesome. When US troops first arrived in Britain, they each received a letter stating that while 'prejudice against the Negro' probably existed, it was not quite the same in England and France as it was in the United States. Implicitly this meant accepting different behaviour on the part of the civilian population (vis-à-vis race mixing).[36] We know from memoirs and interviews that black soldiers routinely encountered racism while serving their country. Wearing military uniform made no difference to the Jim Crow laws in the South. Whether or not they were demonstrably serving and defending their country, black soldiers could not buy a hot dog on home turf. By contrast, German Prisoners of War sent there could sit down and eat in restaurants.[37]

Walter White headed the NAACP from 1931 to 1955. In the *Chicago Defender* in 1948, he recorded German consternation at the US use of a racially segregated army of occupation.[38] Germans asked him how the Americans could 'talk about German racism' when they maintained 'separate white and black armies' within Germany.[39] For contemporaries (German and American alike), segregation was a devastating hypocrisy and a needless, self-inflicted injury. Promoting free elections in Germany stood in sharp contrast to continued restrictions on voting in southern states. In the 1940s, racism was an open, festering sore pitting antagonistic groups against each other. With slurs and physical attacks, white soldiers harassed their non-white contemporaries. When they were stationed in Germany, white Southerners, in particular, took every opportunity to try and demean black troops. Although black troops made up one in nine soldiers by 1948, any problems or failures were blamed on their mediocrity and their intrinsic inability to control their base urges. During World War Two, black troops had generally been kept away from combat roles, because of widely held beliefs about their inherent inferiority.[40] Nevertheless, without their tremendous effort, in hauling supplies day-and-night, the front would not have advanced so quickly.[41] In spite of racism, they had played an important, when not decisive, role in World War Two.

As US Army historian Morris J. MacGregor argues, while justified on the grounds that it could prevent racial trouble, segregation only ended up intensifying it.[42] Given the frequency of racist comments and behaviour directed towards them, the morale of black troops was very low. Although only some had been allowed to fight for their country, nevertheless they had all made sacrifices for the victory. Now they were being made to feel that they did not fully belong to the nation they had been born into. Some muttered about what they would do when given weapons and live ammunition. Others responded to the everyday racism by developing a generalized contempt for white people.[43] After the war, black troops continued to experience severe racism. This left many feeling that they had gained very little for the sacrifices they had made during the war. What seems to have particularly incensed Colonel Miller was that consensual interracial sex was occurring between black soldiers and German women. That white women were attracted to black soldiers was deeply offensive to white racists. They viewed such relationships as inherently sordid and improper.

Conditions in Berlin

The commanding general of the European Theatre of Operations, Dwight D. Eisenhower, may have believed in blacks having equal rights, but many within the high command believed that those rights should be abrogated when it came to 'women and liquor'.[44] Cultural historian Jennifer Fay suggests that the occupation of Germany has been, to some extent, whitewashed.[45] Prominent among the American occupiers in Berlin, despite their limited numbers, were African-American servicemen. A truckload of black GIs caused a sensation when they drove up to the Femina nightclub in 1945. They were quickly 'dancing with the prettiest German girls in the place'. The combination of their 'sharp fitting, immaculate uniforms' and 'pleasant personalities' proved irresistible. Black newspapers speculated whether the attention they attracted was mere curiosity or could constitute 'genuine attraction'.[46]

Despite twelve years of Nazi racism, German civilians retained a certain fascination with these exotic 'Tan Yanks'. Young people throughout Germany reacted with wonder and astonishment when they encountered their first black troops in jeeps. Circumstances encouraged friendly contacts, not least because they had access to food and transport. Sometimes, troops took it upon themselves to distribute food and clothing to hungry and bereft Germans. Like white GIs, in Berlin, black troops enjoyed lives of comparative luxury; everything they needed was provided in abundance.[47] They never had to worry about food, petrol or showers.[48] Members of black truck units, stationed in Templehof, had their own fine mess hall, complete with comfortable club and games rooms. In addition to snack bars, they had access to a photo darkroom and a library. The military put on movies twice a week, together with German-language lessons. They enjoyed baseball matches with other units. For soldiers from ordinary backgrounds, the occupation of Berlin was the closest they would get to a paid holiday. Black troops embraced the freedom to visit shops, restaurants, parks, beaches and bars without 'whites only' signs. One photograph, from 1946, showed Roy Watford, a black private from Brooklyn, at the beach in Wannsee. In front of him, he had a German phonograph playing jazz records. Next to him was a good-looking '*Fräulein*' called Hildegard.[49] With sun and sex on tap, no wonder many GIs did not want the holiday to end.[50] For many readers, black and white, such an image was a stark, jarring, almost revolutionary provocation.

While white troops may have swaggered about like conquerors, black troops were often more circumspect towards German civilians. Conscious of the expectations (spread by white troops) that they were all rapists, black troops went out of their way to convince civilians of their good intentions. They policed their own clubs and ejected troublemakers. News reports in the black press reinforced their sense of themselves as ambassadors for their race. A recurring trope in German accounts of 'zero hour' was 'the friendly black GI', who stepped out of his tank or jeep to hand out chocolate to eager kids. Their politeness and friendliness disarmed many critics. In addition to giving sweets to children, they helped women with their bags and generally acted in a kind and thoughtful way. Knowing what it was like to be the underdog, they may have had more empathy for the downtrodden and defeated German civilians they encountered. Unlike their white peers, they were ready to get along with the ordinary German people. They were less cruel and condescending in their interactions.[51] Their small acts of warmth and generosity helped to ease the burdens and soothe the wounds of a desperate and very damaged population.

The bogeyman of Goebbels's imagination was suddenly near enough to touch. Some saw the chocolate bars, distributed by black troops, as a crude attempt to poison the 'Aryan blood-stream'. For most children (and some adults), however, the contrast between this open-handed generosity and the expectations created by Nazi propaganda served as a fundamental rupture in racial consciousness.[52] The fact that they could be so friendly, despite the hostility and distrust that hung in the air, was jarringly optimistic. Their humanity served not only to belie the Nazi propaganda; it concretely helped to destroy it. In return for their magnanimity, Germans occasionally invited them into their homes, treating these strangers with unprecedented courtesy and respect.[53] Ex-soldier John White argued that black soldiers were nicer to German civilians than their white counterparts. 'We would help them any way we could', including by giving them hardtack rations even though this was contrary to military regulations. German civilians, meanwhile, said that black troops 'had a good heart'.[54] The idea of whites and blacks sitting down at the same table was unheard of in America at this time. Journalist Ruth Andreas-Friedrich recorded her first encounter with a black occupation soldier in July 1945. She described him as 'beautiful like a panther'. His evident passion for Bach and Beethoven exceeded that of most Germans. She loved his cosmopolitanism – the fact that he had travelled all over the world – and had given 'concerts in countless countries'. She could not see him as a conqueror, in spite of his 'elegantly styled American uniform'.[55] Memoir literature like this suggests that African-

American soldiers often made a better impression on German civilians than their white counterparts. Although by no means all Germans were won over, many stopped seeing all black people as enemies and potential threats. While it was still common in the French and Soviet Sectors for black troops to meet stares and apprehension, within the American Sector initial fears disappeared as soon as the local inhabitants got to know their 'Tan Yank' occupiers.[56]

As occupation soldiers, wearing American uniforms, they were treated with unprecedented (and thereby transformatory) respect.[57] As black GI William Gardner Smith put it, the Berliners might have been racists but 'the look in their eyes' was nevertheless one of respect.[58] Hungry Berliners could ill afford to be discriminating in relation to black troops. Germans working under black supervision was an 'amazing paradox' for both parties.[59] Lawrence Johnson, who served in Berlin, saw the developing friendship as a way for ordinary Germans to seek forgiveness for what they, as a nation, had done. It was an unspoken form of atonement (or *Wiedergutmachung*).[60] Toleration and occasional empathy contrasted sharply with the absolute hatred these servicemen had experienced back at home. Whether consciously or unconsciously, the deliberate kindness of these GIs increased their esteem with young women in Berlin and other cities. Such tolerance and friendship could easily be cast as sex by critics. Linking black-market criminality with 'lecherous living', Senate investigator George Meader implied that black troops were uniquely buying favours.[61] It is true that black drivers were particularly difficult to police. Confining black troops to service functions backfired, in providing them with mobility. Nevertheless, *The Negro Star* newspaper insisted that black GIs did not need chocolate or nylons to purchase friendship.[62] Meader had singled out black troops for censure because he was clearly biased and sought only to smear them.[63] The *Plaindealer* suggested that he was more interested in recounting hearsay from former Nazis than in talking to black troops themselves.[64]

Popular songs from the period prove that black soldiers could not just be acceptable; they could be desirable.[65] In the topsy-turvy conditions of postwar Germany, some German women turned the racist indoctrination they had received on its head and began to form romantic attachments with their 'tan' occupiers. It became cool to have a black boyfriend. Despite continued racism by fellow American officers and men, many of these relationships became sexual. Asking what the implications of these dalliances were, African-American journalists reported what was happening for the audience back home. In a seven-page spread in October 1946, *Ebony* magazine pointed to the fraternization which was occurring between black GIs and German women in Berlin and celebrated these interracial relationships as an important achievement of equal rights. The editorial stated that equality and interracial friendship were more available to black soldiers in Berlin than in Birmingham, Alabama, in Dixie or on Broadway. Some of the expressions of respect and esteem were those owed by the conquered to the conqueror. Nevertheless, they rated the 'cordiality and good will' on show from white Germans as genuine. Hitler's ravings no longer influenced most Berliners. After decades of exposure to toxic racism, at home, it felt good to be rated likeable and good-natured.[66]

If this kind of coverage put a positive spin on black troops' experiences, African-American women did not necessarily share the black press's celebration of interracial romance.⁶⁷ Although romantic relationships across the colour line infuriated racists (both German and American), postwar Berlin allowed groups of individuals, from very different backgrounds, to set aside their prejudices and preconceptions and to get to know one another as human beings. With familiarity came recognition and mutual respect. The editorials hoped that racial hatred would eventually fade. Once Berliners had made their acquaintance with black troops, it was even possible for 'interracialism' to flourish.⁶⁸ Noting the number of German girls between the ages of eighteen and twenty-six who had steady Negro boyfriends, *Ebony* recognized that some acted out of self-interest, seeing them as sources of cigarettes, coffee or soap. Nevertheless, love could flourish between Berlin girls and their '*schwarz Amerikaner*'.⁶⁹

On both sides (black male and white female) there was the intoxication which came with breaking a taboo. In some cases, the racist depictions of unbridled black sexuality could increase the allure of African-American soldiers. Young women, in particular, saw them as wonderfully exotic and exceptional examples of style, panache and zest for life. They quickly garnered a reputation as chivalrous and attentive lovers. Often the fascination was mutual: if Europeans had stereotypes about black men, black troops had their own stereotypes about European women.⁷⁰ Often the black press repeated and encouraged these clichés. *Jet* provided its readers with a country-by-country survey of sexual attitudes on the part of European women. It noted that, except for a few prostitutes and 'loose' girls, most French women were quite conservative. It judged German women as profoundly – almost morbidly – swayed by passion. This manifested itself in them falling in love with a man they encountered on the street. The paper suggested that they would wordlessly follow him any place he suggested.⁷¹

In a variety of ways, black GIs had a lot to offer. For women who had not been poisoned by racist indoctrination, the black soldiers were just as dashing, in their crisp uniforms but a whole lot cooler. The jazz they brought with them was more authentic, the dancing more sexual. Black soldiers found German girls excellent 'jitterbug partners'. The hot music that the Nazis had banned was suddenly fashionable again. Dancing was a form of communication requiring no words. The affection they received may only have been 'skin deep'; the underlying racial preconceptions of the German population may not have changed significantly; but black soldiers embraced the opportunities for dalliances and interracial intimacy.⁷² Venereal disease rates, as recorded by the US military, suggested that an awful lot of interracial sex was going on in Berlin (as in the rest of US-occupied Germany). Although only making up 7 per cent of American troops in Berlin, they accounted for as much as 45 per cent of the recorded venereal disease infections.⁷³ However, caution needs to be used in studying these extrapolated figures.⁷⁴ As the NAACP insisted, these figures were designed to smear and denigrate African Americans.⁷⁵ Recorded rates of VD among white troops were probably lower than they were in reality, because officers and men preferred to consult private German doctors rather than submit to official treatment (and exposure) by the military.⁷⁶

Even if the statistics were a true representation of actual VD rates, historian John Willoughby argues that black VD rates were probably higher for several reasons. Black troops were more likely to serve in quartermaster units so had greater mobility than white soldiers. They had ready access to food and other tradable commodities.

Willoughby agrees with the argument that, under segregation, black troops were less easy for white officers to control. He thinks that black troops probably came into the service with higher rates of VD, in spite of screening by the military, because of the absence of medical care for blacks in the South. The women they frequented were more likely to be persecuted by the racist American and German authorities and therefore to avoid treatment. But, above all, he suggests that discriminatory distribution of condoms by the Red Cross probably accounted most for the higher VD rates.[77] Prophylactics played a crucial role in reducing the incidence of VD, but these were distributed in an unequal way. Unprotected sex increased the chances of pregnancy as well as of VD. A cartoon in a Berlin magazine showed a baby conceived during the power cuts; the joke was that it was black.[78] As mixed-race babies began to be born in Berlin and in West Germany, fears grew (both in Germany and among the black community in the United States) about what would happen to these 'wild oats' children.[79]

For racists in the military, such behaviour was an affront. Alvin M. Owsley had been the head of the American Legion veterans' organization. Incensed after seeing a photograph of a black GI fraternizing with a white woman in Germany, he wrote to General Eisenhower: 'My dear General, I do not know . . . where these negroes come from, but it is certain that if they expect to be returned to the South, they very likely are on the way to be hanged or to be burned alive at public lynchings by the white men of the South.'[80] To Southerners, who would lynch a man just for looking at a white woman, these black troops were getting away with murder.[81] Although interracial sex was no longer a crime in Germany, for racists it was an abomination, which threatened the carefully cultivated regime of terror developed in the American South. Having exchanged bodily fluids with a white woman, they believed that a black veteran would find it impossible to remember to jump into the gutter when one approached on the sidewalk. Whites expressed the fear that black veterans would cease to be satisfied with their old status. There would be no possibility of constraining their expectations for white women to acquiesce to their sexual desires.[82] Particularly galling for bigots was the fact that some white women seemed to prefer black to white males. They feared that, once tasted, equality would not easily be forsaken. Having broken the taboo of interracial sex and love, how could they go back to living in constant fear? Many veterans of the occupation had little desire to return to lynchings and segregated slums.[83]

A Shangri-La for African-American soldiers

Although some black servicemen had been fundamentally changed by the experience of fighting for democracy, the country they had served had not. That blacks experienced postwar Germany as liberating says more about how terrible conditions were for African Americans in the United States and especially in the South.[84] Die-hard Nazis were certainly not won over. It was only the toxicity of Southern racism that made Berlin appear such a 'haven of racial tolerance'.[85] Europe only seemed free in comparison to the malignancy of race relations in the United States.[86] As one black GI, who refused to return home, put it: he felt 'like a man' because that was how people treated him. He could never say the same about the place where he had been born and raised.[87] As another black GI put it, in Germany, he had tasted 'absolute freedom' for the first time. The drunken rush it gave meant that he 'never wanted to get sober again'.[88] William Gardner Smith powerfully expressed the sense of dissonance black GIs experienced in Germany. 'I like this goddamn country, you know that? That's right. I like the hell out of it. It's the first place I was ever treated like a goddamned man.' The lesson his principal character learned was that 'a nigger ain't no different from nobody else'. Germany was the place where a black man could be 'treated like a goddamn man'. He had to come to Europe to 'let the Nazis' teach him that. Post-1945 Germany taught black troops to feel truly like men. They ceased to be constantly reminded of their skin colour.[89]

This kind of argument had tremendous resonance with ordinary black soldiers. Reflecting on their experiences, African-American newspapers helped to create the impression that Germany was some kind of 'Shangri-La' or 'racial utopia', where genuine friendship and democracy between the races could be enjoyed.[90] The remnants of the Third Reich became an imaginary space, in which it was possible to dream up an alternative model of life, one where racial boundaries were surmountable. For a nascent black intellectual like William Gardner Smith, Berlin allowed escape from the unending 'social nightmare' of racism in the United States. He and his comrades began to feel 'more equal than the Germans'.[91] Their anomalous position provided unprecedented power and distinction. It was not that racism and prejudice did not exist in Germany; rather, it was that the freedoms black troops enjoyed were unthinkable in the United States.

But if black soldiers could blind themselves to the racism of the German population, it was all too real for their German girlfriends. The *Fräuleins* (or *Veronikas*) experienced at first hand the full force of prejudices against racial mixing.[92] The German police identified 'the negro base (*Negerkaserne*) in the Finckensteinallee' as a key source of danger in relation to prostitution.[93] While contempt was general for 'Ami-hussies', it was much worse for those derided and shunned as 'Nigger-whores'. The German authorities assumed that the women who consorted with African-American troops must be lower-class prostitutes. Consequently, discursively and in terms of practical policing, they fell outside the bounds of what was considered a respectable form of German femininity. Women who were attracted to otherness, despite racism, demonstrated significant insubordination, in dating black men. Those who wanted to marry the mothers of their babies faced nearly insurmountable obstacles. Anti-miscegenation laws in thirty of the then forty-eight states of the Union prohibited interracial marriage. These laws dated back as early as 1661 and were common in many states until 1967. In that year the US Supreme Court overturned the last state anti-miscegenation law. It was common practice among military officials in Germany to transfer black soldiers as soon as they applied for permission to marry.[94] They could be shipped to a different city hundreds of miles away, back to the United States or all the way to the Pacific. The same fate befell men who were known to have fathered a child. They sent desperate and angry letters to the Military Government, demanding to be allowed to return to Germany to be with their lovers and children but to no avail. Black troops with wives and children posed less of a threat. Some adopted the 'brown babies' abandoned to local orphanages.[95]

General Clay's intervention in the racial question

Despite coming from Georgia, finding out what his black troops were up to does not seem to have interested General Clay very much.[96] He later wrote that in March 1947, he inherited some service units containing negro troops. Citing indiscipline, he pointed to excessive levels of incidents involving German civilians. The task of re-educating Germans required a reassessment of prevailing norms of organization and discipline. After transferring them to the infantry and later to Constabulary units, Clay found that their discipline improved significantly.[97] As a consequence, the disparity in offence rates diminished.[98] Clay had told investigator George Meader that he wanted black troops in Germany to be used primarily as parade troops.[99] In spite of War Department reluctance (they supposedly feared the reactions of black leaders), he was able to achieve this. By creating the 7800th Infantry Platoon, as an elite honour guard made up of exceptional black troops, Clay sought to improve morale and discipline and to turn Soviet criticisms of American racism on their head. Howley refers to this special OMGUS Honour Guard as an outstanding unit, made up of 'handsome men, all over six feet' tall. Their precision and smartness on the parade ground was excellent for countering Soviet propaganda.[100] Howley's successor as US Commandant, Maxwell D. Taylor, can be seen in photographs, visiting an integrated classroom at the McNair barracks in November 1949. Nevertheless, under Clay's command, whites continued to use the swimming pool on separate days from blacks and only after the water they had swum in had been comprehensively drained.[101] Höhn insists that the exemplary troops knew that they were being used for propaganda purposes, while continuing to be treated shabbily.[102]

Conclusion

Building on innovative works by Atina Grossmann, Heide Fehrenbach and Jennifer V. Evans, this chapter shows that race came to the forefront of Allied-German encounters in relation to gender and sexuality.[103] The segregated US Army brought its messy and painful 'racial problems' to Berlin. With hindsight, trying to teach democracy to the Germans using a segregated army seems foolish. The Senate investigators from America completely dismissed the notion that General Clay and other senior officers were fearful of dealing with sensitive racial issues. They did not think that the products of West Point were 'terrified' of anything.[104] International romance and interracial sex were not features of the occupation that had been planned for, as the hastily imposed restrictions on fraternization demonstrate. Nevertheless, they became part of the Allied experience in Berlin (and elsewhere in American-occupied Germany). In contrast to the white troops, who behaved with the haughty disdain of a would-be conqueror, many black soldiers exhibited kindness and fairness. In return, many Berliners came to consider occupation by African Americans as something of a blessing. With retrospect, cultural historians emphasize how, through mutual attraction and love, they helped to democratize the defeated German culture they encountered. There was a superficiality to the notion of blackness as a balm for weakened and damaged Aryan white identity, but it nevertheless had potency and traction in the circumstances of 1945. With their smart uniforms and alluring dance music, the 'Tan Yanks' were exotic and attractive. Dating them was daring and taboo. Two downtrodden groups (black GIs and German women) came together and fell in love, in defiance of the colour line. While not without stereotyping and prejudice, their relationships showed that defeat and occupation could give rise to tolerance and understanding.

Much to white racists' horror, soldiers in Germany became forerunners of a new, self-confident black identity. Despite occasional residual racism, many black soldiers experienced their time in Germany as liberating. It provided them with an alternative to the claustrophobic, demeaning, everyday racism back home. Although the occupation experience provided African Americans with certain privileges and freedoms, they knew that they would have to sacrifice these on their return home. Consensual interracial sex was not a crime, but to many Germans, and Americans, it was taboo. African Americans were not all angels. They too could become unruly when drunk; they too could react with violence to perceived slights. As the NAACP insisted, they were neither morally inferior nor superior.[105] The lack of prophylaxis led to the spread of disease and the production of mixed-race children. In denying black fathers the right to marry or to live with their partner and child, the US military demonstrated its cruel application of institutional racism. Parents were shipped away to the other end of the world; in consequence, children grew up not knowing their fathers.

In the crucial postwar years, African-American GIs constituted a nexus between hungry Germans and additional rations. In extreme conditions of scarcity, they provided the moral economy with a modicum of humanity, as well as effectively providing a safety net to the ordinary population. With the onset of the cold war, American racism became a major own goal. It provided the Soviets with a not-so-secret propaganda weapon in the field of discursive combat. African-American soldiers who defected were encouraged to publish books and make speaking tours, describing their negative experiences. Bringing in the perspectives of women and African Americans adds depth to our understanding of policing. This is even more important because, in part, renewal was connected to moral (as well as crime statistical) clean-up.

Notes

1 Such fears were important in the 1940s and 1950s. Maria Höhn, *GIs and Fräuleins: The German-American Encounter in 1950s West Germany* (Chapel Hill, NC: University of North Carolina Press, 2003). Heide Fehrenbach, *Race After Hitler: Black Occupation Children in Postwar Germany and America* (Princeton, NJ: Princeton University Press, 2005).

2 Service Historique de l'Armée de Terre 16N198: Direction de Troupes Coloniales (Mordacq) to Pétain, 'AS emploi des Sénégalais dans les territoires ennemis occupés', 31 December 1918.

3 Fritz Giese, *Girlkultur: Vergleiche zwischen Amerikanischem und Europäischem Rhythmus und Lebensgefühl* (Munich: Delphin, 1925), 64–5.

4 Cornelie Usborne, *The Politics of the Body in Weimar Germany: Women's Reproductive Rights and Duties* (Ann Arbor, MI: University of Michigan Press, 1992), 148f.
5 Dr Franz Rosenberger, 'Gefahr der Mulattisierung', *Münchner Neueste Nachrichten* 163, 18 April 1922.
6 Adolf Hitler, *Mein Kampf* (Munich: Zentralverlag der NSDAP, 1940), 2: 478f.
7 Willi Boelcke, *Kriegspropaganda 1939–1941* (Stuttgart: Deutsche Verlags Anstalt, 1966), 130.
8 Memo, Public Opinion Survey Dept, 15 January 1946, file 4/8-3/16, OMGUS, Landesarchiv Berlin, as cited by William Stivers and Donald A. Carter, *The City Becomes a Symbol: The U.S. Army in the Occupation of Berlin, 1945–1949* (Washington, DC: Center of Military History, United States Army, 2017), 125.
9 'Negro GIs find Equality in Berlin', *The Plaindealer*, 20 September 1946.
10 Interview with Siegfried S-J.
11 'Note d'Information 14 Juillet à Berlin', 16 July 1945, Archives Diplomatiques, GMFB 1/866.
12 Mary Louise Roberts, *What Soldiers Do: Sex and the American GI in World War II France* (Chicago, IL: University of Chicago Press, 2013), 10–11.
13 Maria Höhn and Martin Klimke, *A Breath of Freedom: The Civil Rights Struggle, African American GIs and Germany* (New York: Palgrave Macmillan, 2010), 60.
14 'Nation Aroused Over Meader Report Smearing GIs in Germany', *Plaindealer*, 13 December 1946.
15 Alexis Clark, 'When Jim Crow Reigned Amid the Rubble of Nazi Germany', *New York Times Magazine*, 19 February 2020.
16 Special Committee Investigating the National Defense Program United States Senate. Testimony of Colonel Francis P. Miller. Office of Military Government, United States, 14 August 1946, Washington, DC. This and subsequent testimonies can be found in RG 159, Boxes 34-35, US National Archives.
17 Investigation by Brigadier General Elliot D. Cooke [hereafter known as the 'Cooke Report'], File No. 333.9, Entry 26F, Box 35, RG 159, US National Archives.
18 'Cooke Report'. On rates of rape and murder (together with executions), see Margaret L. Geis, Dorothy Russell and W. H. Maehl, *Morale and Discipline in the European Command, 1945–1949* (Karlsruhe: Historical Division, 1951), 27–8. The fear of arbitrary arrest and court martial was real.
19 Mead Committee investigation headed by George Meader, Chief Counsel of the United States Senate Special Committee [aka 'Meader Report'], 35.
20 Fehrenbach, *Race After Hitler*, 64.
21 Morris J. MacGregor, *Integration of the Armed Forces 1940-1965* (Washington, DC: Center of Military History, U.S. Army, 1981), 210. Cf. Geis, Russell and Maehl, *Morale and Discipline in the European Command*, 27–8, 77.
22 Fehrenbach, *Race After Hitler*, 25.
23 'Nation Aroused Over Meader Report'.
24 'Rumors Blast Our GIs in Germany', *People's Voice*, 7 December 1946.
25 'Report on Berlin Operations Base, 8 April 1948', in *On the Front Lines of the Cold War: Documents on the Intelligence War in Berlin, 1946 to 1961*, ed. Donald P. Steury (Washington, DC: CIA History Staff, Center for the Study of Intelligence, 1999), 11–103, 70. The report went on to argue that CID lacked the manpower and interest in policing the behaviour of the OMGUS personnel.
26 Testimony of Mr O. R. Carlucci, taken at Frankfurt, Germany, on 8 October 1946, by Brigadier General Elliot D. Cooke.

27 Richard M. Dalfiume, *Desegregation of the U.S. Armed Forces: Fighting on Two Fronts, 1939-1953* (Columbia, MO: University of Missouri Press, 1969), 78. Cf. MacGregor, *Integration of the Armed Forces*, 233.
28 Petra Goedde, *GIs and Germans: Culture, Gender, and Foreign Relations, 1945-49* (New Haven, CT: Yale University Press, 2003), 109.
29 E. T. Hall, Jr., 'Race Prejudice and Negro-White Relations in the Army', *American Journal of Sociology* 52, no. 5 (1947): 406.
30 Dalfiume, *Desegregation of the U.S. Armed Forces*, 163.
31 MacGregor, *Integration of the Armed Forces*, ix.
32 Hall, 'Race Prejudice', 401.
33 Maria Höhn, '"We Will Never Go Back to the Old Way Again": Germany in the African-American Debate on Civil Rights', *Central European History* 41, no. 4 (2008): Note 101, 630. Gardner Smith also repeats it in his novel. William Gardner Smith, *Last of the Conquerors* (New York: Farrar, Straus, 1948), 81-2.
34 Joseph McNarney to Chief of Staff, War Department, August 13, 1945. http://www.trumanlibrary.org/whistlestop/study_collections/desegregation/ (accessed 14 June 2013).
35 David Brion Davis, 'The Americanized Mannheim of 1945-46', in *American Places: Encounters with History*, ed. William Leuchtenburg (Oxford: Oxford University Press, 2000).
36 Hall, 'Race Prejudice', 401, 403.
37 Goedde, *GIs and Germans*, 111.
38 Walter White, 'What Negro GIs are Doing in Germany', *Chicago Defender*, 23 October 1948.
39 Clark, 'When Jim Crow Reigned'.
40 Dalfiume, *Desegregation of the U.S. Armed Forces*, 2.
41 Hall, 'Race Prejudice', 404.
42 MacGregor, *Integration of the Armed Forces*, 206.
43 Hall, 'Race Prejudice', 402.
44 Lt. Gen John C. H. Lee as cited by MacGregor, *Integration of the Armed Forces*, 228.
45 Jennifer Fay, 'Germany is a Boy in Trouble', *Cultural Critique* 64 (2006): 228.
46 'First Negro GIs Excite Berliners', *Chicago Tribune*, no date, ca. 1945. 'Investigate Mixed Love of GIs in Germany; Love Life Stirs Army', *Plaindealer*, 13 December 1946.
47 The chief of staff, Brig. Gen. Paul L. Ransom, insisted that the accommodation provided to black units should be of equal standard to that given to white units. Stivers and Carter, *The City Becomes a Symbol*, 124.
48 Gardner Smith, *Last of the Conquerors*, 53, 62. This was a novel about the romantic relationship between a black GI and a German woman. Smith was just twenty-one years old when he wrote the novel. He used his own service, as an occupation soldier, as the basis for this fictional account of a black Sergeant in Germany. Goedde, *GIs and Germans*, 110. Serving in Berlin and West Germany 'exposed Smith to new opportunities and a new sense of freedom'. Alex Lubin, *Romance and Rights: The Politics of Interracial Intimacy 1945-1954* (Jackson, MS: University of Mississippi, 2005), 127.
49 'Germany Meets the Negro Soldier: GIs find more Friendship and Equality in Berlin than in Birmingham or on Broadway', *Ebony* 1, no. 11 (October 1946): 5-9, 6-7, 9.
50 'Found Freedom in Germany: Few GIs Eager to Return to States', *Pittsburgh Courier*, 22 February 1947. 'Why Negroes Leave America: Many GIs Find More Freedom Overseas Than in Their Native Land', *Negro Digest*, March 1949, 10-11.

51 Some Germans saw a similarity between the way white Americans treated blacks in the United States and the shabby way they behaved towards German civilians during the occupation.
52 Referring to the transformative effect of Goethe's discovery of classical literature, Eduard Beaucamp called his first encounter with black troops a '*Griechenerlebnis*'. Eduard Beaucamp, 'Befreit. Aachen vor fünfzig Jahren', in *Frankfurter Allgemeine Zeitung*, 21 October 1994.
53 'A Lot of Pleasure in Berlin' – Interview with Lawrence Johnson. http://www.aacvr-germany.org/ (accessed 1 May 2013).
54 Interview with John White Sr: 'Black Army soldiers eating Christmas dinner with German civilians'. http://www.youtube.com/watch?v=BJBtY4iP3oI (accessed 16 May 2013).
55 Ruth Andreas-Friedrich, *Battleground Berlin: Diaries 1945-1948*, trans. Anna Boerresen (New York: Paragon, 1990), 76.
56 'Germany Meets the Negro Soldier', 6, 7.
57 Fehrenbach, *Race After Hitler*, 34–5.
58 William Gardner Smith, 'An American in Paris-III', *New York Post*, 29 September 1959, as cited by Höhn, 'We Will Never Go Back to the Old Way Again', 619.
59 'Negro GIs find Equality in Berlin'.
60 'A Lot of Pleasure in Berlin'.
61 *Plaindealer*, 20 December 1946. 'Socializing with German Women Main Charges against Negro GIs', *People's Voice*, 14 December 1946.
62 'Negro Soldiers Still Popular in Germany', *The Negro Star*, 4 January 1952.
63 'Marcus Ray Gives Lies to Meader Report on GIs', no details, 28 December 1946.
64 'Nation Aroused Over Meader Report'.
65 'Negro GIs find Equality in Berlin'.
66 'Germany Meets the Negro Soldier', 5.
67 Letters to the Editor, *Ebony* 2, no. 2 (December 1946) as cited by Lubin, *Romance and Rights*, 118.
68 'Germany Meets the Negro Soldier', 5. See also 'Racial: Mädchen and Negro', *Newsweek*, 16 September 1946, 29–30; 'The New Germany and Negro Soldiers: The Tan Yanks Still Popular with Germans Although Chocolate Bars No longer Buy Friends as in Early Occupation Days', *Ebony*, January 1952.
69 'Germany Meets the Negro Soldier', 5.
70 Lubin, *Romance and Rights*, 108.
71 'How Europe's Women Make Love', *Jet* 4, no. 11 (23 July 1953), as cited by Lubin, *Romance and Rights*, 113.
72 See advertisement for the *Ebony* story in the *Chicago Defender*, 14 September 1946, 7 as cited by Höhn, 'We Will Never Go Back to the Old Way Again', 626.
73 Berlin Command, OMGUS: 'History of Activities', 1 November 1946–30 June 1947, 88, 87. US National Archives, 390/50/23/3, BOX 19, 94. Although making up only 9 per cent of the men in the European Theatre, Geis and Gray argued that black troops accounted for 25–30 per cent of the cases of VD. Margaret L. Geis and George J. Gray, *The Relations of Occupation Personnel with the Civil Population, 1946-1948* (Karlsruhe: Historical Division, European Command, 1951), 36.
74 John Willoughby, 'The Sexual Behavior of American GIs during the Early Years of the Occupation of Germany', *The Journal of Military History* 62, no. 1 (1998): 161.
75 'Nation Aroused Over Meader Report'.

76 MacGregor, *Integration of the Armed Forces*, 209.
77 Willoughby, 'The Sexual Behavior of American GIs', Note 31, 166.
78 *Frischer Wind*, 1 November 1946.
79 Douglass Hall, 'What's Become of Them? Berlin's "Wild Oats" Babies', *Afro-American*, 25 October 1947. 'How Many "Wild Oats" Babies in Germany?', *Afro-American*, 8 May 1948. 'German Brown Babies Won't Be Segregated', *Plaindealer*, 14 September 1951.
80 Alvin M. Owsley, 'Chairman of the American Legion National Americanism Endowment Fund to General Eisenhower', 16 September 1946, as cited by Dalfiume, *Desegregation of the U.S. Armed Forces*, 133.
81 Cf. Lubin, *Romance and Rights*, 144.
82 Hall, 'Race Prejudice', 403.
83 Ralph G. Martin, 'Where is Home?', *New Republic*, 31 December 1945, as cited by Höhn, 'We Will Never Go Back to the Old Way Again', 636.
84 'Nazis in Germany treated me better than the white folks in Virginia, where I was born', was a common sentiment expressed. See Höhn and Klimke, *A Breath of Freedom*, 45.
85 Goedde, *GIs and Germans*, 108.
86 Lubin, *Romance and Rights*, 105.
87 'Why Negroes Leave America: Many GIs Find More Freedom Overseas Than in Their Native Land', *Negro Digest*, March 1949, 10–11 as cited by Höhn, 'We Will Never Go Back to the Old Way Again', 622.
88 'Found Freedom in Germany'.
89 Gardner Smith, *Last of the Conquerors*, 65–8.
90 See Walter White, 'People, Politics, Places', *Chicago Defender*, 18 May 1946, as cited by Höhn, 'We Will Never Go Back to the Old Way Again', 621.
91 Smith, 'An American in Paris-III'.
92 Lubin, *Romance and Rights*, 103.
93 KJ. M. III: 'Weibliche Kriminalpolizei: Bericht', 27 June 1947, Landesarchiv Berlin, C Rep 303-09, Nr. 249, 28f.
94 Lubin, *Romance and Rights*, 99, 103.
95 'Negro Soldiers Still Popular in Germany'.
96 Clay called his black cocker spaniel 'Sambo'.
97 'Bishop Walls Home from Europe', *The New York Age*, 9 August 1947. Bishop Walls found Clay a fair man trying to do the right thing. 'Bishop Walls Reports on Tour of Europe', *Sunday Chicago Bee*, 10 August 1947.
98 Lucius D. Clay, *Decision in Germany* (Westport, CT: Greenwood, 1970), 230–1.
99 'Meader Report', 35.
100 Frank L. Howley, *Berlin Command* (New York: Putnam, 1950), 190. *Time*, 12 July 1948 featured Clay's honor guard.
101 'Bishop Walls Blasts Army German Jim Crow Policy', *Chicago Defender*, 1 November 1947, as cited by Höhn, 'We Will Never Go Back to the Old Way Again', 633.
102 Clark, 'When Jim Crow Reigned'.
103 Atina Grossmann, *Jews, Germans, and Allies: Close Encounters in Occupied Germany* (Princeton, NJ: Princeton University Press, 2009). Jennifer V. Evans, 'Protection from the Protector: Court-Martial Cases and the Lawlessness of Occupation in American-Controlled Berlin, 1945-1948', in *GIs and Germans: The Social, Economic, Cultural and Political History of the American Military Presence*,

ed. Detlef Junker and Thomas W. Maulucci (New York: Cambridge University Press, 2013).
104 Testimony of Brigadier General Robert A. McClure, USA, taken at Berlin on 19 October 1946.
105 'Nation Aroused Over Meader Report'.

Part II

Cutting the Gordian knot of overlapping, entangled jurisdictions. The policing implications of ripping a town in two in the opening battles of the 'cold war'

5

Initial cooperation and attempts at four-power government

Some American journalists believed that by splitting the atom, their scientists had effectively shortened the war. In Berlin, however, the generals representing the four powers were attempting an even more difficult task, that of conjuring up the political atoms of peace.[1] In 1945, the Allies created a novel form of 'civico-military' governance for occupied Germany, centred on Berlin. The demands on it were far greater than even the exceptional postwar conditions stretching the civilian governments at home.[2] At the Moscow conference in October 1943, the three foreign ministers of Britain, the United States and the Soviet Union had agreed that disarming, demilitarizing, denazifying and democratizing Germany were crucial. Once these far-reaching principles were established, the only real sticking point was reparations. At Yalta, the big three had agreed to an overall figure of $20 billion (half of this would go to the Soviet Union). Nevertheless, Winston Churchill refused to allow discussion of the details at this stage.[3] The technicalities were to be hammered out at Potsdam (without the French) in July 1945. General Lucius D. Clay thought that re-establishing the central all-German governmental machinery was an essential prerequisite before beginning to restore the German economy and thereby settling the reparation claims.[4] Nevertheless, there was a consensus among the victors that Germany had to be thoroughly denazified and reformed before it could once again be treated as a single political unit. So, there was a chicken-and-egg problem: Which would come first, denazification or reparations?

The French government was particularly aggrieved to be left out of the Potsdam negotiations because they wanted compensation for all the damage German occupation had caused to their people and infrastructure. However, by the time they met at Potsdam, the British and Americans had realized that the only way to prevent starvation in Germany was for the Allies to supply their zones with food. In the circumstances, neither power wished to foot the bill for reparations, by taking food and other essential supplies out of their zones.[5] Political division complicated the economic situation and vice versa. For his part, Winston Churchill refused to accept starvation in the industrial Ruhr because the Soviets had given the Poles the breadbasket of Pomerania and Silesia.[6] He and President Harry Truman insisted that reparations could only come once German basic needs had been assured. However, the formula for calculating what was an acceptable level of reparations from the individual zones was fiendishly complicated and inevitably gave rise to misunderstandings once the occupation was less precarious.

For much longer than the British and Americans, the French and Soviet governments were preoccupied with obtaining reparations from the Germans.[7] This planted the seeds of future discord. The Soviets demanded that reparations be paid before they would consider any resolution of the issue of German unity. For the other Allies, political and economic unity should precede payments. What was the point of supplying Germans made hungry and needy by the Soviets? To Moscow, this sounded suspiciously like the British and Americans were trying to welch out of their agreements. In May 1946, Clay demonstrably refused to deliver reparations from the US Zone to the Soviets. He did not see why the United States should deprive their Zone of resources to fund reconstruction in the Soviet Union.[8] In his view, reparations now undermined the goal of reactivating German industry and thereby reviving the economy of Western Europe. However, his papers reveal that the power whose actions caused him to cut off reparations deliveries was France, not the USSR. In the beginning, Paris was as important as Moscow in impeding any move towards German economic unity.[9] Nevertheless, understandably the move did not go down well in the Kremlin. While the British and Americans came away from the negotiations believing that the Soviets intended to turn Germany into an economic wasteland, Stalin became convinced that the Western Allies were interested only in restoring Germany's military might.[10] As this chapter will show, disputes over governing Germany, as a single entity, created and then widened an East-West schism emerging in the prostrate former capital.

Four-power government institutions

On 5 June 1945, General Eisenhower, General de Lattre de Tassigny, Field-Marshal Montgomery and Marshal Zhukov met in Berlin and signed the Allied Control Council into being. This was to be the chief instrument for the four-power government of Germany. Decisions were to be made unanimously. This was intended to build in limitations on unilateral action and to ensure continued Allied cooperation. Not interested in the details, General Eisenhower left the nitty-gritty of negotiations to General Clay. Clay has subsequently been heavily criticized for not getting a firm commitment from the Soviets on the Western Allies' rights of access to West Berlin. Neither the American nor the Soviet negotiators had demonstrated any desire to discuss access in the European Advisory Committee (EAC). The lack of a written agreement with the Soviets for Allied access to Berlin is even more surprising given the detailed negotiations and watertight agreements the Americans made with the British and French for access to the American Zone.[11] Clay believed that he had secured a gentleman's agreement with Marshal Zhukov but did not want to box himself in with entry routes that were too narrowly defined. He did not realize that, while theoretically possible, the requirement for unanimity meant that the Soviets could veto any subsequent attempt to alter the situation. With hindsight, he believed that he should have made access to Berlin a precondition for American troops to begin withdrawing from the Soviet Zone.[12] It is surprising that such a momentous decision could be based on a verbal agreement and a handshake.[13] The fact that Clay, who had not been part of the detailed, careful planning for the occupation, should have to take it demonstrates problems with the American preparations. With the talks taking place just two days before the main body of troops arrived in the city, the Anglo-American lack of leverage in negotiations, at this stage, was tangible.

Gentlemen's agreements from 1945

The chaotic and disorganized nature of life in Berlin in 1945 meant that the Allies overlooked certain anomalies, amid the desperate need to prevent starvation and disease. The Allies accepted the boundaries of Greater Berlin from 1920 as the basis for the division of Berlin into three (and then four) sectors. In a spirit of goodwill and cooperation, during the first weeks of the occupation, the Western Allies also struck certain deals with the Soviets. These deals were made in the expectation that the details could be ironed out later. At the time, the Allies did not always realize that they were creating binding agreements, regarding these anomalies, which would be impossible to undo later. Airfields were particularly difficult to fit inside the circumscribed confines of quadripartite Berlin. The British did a deal with the Soviets, allowing extra room for their airport in Gatow, in exchange for territory provided to lengthen an airport in the Soviet Sector.[14] In November 1945, the Soviets agreed to a slight extension of the French Sector to the north of Frohnau so that they too could build an airfield.[15]

Had they known what they were getting into, the British and Americans might have been more suspicious of Soviet intentions from the beginning. Misunderstandings were put down to language and/or cultural differences rather than signalling a malign intent. In the early days of the occupation, it was common for all four powers to meet up nearly every night at the state opera in East Berlin. The Western Allies did their best to accommodate the Soviets, having needed their help during the long war against Hitler. They encountered officers who were exceptionally clever, charming and urbane, who talked so delightfully about culture. It was only subsequently that they realized that their Soviet opposite numbers were wearing masks and were skilfully engaged in manipulating them. Afterwards, there was a palpable sense of grievance and embarrassment that they had been so easily hoodwinked.[16] When he assessed the early four-power cooperation, journalist George Bilainkin noted disunity and lack of direction.[17] The essential problem was that the Western Allies had been winging it, while the Soviets appeared to have had a clear and coordinated plan from the outset. Although the execution may at times have been shoddy, the Soviets always had a clear and coherent vision of what they wanted to achieve in Berlin.

Allied *Kommandatura*

If the Control Council was responsible for governing Germany as a whole, the Allied *Kommandatura* was the four-power governing body for Greater Berlin. It first met at the Soviet headquarters on 11 July 1945.[18] This was the first time in history that four powers had come together to govern a foreign city. To Anglo-American ears, its title was a curious amalgam of Russian and German, halfway between *Komendatura* and *Kommandantur*.[19] This summed up its potential to produce mixed messages and misunderstandings. For American-German journalist and ex-psychological warrior Curt Riess the ugly linguistic compound indicated a mixture that would prove difficult to digest as well as to pronounce.[20] Only on the day of its first meeting did the Allies begin to discuss how it should be organized. Howley claims to have possessed a carefully thought-through plan not to give the Soviets a veto. However, General Clay crushed his plan, saying that the orders had come from Washington.[21] Clay had already given a press conference in Paris, at which he optimistically saw Berlin as the testing ground for international cooperation. 'It's got to work. If the four of us cannot get together now in running Germany, how are we going to get together in an international organization to secure the peace of the world?'[22] Clay's eventual anti-Soviet attitude was even more powerful because he had begun the occupation with a large degree of goodwill and an open mind. The British Foreign Secretary, Anthony Eden, also stressed the importance of achieving Allied unity in Germany.[23]

In the *Kommandatura*, each occupying power was represented by its sector's commandant. Howley argues that this gave him considerable authority despite his lowly rank.[24] Below them were twenty sub-committees composed of quadripartite experts. Employing specialists in everything from 'fertilizers to culture', the US Military Government had hundreds of departments; this important machinery cost upwards of $200 million a year.[25] Though less well resourced, the other Allies had comparable bureaucracies. Of the *Kommandatura* committees, 'Public Safety' (concerned with policing) was by far the most important. The Western Allies brushed aside their concerns about the continued Soviet encroachments on their sectors and resolved to cooperate with their homologues. The Western Allies did everything they could in the hopes of winning over the Soviets, allaying their suspicions, and convincing them that they were friends: 'We were going to get along with the Russians and we were quite willing to start off on their terms.'[26]

Their ten weeks of sole occupancy had allowed the Soviets to make their mark on the city. While they had had exclusive control of Berlin, the Soviets had been busy establishing institutions unilaterally, creating semi-permanent institutional solutions to a whole range of important questions. In the process of getting its administration going again, the Soviets had developed an impressive, in-depth understanding of the complex workings of the city. They appointed a number of personnel to administrative and policing positions; they unilaterally decided which parties and unions could form. With hindsight, it was clear that the Soviets had shown exceptional foresight in having the city government's executive (called the *Magistrat*) established in their Sector. When the other Allies arrived, they could not reverse these decisions without Soviet approval. Parties that the Soviets had created could not subsequently be banned. The Soviets had, in effect, achieved several faits accomplis. Instead of questioning these decisions, the other powers approved all of them in the first meeting of the Allied *Kommandatura*. Getting along with the wartime ally meant trying to understand and appreciate peculiar Soviet economic and political arrangements. The circumstances seemed to dictate forbearance. Nevertheless, with hindsight, the Americans felt that they had given too much leeway, in effect acquiescing to Soviet control of Berlin. Only later did the Western Allies realize that they were confirming Soviet-appointed administrators and police officials.[27] Too late, the Western Allies realized that they were stuck with Communist government officials, who they could not dismiss unless the Soviets decided not to exercise their veto.[28]

The Soviets did not have a monopoly on diffidence or truculence. From the start, the French pushed for citywide cooperation as a way of undermining German unification. Between May 1945 and September 1949, the occupying powers provided Germany's de facto government. Although each power was sovereign – master in his own house – in its own zone, they sought to act jointly in matters affecting the country as a whole. The respective Military Governments wielded immense power. As well as keeping the population fed, the Allies now represented the main source of law and order. The four-power occupation agreements allowed for four different sets of Allied military law to function, in Berlin, in addition to the continued operation of German law.[29] Looking back, Clay described the position of Military Governor as the closest thing to 'a Roman proconsulship' that the modern world could offer. He merely needed to turn to his secretary and say, 'Take a law' and henceforth the law existed, impacting on German society in a matter of two or three weeks. Recognizing his somewhat limitless ambitions, he nevertheless argued that he had tried to act as a benevolent despot.[30] For their part, the local press mocked Clay for instituting a 24-hour razzia after his car was stolen.[31] The would-be emperor had seemingly been caught not wearing his toga. For a British official, Clay not only resembled a Roman emperor but also tended to act 'like one, too'.[32] To some extent, the power wielded by Clay was even greater than that possessed by his Soviet opposite numbers, Zhukov and Sokolovsky.[33] In 1948, Secretary of State George C. Marshall suggested that Clay was prone to 'localitis', getting distracted by events in Germany and losing sight of the big picture.[34] Clay later suggested that the initial attempts to foster quadripartite cooperation led the Western Allies to make too many compromises with and concessions to the Soviets, sowing the seeds for the eventual breakdown. Nevertheless, at the time, he felt that 'four-power harmony' was what President Roosevelt's government had signed up to at Yalta.[35]

Four-power government in operation (1945–6)

The initial *Kommandatura* sessions were marked by variety as well as goodwill, with a thousand and one practical detailed matters to settle. The issues that preoccupied the Allies in the early days were getting the city functioning again; organizing food supplies, transport and sewerage; preventing outbreaks of disease; preparing for the onset of winter; holding elections and re-establishing local government for Berlin; and dealing with a flood of refugees and expellees from the East. One of the most important was re-establishing a functioning police force to bring order to the post-conflict city.[36]

Four-power Military Government was cumbersome and slow moving. From the outset, there was significant confusion about areas of responsibility between the *Kommandatura* and its superior, the Control Council. The *Kommandatura* had no legislative authority and routinely had to pass matters on to the Control Council for approval.[37] The Allies thereby managed to create an incredibly complex, but slow-moving, administrative machine, with significant potential for confusion and misunderstanding. From its inception, the *Kommandatura* witnessed the clash of divergent cultures and ideologies. Language differences could act as a considerable barrier, exacerbating ideological differences. Words like 'democracy' could mean very different things in the different lingos. To French and Soviet amazement, even the British and Americans disagreed on the meaning of certain terms.[38] Often stalemate occurred because the translations failed to match. The need for every matter discussed to be translated slowed deliberations down to a snail's pace. Every directive, however trivial, had to be intensely debated and discussed before unanimous agreement could be reached. Many hours were wasted on seemingly trivial directive 23. At a time of deprivation and hunger, this forbade Germans from swimming, sailing or skiing.[39] On another occasion, a notorious Soviet representative spent over an hour assessing the food group to which nuts and berries belonged. Once the Allies had finished discussing an issue in their three languages, they made a decision that was then issued in German. It is a sign of the reversed hierarchy that the language of Goethe and Hölderlin, not to mention that of *Ordnung und Sicherheit*, now constituted the fourth most important language in the country.

Intractable problems that could not be solved in the *Kommandatura* were referred to the Control Council. There were also often delays while Military Government officers consulted their governments at home. From the start, four-power government – involving four national cultures, three languages and two contrasting ideologies – proved highly unwieldy. With the United Nations still in its infancy, the *Kommandatura* represented the most radical attempt of different nations to surrender their differences by working together. Howley disliked the British habit of mincing words, for example referring to the Socialist Unity Party (SED) as a 'certain party'. The French delegates were often caught between Germano- and Russophobia. Nevertheless, for nearly two years, the four powers struggled to try and make it work. They valiantly overlooked their differences and tried to find a 'quadripartite modus vivendi' in the beleaguered capital.[40] The cumbersome quadripartite machine could not function without plenty of give and take and an occasional, strategic blind eye. The British often saw the Americans as naive and unworldly. Howley claimed that his countrymen were driven by pragmatism and the French by logic. With hour-long tirades, the Soviets laboriously sought 'to sap the other Allies' will to resist. He was surprised to find the British, 'oddly enough' the 'most emotional' of the four Allies. Having fetishized fair play, anything 'smacking of twisted truth' enraged them. Given the Soviets' propensity for 'twisting facts, figures, and even the words of their colleagues to suit their needs', they were continually outraged by such uncricketing behaviour.[41] With his boxing and footballing analogies, Major-General Herbert seemed to fit the British 'fair play' stereotype. He said that it would be 'rather off-side' to discuss the Soviet personalities he had battled with and batted against.[42] His successor, Geoffrey Bourne, had lost an arm in a bobsleigh accident but persisted in playing golf with considerable skill. The outlook his injury gave him was no handicap in dealing with four-power imbroglios.

General Charles De Gaulle had found his absence at Yalta and Potsdam both humiliating and absurd, a view shared by many of his countrymen. Consequently, the French representative on the Control Council routinely used his veto to remind the others that there were consequences for not having invited his government to the conferences aimed at planning the postwar world.[43] Nevertheless, the fact that Germany had invaded France three times during the previous seventy years showed that the diplomats had legitimate security concerns about their neighbour as well as a sense of grievance. By paralyzing and stymying the Control Council, the French initially constituted the chief obstacle to four-power cooperation. This galled the British and Americans because it flew in the face of pressing realities. With rampant inflation and a cigarette economy, the failure to create central agencies threatened to sink an already prone and divided Germany into disastrous economic and financial havoc. Each occupying power initially pursued its own approach to reviving trade and industry, as well as to reforming political life. In November 1945, Field-Marshal Sir Bernard Montgomery saw the French as the 'chief obstacle' to unity. Without progression towards a central government, he feared the Germans would rise up during the expected harsh winter.[44] For Howley, Soviet policy seemed to be dictated by greed, while British policy expressed fear. French notions were dominated by national honour while the Americans simply wanted to get things over so that they could pack up and go home.[45]

Berlin was not a blank slate on which the occupiers could easily impose their models. Only the *Kommandatura* (and not the Berlin *Magistrat* or local government) could issue orders to the police, but decisions had to be unanimous in order for them to be binding. For example, unanimity was required for the appointment or dismissal of senior policemen.[46] From the start, members of the *Magistrat* criticized their lack of influence on or control of the Police President.[47] More than any other branch of the newly re-established city government, the police force was the cause of frictions and disagreements between the Allies. The victors were united in believing that the police should be denazified and that there should be no secret police, but they differed on the precise implementation of reforms. Expecting the British and Americans to share conceptions of policing, let alone the Soviets and the French, was overly idealistic. Despite repeated attempts to put policing reform on the agenda, the Western Allies found it difficult to influence and get sense from the Soviet-appointed Police President. The Public Safety Committee could require Markgraf to attend meetings, where he had to answer questions about his force's decisions and activities. He later complained that he was only allowed to speak when asked a direct question. He found the French representative generally friendly and cooperative towards him, but he struggled to get on with the British and Americans, who expressed increasingly overt hostility.[48]

Howley rated Ray Ashworth, the head of the US Public Safety Branch, as 'a giant of a man', who almost single-handedly rebuilt the Berlin police as a strong and democratic force.[49] Ashworth later argued that it was above all the Western Allies who had pressed for democratization of the police. Despite Soviet opposition, they had pushed for better pay and pensions, together with improved equipment.[50] It is possible that, in the early days, western Public Safety officers were more worried about Nazis, criminals and incompetents in the police than about Communists. The latter had initially appeared disciplined and vigorous in challenging remnants of Nazi ideology. At great length, the

Kommandatura's Public Safety Committee discussed how to arm the fledgling police. From February 1946, they were able to create a motorized flying squad.

Deterioration of four-power relations

During 1946, the honest misunderstandings of the early days increasingly gave way to outright Soviet prevarication. With hindsight, the initial cooperation appears to have been based on the conviction that the Communist-controlled Socialist Unity Party (SED) would triumph at the polls. Clay believed that he had established a relationship of trust with Zhukov, but in March 1946, Stalin replaced Zhukov with the 'hardline' Marshal Vasily Sokolovsky. Although retaining a semblance of cordiality, relations became markedly frostier.[51] At six feet four in height, with a chest full of decorations, Sokolovsky was as determined as he was sturdy. He personified the Soviets' newfound determination not to compromise. Access to their Soviet opposite numbers became more difficult and relations were increasingly strained. Nevertheless, in the view of Colonel John B. Hughes, Clay too was inconsistent, in the approach he took to the Soviets. His underling suggested that he should stick to one policy – gentle or strict – and stop switching from one to the other.[52]

The lawless limbo of the European 'Shanghai'

Even when they were ostensibly engaged in cooperation, the Soviets were wilful and arbitrary. They routinely arrested Allied soldiers and officials who exercised their right to visit the eastern sector. For dyed-in-the-wool democrats, the Soviet tendency to have opponents disappear was disturbing. It is true that the NKVD showed little concern for borders or for the niceties of four-power government. Also worrying was the arrest of two municipal judges in the western sectors by German police, in the middle of the night. The only crime the judges had committed was to rule against local German Communist leaders.[53] Habeas corpus was not a concept that the Soviets generally understood.[54] Long after the Western Allies had taken over their sectors, the NKVD continued to carry out arrests there. It was common for Berliners to describe the lawless limbo of the postwar city they lived in as a 'Shanghai'.[55] The blurred boundaries of both cities – with a clash of legal cultures and the juxtaposition of dangerous and safe sectors – served to create a legal vacuum. Nevertheless, there were distinct differences between postwar Berlin and concessionary Shanghai. Germans in all four sectors were roughly subject to the same laws. Trials were supposed to take place in the sector where the arrest had occurred. At times, it is true, Allied Military Governments could act in an ad hoc, extra-legal manner. However, exceptional cases of military courts trying German suspects according to Allied military justice only occurred in the first months of the occupation. At that time, justice had been swift and merciless. Nevertheless, long after the initial emergency, Military Government could transfer any case it chose to the jurisdiction of its own Courts. This meant that Berliners could not question Military Government decisions or seek redress for their grievances in a German court.[56] In addition to maintaining order, the specific goal of Military Government Courts was to protect Allied government interests. Laws made by the Allies as occupying powers overrode the pre-existing laws of Berlin. For example, Ordinance 501 forbade Berliners from uttering 'derogatory statements' about any of the occupying powers. The Allies operated according to the principle that the victors would not be subject to the laws of their defeated enemy. This immunity was vexing for Germans, who saw the foreigners as being above the law.

Although both were increasingly critical of Soviet behaviour, Clay and Howley did not always see eye-to-eye on police tactics in the American Sector. At times, Clay demonstrated more concern to outflank Howley than to outsmart his Soviet counterparts. As late as September 1947, Clay criticized Howley for temporarily locking up Communists, who had been due to speak at a mass meeting in Kreuzberg. When Howley affirmed that he could break up demonstrations not authorized by the Military Government, Clay accused his Deputy Commandant of 'running a Gestapo city'.[57] Police historian Eugene Jones likewise accuses Howley of overstepping his authority and of misusing control of the police, to make raids on Communist offices. He sees Howley as exercising 'a form of martial law', in which temporary arrests could be made without bringing charges. In this way, Howley used detention as an intimidatory tactic in a similar fashion to the operation of 'dictatorial regimes'.[58] Howley, however, felt that Clay was overreacting to his pre-emptive action in throwing 'a handful of Communists in jail overnight'. He insisted that that the original Supreme Headquarters Allied Expeditionary Force (SHAEF) legislation was still in effect, requiring advance approval of any meetings, and that the Communists 'knew the rules'. Technically, any gathering of three or more persons required Military Government approval.[59]

Although Howley probably intended to use the police intervention to impede and harass German Communists, and thereby to annoy the Soviets, he was acting in accordance with his rights and duties as Deputy Commandant of the US Sector. As an extrovert and an introvert, Howley and Clay were polar opposites. Nevertheless, both had absolute conviction that they were right. Although Howley was prone to emotional fits of pique, as well as of mischief, all four Allies had granted themselves wide-ranging powers to police demonstrations, in their sectors, as they saw fit. The Americans had gone into Berlin expecting to encounter a vicious and ruthless insurgency, together with riots and civil unrest. If they faced sniping or mass sabotage, they had laws permitting them to take and shoot hostages.[60] Therefore, Military Government had granted itself wide-ranging aspects of 'martial law' from the very beginning. Requiring authorization for the tiniest of demonstrations and imposing a curfew at night-time was relatively mild in comparison. Even if Howley occasionally let the wide-ranging powers go to his head, in his vendetta against communism, his excesses were still minor peccadillos compared to how the Soviets dealt with dissidents in their Sector and Zone. There is a sense in which the West Berlin authorities are held to a higher standard of probity than their Communist enemies.[61] That Clay was concerned to ensure that Howley was behaving in a decent, non-Gestapo-like manner is laudable. But a similar discussion is unlikely to have occurred within the ranks of the Soviet military administration. On this occasion, by nipping the demonstrations in the bud, Howley prevented the need for violent clashes between police and demonstrators.

Increasing tension (1946–7)

In the beginning, the Allies had agreed to prevent media criticism of any occupation power. In spite of increasingly overt Soviet anti-western propaganda, in late 1946 and early 1947, the Western Allies were still trying to reason with their Soviet opposite numbers. They investigated criticisms and sought to act in a way which would maintain faith, but they were seriously beginning to doubt the Soviets' sincerity. This lack of good faith was not helped by differential interpretation of agreements in the individual zones and sectors. As the son of a General, Jean Ganeval was destined for a military career. More than any of the other Allies, he understood the need to denazify Germany. In 1940, he had become one of the first resistance fighters and, once captured, spent several months in Buchenwald Concentration Camp. In December 1946, Ganeval agreed that the French-Sector newspaper, *Der Kurier*, had published 'tendentious information' about an Allied power. To punish the editors and to prevent a recurrence, he closed the presses for twenty-four hours and promised to keep a close watch on it in future.[62]

Given Markgraf's slavish obedience to the Soviets, the other Allies were keen to diminish his influence in their sectors. The Commandants retained significant responsibility for law and order within their sectoral boundaries. After much wrangling in the *Kommandatura*, in October 1946, the Western Allies managed to obtain agreement for the appointment of Assistant Chiefs of Police (one in each sector).[63] Although directly responsible to the military commanders of each sector, in the event of an emergency, in practice they served to increase sectoral divergence. Sector variations in legal norms demonstrably undermined the principle of joint rule. The Assistant Chiefs of Police began to behave more and more like 'sovereign heads of state' within their sectors, encouraging a decentralization of policing.[64] By March 1948, for example, Markgraf had long since ceased to influence day-to-day police activities of the 3,353 policemen in the American Sector.[65] In January 1948, the head of the uniformed police, Hans Kanig, criticized these Assistant Chiefs of Police for creating their own little fiefdoms.[66] Once they had obtained control of the police in their own sectors, the Western Military Governments manifested less interest in reforming the overarching police authority. Markgraf continued to issue orders but found it increasingly difficult to influence how such orders were carried out in the three western sectors. Transfers of policemen from one sector to another were no longer possible without the permission of the Allies.

As the Allies made slow progress in meeting their objectives, the stumbling blocks multiplied, and their four-power meetings became increasingly long-winded and fractious. To their cost, the Western Allies discovered that the Soviets were masters at both hair-splitting and invective. In an increasingly fraught atmosphere, exacerbated by propaganda following the election of October 1946, the victorious Allies frequently lapsed into mutual accusations. Despite concerted efforts at cooperation, relations were steadily souring. As Clay put it, it was difficult to retain a cool head when Soviet media continuously chanted that the Anglo-Americans were imperialists, monopolists and capitalist exploiters.[67] Although Clay blamed the French and the

Soviets for the lack of progress, it is clear that his own priorities were also changing. From initially wanting to punish Germany (with the Morgenthau Plan), American officials began to see sanctions and reparations as less important than trying to resurrect German administrative functions and get the economy going again. The Soviets insisted that reparations should precede unity, but the British and Americans thought it should be the other way round. Given the scale of Nazi influence, self-rule had initially appeared a distant possibility. Stivers and Carter argue that Clay failed to 'respect the fact' that Berlin constituted an enclave within the Soviet Zone and therefore needed to be sensitive to Soviet needs. Although restoring self-government to Berlin was a laudable aim, it was also a move clearly intended to reduce Soviet influence.[68]

The dismantling carried out in all sectors in May–June 1945 showed that Stalin had been in a hurry to extract the maximum possible reparations from Germany, in the shortest amount of time.[69] Soviet administrators were determined to strengthen their homeland and to weaken Germany. Behind the scenes, Clay came round to the idea that only 'a strong, stable, democratic Germany' could act as a bulwark against communism in Central Europe.[70] As early as September 1946, US Secretary of State, James F. Byrnes, gave a speech in Stuttgart about allowing Germany to develop a democratic constitution. Remarkably soon after the armistice, and with the Nuremberg Trials ongoing, he spoke in favour of allowing Germany to rebuild and once again to govern herself. The speech was broadcast throughout Germany.[71] Many Germans saw self-government as the only way to improve the dire economic situation. For his part, Clay was determined to restore the German economy despite Soviet and French foot-dragging on reform. He had begun to see economic recovery as a crucial stepping stone to the creation of a stable West German government.[72] In September 1946, the British and Americans agreed to merge their zones into a 'Bizone', in the hopes of reviving the economy and of stimulating democratization.

Reversing the traditional explanation of the cold war, revisionist historian Carolyn Eisenberg argues that it was American, not Soviet, non-cooperation that impeded German unification. In her view, the Americans preferred division to accepting the unity of Germany on Soviet terms.[73] However, this neglects the role played by the Communists' attempt to impose fusion on the Social Democratic Party (SPD) in Berlin and in the Soviet Zone. With this action, and American resistance to it, clear ideological positions began to crystallize that had a lasting impact on Allied (non)cooperation in Berlin.[74] The Americans shifted from hostile aloofness to close cooperation with indigenous political actors, thereby embroiling themselves in local politics by taking sides.[75] From a 'Kraut is a Kraut is a Kraut', they began to see Christian and Social Democrats as valid and valuable allies. Clay came to realize that 'implanting democracy' involved cultivating local democrats. An international consensus began to develop around shared anti-Communist ideals.[76] The alliance between the Americans, as defenders of capitalist freedoms, and the Social Democrats, as fierce defenders of organized labour, was unexpected. From 1946 onwards, freedom of thought' became the key feature distinguishing social democracy from communism.

The Iron Curtain and the impact of the October 1946 elections

Historians continue to be divided over whether Stalin's moves in Eastern Europe were a sign of aggression or rather evidence of his 'insatiable craving' for security.[77] Early on, Winston Churchill had come to see the situation in Berlin as part of an attempt at Communist manipulation throughout Eastern Europe. Everywhere, the Soviets and their stooges sought pre-eminence and totalitarian control.[78] In his famous Iron Curtain speech, in March 1946, Churchill specifically referred to Berlin as a principal area of concern. He saw the forced merger of the SPD and KPD as a prelude to the creation of a separate Communist Germany, which would prevent unity and damage East-West relations. Stalin countered by arguing that Berlin continued to be under four-power administration, making it absurd to suggest that the USSR had exclusive control. Deliberately misinterpreting Soviet veto power in the Control Council and *Kommandatura*, he argued that the USSR had only one-quarter of the vote.[79]

A colossal 82 per cent of Social Democrats in West Berlin opposed fusion with the Communists in April 1946. Unification of the two left-wing parties in the Soviet Zone dramatically increased the division between East and West. The forced merger destroyed attempts to create a broad, left-wing consensus in both West and East Germany. It turned West Berlin's Social Democrats into implacable enemies of communism, who would rather work with the Christian Democrats over the SED. The Soviets appear to have genuinely believed that Berliners would elect Communists to the City Executive. With a turnout of over 90 per cent, the elections of October 1946 were the first free elections in Berlin since 1933. Quadripartite inspection teams provided citywide supervision. With hindsight, British observers traced later Soviet obstruction – with repeated use of the veto in the Allied *Kommandatura* and culminating in mob violence – to 'the shattering defeat of the SED'. It obtained a humiliating 19.8 per cent of the votes cast, compared to the SPD's whopping 48.7 per cent.[80] Even in the Soviet Sector, the SPD trounced the SED. These elections conclusively proved that most Berliners had a clear preference for western-style democracy over Soviet communism. Referring to Soviet depredations in 1945, the voters manifestly rejected the overtures of communism, with Berliners defacing Communist posters with '*Frau komm*' and '*Uri, Uri*'. Some wits referred to the SED as an expression of 'Mongolian culture'.[81] General Clay's refusal to accept the merger of the KPD and SPD in the western sectors, unless a majority of SPD members voted for it, seemed to be vindicated. In getting involved in the skirmishes between the rival left-wing parties, Clay had shifted from his initial position of dispassionate, neutral umpire. He now saw the socialists as the city's 'real democrats'.

The massive defeat at the polls made the Soviet authorities realize that their manipulations of Berlin's political system were insufficient. The new City Executive (*Magistrat*) tried to oust the 'Soviet-appointed Communist officials', with Soviet attempts to retain them leading to dissension in the Allied *Kommandatura*.[82] After the election, neither side was as ready to make concessions; bridging the gap between the two sides seemed more difficult. The Communists blamed their humiliating defeat on the 'anti-Communist atmosphere' fostered by the Western Allies. The new SPD Mayor,

Otto Ostrowski, immediately earned the hostility of members of his own party by trying to cooperate with the SED as well as with the four occupation powers.[83] He was a technocratic municipal manager rather than an experienced, career politician. Under the leadership of Drs Ernst Reuter and Otto Suhr, the Berlin SPD unmistakably emerged as the most vociferously anti-Communist force in Germany. Neither spokesman had time for Ostrowski's inopportune neutralist, bipartisan approach, seeing it as a Trojan horse for the Communists. When he was forced from office, he blamed 'American intrigues'. His attempts to maintain bridges across the opening chasm came to seem anachronistic and inopportune.[84]

For their part, the French had supported Ostrowski's difficult position. They considered his attempt to find a third way between East and West laudable and felt that attacks on any of the victors damaged all the occupying powers.[85] According to the western view, while protecting their own incompetent place holders, the Soviet authorities harassed and hampered non-Communist politicians in their Sector. West Berlin represented not just a stronghold of independent Social Democrats; it also acted as a beacon for democrats of all stripes still trapped in the Soviet Zone. Newspapers like the *Tagesspiegel* and *Telegraf*, licensed by the Americans and British respectively, began to act as forums for anti-Communist arguments. The new *Magistrat* was western dominated but continued to meet in the Town Hall in the Soviet Sector where it was vulnerable to agitation and intimidation. The Soviets routinely interpreted democratic opposition to Communist policies as the work of 'reactionary forces'. They accused the Americans of stirring up anti-Communist demagogy. At times, they found it difficult to differentiate between Social Democrats and fascists. The increasingly bitter political battle in Berlin had implications for four-power government. With *Kommandatura* meetings degenerating into ill-tempered shouting matches, amplified by external propaganda campaigns, each commandant began to ignore four-power responsibility and to act unilaterally in his own sector. Despite the continued existence of four-power government agencies, and the election of a citywide *Magistrat*, experiences of life in the different sectors increasingly diverged. The Western Allies accused the Soviets of leaking confidential information, from the *Kommandatura*'s four-power discussions, to their press.[86]

While tensions peaked in Berlin, on the international plane, agreement on what to do about Germany or reparations proved impossible. The Foreign Ministers could not agree to a German peace-treaty or to any concrete steps towards German reunification.[87] In the light of Truman's new policy of containment, encouraging West German political and economic recovery made sense. On 5 June 1947, Secretary of State George Marshall announced his plan for the economic recovery of Europe, including Germany. Also in June 1947, the City Assembly representatives of Berlin overwhelmingly voted for SPD politician Ernst Reuter to be appointed Mayor. With battle lines drawn, local government quickly became gridlocked. The British felt that the Mayor should ideally be someone who could gain the approval of all four powers. Reuter would not have been the French Military Government's first choice, but they did not openly oppose his appointment. In the event, he was not allowed to take office because the Soviets vetoed his appointment in the *Kommandatura*. Seeing it as a good 'Communist' tactic to adopt, henceforth the British encouraged Reuter to act as the power behind the throne. This he did, causing no end of trouble for the Soviets. His anomalous position as unconfirmed Governing Mayor gave his voice weight, even though he lacked responsibility. In his new role as obstinate cold warrior, Reuter played an important role in fomenting division within the city administration.

Dubbed 'the Mayor Russia hates', Reuter did not need a position of power to influence others. His Deputy Mayor, Louise Schroeder, was appointed Acting Mayor. At first, Clay underestimated the strength of 'this quiet, motherly-appearing woman'.[88] After a few months, however, both he and Howley came to see her as a lioness, with the requisite protectiveness towards her cubs. Despite her mild manner and increasing ill health, Schroeder was no pushover or puppet. With the press dubbing their first female Mayor 'Auntie Louise', the hit song that summer was '*Oh, Louise, keine Frau ist so wie diese!*'[89] Although it had been brewing for some time, when it took hold with great suddenness in late 1947, the cold war took Clay and his Allied colleagues by surprise. Although it was technically part of the separate, four-power Greater Berlin area, the Soviets increasingly integrated East Berlin with the economy of the Soviet Zone. After some hesitation, in September 1947, the Soviet leadership rejected the Marshall Plan and let it be known that they had entered a new and intense phase of confrontation with the United States. Pressing ahead, Marshall proclaimed that German economic revival was essential for the recovery of Western Europe's economy. A number of historians see the Marshall Plan as a crucial turning point, in causing a cold war, by threatening Stalin's control over his own sphere of influence.[90] Feeling existentially threatened throughout Eastern Europe, the Soviets in Berlin now engaged in systematic, across-the-board non-cooperation, marked by an increasing number of 'war of nerves' stunts and prevarications.[91]

Mirroring and echoing George Kennan's infamous Long Telegram of February 1946, in September of that year Soviet ideologue Andrei Zhdanov emphasized that the world was now divided into two hostile camps.[92] Even though they found their Soviet counterparts to be trickier and deafer than usual, on the ground, the Western Allies continued to go through the motions regarding quadripartite government of Berlin. However, American newspaper correspondents and some officials were convinced that America was losing the 'Battle for Berlin'. When Assistant Deputy Military Governor, General Cornelius E. Ryan, spoke of 900 agreements in the *Kommandatura*, the reporter for the *New York Times* asked whether he actually meant '900 American concessions'.[93] As well as unlocking investment, the British and Americans pushed ahead more openly with plans for rebuilding political institutions in West Germany. It appeared that they had begun to see the Soviet Union as representing more of a threat than the defeated Germans. In the eyes of the British Military Governor, Sir Brian Robertson, Germany was clearly already sprawling in the dust, and it made no sense to keep battering her down. Saving Germany from desperate 'squalor and penury' was the best way of insulating her, spiritually, from despair and its bedfellow, communism.[94]

Open propaganda war

In September 1947, Colonel Sergei Tulpanov addressed the second SED party conference in Berlin, which was also attended by Police President Markgraf. Tulpanov stated that the United States was aggressively seeking war.[95] Although disagreements had been happening in private, for some time, this was the first time that an Allied occupying power had openly criticized another in front of a German audience. General Clay was deeply disturbed by this development and immediately demanded an apology. He warned the Soviets that people who lived in glass houses should not throw stones. Smarting at the vicious propaganda and lack of courtesy shown by his Soviet counterparts, he authorized American intelligence operatives to gather dirt on the Soviets.[96] In October 1947, he gave the green light for Radio in the American Sector (RIAS) to begin criticizing Soviet methods and Communist ideology, whenever and wherever possible. This move was called 'Operation Talk Back'.[97] At this point, Clay still saw no alternative to quadripartite governance of Berlin. Nevertheless, he was growing increasingly impatient with the incessant barrage of negative propaganda being churned out in East Berlin. Because they saw at first hand where such an ideology led, Clay now placed weight on American representatives in Germany expressing their own personal views on communism. While they would not resort to 'name calling', or attacks on other Allied governments, American propaganda would defend the democratic system in a direct and forthright manner. Clay insisted that American forces would no longer avoid 'making unfavourable comparisons' between communism and alternative forms of government or political thought. Journalist Melvin J. Lasky suggested that this meant that the 'kid gloves' had been swapped for 'brass knuckles'.[98]

Conclusion

At times, life in Berlin under four-power governance could be almost surreal. The clash of four different languages, and five distinct cultures, frequently caused confusion and chaos. While mingling on the black market and, after hours in speakeasies and dives, the four Allies also sought to come together to govern defeated Berlin. Although there were parallels with the International Settlement in Shanghai, never had such different ideologies and cultures tried to cooperate in international government. The arrangements for dividing Berlin into sectors were predicated on a continued spirit of 'friendship and cooperation' existing 'between the occupying powers'.[99] Cohesive and effective government was almost impossible for such a hodgepodge of blurred boundaries and overlapping jurisdictions to achieve.

Although Churchill had grown suspicious and wary of Stalin, between Yalta and Potsdam, Roosevelt's replacement, Harry Truman, stuck to America's earlier agreements. As veteran diplomat Charles E. Bohlen stated, at the Potsdam Conference, there was a distinct feeling that 'from the President down, the American delegation was feeling its way' through unfamiliar territory.[100] Whether or not they were genuine in seeking four-power cooperation, from the start, the Moscow-appointed officials were also determined to Sovietize their Zone. By refusing to provide the Soviet economy with the reparations they had promised and which it desperately needed, the western powers served to increase Stalin's suspicions.[101] Cohesion was always fragile in divided, four-power Berlin. Nevertheless, the Western Allies initially tried to work with and to understand their Soviet counterparts. In 1945, the evidence of the costs of the struggle it had taken to defeat Hitler appeared omnipresent. The western powers overwhelmingly recognized the Red Army's sacrifices in defeating Nazi Germany. Assuming that all Berliners were corrupt and tainted former Nazis, the Western Allies went into the city determined to cooperate with the Soviets and to remain aloof from the Germans. Nevertheless, from the start, there were important differences in ideology and behaviour, particularly in relation to policing. Quadripartite government was imperfect, with plenty of room for disagreements based on diverging perspectives and interpretations. The Americans initially underestimated the Soviets, seeing them merely as hardbargainers. Nevertheless, with prolonged exposure to underhand Soviet and devious Communist tactics, pragmatism shifted to cynicism and suspicion. If, in the beginning, the enemy was chaos and disorganization, increasingly it manifested itself as communism as refracted through Soviet machinations.

Despite their differences, Berlin's political leaders came to see the western occupation of the city as a guarantee of democracy. In particular, Soviet attempts to neutralize the SPD by taking it over in April 1946 had stimulated vociferous and lasting opposition in Berlin. Over the next eighteen months, the Americans shifted from private support for such resistance to unambiguous and overt endorsement. In contrast to the unambiguous positions of the British and Americans, the French tried to maintain a non-partisan, neutral stance in relation to Berlin power politics for longer. Keen to understand the Soviet attitude, they saw clear dangers for the occupation regime, in stoking up populist politicians like Ernst Reuter.[102] With hindsight, the misunderstandings and discord can appear pre-programmed. Although the collapse of four-power government came to seem inevitable, all sides did briefly invest in trying to make the experiment work. Despite obstructionism and misunderstandings, these initial attempts at cooperation were genuine. Even at the height of the cold war, the Western Allies retained some residual, grudging respect for the Soviets as fellow victors in World War Two. Howley was not alone in coming to see acquiescence on unfavourable terms as tantamount to appeasement. Increasingly, he saw the Soviets as blackmailers, who would never be satisfied until they had extorted absolutely everything.[103]

Notes

1 J. P. McEvoy, '4 Strange Bedfellows of Berlin', *Hearst's International Combined with Cosmopolitan* 119, no. 6 (1945): 28–9, 220–1, 225–6, 28.
2 Frank S. V. Donnison, *Civil Affairs and Military Government* (London: HMSO, 1966), 7, 20.
3 Geoffrey Roberts, 'Stalin at the Tehran, Yalta, and Potsdam Conferences', *Journal of Cold War Studies* 9, no. 4 (2007): 9–10, 25, 33.
4 Jean Edward Smith (ed.), *The Papers of Lucius D. Clay: Germany, 1945-1949* (Bloomington, IN: Indiana University Press, 1974), I: 37, 41.
5 Lucius D. Clay, *Decision in Germany* (Westport, CT: Greenwood, 1970), 38.
6 Winston S. Churchill, *The Second World War*, vol. 6, *Triumph and Tragedy* (London: Cassell, 1954), 581.

7 Wilfried Loth, 'Die französische Deutschlandspolitik und die Anfänge des Ost-West-Konflikts', in *France-Allemagne 1944-1947*, ed. Klaus Manfrass and Jean-Pierre Rioux (Paris: Institut d'histoire du temps present, 1990), 83.
8 Clay, *Decision in Germany*, 120.
9 Smith (ed.), *The Papers of General Lucius D. Clay*, xxvii.
10 Anne Whyte, 'Quadripartite Rule in Berlin: An Interim Report of the First Year of the Allied Control Authority', *International Affairs* 23, no. 1 (1947): 34.
11 T. H. Elkins and B. Hofmeister, *Berlin: The Spatial Structure of a Divided City* (London: Methuen, 1988), 34.
12 Clay, *Decision in Germany*, 22, 26.
13 Stivers and Carter insist that there was as little the Western Allies could have done to stop the Soviets violating a written protocol either. William Stivers and Donald A. Carter, *The City Becomes a Symbol: the U.S. Army in the Occupation of Berlin, 1945-1949* (Washington, DC: Center of Military History, United States Army, 2017), 60.
14 'Stenographie de la 30ème Seance du Comité de Securité Publique, 3 October 1950 à la Kommandatura Alliée'. French Archives Diplomatiques, KI /626.
15 Agreement reached 27 November 1945. Archives Diplomatiques, GMFB 1/2405.
16 Reginald Colby, 'Exit Tulpanov', *Spectator*, 13 October 1949.
17 George Bilainkin, 'The Allies in Berlin', *Contemporary Review* 168 (1945): 345.
18 'Russians in Berlin get their way', *Daily Mail*, 12 July 1945.
19 Brigadier C. E. Ryan, 'The Kommandatura's Debut', *Journal of the Royal United Service Institution* 96, no. 582 (1951): 267.
20 Curt Riess, *The Berlin Story* (London: Frederick Muller, 1953), 90.
21 Frank L. Howley, *Berlin Command* (New York: G. P. Putnam's Sons, 1950), 53–4.
22 'International', *Time*, 25 June 1945, 23.
23 UK National Archives, Allied Reparation Commission in Moscow, FO 371/45775/UE 1118.
24 Stivers and Carter, *The City Becomes a Symbol*, 90.
25 William Murray, *Germany Today* (Pathe, 1947).
26 Howley, *Berlin Command*, 56.
27 Mr. Hall and Mr. Mittendorf. Secret. 'Survey Report of the Public Safety Branch', USCOB [ca. 15 March 1950], US National Archives, RG 466, 250/72/8/7, Box 1.
28 'Public Safety, July 1945 to 31 August 1949', 2, US National Archives, RG260, 390/48/27/2, Box 893.
29 Dorothea Führe, *Die Französische Besatzungspolitik in Berlin von 1945 bis 1949: Déprussianisation und Décentralisation* (Berlin: Weißensee-Verlag, 2001), 81, 73.
30 Smith (ed.), *The Papers of General Lucius D. Clay*, xxv.
31 Landesarchiv Berlin, C Rep. 303-09, Nr. 90 as cited by Jens Dobler, 'Die Berliner Polizei und die Nachkriegsdelinquenz', in *Großstadtkriminalität: Berliner Kriminalpolizei und Verbrechensbekämpfung 1930 bis 1950*, ed. Jens Dobler (Berlin: Metropol, 2013), 250.
32 Lyford Moore, 'The Man in the Goldfish Bowl', in *This Is Germany: A Report on Post War Germany by 21 Newspaper Correspondents*, ed. Arthur Settel (New York: William Sloane, 1950), 26.
33 Norman Naimark, *Russians in Germany: A History of the Soviet Zone of Occupation, 1945-1949* (Cambridge, MA: Belknap Press of Harvard University Press, 1995), 25.
34 Stivers and Carter, *The City Becomes a Symbol*, 206.
35 Clay, *Decision in Germany*, 29.
36 Whyte, 'Quadripartite Rule in Berlin', 30.

37 Führe, *Die Französische Besatzungspolitik in Berlin*, 53, 84.
38 Ryan, 'The Kommandatura's Debut', 268.
39 Whyte, 'Quadripartite Rule in Berlin', 31.
40 Ambassador in the Soviet Union (Smith) to the Secretary of State, 17 August 1948, United States Department of State, *Foreign Relations of the United States (FRUS), 1948, vol. 2, Germany and Austria* (Washington: United States Government Printing Office, 1973), 1045.
41 Howley, *Berlin Command*, 158–9.
42 Major-General E. O. Herbert, 'The Cold War in Berlin', *Journal of the Royal United Service Insitution* XCIV, no. 574 (1949): 175.
43 Clay, *Decision in Germany*, 39.
44 'Montgomery Sees Dangers in Reich. French Blocking of Central Rule and Shortages May Cause Uprising, He Says', *New York Times*, 12 November 1945.
45 Howley, *Berlin Command*, 103.
46 Norbert Steinborn and Hilmar Krüger, *Die Berliner Polizei 1945 bis 1992: von der Militärreserve im Kalten Krieg auf dem Weg zur bürgernahen Polizei?* (Berlin: Arno Spitz, 1993), 24–5.
47 '34. Magistratssitzung vom 10. Dezember 1945', LAB (STA), Rep. 100, Nr. 764, Bl. 40-45 in *Die Sitzungsprotokolle des Magistrats der Stadt Berlin 1945/46*, ed. Dieter Hanauske (Berlin: Arno Spitz, 1995), vol. 1, 688–703.
48 Peter Rhode, 'Lebensbild des Genossen Oberst der VP a.D. Paul Markgraf' (Diplomarbeit, 1988), Anlage F/2, Police Museum, Paul Markgraf File.
49 Howley, *Berlin Command*, foreword, 248.
50 'Public Safety, July 1945 to 31 August 1949', 4.
51 Donald P. Steury (ed.), *On the Front Lines of the Cold War: Documents on the Intelligence War in Berlin, 1946 to 1961* (Washington, DC: CIA History Staff, Center for the Study of Intelligence, 1999), 125.
52 Testimony of Colonel John B. Hughes, CE, taken at Washington DC, on 20 September 1946 by Brigadier General Elliot D. Cooke, USE and Lt Col Curtis L. Williams, IGD. RG 159, Boxes 34-35, US National Archives.
53 Clay, *Decision in Germany*, 133–4.
54 'The Breakdown of Four-Power Rule in Berlin', *World Today*, 1 August 1948, 326.
55 'Berlin ist nicht Schanghai. Der Fall Friede vor dem Stadtparlament. Mißtrauen gegen die Polizei', *Kurier*, 14 November 1947. 'Schanghai mitten in Berlin', *Tribüne*, 21 August 1948.
56 SHAEF, *Handbook for Military Government in Germany: Prior to Defeat or Surrender*, December 1944.
57 Howley, *Berlin Command*, 155–6.
58 Eugene Gilbert Jones, 'The Allied Reconstruction of the Berlin Police, 1945-1948', PhD, University of California, San Diego, 1986, xiii, 162–4.
59 Howley, *Berlin Command*, 156.
60 Peter M. R. Stirk, 'Benign Occupations: The Allied Occupation of Germany and the International Law of Occupation', in *Transforming Occupation in the Western Zones of Germany: Politics, Everyday Life and Social Interactions, 1945–55*, ed. Camilo Erlichman and Christopher Knowles (London: Bloomsbury Academic, 2018), 45.
61 Mark Fenemore, *Fighting the Cold War in Post-Blockade, Pre-Wall Berlin: Behind Enemy Lines* (London: Routledge, 2019), 245.
62 'Allied Kommandatura Berlin, Minutes of the thirty-third meeting held in Berlin on 6 December 1946', UK National Archives, FO 371/64432.

63 BK/0 (46) 391 from 4 October 1946. Legal Division, OMGUS, 'Enactments and Approved Papers of the Control Council and Coordinating Commmittee. Allied Control Authority Germany. 1 July 1946–30 September 1946', Vol. IV, 70.
64 Steinborn and Krüger, *Die Berliner Polizei*, 63.
65 Smith (ed.), *The Papers of Lucius D. Clay*, 2: 567.
66 'Berliner Polizei-Probleme. Von Hans Kanig, Kommandeur der Schutzpolizei', *Die Welt*, 15 January 1948.
67 Clay, *Decision in Germany*, xi, 158.
68 Stivers and Carter, *The City Becomes a Symbol*, 181.
69 Eric Morris, *Blockade: Berlin and the Cold War* (London: Hamish Hamilton, 1973), 54.
70 Roger G. Miller, *To Save a City: The Berlin Airlift 1948-1949* (Washington, DC: Air Force History and Museums Program, 1998), 4–5.
71 James F. Byrnes 'Speech of Hope', http://germany.usembassy.gov/speech-hope.html (accessed 11 June 2015).
72 Clay, *Decision in Germany*, 164, 176.
73 Carolyn W. Eisenberg, *Drawing the Line: The American Decision to Divide Germany, 1944-1949* (New York: Cambridge University Press, 1996), 316.
74 Führe, *Die Französische Besatzungspolitik*, 104–5.
75 Stivers dates the shift from an occupation based on 'punitive control' to one primarily aimed at 'restoring democracy' to 1946. William Stivers, 'Victors and Vanquished: Americans as Occupiers in Berlin, 1945-1949', in *Armed Diplomacy: Two Centuries of American Campaigning*, ed. US Army Training and Doctrine Command and Combat Studies Institute (Fort Leavenworth, KS: Combat Studies Institute Press, 2003), 167.
76 Smith (ed.), *The Papers of Lucius D. Clay*, 2: 453–4.
77 Vojtech Mastny, *The Cold War and Soviet Insecurity: The Stalin Years* (New York: Oxford University Press, 1996), 23.
78 'The Sinews of Peace ('Iron Curtain Speech'), 5 March 1946, winstonchurchill.org (accessed 21 December 2020).
79 *Pravda*, 14 March 1946.
80 'Head of Chancery: Draft Intel: Legal Basis of Occupation of Berlin', 21 January 1955, UK National Archives, FO 1008/327.
81 Paul Steege, *Black Market, Cold War: Everyday Life in Berlin, 1946-1949* (Cambridge: Cambridge University Press, 2007), 91.
82 Clay, *Decision in Germany*, 139.
83 See Norbert Podewin, *Otto Ostrowski - der gelöschte Oberbürgermeister: ein Schicksal im Berlin des Kalten Krieges* (Berlin: Luisenstädtischer Bildungsverein, 2004).
84 Steege, *Black market*, 113–16. Riess, *Berlin Story*, 97.
85 Führe, *Die Französische Besatzungspolitik*, 150–2.
86 Walter Krumholz, *Berlin-ABC* (West Berlin: Verlag Documentation, 1969), 700.
87 D. M. Giangreco and Robert E. Griffin, *Airbridge to Berlin: The Berlin Crisis of 1948: Its Origins and Aftermath* (Novato: Presidio, 1988), 72.
88 Clay, *Decision in Germany*, 144.
89 Riess, *Berlin Story*, 106.
90 Melvyn Leffler, 'The Cold War: What Do "We Now Know"?', *American Historical Review* 104, no. 2 (April 1999): 516. Scott Parrish, 'The Marshall Plan, Soviet-American Relations and the Division of Europe', in *The Establishment of Communist Regimes in Eastern Europe, 1944–1949*, ed. Norman Naimark and Leonid Gibianskii (Boulder, CO: Westview, 1997), 267–90.

91 Fenemore, *Fighting the Cold War*, 26–7.
92 Andrei Zhdanov, 'Report on the International Situation to the Cominform', 22 September 1947. http://www.csun.edu/~twd61312/342%202014/Zhdanov.pdf (accessed 5 June 2015).
93 'Memorandum for the Chairman, Joint Chiefs of Staff, General of the Army Omar Bradley', 31 July 1947, in *On the Front Lines of the Cold War*, ed. Steury, 133–5, 134. Cf. 'U.S. to be Firmer in Berlin Council', *New York Times*, 8 July 1947.
94 Lord Robertson of Oakridge, 'A Miracle? Potsdam – Western Germany 1965', *International Affairs* 41, no. 3 (1965): 403.
95 Wilfried Ranke, German Historical Museum Chronicle, http://www.dhm.de/magazine/heft7/chronicle1.htm (accessed 15 October 2013).
96 David E. Murphy, Sergei A. Kondrashev and George Bailey, *Battleground Berlin: CIA vs. KGB in the Cold War* (New Haven, CT: Yale University Press, 1997), 9.
97 Michael Derenburg, *Streifzüge durch vier RIAS-Jahrzehnte: Anfänge und Wandlungen eines Rundfunksenders* (Berlin: Presse- und Informationsamt des Landes Berlin, 1986), 20.
98 Smith (ed.), *The Papers of General Lucius D. Clay*, 2: 451–8.
99 'Pressure on Berlin', *The Times*, 22 October 1951.
100 Charles E. Bohlen, *Witness to History, 1929-1969* (New York: Norton, 1973), 229.
101 Parrish, 'The Marshall Plan', 273.
102 Führe, *Die Französische Besatzungspolitik*, 144–5, 156.
103 Howley, *Berlin Command*, 12–13.

6

The splitting of the police, 1948

As the previous chapter showed, during the course of 1946 and 1947, the British and Americans shifted from wanting to punish Germany to seeing the need to build it back up, as a possible ally against the Soviets. As the latter continued to press for reparations, the Western Allies belatedly began to become alarmed about their erstwhile Ally's intentions. The suspicion was mutual, however. By distributing Cooperative for American Remittances to Europe (CARE) packets to Germans, from August 1946, the Americans appeared to be conspicuously purchasing indigenous goodwill. Ignoring and bypassing existing shared provisioning structures, this move greatly 'unnerved the Soviets'.[1] Such unilateral actions undermined four-power unity and embarrassed less munificent powers. The Allies differed markedly in the degree to which they wanted to divert resources from an already weak economy to pay for postwar reconstruction. Unlike their Western Allies, the French were initially keen to dismantle industry in their Sector and Zone for it to be sent home as reparations. French willingness to support economic recovery in Germany was tempered by their desire to prevent German resurgence and to receive appropriate indemnification for the damage Nazi Germany had done to France. As the previous chapter showed, smarting at not having been included in the discussions at Potsdam, the French consistently blocked any moves to form centralized German economic agencies.[2] Even though the Soviets had been just as keen to strip Berlin (both East and West) of essential machinery, French dismantling of the Borsig factories got a lot of attention in the Soviet-licensed press.[3] For their part, the Soviets desperately feared a resurgent, revanchist Germany and were prepared to do anything to block it.[4]

Seeing it as a prerequisite for establishing a peaceful and democratic Germany, by early 1947, General Clay had become convinced that currency reform across Germany was essential. Without it, economic recovery would not progress very far.[5] Moscow recognized that there was a problem with inflation that was hampering German economic recovery, but failed to offer any credible solution. While continuing to go through the motions of four-power consultation, behind the scenes, the British and Americans moved beyond economic unification, in the form of a 'Bizone', to envisaging full-scale currency reform. The Soviets saw such moves, designed longer term to facilitate the creation of a West German state, as unwarranted and aggressive. While many western historians dismiss Soviet fears of resurgent German militarism as mere propaganda ploys, even at this stage, Soviet concerns about German ambitions were 'genuine and deep-seated'.[6] Stalin perceived any revival of German sovereignty as a threat to the delicate balance of power – achieved through no fewer than twenty-six million Soviet deaths – which could fatally undermine the Soviet Union's still fragile hold over Eastern Europe.

As the previous chapter showed, during the course of 1947, the increase in suspicion and tension was reflected in both the Control Council and the *Kommandatura*. Tensions were already at a new level of distrust, in January 1948, when the four Military Governors met. In Clay's recollection, the stormy Control Council meeting was marked by interminable 'fruitless discussions' and much unnecessary 'vituperation'.[7] Marshal Sokolovsky refused to consider the American Military Governor's proposals for currency reform within occupied Germany. In his eyes, currency reform in one-half of Germany threatened to increase the divide between the Soviet and western zones, by highlighting the differences between the two economies (planned vs. capitalist). Sokolovsky called Bizonia (the merging of the British and American Zones, combined with greater self-rule powers for the Germans living there) a flagrant infringement of the Potsdam Agreements.[8] In theory, at least, the Soviets opposed any dismemberment of Germany. Sokolovsky was most aggrieved that the other Allies appeared to be acting behind the Control Council's back. He saw it as a first step towards the establishment of a 'separatist' (and thereby hostile) West German government. But blatant Soviet pressure to push for communism in their Zone also served to heighten the political-economic division of Germany.[9] While continuing to preach German unity, at least in abstract form, in reality, the SED pushed for a separate East German state.[10]

Soviet interference with access to Berlin

In January 1948, Soviet troops suddenly demanded to inspect all trains travelling between West Berlin and the western zones. In February, forces loyal to Stalin blatantly orchestrated a coup in Czechoslovakia, which ousted the few remaining democrats from government. 'From Sokolovsky down', the Soviets presented a new, more rigid attitude in the four-power bodies. They were unabashed in their (not newfound but nevertheless radical) contempt for democracy. They seemed more arrogant and assured in pursuing their objectives.[11] On 5 March, General Clay sent a telegram to Washington, which made his government sit up and take notice. He had previously assessed the prospect of war as 'unlikely for at least ten years'. In the previous fortnight, however, he had noticed subtle, but distinct, changes in the Soviet attitude. Although he still had difficulty defining it, he now felt that war could come 'with dramatic suddenness'.[12] In Washington, President Truman asked his armed services chiefs to assess whether they thought that war was really on the cards.[13] Cut off in Berlin, Clay and his staff were startled by the excitement his cable had caused in Washington when it rippled back to Berlin. For them, it was very much business as usual, despite the increased tension. In the interval, Clay had come back to the opinion that the Soviets were bluffing and did not want war.

In March 1948, General Sir Brian Robertson, the British Military Governor of Germany, challenged the Soviets to lift what Churchill had dubbed the Iron Curtain in Germany. Lifting the zonal barriers would provide proof that the 'reports of arbitrary arrests' and 'large-scale deportations' were untrue. He dared to suggest that the Soviets were erecting Concentration Camps in their Zone.[14] A week later, on 20 March 1948, the Soviets withdrew from the Allied Control Council, ostensibly in protest at western moves to unite their zones. They argued that these moves were in clear violation of the Potsdam Agreement and other four-power decisions. Marshal Sokolovsky issued a statement arguing that the Control Council was no longer functioning as a four-power organ of government or as 'the supreme body of authority in Germany'. Through their actions, the Western Allies had demonstrated that the Control Council only existed on paper; they alone were responsible for its breakdown.[15] For the British and Americans, the Soviet walkout was a propitious opportunity to press ahead with plans for a separate West German state and currency. On 31 March 1948, Sokolovsky announced stringent new rules on ground access to West Berlin. The Soviet authorities now required identification papers for all civilian and military personnel using trains into or out of Berlin. In addition, they insisted on being able to inspect the personal belongings of passengers. While the American Military Government categorically refused to allow the Soviets to inspect their trains, the French did and were consequently allowed to travel back and forth to Berlin without further hindrance.[16] Although the guards continued to raise the flags of the victorious nations every morning, at the Control Council building in Kleistpark, four-power government had clearly become unworkable. The abrupt Soviet move caused the French to bury the hatchet and fall in line with the British and Americans. French representatives ceased to believe that France alone constituted the means of bringing East and West together. Although they continued to worry about resurgent German military power, French officials began to see the necessity of a West German state. Even if they continued to fear their German neighbour, they did not want to be left with an isolated, non-viable French Zone remnant.

Continued tension over currency reform

In Berlin, the lack of a stable currency and the persistence of the black market caused no end of problems for officials and the police. And yet, American moves to reform the currency threatened to make the Soviet political and economic position untenable. For the *Tägliche Rundschau*, split currencies would mean that the two halves of the city irrevocably became foreign powers to one another. Separate currencies would create a tense economic as well as ideological border within the city, effectively ripping it in two. The newspaper speculated that, in order to prevent speculators from exploiting differences in the exchange rate, the authorities might have to seal the border hermetically.[17] The existing common currency, worthless though it was, was the last remaining link between all four zones. The Soviets demanded a set of plates for the new currency, but Clay had no wish to repeat the mistake the Allies had made in 1945. He offered to set up a special 'quadripartite enclave' within the United States Sector, which would house the currency mint, but the Soviets rejected this proposal.[18]

A tit-for-tat conflict occurred throughout March and April 1948, as the Soviet authorities continued to interfere with military rail transport. The Soviets demanded the right to inspect identity papers and to search British and American trains in the same way that they were doing on French transports.[19] At the same time, they established guard posts on seventy-one crossing points and seventeen stations leading out of West Berlin. This was accompanied by a press campaign designed to create the impression that the western powers were on the verge of leaving the city. Convinced that each train was de jure moving 'American territory', Clay had machine guns mounted on his trains. In his view, American trains should be as inviolate as American Sector territory. The Central Intelligence Agency (CIA) secretly admitted that their principal method of moving agents, between Berlin and the American Zone, was by rail. The American spooks criticized their British Allies for taking 'literally hundreds' of secret agents on their trains, and thereby bringing the military-train system into disrepute. In American eyes, the British then compounded this error, by buckling in the face of Soviet demands for German civilians to have interzonal passes, if they wished to travel on military trains.[20]

Having warned Washington about the prospect of war in April, General Clay now made increasingly belligerent noises. As well as threatening to order the guards to open fire if Soviet soldiers attempted to enter his trains, he refused to countenance withdrawing American dependents from West Berlin.[21] Such a move could only create hysteria among the German population, left behind without protection. Although he knew that a wrong move could cause war, he said he would rather risk ending up in Siberia than fall on his sword by evacuating Berlin. For their part, CIA operatives rightly worried about the predominantly young and inexperienced troops overreacting to one of the many Soviet provocations. Perceived insults or minor acts of violence could easily cause serious incidents, street fights or brawls. Such public disturbances could have grave repercussions. As an April Fools' Day prank, the Soviets set up a control point within the British Sector. While British Hussars surrounded and escorted the Soviet troops back to their own Sector, the Americans surrounded the *Reichsbahn* headquarters at the heart of their Sector.[22] US troops established their own 'check point' on the main road between Berlin and Potsdam. This forced Marshal Sokolovsky and his officials to make a long detour. Only the utmost tact was preventing the grassroots 'war of nerves' or pinpricks from escalating beyond the local sectoral authorities' control.[23] One battalion was no match for twenty Soviet divisions; in theory as well as in practice, West Berlin appeared indefensible.

In the end, rather than submit to Soviet inspection, Clay halted military trains and resorted to a mini-Airlift in order to supply his troops in West Berlin. Rather more seriously, at the height of East-West tension, a Soviet fighter buzzed a British airplane, causing both to crash. Twelve Britons and two American passengers were killed. Sokolovsky immediately insisted that the British pilot was at fault. He interpreted British radio reports, attributing blame to the Soviet pilot, as mendacious and malicious.[24] Many people within the British and American governments thought that the world was now on the verge of war and that any concessions to the Soviets over Berlin would constitute a return to appeasement. From the side-lines, Winston Churchill continued to chunter about pushing the Soviets out of Germany altogether, by holding out the threat of razing their cities with atomic bombs.[25]

Conflict over policing in the *Kommandatura*

While the Control Council was now in hiatus, the *Kommandatura* continued to meet monthly. By the spring of 1948, policing had become the issue that caused the most acrimony and division within the city. According to its detractors, the police in the eastern sector seemed more preoccupied with acting as a lap dog for the Soviets than with fighting crime. Police President Markgraf manifestly had to keep his Communist comrades and the Soviets happy, at the same time as feigning to serve the Western Allies.[26] Later Markgraf recalled the Soviets having provided him with constant help and guidance, while Walter Ulbricht had given him 'almost fatherly' guidance.[27] Markgraf refused repeated requests to take part in press conferences. He saw no point in answering questions about his military record or involvement in the Battle of Stalingrad. He did not want to be probed about his lack of police training or experience or the fact that he had flown to Berlin by airplane in 1945.[28] From spring 1948 onwards, Markgraf's police force operated increasingly unilaterally, with little pretence of non-partisanship. In the new climate, the Allied representatives of the Public Safety Committee struggled to impose their vision for how the police should be reformed, based on their understandings and experience. The CIA pointed to Charles Bond's notable success in the sphere of Public Safety.[29] As a professional police officer with decades of experience in the United States, he had spent two and a half years building the police force in the American Sector into a reliable and efficient organization. Although hampered by shortages of personnel and equipment, it was beginning to return to prewar standards.

For ordinary policemen, the differences in outlook possessed by the four Allies, with regard to law and order, made the concrete work of policing more confusing. Or it would have done if they had paid any attention to it.[30] The only unity of vision they could see was in the emphasis on the police having a civilian rather than a military outlook.[31] Discursively at least, police in both the British and American Sectors took the English bobby as their ideal beat policeman.[32] Compared to Continental (German and French) approaches, the police in Britain and America were much more limited in the scope of their actions. British bobbies were above all civilian rather than military in approach. They were not required to have served in the military before joining the police. They did not have a special civil-servant status that differentiated them from civilians. They focused above all on maintaining law and order. There had been some limited attempt to alter policing, in accordance with Anglo-American concepts, but the need for quadripartite approval meant that little reform had proven possible. Many of the administrative functions of the German police were strange to the British and Americans. Nevertheless, the Military Governments were willing to make use of these extensive powers when it suited them.[33] From an Anglo-American perspective, there were fewer limits or safeguards on the police's exercise of power in Germany and elsewhere on the continent. German policemen did not need warrants to make arrests or to conduct searches. They could jail suspects without worrying about a hearing or considering habeas corpus. For the Office of Military Government, United States (OMGUS), this put them in an almost 'dictatorial position'. The outsiders assumed that the police's continued possession of unbridled powers could only cause distrust, fear and animosity on the part of ordinary German citizens.[34]

In a move designed to try and dampen Communist activity within the police operating in their Sector, the American Public Safety branch banned policemen from undertaking political activity in May 1946. Policemen could vote and join parties but could not hold political functions or stand in elections.[35] For the British and Americans, the impartiality of the police was very important. Nevertheless, Jones argues that this ban on 'police activism' in their sectors only served to confuse the Germans and to incense the Soviets, who used the measure to suggest that the police operating in the western sectors were dictatorial and anti-democratic.[36] Policemen, who had served before 1933, were keen to rebuild a police union on the model that had existed in the Weimar Republic. This German ideal clashed with Allied plans. Nevertheless, when work council elections were held in early 1948, the Soviets were disappointed to find that, despite housing the Police Presidium, the Soviet Sector elected no fewer than thirty-two non-Communists.[37] For their part, the Soviets had no intention of allowing an apolitical police force. In 1948 as in 1945, they saw Communists as the driving force behind progressive, democratic policies. Vigorously defending the senior policemen and local government administrators they had appointed before the other Allies arrived in Berlin, they now went onto the offensive, attacking aspects of police practice in the western sectors. The Soviets believed that, in their sectors, the Western Allies were removing progressives and replacing them with reactionaries. Left-wing historians Steinborn and Krüger echo these criticisms. Based on a report in the eastern newspaper *Vorwärts*, they claim that, by February 1948, one in four uniformed policemen in the British Sector had served during the Nazi dictatorship.[38] Nevertheless, if anything, such propaganda proved counterproductive; citizens of West Berlin largely trusted 'their' police. In tit-for-tat battles, the Western Allies dismissed Communists who dared criticize the police hierarchy in union meetings. They quickly found employment in the Soviet-Sector police.[39]

Five thousand missing Berliners

As far as the Western Allies were concerned, most of the policemen they dismissed had been unqualified political appointees. Their chief qualification had been their willingness to do 'whatever the Russians told them to do'.[40] At the beginning of 1948, the Western Allies tried to have Police President Markgraf dismissed. They accused him of being completely inexperienced in police matters, of abusing his power and of committing acts of insubordination in relation to the Allied *Kommandatura*. In particular, they accused him of turning a blind eye to the kidnappings, arbitrary arrests and illegal detentions that were occurring daily. The Soviets were not just abducting people from West Berlin in the fog of night; they also kidnapped in broad daylight. The western press accused the Police President of abetting the Soviets in unlawful arrests. It is true that, disregarding legal niceties, the NKVD never really accepted that they had to ask permission to carry out the arrest of a wanted criminal outside their area. The Social Democrats claimed to have a list of 5,413 people, who had been 'disappeared' by the Soviet-controlled police.⁴¹ However their figures went back to the summer of 1945 and contained nearly 3,000 Nazis as well as assorted war criminals. A case which attracted a lot of attention was the disappearance of Dieter Friede. He was a journalist for *Der Abend*, a newspaper licensed by the American authorities from October 1946. Friede went missing in the Soviet Sector in November 1947. He had received a telephone call stating that he should meet someone in the eastern sector. *Neues Deutschland*'s initial report, that Friede was in all likelihood getting drunk somewhere in the western sectors, was an expression of abject cynicism.⁴² The East Berlin authorities subsequently revealed that they had indeed arrested him, accusing the forty-year-old of spying for the United States and Britain.

Clay believed that the kidnapping situation was worsening. In his view, it was exacerbated by the sense of obedience Germans felt towards all authority. Such was 'their instinct to obey', that they could not refuse a request to accompany a police officer, even if he insisted that they accompany him over the border.⁴³ Therefore, the Americans used a campaign in their radio and newspapers to warn citizens of the dangers of blind obedience. Henceforth, western media exhorted Berliners only to obey the police of their own sectors. As relations deteriorated between the Soviets and their Western Allies, the continued incursions and illegal arrests acted as a source of additional misunderstanding and tension. The Western Allies repeatedly raised this as a problem in four-power governing agencies like the Public Safety Committee. Even though Berlin was supposedly still policed by a single, unitary agency, the western powers now argued that German policemen operating outside their jurisdiction were liable for arrest and imprisonment.

Whistle-blowers accused Markgraf's police HQ of pressuring them to spy on their fellow officers for the Soviets.⁴⁴ On 13 November 1947, the majority of the *Magistrat* had taken the bold step of expressing their lack of confidence in him as Police President. On several occasions, Mayor Friedensburg (Christian Democratic Union, CDU) tried to mediate, but succeeded only in engendering the suspicion of both sides.⁴⁵ Although he saw himself as an umpire or equalizer, Friedensburg seems to have had a remarkable ability to alienate people, whatever their political position.⁴⁶ He repeatedly flip-flopped in the spring and summer of 1948, sometimes declaring eastern police actions 'irreproachable' and, at other times, making bellicose noises.⁴⁷ With a continued lack of effective, impartial leadership, Markgraf refused repeated requests to attend press conferences to discuss the disappearances. He said that he did not interfere in Allied Military Government decisions and would not therefore allow interference by the *Magistrat* in police business.⁴⁸ Although expressing disapproval, the Western Allies needed a unanimous decision by the *Kommandatura* to dismiss the Police President; with the Soviet veto, this would not be forthcoming. This left the police force in a thorny and entangled legal limbo. On 3 March 1948, Markgraf categorically stated that he was under no obligation to accept any orders from the city government.⁴⁹ His only responsibility was to the Public Safety Committee.⁵⁰ Encouraged by Mayor Friedensburg, members of the *Magistrat* increasingly claimed that the constitution of Berlin gave them the authority to appoint and dismiss the Police President, but the legal foundations for this act were tenuous.⁵¹ The western democrats claimed that Markgraf had acted in contempt of the law when he had dismissed several hundred non-Communist policemen from the police in the eastern sector. For their part, the Soviets insisted that the lack of unity, demonstrated by the Public Safety Committee in coordinating citywide police measures, was rendering it worthless.[52]

Later than their Allies, in April 1948, the French Military Government authorities became conscious of the need to purge the police in their Sector of Communists and criminals. They desperately needed French policemen, who could speak German, to sort out the mess they had inherited. They realized that the policemen recruited by the Soviets were still slavish to them. The Wedding precinct remained 'seriously infiltrated by members of the SED'. Determined to purge their Sector's police force, they anticipated a 'number of defections'.[53] In all four sectors there was an increase in dismissals in the weeks and months leading up to the eventual rupture. In April, *Tägliche Rundschau* accused the US authorities of unilaterally setting up a photographic lab and of providing fifty-nine radio cars to the police of their Sector. The Allied *Kommandatura* had not given permission for such a move.[54]

On 13 May 1948, the Soviet representative on the Public Safety Committee withdrew in a huff. The Western Allies had rejected the Soviet explanation that their Sector Assistant was resigning due to ill health. Instead, they had asserted that he had four convictions and continued to be involved in criminal activity.[55] The Soviets refused to permit their member of the Public Safety Committee to attend any further meetings unless General Herbert, the British Commandant, explicitly apologized for his representative's misconduct. This breakdown of the Public Safety Committee set the stage for the rupture of the police force. Nevertheless, despite recognizing that it was a farce, for the time being, the Western Allies clung to the fiction of quadripartite government. Behind the scenes, the American authorities initiated plans to use the police to protect Radio in the American Sector (RIAS) alongside food warehouses and public utilities. Together with the prospect that the *Magistrat* might urgently need to relocate to West Berlin, they began to prepare for potential cases of sabotage, widespread public disorder or acts of terrorism.[56] Amid much recrimination (aired in the newspapers), the four occupation powers spent the spring of 1948 accusing one another of abusing their police powers in a criminal way. If, for convenience, a policeman living in the French Sector arrested a West Berliner in the precinct he worked in (the Soviet Sector), this could provoke a major diplomatic incident. There was a definite East-West split developing. Where previously the French had taken the role of umpire, they now openly began to align with the British and Americans.[57]

Attempted 'kidnapping' of Hans Kanig

In April 1948, the Markgraf police tried to arrest West Berlin *Schupo* chief Hans Kanig for insulting the Soviet occupation power. He had dared to use the word 'kidnapping' in a teletype message, referring to Soviet-Sector police actions.[58] Prior to 1933, Kanig had reached the rank of Lieutenant before being ejected by the Nazis for what they saw as political unreliability.[59] He returned to the police after the Soviet capture of Berlin and was made head of the 11,000-strong *Schutzpolizei* (uniformed patrolling police) after Karl Heinrich disappeared. The French underlined Kanig's value to them and to the other Western Allies: as a member of the SPD, he was of crucial democratic importance and represented 'one of Markgraf's most formidable adversaries'.[60] After the 1946 elections, the Soviets saw him as an opponent and subjected him to repeated attacks in the *Kommandatura*. They accused him of having profited from the black market and of having illegally used police vehicles for his own enrichment.[61] As the American Public Safety officer argued, the three western powers had reluctantly supported this corrupt waverer. Although they judged his deputy Wagner a better police officer than Kanig, the fact that his underling was an ardent Communist prevented them from replacing 'their' man. Faced by a choice between an inefficient Social Democrat and an efficacious Communist, they chose 'the lesser of two evils'.[62] By introducing charges against both Markgraf and Wagner, the Western Allies succeeded in preventing Kanig's case from being discussed again in the *Kommandatura*. Nevertheless, they suspected him of having renounced his SPD membership and of secretly having joined the SED just before the 1946 elections. Their sources suggested that he was a card-carrying member of both parties. Privately, Ray Ashworth, the head of the American Public Safety Branch, was highly critical of Kanig, viewing him as lacking courage or intelligence. He was a poor administrator, who connived to enrich and aggrandize himself.[63] Kanig gave the comic impression of someone attempting to ride two different gravy trains, which were heading in opposite directions. He demonstrated a willingness to shirk battles and then to side with the winning side.[64] Ashworth wanted to get rid of Kanig, but the logic of the developing cold war conspired to keep him in place.

In April 1948, Markgraf called Kanig to attend a meeting with Colonel Kotichev and himself. Markgraf stated that during the heated meeting Kotichev called his German underling a criminal.[65] Fearing that this meant that he was about to be arrested, Kanig made an excuse to leave the room. Saying that he needed to consult with his translator, who was outside in the corridor, he managed to get past the sentries and fled head over heels to the American Sector.[66] Kanig feared suffering the same fate as his predecessor, Karl Heinrich.[67] Not only did he refuse to return to the Soviet Sector, but he voiced his fears to western newspapers. He claimed that the Communists were determined to dismiss him because he was a Social Democrat. He referred to himself as 'pretty much the only non-Communist' who continued to occupy in an important position in the Berlin police force.[68] The eastern press mocked Kanig as a cowardly bungler, who was a victim of his own propaganda and psychological warfare. Markgraf said that had the Soviets wanted to arrest Kanig, then the sentries would have stopped him from leaving the building.[69] Eastern policemen, loyal to Markgraf, demonstratively marched behind the banner 'Dismiss the provocateur Kanig from the police'.[70] Although he was out of action from April, Markgraf did not officially dismiss him until 12 July 1948.[71]

The eastern press now accused the US military authorities of unlawfully placing the police of their Sector under their 'own direct control', having effectively withdrawn them from the oversight of the Police Presidium of Berlin.[72] Relations within the *Kommandatura* became increasingly strained. Both sides accused each other of misusing the police to impose terror on Berlin's citizens. Never particularly fond of Soviet negotiators' dialectical double-talk, the Western Allies found Soviet mental gymnastics even harder to bear. Stymying the *Kommandatura*'s work with incessant prevarications and delay, every proposal was blocked by hot air, irrelevancies and obtuse counterproposals. The Americans accused the Soviets of using four-power meetings as a 'propaganda forum'. They found having to answer 'wild claims', based on demonstrably disingenuous allegations, tedious and exhausting. The Soviet representatives seemed to be just waiting for an excuse to break into lengthy prepared statements. In April, Howley poured gasoline on the fire, by accusing the Soviets of misusing the police in their Sector: he voiced strong criticism of what he called Soviet-orchestrated kidnappings.[73] For their part, the Soviets accused the Anglo-Americans of trying to annex their sectors to the economy of the Bizone, with the complicity of the Berlin *Magistrat*. Steered from Moscow, Soviet representatives began to read out long prepared statements, filled with propaganda point-scoring and accusations, which made the fifteen-hour meetings even more fractious and difficult to bear. The constant horse trading was gruelling as well as cumbersome. The other Allies complained that the Soviets were ignoring the issues at hand while rigidly sticking to their own line. Four-power government depended on goodwill and cooperation. From the spring of 1948 onwards, neither side was prepared to budge. For the French Commandant, Ganeval, the Soviets had ceased to play the game. Nevertheless, the other Allies appeared helpless. Maintaining the rules was impossible when one party ceased to express any conscience or shame, despite clearly acting in bad faith. Ganeval felt that the Soviet Commandant, General Kotikov, was openly laughing at the *Kommandatura* procedures.[74]

In subtle, but important, ways, the brass-necked Soviets were undermining the *Kommandatura* and turning it into a farce. For their part, American participants noticed that the Soviet Deputy Commandant, who used to listen attentively and to take extensive notes, had begun doodling during *Kommandatura* meetings.[75] The Western Allies saw a definite shift from the usual Soviet prevarication and misinterpretation to a new Moscow-orchestrated effort designed completely to stymy four-power government. Whenever they could, the Soviets breached the rules and unilaterally messed around with procedures. They altered the running order and reassigned interpreters without consulting the others. The need to interpret every statement twice (into English and French) made the incessant and acerbic Soviet propaganda attacks even harder to endure. The Soviets were sacrificing quadripartism by turning the meetings from those of a practical, decision-making body into a theatre of the absurd. Playing to the German gallery, every statement made in the *Kommandatura* appeared designed for the headlines the next day. The Soviets no longer discussed issues with their erstwhile Allies. They simply read out prepared propaganda statements, without any concern for whether they were relevant or accurate. Like stuck records, or a particularly grating loudspeaker truck, they tried to wear the other Allies down.[76] Throughout the long and interminable meetings, Kotikov had an adviser constantly whispering in his ear. Already in May 1948 Ganeval was asking if, as Chairman, he would 'preside over the funeral of the *Kommandatura*'. He had tried to remind the British that being provoked was as bad as showing weakness. The Soviet representatives were just looking for a sign of 'legitimate impatience' to engineer a walkout.[77]

Ganeval characterized the previous month's meeting as an episode in 'the war of nerves'. Colonel Howley had accused Markgraf's men of being political appointees rather than policemen.[78] General Kotikov accused his American counterparts of employing SS and Gestapo officers for their police force. In his view, all 'the bandits of Berlin' were flocking to the US Sector in search of sanctuary.[79] Howley protested about Soviet-Sector police continuing to make arrests in his Sector. Kotikov responded that the citizens of the American Sector regularly witnessed all sorts of shooting from rifles, revolvers and submachine guns. When not needlessly smashing crockery, like the perpetrators of *Kristallnacht*, out-of-control (and fascist) bandits in uniform were manhandling the citizens of Steglitz or of Charlottenburg. The Soviet complaint ended with the statement that such boorish American oafs targeted old women in particular. Unfortunately, instead of Americans beating old women, the translator said that they bit them. Ganeval reported that the suggestion of 'gerontophilic sadism' was too much for Howley's composure. He declared that he had participated in several fights in his time but had never once witnessed an American belligerent over the age of five bite his adversary.[80]

Although tensions had been high for months, the precise trigger for the breakdown of four-power cooperation in the *Kommandatura*, came during the meeting of 16 June 1948. Ganeval thought that the Soviets were just looking for an excuse to walk out and end quadripartite government.[81] Ironically, up until that point the meeting had proceeded innocuously. The usual insults had been relatively courteous. Although accusing their Allies of being cynics, liars, enemies of the people, fascists and reactionaries, the Soviets were doing so relatively calmly and affably. The meeting had started at 10 am and had reached 11 pm when Deputy Commandant Colonel Alexei Yelizarov began a lengthy, lugubrious speech. Pleading exhaustion, Colonel Howley stood up and announced that he was leaving. He said that he had to be in his office early the next morning. He felt that the 'never-ending tirades' were undermining the dignity of the *Kommandatura* as a four-power body. He nevertheless stated that his Deputy, Colonel Bill Babcock, was free the next day and would take his place. Ganeval opined that, on leaving the room, Howley had closed the door without much care and attention, but that he had not slammed it. Babcock – also tired – did not have the presence of mind to jump up straight away to take Howley's place at the table. After his political adviser whispered something in his ear, Colonel Yelizarov stated that Howley's actions made continuation of the session impossible. As long as the American Commandant failed to present his apologies, he would no longer sit in the *Kommandatura*. Ganeval stated that the new Soviet political adviser Maximov literally pushed Yelizarov out of the door. In the press, the Soviets immediately accused Howley of a deliberate 'hooligan action'. Afterwards, Howley and the other Allies at the meeting were convinced that the Soviet walk out was a premeditated move.[82] Nevertheless Clay was furious at his Commandant's rashness. Fully preoccupied by a late-night meeting with UK and French representatives concerning currency and tax reform, Clay felt that his subordinate should have shown more stamina and patience.[83] The British shared the belief that Howley had scored an important own goal.[84] In the next weeks, Soviet guards and the Red Flag remained, while they extracted records, but the era of feigned cooperation was definitively over.[85]

Suspension of Markgraf and rupture of the police (July 1948)

With the Soviet walkout of the *Kommandatura*, the splitting of the police was now irrevocable. Unable to dismiss the Police President without Soviet assent in the *Kommandatura*, Mayor Friedensburg sent a letter to Markgraf, on 26 July 1948, suspending him from his functions.[86] Accusing the Police President of 'illegal and anti-constitutional' acts, not least in refusing to follow instructions issued by the *Magistrat*, Friedensburg accused Markgraf of deliberately disregarding the Berlin Constitution.[87] Then as before, the Police President saw no need to obey the order because it had not been issued by the *Kommandatura*.[88] The Western Allies unilaterally declared that the 51-year-old former acting Vice-President of Berlin's police, Dr Johannes Stumm, was the new Police President.[89] The eastern authorities insisted that Stumm had been planning the splitting of the police from the beginning of 1947.[90] For the Americans, Stumm represented everything that Kanig was not. Praising his clear and proven democratic sentiments, they stressed his professionalism and police experience.[91] He set up his new headquarters in a bomb-damaged fifty-year-old army barracks in Friesenstrasse in Kreuzberg. His first act was to send another letter to Markgraf, dismissing him from his post and threatening legal action.[92] On 28 July 1948, Stumm used RIAS to call upon police officers, as public servants, to demonstrate their loyalty to the constitution, by taking up their duties with him. About two-thirds of the Berlin police deserted Markgraf and joined Stumm.[93] A total of 9,491 police officers, 971 assistants and 2,200 watchmen were immediately available to police West Berlin.[94]

RIAS broadcaster and later speech writer for Mayor Willy Brandt, Egon Bahr, remarked that once they ceased to maintain the pretence of unity, the Germans embarked on the process of dividing the city with pedantic thoroughness.[95] Members of the *Magistrat* went to see the new police headquarters for themselves. Dr Friedensburg declared that West Berlin finally possessed a democratic police force that could prioritize German interests, without fear or favour.[96] Nevertheless, the criminal records, mugshot albums and card indexes all had to be built up again from scratch, while most of the relevant files lay in East Berlin. The administrative impact of rupture was thus hugely disruptive. The renegade policemen began work without furniture or office supplies. At this stage, postwar recruits made up 75 per cent of Stumm's police force.[97] The eastern authorities and press dismissively referred to the new police force as the '*Stummpolizei*'. The neologism had the advantage of suggesting both stupidity and collusion. The Western Allies announced that any policemen, who had not joined Stumm in the Friesenstrasse HQ, were dismissed. They took the opportunity to purge any remaining suspected Communists from the police in their sectors.[98] Likewise, Markgraf dismissed known or suspected anti-Communists from what was left of his force.[99] On both sides of the new yawning political chasm, policemen could be dismissed based on 'anonymous denunciations' or mere rumours. Those who remained in the 'Markgraf police' did not necessarily do so out of conviction. One was heard saying, 'I'm not a "Markgraf policeman". I don't like to be called that, I'm a policeman that's all. I don't particularly want to be on the eastern sector force, but what can I do? I cannot move my family to Western Berlin. And even if I did, it might be worse for me later.'[100] At first, both sides refused to see their opposite numbers as legal and did everything they could to disrupt their work.

Several policemen now served in the western sectors but continued to live in the eastern sector. With cold-war tensions now at fever pitch, they risked harassment and arrest on their way to and from work.[101] Seven hundred and thirty five were still living in the Soviet Sector in 1950.[102] Initially, their uniforms were identical to those of the eastern sector police. The western authorities permitted them to remove the number badge from their collars, thereby making themselves a less conspicuous target.[103] The eastern authorities arrested one policeman after he entered their sector armed with a pistol.[104] Stumm initially advised his men to move their families to the western sectors. However, the SED deliberately hindered them when they sought to bring their furniture and belongings over the border.[105] Stumm himself began his Presidency with just the clothes on his back. After initially opposing unionization, the Western Allies abruptly decided to encourage the police in their sectors to join unions independent of Communist control.[106] The goal was to imbue the new force with the spirit of democracy. The union sought to combat any resurgence of Nazism or militarism.[107]

Police President Stumm

Dr Johannes Stumm was born on 27 March 1897. He was the son of a policeman, who had served under the Kaiser. He attended a higher vocational school and subsequently obtained a doctorate in law and political science. From 1920 to 1933, he belonged to the criminal police of the Weimar Republic. As a member of the political police, based in Berlin, he had investigated the murders of the government ministers Walter Rathenau and Matthias Erzberger. He was part of the fight against the 'Black Reichswehr' (the covert paramilitary formations organized by the German Army High Command). In the early 1930s, he became head of the Prussian police section tasked with fighting the NSDAP. Despite clear evidence of his anti-Nazi credentials, the Communists later refused to believe that he had pursued this fight with any vigour. The Communists blamed Stumm for Hitler being allowed to speak unhindered and for Goebbels's *Der Angriff* (Attack) newspaper not being banned in Berlin. He was nevertheless forced out of the police in February 1933. Out of uniform, Stumm found work as an insurance and tax adviser. The Stasi insisted that he also profited as the administrator of property and businesses stolen from the Jews.[108] He briefly served in a logistics unit during the invasion of Poland. Although he joined the National Socialist Association of Legal Professionals (NSRB), he also participated in the Kreisau Circle (the anti-Hitler resistance grouping connected to Count von Moltke).[109]

Returned to police service by the Soviets in May 1945, Stumm did what he could to achieve the reemployment of former Weimar police officials. The Stasi later accused him of hindering the removal of residual Gestapo officers and agents, like the former police Vice-President Dr Heinz Kionka, a notorious member of the NSDAP and the

SS. However, it seems that Stumm had little reason to defend a competitor. In any case, it was the Soviets who appointed Kionka. If anything, the evidence suggests Stumm's anti-Nazi credentials. Stumm did defend his deputy, Dr Hans-Georg Urban, allowing him to become a pillar of his police force.[110] Above all, the Stasi accused Stumm of sabotaging the recruitment of progressive people (in other words Communists), on the grounds that they had no police experience. Initially, SPD politicians welcomed the appointment of a member of their party. However, Stumm quickly turned down an offer to play an active role in the police committee of the SPD. The Western Allies had advised him that this would be illegal, but several SPD politicians, including Mayor Reuter, were peeved. In particular, Reuter resented the Allied *Kommandatura*'s continued powers to hire and fire senior policemen. For Ashworth, this was evidence of Stumm resisting pressure to promote SPD members.[111]

Financially, the splitting of the police presented the Western Allies with serious additional burdens. They had to fund the creation of duplicate offices. As well as a new forensics lab and card indexes, they needed a new morgue. Stumm's collaborators had been forced to leave behind all their case reports, mugshots, fingerprint files and nickname reference indexes. To rub their noses in it, the East German 'Augenzeuge' newsreel recorded the highly modern records room left behind.[112] The western police had to start again from scratch. Some of Stumm's police tried to bring material over the border but were arrested.[113] The conspicuous Soviet threat helped to weld all the democratic forces – from police to occupation soldiers – together and to win the support of the population. While in previous years, the Allies had been standoffish towards the German police, now they treated them as 'comrades in arms', with an essential part to play in western defence plans.[114]

Conclusion

Beginning in 1947, Berlin became the dramatic stage, on which the East-West conflict would play out. Certain warning signs were there from the very start: the way the Soviets located all important institutions in their Sector and stripped the western sectors of anything of value gave indications of how they would operate. The proviso that *Kommandatura* decisions had to be unanimous meant that such decisions were almost impossible to overturn. With the growing antagonism, unanimity about how to revive Germany was almost impossible to achieve. This chapter has shown how four-power cooperation ultimately broke down in an atmosphere of mutual suspicion and increasingly overt hostility in the spring of 1948. The ambience within Berlin influenced and was shaped by the wider collapse in East-West relations. As Allied collaboration broke down, Berlin was at the forefront of these developing tensions. In three short years, the police force had been subject to buffeting and battering, both concretely and ideologically, from all sides. Few Police Departments have ever faced such an array of problems in such a tight timeframe. If anything, this diluted and undermined Allied attempts to reform policing. Disagreements about how to police the city were both a product of and a catalyst for worsening tensions, which ultimately led to full-scale, war-of-nerves-style cold war. Left-wing historians Steinborn and Krüger criticize the western press for not having been more critical of the western powers and for employing police who had served in the Third Reich.[115] Nevertheless, this was largely an example of pots calling kettles black. In June 1948, the cold war came to a head: the police force, which up until that point had been a single entity covering the whole of Berlin, now ruptured into two. The eastern police now had no business whatsoever entering the western sectors, except those who policed the S-Bahn. But many western policemen continued to live in the East, so it was common for them to be arrested on their way to or from work. In an effort to drive them out, the Soviets also reduced their ration allocations.[116]

Suspicions gave rise to the 'war of nerves', with border incidents used by the Soviets, in particular, as a way of needling their former Allies. The key issues which split Berlin's government were the Soviet veto on the democratically elected Mayor taking office and Allied pressure to have Paul Markgraf removed as Police President. The splitting of the police force was the final blow to an already infirm and wounded four-power government. The Soviet-appointed police chief had been operating in an increasingly one-sided and arbitrary way. Up to this point a single police force, reporting to the Allied *Kommandatura*, had operated in Berlin. The Markgraf affair had been rumbling since the winter of 1947 and stretched relations between the Americans and the Soviets beyond breaking point. When the police force finally split, on 28 July 1948, a new West Berlin police command was created from scratch. Nevertheless, important elements of Berlin's fragile democracy, together with major economic thoroughfares, either straddled or lay on the eastern side of the border.

Notes

1 William Stivers and Donald A. Carter, *The City Becomes a Symbol: The U.S. Army in the Occupation of Berlin, 1945-1949* (Washington, DC: Center of Military History, United States Army, 2017), 169.
2 D. M. Giangreco and Robert E. Griffin, *Airbridge to Berlin: The Berlin Crisis of 1948: Its Origins and Aftermath* (Novato, CA: Presidio, 1988), 72.
3 'Rapport Mensuel du mois d'avril 1948 (7.5.1948)', Archives Diplomatiques, GMFB 1/537.
4 'General Hays: keine Krise, sondern Nervenkrieg. Eine Erklärung zu den Differenzen im Allierten Kontrollrat', *Tagesspiegel*, 28 March 1948.
5 Lucius D. Clay, *Decision in Germany* (Westport, CT: Greenwood, 1970), 208.
6 Caroline Kennedy-Pipe, *Stalin's Cold War: Soviet Strategies in Europe, 1943 to 1956* (Manchester: Manchester University Press, 1995), 162.
7 Clay, *Decision in Germany*, 350–3.
8 '"End Bizonia" - Sokolovsky', *Daily Mail*, 21 January 1948.
9 'Les Russes prétendent contrôler militairement les communications alliés avec Berlin', *Le Monde*, 2 April 1948.
10 Paul Steege, *Black Market, Cold War: Everyday Life in Berlin, 1946-1949* (Cambridge: Cambridge University Press, 2007), 161, 178f.
11 Clay, *Decision in Germany*, 354.
12 Clay's cable to the Joint Chiefs of Staff in Washington, 5 March 1948, as reproduced in *The Papers of General Lucius D. Clay*, ed. Jean Edward Smith (Bloomington, IN: Indiana University Press, 1974), 2, 567–8.

13　William R. Harris, 'March Crisis 1948, Act II', *CIA Studies in Intelligence* 11 (1967): 9.
14　'C-in-C Challenges: "Lift Iron Curtain"', *Daily Mail*, 11 March 1948.
15　Statement by Vasily Sokolovsky, 20 March 1948, as cited by Carolyn Eisenberg, *Drawing the Line: The American Decision to Divide Germany, 1944-1949* (Cambridge: Cambridge University Press, 1996), 391.
16　Gerhard Keiderling, *Berlin 1945-1986: Geschichte der Hauptstadt der DDR* (East Berlin: Dietz, 1987), 255.
17　*Tägliche Rundschau*, 30 May 1948.
18　Clay, *Decision in Germany*, 156.
19　David E. Murphy, Sergei A. Kondrashev and George Bailey, *Battleground Berlin: CIA vs. KGB in the Cold War* (New Haven and London: Yale University Press, 1997), 56.
20　'Report on Berlin Operations Base, 8 April 1948', in *On the Front Lines of the Cold War: Documents on the Intelligence War in Berlin, 1946 to 1961*, ed. Donald P. Steury (Washington, DC: CIA History Staff, Center for the Study of Intelligence, 1999), 85-6.
21　Clay to Bradley, 31 March 1948, in Clark Clifford Papers, Subject File 1945-54, 'Russia [5 of 8]', Truman Library, as cited by Deborah Welch Larson, 'The Origins of Commitment', *Journal of Cold War Studies* 13, no. 1 (2011): 189.
22　Brian Connell, 'Hussars Win a Victory in Berlin Battle of Words. Russians In – and Out. Post Set Up in British Sector. Encircled by Troops and Told to Quit', *Daily Mail*, 2 April 1948.
23　'Memorandum for the President', 16 March 1948, in *On the Front Lines of the Cold War*, ed. Steury, 145.
24　Murphy to the Secretary of State, 6 April 1948, United States, Department of State, *Foreign Relations of the United States (FRUS), 1948*, vol. 2, *Germany and Austria* (Washington, DC: United States Government Printing Office, 1973), 2, 890-1.
25　The Ambassador in the United Kingdom, (Douglas) to the Under Secretary of State (Lovett), 17 April 1948, *FRUS, 1948*, 2, 895-6.
26　This comes out in 'Diskussionsauszüge aus Tonbandaufzeichnungen einer Beratung der Forschungsgruppe der Hochschule der DVP im Jahre 1964 zur "Geschichte der Deutschen Volkspolizei"', Police Museum, Paul Markgraf File.
27　Peter Rhode, 'Lebensbild des Genossen Oberst der VP a.D. Paul Markgraf', (Diplomarbeit, 1988), 27, Police Museum, Paul Markgraf File.
28　'Liaison Officer of the Police President to the American Headquarters', 27 April 1948, US National Archives, RG260, box 893.
29　Steury (ed.), *On the Front Lines of the Cold War*, 67.
30　Alice Hills, *Policing Post-Conflict Cities* (London: Zed, 2009), 211.
31　Polizeiinspektor Metz, Beamtenvertreter des Landes Nordrhein-Westfalen, speaking at the 'Großkundgebung der Berliner Polizei', *Die Berliner Polizei* 2, no. 7 (1950): 126.
32　'Ein Rückblick', *Die Berliner Polizei* 1, no. 1 (1949): 13.
33　Eugene Gilbert Jones, 'The Allied Reconstruction of the Berlin Police, 1945-1948', PhD, University of California, San Diego, 1986, 56, 128, 8, 12, 21, 150.
34　OMGUS, Interdivisional Reorientation Committee, 'Cultural Exchange Program', February 1949.
35　Norbert Steinborn and Hilmar Krüger, *Die Berliner Polizei 1945 bis 1992: von der Militärreserve im Kalten Krieg auf dem Weg zur bürgernahen Polizei?* (Berlin: Arno Spitz, 1993), 36, 41.
36　Jones, 'The Allied Reconstruction', 180.

37 'Public Safety, July 1945 to 31 August 1949', 2, US National Archives, RG260, 390/48/27/2, Box 893, 5.
38 Steinborn and Krüger, *Die Berliner Polizei*, 39–40. While giving no further evidence to corroborate this figure, these authors condemn the western press for not having been more critical of the western powers for employing police who had served in the Third Reich.
39 Steinborn and Krüger, *Die Berliner Polizei*, 43. Similarly, known SPD members in the eastern sector were either dismissed or demoted to foot patrol.
40 Curt Riess, *The Berlin Story* (London: Frederick Muller, 1953), 107.
41 'Mißtrauen gegen Berlins Polizeichef. Fall Friede vor dem Stadtparlament. 5413 Berliner verschwunden', *Sozialdemokrat*, 14 November 1947. Stadverorentenversammlung vom Groß-Berlin, 47. Ordentliche Sitzung vom 13. November 1947. Landesarchiv Berlin, C Rep. 001, Nr. 47.
42 'Ernüchternder Polizeibericht', *Der Tagesspiegel*, 19 November 1947.
43 Clay, *Decision in Germany*, 158.
44 Steege, *Black Market*, 137.
45 'La Situation à Berlin', no date, ca. 1948, Archives Diplomatiques, GMFB 1/214.
46 Ferdinand Friedensburg, *Es ging um Deutschlands Einheit: Rückschau eines Berliners auf die Jahre nach 1945* (West Berlin: Haude and Spenersche, 1971), 263.
47 'Zwei Seelen in seiner Brust', *Der Kurier*, 24 August 1948.
48 Steinborn and Krüger, *Die Berliner Polizei*, 61.
49 W. Phillips Davison, *The Berlin Blockade: A Study in Cold War Politics* (Princeton, NJ: Princeton University Press, 1958), 52.
50 Jones, 'The Allied Reconstruction', 175–6.
51 L. Schroeder, Deputy Oberbuergermeister to Major-General Kotikow, Central Kommandatura of the Soviet Sector of Greater Berlin, 27 July 1948, US National Archives, RG260, 390/48/27/2, Box 893.
52 Edward A. Morrow, 'New Dispute Mars Berlin Air Inquiry', *New York Times*, 14 April 1948.
53 'Mr. J. Tarbe De Saint Hardouin, Ambassadeur de France, Conseiller Politique en Allemagne à Son Excellence Monsieur G. Bidault, Ministre des Affaires Etrangères', 3 April 1948, Archives Diplomatiques, GMFB 1/537.
54 'Einseitige Polizeimaßnahmen der amerikanischen Behörden', *Tägliche Rundschau*, 1 April 1948.
55 'Public Safety, July 1945 to 31 August 1949', 4.
56 Ray Ashworth, 'Plan should Berlin be divided', 22 March 1948, US National Archives, RG466, 250/72/9/1-3, Box 2.
57 Dorothea Führe, *Die Französische Besatzungspolitik in Berlin von 1945 bis 1949: Déprussianisation und Décentralisation* (Berlin: Weißensee-Verlag, 2001), 13.
58 'Liaison Officer of the Police President'.
59 Ray Ashworth, Chief, Public Safety Branch: 'Report on Hans Kanig, Kommandeur of the Schutzpolizei Berlin', 21 April 1948, US National Archives, RG260, 390/48/27/2, Box 893.
60 'Rapport Mensuel du mois d'avril 1948'.
61 'Einträgliche Nebenbeschäftigung. Polizeikommandeur Kanig jagt Tantiemen statt Verbrecher', *Berliner Zeitung*, 14 May 1948.
62 'Report on Hans Kanig'.
63 'Public Safety, July 1945 to 31 August 1949', 3.
64 'Report on Hans Kanig'.

65 Der Polizeipräsident in Berlin to the Allied Kommandatura, Public Safety Committee: 'Verhalten des Kommandeurs der Schutzpolizei, Herrn Kanig, gelegentlich seiner Besprechung in der sowjetischen Zentralkommandantur', 10 May 1948, Landesarchiv Berlin, C Rep 303–09, Nr. 2, 345f.
66 'Rapport Mensuel du mois d'avril 1948'.
67 'Ein neuer Fall Heinrich?', *Sozialdemokrat*, 27 April 1948.
68 'Les enlèvements continuent à Berlin', *Le Monde*, 29 April 1948.
69 'Held Kanig verfällt in Panik. Fingierte "Flucht" als Auftakt zur Spaltung der Polizei?', *Neues Deutschland*, 28 April 1948; 'Opfer eigenen Nervenkrieges. Berlin lacht über den Schildbürgerstreich seines Schutzpolizeikommandeurs Kanig', *Berliner Zeitung*, 28 April 1948.
70 Police Museum, Paul Markgraf File.
71 Steinborn and Krüger, *Die Berliner Polizei*, 54.
72 'Extract from Minutes of the Deputy Commandants', Meeting held on 7 May 1948, UK National Archives, FO 1012/738.
73 'Howley über den Menschenraub. Debatten in der Sitzung der alliierten Kommandanten. Kotikow lehnt Untersuchungskommission ab', *Tagesspiegel*, 24 April 1948.
74 'Compte-rendu personnel du Général Ganeval de la séance des Commandants du 13 Mai 1948', Archives Diplomatiques, GMFB 1/838.
75 Acting U.S. Political Adviser for Germany (Chase) to the Secretary of State, 29 April 1948, *FRUS, 1948*, vol. 2, 901.
76 Frank L. Howley, *Berlin Command* (New York: G. P. Putnam's Sons, 1950), 179.
77 'Compte-rendu ... du 28 Mai 1948'.
78 Although known for his blunt and undiplomatic language, Howley had hidden depths. He had studied at the Sorbonne and went on to be Vice Chancellor of New York University. Howley, *Berlin Command*, 19.
79 'Compte-rendu personnel du 28 Avril 1948'.
80 Ibid. Howley confirms the story. Howley, *Berlin Command*, 160.
81 'Compte-rendu personnel du 16 Juin 1948'.
82 See 'Stenographic Notes on meeting of Chief of Staff, Allied Kommandatura', 1 July 1948, US National Archives, RG 260, 390/40/18/6-7, Box 7. Ganeval had been wondering about a rupture since April 1948.
83 Murphy to Secretary of State, 17 June 1948, *FRUS, 1948*, 2: 908–909, 909.
84 Howley, *Berlin Command*, 183.
85 'Stenographic notes on meeting of ... Allied Kommandatura'.
86 Jones argues that Friedensburg suspended Markgraf without seeking the prior approval of the Western Allies. Jones, 'The Allied Reconstruction', 178, 190.
87 'City Assembly of Berlin Condemns Soviet Blockade', *Stars and Stripes*, 30 July 1948.
88 'The Police President of Berlin to Bürgermeister Dr. Friedensburg', 27 July 1948, US National Archives, RG260, box 893.
89 The Allied *Kommandatura* had not approved Stumm's appointment to the position of Vice-President of the Berlin police because of the opposition expressed by the Soviet delegation. Press Branch, British Element, Control Commission for Germany: 'Western Military Governments confirm Berlin Police President's Suspension', 28 July 1948, Archives Diplomatiques, GMFB 1/214.
90 BStU MfS AP 10187/56, 6.
91 Mr. Hall and Mr. Mittendorf. Secret. 'Survey Report of the Public Safety Branch', USCOB [ca. 15 March 1950], US National Archives, RG 466, 250/72/8/7, Box 1, 2.

92 Stumm to Markgraf, 28 July 1948, Landesarchiv Berlin, C Rep 303–09, Nr. 2, 102.
93 'OMGUS Political Report No. 9', 7 August 1948, US National Archives, RG 260, Box 903.
94 Berlin Police Museum Chronicle, http://www.berlin.de/polizei/wir-ueber-uns/historie/geteiltesberlin.html (accessed 27 September 2013).
95 Egon Bahr, *Zu meiner Zeit* (Munich: K. Blessing, 1996), 37.
96 *Welt im Film* 169/1948, 20 August 1948.
97 'Polizei – Freund der Bevölkerung. Gespräch mit dem Polizeipräsident Dr. Stumm', *Telegraf*, 3 February 1950.
98 Präsidium der Volkspolizei (ed.), *Zeittafel zur Geschichte der Volkspolizei Berlin 1945–1961* (East Berlin: Präsidium der Volkspolizei, 1985).
99 Ursula Nienhaus, '"Für strenge Dienstzucht ungeeignete Objekte . . ." Weibliche Polizei in Berlin 1945-1952', in *Nachkriegspolizei: Sicherheit und Ordnung in Ost- und Westdeutschland, 1945–1969*, ed. Gerhard Fürmetz, Herbert Reinke and Klaus Weinhauer (Hamburg: Ergebnisse Verlag, 2001), 149.
100 'East Berliners Forced to Demonstrate, "Soviet" Cop Says', *Stars and Stripes*, 28 August 1948.
101 'Vier entführte Polizisten wieder frei', *Der Tagesspiegel*, 24 August 1948. 'Political Report No. 10', 14 August 1948, US National Archives, RG260, 390/48/27/3, Box 903.
102 'Präsidialabteilung an den Leiter der Präsidialbabteilung Dr Urban: Einstellungen und Entlassungen in der Zeit vom 1.7.1949 bis 1.3.1950', 3 April 1950, Landesarchiv Berlin, E Rep 200-25, Nr. 157–8.
103 'Eine Eroberung!', *Volksblatt*, 24 August 1948. 'Eine Schutzmaßnahme', *Der Abend*, 24 August 1948.
104 'Polizist freigelassen', *Der Abend*, 25 August 1948.
105 Walter Krumholz, *Berlin-ABC* (West Berlin: Verlag Documentation, 1969), 494.
106 On hostility to unionization, see Jones, 'The Allied Reconstruction', 166.
107 On the subsequent reversal, see Mark Fenemore, *Fighting the Cold War in Post-Blockade, Pre-Wall Berlin: Behind Enemy Lines* (London: Routledge, 2019), 92–3. 'OMGUS, Public Safety Branch: Statutes of proposed Police Union', 18 June 1948, US National Archives, RG260, box 893.
108 The British merely referred to him having worked as an industrial employee. 'Western Military Governments confirm Berlin Police President's Suspension'.
109 BStU MfS AP 10187/56.
110 BStU MfS AP 10187/56, 8.
111 Ray Ashworth, Chief, Public Safety Branch: 'Stumm-Reuter Relationship', 15 October 1949, US National Archives, RG260, 390/48/27/2, Box 893.
112 *Die Gladow-Bande: Chicago in Berlin*, directed by Ute Bönnen and Gerald Endres (ARD, 2000).
113 Steinborn and Krüger, *Die Berliner Polizei*, 78. 'La guerre des deux polices sévit à Berlin', *Le Monde*, 3 August 1948.
114 Jones, 'The Allied Reconstruction', 154–4. Cf. Fenemore, *Fighting the Cold War*, chs 4 and 5.
115 Steinborn and Krüger, *Die Berliner Polizei*, 59.
116 Davison, *The Berlin Blockade*, 212.

7

Policing public order without East-West cooperation

West Berlin's position was anomalous in the summer of 1948. The local authorities had managed to push for greater self-government and a separate police force for the western sectors, but the City Executive (*Magistrat*) had no alternative but to continue to meet in East Berlin. The breakdown of four-power rule – with the Soviet walkout from the *Kommandatura* and the splitting of the police – had important implications for public order. Demonstrations and protests near the (still largely invisible) frontier between East and West became very difficult to police. The task was made harder by full-blown cold war, expressed increasingly vociferously in propaganda, in which neither side was ready to compromise. Rather than mediating border disputes, the Soviets and their police allowed their tame mass media to exploit them. Both sides blew up minor conflicts over jurisdiction to serve as a pretext for dividing the city along political and ideological lines.[1] Every step either of the authorities took was now judged according to hostile propaganda reports. Although the police on either side of the sectoral boundary no longer cooperated, important unitary institutions like the City Assembly and *Magistrat* continued to be located in the eastern sector. The need for political representatives to cross the border to exercise their democratic rights substantially complicated the public-order situation. This chapter assesses the period of political turmoil in the summer and autumn of 1948. From a western perspective, the increase in Communist-orchestrated mob violence eventually forced the city government to abandon its seat in East Berlin and to relocate to the western sectors.[2] Although Soviet propaganda claimed that western interests covertly orchestrated the political cleavage in Berlin, most of the impetus for division came from their own side. Despite clear problems with the *Kommandatura*, and the rupture in citywide policing, the other Allies tried vainly to save at least the pretence of four-power government.

So-called 'Black Guards'

In the summer of 1948, policemen became the principal protagonists of a propaganda war, waged between East and West. Smarting at repeated American accusations of kidnapping, in 1947 and 1948, the Soviets countered with claims of wanton terror occurring in the American Sector. Prior to the rupture of the *Kommandatura*, they claimed that these were carried out by a shadowy state-terror organization known as the 'Black Guards'.[3] These were German guards patrolling US installations, who wore black uniforms to distinguish them from the blue/green uniforms of the standard police. In December 1947, the Soviet newspaper *Izvestia* claimed that the American authorities had deployed the Black Guards for attacks on German civilians in the American Sector.[4] Thereafter, Soviet propaganda reports built up the Black Guards to mythic proportions. In March 1948, the Red Army's broadsheet, *Tägliche Rundschau*, accused the Americans of carrying out Gestapo-like attacks on SED offices in the working-class districts of Kreuzberg and Neukölln.[5] The following month, the Soviet Commandant, Alexander Kotikov, spent four hours accusing the Americans of employing SS members and Nazi activists in the police in their Sector.[6] Soviet propagandists suggested that the Americans were using this sinister body to carry out armed raids on assorted democrats, trade unionists and pro-unification patriots. For example, on 26 April 1948, an armed unit of the 'Black Guard' had swooped on a Communist-orchestrated Free German Youth (FDJ) meeting.[7] In breach of four-power agreements, the Americans were evidently dismantling democracy in their Sector. The Soviet representative in the *Kommandatura* stated that 'if this was freedom, he would like to know the meaning of oppression'.[8]

Trying to play on differences between the Western Allies, the Soviet representative reminded the French delegation of the effects German militarization had had on his country. The British representative challenged the Soviet report's objectivity and accuracy. Asking whether the Soviet representative was talking about the US Sector's Industrial Police or the so-called 'Paulus' army, he made a subtle dig at the Soviets. The latter had been actively recruiting former *Wehrmacht* officers (not least Police President Markgraf), who were willing to serve Stalin. As far as the American representative was concerned, the Soviet report was jumbling together fact and fiction: it deliberately blurred the lines between different policing bodies. Any raids on FDJ or SED offices had been carried out by the authorized Berlin police. The British chairman asked why, if such a 'terror' existed in West Berlin, democratic citizens were not leaving en masse for the safety of the Soviet Sector. The Soviets said that the creation of the 'Black Guard' contravened four-power agreements, insisting on demilitarization.[9] In reality, the 'Black Guards' were private security guards for watching military installations and supply dumps. It was their task to guard Allied warehouses and vehicle parks against fire and theft. Despite Soviet insistence that they illegally carried on the German military tradition, they were not employed in any military capacity and did not receive infantry training. It was true that many of them had served in the *Wehrmacht*, but few German men of their age had not. Nevertheless, the name was well chosen by the Soviets because contemporaries instantly associated the Communist-invented term with Hitler's black-uniformed *Schutzstaffel* (Protection Squads). Having established the trope that the American-Sector police were little more than SS men, the Soviets used it at every opportunity.

The breakdown of local government

With the police split, the breakdown of local government became inevitable but not yet conclusive. The tenuous threads that bound the city (and its civic institutions) together began to unravel. Nevertheless, with neither side willing to give their adversary moral superiority, it was a slow and agonizing death. In 1945, the Soviets had ensured that the city government – made up of the *Magistrat* and the City Assembly – were all located in the Soviet Sector. During June and July 1948, the three Allies met nearly daily and remained in close contact with Mayor Reuter. For Clay, the Soviets were deliberately stymieing negotiations while pursuing violent and virulent 'propaganda attacks'. Immediately following a four-power conference to discuss currency reform, on 22 June 1948, the Soviets used their press and radio to publish their own, unilateral currency reform. The Western Allies refused to allow the Soviets to exert financial control over any part of Berlin because, in their eyes, this would have meant accepting 'Soviet sovereignty' over the whole city.[10] The Communists then cynically whipped up a mob to disrupt the *Magistrat* and the City Assembly in the following days. Bolstering the Soviet fait accompli, the angry crowd demanded a single currency (the *Ostmark*) for the whole of Berlin.[11] The mass of angry, aggrieved people was clearly organized and steered by the SED. The East German government was ready to use public disorder to compensate for its geopolitical weakness.

Without consulting the *Magistrat*, the Western Allies introduced their Deutschmarks, on 24 June. At the same time, they authorized the creation of *bureaux de change* in the western sectors, which were operational from the beginning of August.[12] The currency exchange was largely successful, if somewhat chaotic. Despite queuing for thirty-six hours, when the new currency was issued, some West Berliners were turned away at the bank counter and left moneyless. It was unclear whether the city treasurer would have enough money to pay the policemen's wages, threatening continued law and order.[13] Some prophesied impending economic collapse for West Berlin. However, Mayor Reuter felt that those who controlled the currency possessed the power. He assured Clay that the Berliners would stand up and be counted in defence of their freedom. The impact of the reform was dramatic: no longer having to hoard goods and foodstuffs, the shop windows were suddenly full again. Their owners could be sure of getting a reasonable return for their goods, in a currency that was now worth something. Abandoning the notion that Germany would function as a single economic unit allowed the West German economy to begin recovery. In the coming weeks, the competition of the currencies began to favour the economy based on free trade. 'East' and 'West Berliners' increasingly became defined by whether or not they had access to the goods and services that could be bought with western money. Currency reform thus served to create a very real and tangibly experienced division between the 'haves' (those with the new Westmarks) and 'have-nots' (those without) (Figure 2).

For the western press, there was no question that the actions of the authorities in East Berlin, in whipping up anger against the politicians, were undemocratic. For its part, the SPD newspaper, the *Telegraf*, called the first demonstration on 23 June 1948 a pogrom.[14] As Dr Friedensburg wrote to Markgraf, the throng of demonstrators invaded the City Hall and prevented the City Assembly from sitting. Orchestrated by the Communist authorities, this siege of the local parliament was deliberately intimidating for the representatives. As well as insults and threats, there was some physical manhandling of the deputies. Although aware of the illegal disruption, Markgraf ordered his men not to intervene. The French felt

Figure 2 As the western press condemns Soviet tyranny in the form of the Blockade, the Western Allies impose their own form of anti-democratic and patronizing oppression. *Frischer Wind*, 1.11.1948.

that the report Markgraf later sent to the *Magistrat* was a deliberate provocation, aimed at mocking the democratic process.[15] The other Allies accused the Soviets of deliberately instigating and fomenting disorder to undermine the work of the Berlin local government. Not surprisingly, the Soviets cared little about the legal niceties of bourgeois self-government. Karl Litke, the SED leader in the City Assembly, described that body as little more than a 'colonial dependency', imposed by foreign imperialists.[16] For democratic politicians, the use of mob intimidation had unpleasant parallels with what happened at the Kroll Opera House, in March 1933, when the Nazis surrounded the German parliament with storm troopers. In a move equated to the Nazi Enabling Act, in June 1948, the Soviet-orchestrated crowd repeatedly manhandled, cursed and spat at democratic politicians. According to the accounts of contemporaries, it was a terrifying ordeal. The unwillingness of the Soviet Sector police to intervene left the elected representatives at the mercy of a baying rabble. Communist agitators denounced city councillor Jeanette Wolff (SPD) as a traitor to the VVN, the left-wing Association for Persecutees of the Nazi Regime.[17] People with VVN badges swore at and kicked the sixty-year-old.[18] Being part of a mass of people allowed the release of pent-up frustrations, directed at a range of scapegoats.

Wolff had been a founding member, and chairwoman, of the VVN.[19] From 1946, she led the American Denazification Committee in Neukölln and testified against Nazi war criminals. For her vociferous opposition to Nazism, from the 1920s onwards, the five-foot-tall bundle of energy had been nicknamed 'the trumpet'.[20] The Holocaust had robbed her of no fewer than twenty-four close relatives. Although Communist politician Franz Dahlem criticized her as overly diplomatic and insufficiently militant, she continued to defend the VVN against SPD criticism until May 1948. Wolff resigned from the VVN in June 1948, after it began criticizing the *Magistrat*.[21] *Neues Deutschland* argued that the crowd had booed Wolff because she was saying 'particularly nasty' things about the workers. In their eyes, she was guilty of outrageously shameless, calculated attacks. Berliners owed their respect to the Soviet Red Army that had freed them, not to pseudo-democratic lackeys, who were prepared to sacrifice Berlin's unity for a few banknotes. The 'Organ of the SED' juxtaposed formal democracy – as it existed in the City Assembly – with the 'true' democracy of the people, exercising their rights in the street. Claims that a sixty-year-old, disabled woman (Wolff) had been the principal victim – kicked in her injured legs and beaten while on the ground – was just grist to the propagandists' mill. ND denounced the accusations of manhandling by the crowd as audacious in their mendacity. Talk of terror from the street was just the fearful expression of 'hysterical women'. The paper linked the actions of the workers in East Berlin in 1948 with those who had erected barricades in 1848.[22] For many historians, the treatment of this courageous Jewish Concentration Camp survivor, at the hands of the Communist rabble, is evidence of the SED's totalitarian methodology and outlook. Members of the crowd supposedly called her an 'old Jewish sow' and derided her as a 'betrayer of the working class'.[23] This ill-treatment of a survivor of Nazi persecution made clear to many Berliners the parallels between the Third Reich and the Stalinist dictatorship. Wolff declared herself unafraid of death – whether from the Gestapo or the Soviets – as SED Assembly members tried to heckle her. Other Communists allegedly attacked a British photographer, with the words, 'You bombed our cities'.[24] Eastern propaganda said that this was merely an expression of the righteous anger of working-class Berliners. The Communists condemned what they called 'reactionary machinations in the City Assembly', aimed at splitting the police at the behest of the western powers.[25]

In the increasingly divided ex-capital, the cold war offered ample opportunities for dissensus (or disputatious disagreement). In such a context, coercion is routinely dressed up as consent. Deciding who can legitimately deploy violence determines who is inside and who is outside the realm of legitimate authority (or *Herrschaft*). In the case of demonstrations against the local government's authority, the eastern authorities dropped legitimate-violence arguments in favour of those stressing the legitimacy of street protest.[26] In the view of the eastern press, a united Berlin unequivocally required a single currency. The possibility of two currencies existing within the same city was too absurd to consider. In a bold pivot, *Neues Deutschland* presented the claims, made by demonstrators it described as robust and vocal, as expressions of genuine, unfiltered democracy. The Communists presented the street rather than the ballot box as the source of sovereignty and basis of legitimacy. As the last defence against an artificial and unfair division of the city, these demonstrators constituted a legitimate challenge to the remotely controlled *Magistrat*. The crowd was made up of hundreds of ordinary, 'decent' workplace delegates. The 'people' were sending the politicians a potent reminder (in the form of a deputation from the workers) that true power lay with them, not with the elected representatives. Given the dire economic situation, the Berliners were reaching the 'limits of their patience'. Accusing members of the three western parties – the SPD, Christian Democratic Union (CDU) and Liberal Democratic Party (LDP) – of digs and provocations, the true voice of the people demanded concrete actions to end division.[27] Unused to such directness from ordinary people, the city elders seemed stunned.[28] Refusing to be ignored, the workers would resist attempts to get them to leave. For the first time, the mighty *Internationale* could be heard thundering from the City Assembly chamber. ND presented a picture of a united front of workers – young and old, male and female – joining together with People's Policemen against the division of Berlin. It blamed the violence on an American car that had rammed the crowd, knocking two women to the ground. Naturally, those who witnessed this act were outraged by the reckless actions of the driver.

According to the eastern press, western journalists and politicians tried to slip away – or to take 'French leave'. The workers cried out that they were not representatives of the people, but traitors. 'You have torn Berlin asunder.... We will teach you to fulfil the wishes of the Berliners.' ND argued that the People's Police did try to calm the crowd, but it was worked up by the undemocratic behaviour of the western politicians. A man with the insignia of a former Concentration Camp inmate proclaimed that Berliners wanted their city to remain undivided. In the chamber, only the SED 'emphatically and vigorously' defended the workers' interests. What was offensive, to both the working class and its representatives, was the City Assembly's acceptance of two currencies for Berlin, a situation that would make life in the city unbearable. For the SED, former Deputy Mayor Karl Maron stated that separate currencies would not just cause economic chaos but would make life impossible for the workers.[29] It was the *Magistrat* that was behaving irresponsibly. By acting as an enemy of the people, it was behaving undemocratically. The western parties may have made up the majority, but in the eyes of the eastern press, they were a remote-controlled, servile, manipulated oligarchy. For his part, Franz Neumann (SPD) countered by denouncing the actions taken by the eastern worker delegations as a form of circus. *Neues Deutschland* suggested that the western parties already planned to move the City Assembly to Schöneberg. It argued that the *Magistrat* should flee straight to West Germany without pausing in West Berlin.[30] With a surfeit of imagination and a lack of common sense, one SPD representative suggested turning the entire borough of Mitte, where City Hall was located, into an extraterritorial enclave. Mayor Friedensburg found little support for his suggestion of Berlin taking on a would-be neutral, 'intermediary role between East and West'.[31]

Leaks in the Blockade: Clashes at the border

If the Town Hall was one trouble spot, the border was another. In the immediate aftermath of western currency reform, the Soviets declared possession of Westmarks to be a criminal offense for East Berliners and residents of the Soviet Zone. Nevertheless, for Berliners from both sides of the beleaguered city, black-market money changing became an everyday experience. ND complained that the western press was deliberately spreading false rumours, to make the population jittery and submissive. It praised the newly printed currency, introduced by the Soviets, as tasteful as well as stable. It argued that the eastern currency reform only impacted on the black marketeers. Naturally, the latter feared what would happen to their ill-gotten bundles of cash. Taking pleasure in their nonplussed faces, ND prophesied that the divisive 'Clay Mark' would soon be worthless.[32] In reality, the introduction of a new, more stable western currency heightened the already dire economic problems present in East Berlin. East Berliners were willing to trade scarce goods to get hold of the new western money. The day after the demonstration and disruption at the Town Hall, on 24 June, the Soviets imposed a Blockade on West Berlin. Nevertheless, Berlin was such a large and complex city that the Soviets could not attempt to seal the border hermetically. So many people continued to cross the border between East and West Berlin that it was almost impossible to prevent minor smuggling. *Tägliche Rundschau* estimated that 420,000 foragers were smuggling up to 7,000 tons of supplies a week.[33]

In mid-August 1948, the People's Police launched a high-profile clampdown on illegal trading. The focus of their razzias was the centrally located Potsdamer Platz.[34] Mainly ruins, the square had once been one of Berlin's main thoroughfares, akin to Piccadilly Circus or Times Square. Even at the best of times, it was difficult to control the movement of so many people and vehicles in this area. It was also the point where three sectors (British, American and Soviet) met, making it highly sensitive in geopolitical terms. With the cold war unleashed, the border now slashed Potsdamer Platz in two.[35] Its position, straddling the border, made it a haven for smugglers of all stripes, threatening ordinary citizens with violence and crime. Throughout the eleven-month Blockade, smuggling and black-market trading persisted. Scarcity made commodities like coffee, chocolate and tobacco even more precious resources. Smuggling these stimulants avoided tax and had an exorbitant mark-up. A circuitous route swapped precious metals in the East for western hard currency. The ease with which smugglers could cross over the sector borders was a significant disadvantage for the east-sector police, who sought to crack down hard.[36] The *Tagesspiegel*, published in West Berlin, equated the mid-August razzia with arbitrary 'harassment and terror'. In total, the East Berlin authorities claimed to have seized millions of cigarettes and tons of coffee beans. In addition, they took large quantities of cocoa powder, corned beef, condensed milk and sardines out of the speculators' rucksacks. Everything from matches and razor blades to women's stockings were sold at outrageous prices. The police raid netted no less than 246,867 Westmarks. The raids marked the determination of the police of the eastern sector to eradicate the black market on their side of the border root and branch.[37]

For Soviet-controlled media, the splitting of the Berlin police had paved the way for crime. Depicting the western police as being in cahoots with the criminals, they argued that all the People's Police wanted was order at the border. Nevertheless, unilateral action by the Markgraf police was bound to fail, because of the open border and the lack of cooperation of the west-sector police.[38] Eastern propaganda accused the *Stummpolizei* of offering black marketeers asylum.[39] Arguing that Stumm had encouraged his men to make free use of their truncheons on Communist demonstrators, the eastern press claimed that his police were doing nothing to stop the trading in chocolate, cigarettes and silk stockings.[40] By impinging on these razzias, the splitting of the Berlin police force went against the interests of the working population. Showing traders arm in arm with the US Military Police, Soviet propaganda insisted that the western authorities were actively protecting the criminals (Figure 3).

Figure 3 'Black Guard' illicit traders in league with the US Military Police. Now exchanging butter and cigarettes for hard cash. *Frischer Wind*, 1.9.1948.

On 19 August 1948, the eastern police tried to carry out yet another razzia at Potsdamer Platz, but this time the situation exploded.[41] One young man escaped arrest, by the *Volkspolizei*, by fleeing into the US Sector. A Markgraf policeman pursued him over the border, seized him and was in the process of dragging him back to the Soviet Sector. However, seeing her son arrested, his mother rushed after him. At that moment, Markgraf's *Schutzpolizei* commander, Rudolf Wagner, appeared in a car. Snatching a rubber truncheon from the nearest policeman, he went towards the old woman, with a pistol in one hand and the truncheon in the other. Seeing this unfair fight, the outraged crowd threw stones at the eastern policemen.[42] Eastern reports alleged that young men wearing black trousers and high boots led the black-market traders. The People's Police responded to the stone throwing by firing shots back. Markgraf's police fired an estimated fifteen to twenty shots, injuring six to eight people.[43] *Berliner Zeitung* claimed that they were responding to a 'systematic barrage of stones' from a 'howling mob'. A stone hit a Constable in the face; a woman received one in the chest. The newspaper claimed that up to a thousand people were shouting Nazi slogans. The American Associated Press agreed that the crowd was laughing at and insulting the People's Police. A well-organized mob tried to storm a branch of the *Konsum* department store, but forty Soviet MPs managed to stop them. Protected by 'their' police, the traders carried on trading regardless, just over the border.[44] Armed Military Policemen from the western sectors just stood and watched the attack on the People's Police. Major Bond, the American Assistant Chief of Public Safety, and Dr Stumm arrived to monitor the situation. The eastern press then suggested that their arrival proved that this was an orchestrated 'fascist provocation' by the sinister Black Guard.[45] Only with the arrival of a substantial body of troops, under the command of the Soviet Commandant, did the rioting end.

Journalist and diarist Ruth Andreas-Friedrich was horrified at the idea of Germans shooting at Germans or Berliners at Berliners.[46] But injuries to pride easily led to violence. British Military Police detained some of the stone-throwers. According to the western press, Soviet officers made the situation considerably worse when they arrived on the scene, not least by ignoring the border.[47] Refusing any cooperation with the western police, they blocked access to the American and British Sectors. As they faced off with the police on the other side of the border, the crowd of 'flashy young German spivs' howled and jeered with derision. For the West Berlin newspaper *Der Abend*, the stone throwing was the explosion of pent-up anger. The shots fired by the eastern police had also injured harmless citizens going about their business.[48] *Neues Deutschland* claimed that several policemen had been injured by the stone throwing, two of them seriously. It admitted that three people had also been lightly injured by the 'warning shots', one seriously.[49] The *Kurier* claimed that the incidents occurred only because the police in the western sectors were not informed beforehand about the razzia.[50] *Der Tag* agreed that unless coordinated, razzias were useless. Attempts to round up black-market traders in the Soviet Sector only caused them to flee over the border. The copious rubble offered several hiding places as well as missiles. If the police of the British Sector tried a razzia, then the migration across the sector boundary just occurred in reverse.[51]

Refusing to pick a side, Mayor Friedensburg called for a 'united front' in the struggle against the black market. Nevertheless, the eastern press saw his actions, in splitting the police, as directly responsible for the shameful situation at Potsdamer Platz. *The Times* suggested creating a 'no-man's land' where soldiers were banned.[52] Representing the previous message of paramilitary fascist intimidation, *Vorwärts* (Forwards), published in East Berlin, claimed that the young men in black trousers and high boots were members of the sinister Black Guard.[53] The riffraff was made up of former Nazis, who wore SS-boots. This rabble of SA and SS men were parasites, feeding off the 'corrupt Clay Mark'. They stood in direct contact with the 'Stumm Garde', a propitious amalgam of Stumm police and Black Guard. The *Magistrat*'s actions, in undermining unity, had given them a chance. The tune had changed substantially from June. Far from letting 'the people' express themselves as a progressive historical force, in the street as they chose, the eastern press now argued that 'All respectable Berliners want to live in peace'.

US Commandant Frank L. Howley admitted that the eastern police had the right to defend themselves against attacks. However, at no point was violence against unarmed civilians helpful or necessary. He affirmed his Military Government's support for the effort to eliminate the black market. Nevertheless, he pointed to the Soviet Blockade as the cause of much of the illegal trade.[54] The best way for the East Berlin authorities to deal with the black economy would be for the Soviets to lift the artificial and punishing tourniquet of West Berlin. Howley then accused several leading East Berlin policemen of being criminals (for assisting the removal of people by the Soviets).[55] *Der Abend* made similar attacks; it called Markgraf's police a Soviet-German criminal agency, led in part, by kidnappers and hoodlums.[56] Several tit-for-tat border incidents occurred in late August. Soviet soldiers dragged a German photographer over the sector boundary, despite attempts by the western police to save him.[57] The Soviets also arrested western policemen, in plain clothes, who were in possession of pistols and cameras.[58] State symbols and signs are extremely important in creating a bordering narrative. Up to this point, the Western Allies had done little to mark their territory. At this tense point in the cold war, they erected the now iconic warning signs (in four languages) at the sector borders. These alerted people to the fact that they were about to leave the safety of the western sectors. The western authorities positioned bollards to stop cars easily crossing the sector border. For a time, a barbed wire fence separated the sectors at Potsdamer Platz. In this way, the western authorities sought to prevent confrontations occurring between black-market traders and the newly aggressive People's Police.[59] The *Telegraf* adopted an uncharacteristically sober and neutralist position. It argued that both the Soviets and the western powers should pull their armed sentries back from the sector boundary and leave policing it to the German police. The SPD newspaper suggested that the police chiefs of the neighbouring precincts should meet to discuss a planned razzia. This would prevent this sort of dangerous incident.[60]

Renewed violence impeding the City Assembly

On 26 August 1948, the Communists again prevented the City Assembly from meeting. While the bussed-in 'hooligan elements' were allowed to run amok, the eastern police again refused to intervene.[61] They ignored requests from the President of the Assembly, Dr Otto Suhr (SPD), for them to remove members of the mob. Armed with sticks and axes, the crowd was able to invade the chamber.[62] The eastern press accused western politicians of defaming the Soviet occupiers as primitives and wishing violence on them. Jeanette Wolff's supposed condemnation of them as lawless Asians was presented as a blatant return to Hitler's racial theories. In the eyes of Communist propagandists, the SPD wanted nothing less than the unleashing of World War Three.[63] The invasive multitude made the transaction of business impossible. Mayor Louise Schroeder (SPD) entreated the crowd to be reasonable and to go home. Saying that they could listen to the debate on RIAS, her words prompted scorn and derision. Her plea for the crowd to behave democratically was in vain.[64] The Communists, backed by the Soviets, were in the process of seizing control of the freely elected and overwhelmingly anti-Communist Berlin City Assembly and the east-sector police were doing absolutely nothing to stop them. The Western Allies viewed it as particularly perfidious for the Soviets to use street demonstrations while, behind closed doors, negotiations about the Blockade were ongoing.[65] Dr Friedensburg condemned the People's Police as only representing a minority interest and of clearly failing to act in a fair or democratic way.[66] Western commentators accused senior policemen of directing the crowd, by pointing out individual politicians as targets. Dr Suhr asked the Soviet Commandant, General Kotikov, to ban demonstrations near the City Assembly, but he received no answer.[67] During the Weimar Republic, the Reichstag had possessed an exclusion zone (*Bannmeile*), though this did not stop the Nazis from intimidating their opponents once Hitler was made Chancellor. General Kotikov demanded of Mayor Schroeder that Stumm be dismissed for trying to disrupt and disorganize the police in Berlin. Under the strain of tempestuous meetings, which often lasted long into the night, Frau Schroeder's health began to break down.

The ultimate rupture of local democracy and city government

The western press was quick to condemn the Soviet-orchestrated mob violence as an attempted 'terrorist putsch' in the city or a *Stadtstreich* (overthrow of the local government).[68] The Soviets chose to unsettle city officials, by threatening to arrest them on charges of espionage if they went into the eastern sector to perform their duties.[69] Commander Wagner stated that the crowd that had invaded the chamber constituted the 'voice of the people'. They had as much right to be in the building as the shiftless politicians.[70] For what turned out to be the last meeting of the City Assembly, on 6 September, Dr Friedensburg decided to recruit extra stewards to protect the meeting. Young members of the SPD and the CDU volunteered to help protect the Assembly building in the Soviet Sector. They were joined by fifty young, off-duty policemen from the US Sector. Friedensburg believed that, even if they were unarmed and wearing plain clothes, the policemen could be particularly useful. They wore white armbands with the word 'steward' on them.[71] *Neues Deutschland* subsequently claimed that he had smuggled them into the building with forged papers.[72] *Tägliche Rundschau* denounced them as a 'raiding party', deployed for a deliberate provocation.[73] Echoing their earlier propaganda, the Soviets naturally dubbed them the 'Black Guard'.[74] The eastern press claimed that the policemen were illegally armed with knuckledusters as well as wooden truncheons.

Strangely, Friedensburg informed the Soviets of his plans, but not the Western Allies.[75] The Soviets accused the off-duty policemen, who tried to protect the politicians, of illegally usurping authority outside their jurisdiction and made moves to arrest them as 'criminals'.[76] A standoff occurred as Allied officers tried to protect the remaining stewards, while the eastern police surrounded the building. The Soviets detained Allied representatives, who attempted to reach their men, for supposed speeding offences. *Stars and Stripes* called this a 'fantastic Soviet Blockade-within-Blockade'.[77] Some of the policemen allegedly tried to escape over a wall from the rear courtyard of the building. RIAS attempted to broadcast live from East Berlin, but the Soviets cut the transmission cable. The journalists managed to escape out of a toilet window into a waiting US jeep.[78] At this moment of high tension, the French Liaison Officer, Captain Hector Ziegelmeyer, demonstrated his mettle by pulling out his pistol to protect the stewards. He alone staved off the arrest of twenty young people. They spent the night besieged in his office.[79] Although Ziegelmeyer's bold action provided temporary refuge, the siege lasted thirty-six hours. When it ended, the US Political Adviser in Germany, Robert D. Murphy, was uncharacteristically alarmist in his report to Washington. He condemned Friedensburg's decision to deploy western plain-clothes policemen over the border as desperately foolish. He believed that the People's Police were taking the 'poor devils' off to their 'death or worse'.[80] Viewing it as dangerous and completely pointless, the British Commandant, General Otway Herbert, was furious at Friedensburg's unauthorized action.[81] He berated the Deputy Mayor for having taken unilateral action without consulting the Western Allies.[82] For his part, the French Commandant, Jean Ganeval, tried to negotiate the stewards' release and safe passage back to the western sectors. To his chagrin and fury, both Kotikov and Sokolovsky broke their personal promises to him.[83] The Soviets subsequently claimed that they had found his officers to be in a state of intoxication. In this condition, they posed a danger for the health and safety of the building located in the Soviet Sector.[84] Kotikov accused the western policemen of attacking peaceful workers. For his part, the unappointed Mayor, Ernst Reuter, criticized the 'tragicomic' spectacle of cold-blooded cynicism, dressed up in sham revolutionary gestures. The systematically arranged demonstrators possessed no spark of genuine grievance.[85]

Howley stated that the policemen were 'sobbing and screaming' when the Soviets arrested them.[86] They did not know whether they would be released in a few days or if they would be shipped off forever to Siberia. In the end, all but three were released after being held for six weeks without trial. Two received six months in prison and one was sentenced to a year.[87] Twenty-one-year-old *Tagesspiegel* journalist, Wolfgang Hansske, was not so lucky. He returned to Berlin only after seven years in Siberia.[88] Henceforth, the rump City Executive, dubbed the 'splitter *Magistrat*' by the eastern press, was forced to meet in West Berlin. City Assembly leaders asked the British Commandant to be allowed to use the old Reichstag building, but, when he refused, they agreed to meet in the Technical University refectory in the British Sector.[89] The first decision the new democratic organ for West Berlin took was to confirm the removal of Markgraf as Police President. Berlin could now boast two different mayors, two competing police forces and two uncooperative bureaucracies, in addition to the dual currencies circulating in the city. The lone voice of Eastern-CDU member, Helmut Brandt, criticized the move as unnecessary. The eastern authorities later rewarded him for this demonstration of loyalty with an eight-year prison sentence.[90]

Reichstag demonstration

On 9 September 1948, the burnt-out Reichstag building provided the backdrop for hundreds of thousands of Berliners to demonstrate for freedom on the Platz der Republik. Smarting from his humiliation and public condemnation by the Western Allies, Friedensburg condemned the machinations of the 'ludicrous Markgraf police'. He claimed that the City Assembly had defended the sacred task of eventually reuniting Germany.[91] Next, the man the Soviets had vetoed as Mayor, Ernst Reuter, asked the people of the world, wherever they were, to look to his city and to express solidarity with its people. Reuter called on the world not to forget or to abandon Berlin. Standing together was the only way to defeat the combined 'powers of darkness'.[92] Translated and broadcast around the world, the speech served to highlight the plight of those on the frontline of the cold war. The speech helped to rebrand the Berliners as people suffering for democracy rather than as supporters and defenders of Nazism. Three years after the collapse of Hitler's murderously dystopian Gestapo state, the image of Germans standing up for themselves, in the name of constitutional government, was tremendously important, both politically and psychologically.

Reuter had some knowledge of the enemy he was talking about.[93] He had inside information about how the Communist machinery operated.[94] During World War One, he had fought as a soldier against Russia. After being wounded and taken prisoner in 1916, he was liberated as a result of the October Revolution. He went to Moscow and Petrograd, met Vladimir Lenin and became an active member of the Bolshevik Party. In 1918, Lenin named him the first People's Commissar of the Volga German autonomous workers' commune.[95] Lenin was pleased with his work but found Reuter a tad too independent. Reuter claimed always to have disliked the Bolshevik Commissar for the Nationalities, Joseph Stalin.[96] Returning to Germany, he briefly became Secretary for Berlin and then General Secretary of the German Communist Party (KPD), but subsequently renounced communism and returned to the SPD in 1922. He came to see social democracy and communism as completely opposed, alien political movements. The Soviets never forgave Reuter for his refusal to accept the authority of the Comintern. For his part, West Berlin's Mayor said he could not stand the fundamental lack of morality of the Moscow-dominated international Communist movement. Historian and ex-occupier Michael Balfour argues that it was the fact that Reuter was a renegade Communist 'who had seen the light' that made him so irritating for the Soviet-backed East Berlin leadership.[97] In the 1920s, he had worked in local government (mainly concerned with transport) and had been a popular Mayor of nearby Magdeburg. To escape imprisonment when Hitler came to power, he went to England and then, unusually, to Turkey.[98] However, this was not before he received injuries in a Concentration Camp. With his trademark Basque beret, Reuter emphasized his civilian, anti-Nazi credentials. He was first and foremost a democrat, but he also had shades of a demagogue. Because he knew how to play to his Berlin audience, his

Communist opponents routinely compared him unfairly to Joseph Goebbels.[99] Having met Stalin, he condemned him as having the mentality of a jumped-up Sergeant-Major. British occupation soldier Richard Brett-Smith praised Reuter's incredible shrewdness combined with no-nonsense Berlin directness. As an exceptionally gifted politician, some of his schemes had a rogue-like quality.[100] Looking back on his time in Berlin, the US Commandant, Maxwell D. Taylor, said that he could think of 'no better cold war fighter' anywhere in the western world than Ernst Reuter.[101] *Time* profiled him on their cover as the man capable of stemming the red flood. However difficult the situation got, Berliners and the Allies knew that he would not flinch or cave.

Reuter's speech, using the ruined Reichstag as a dramatic backdrop, on 9 September, managed to focus world attention on his beleaguered city. Almost single-handedly, he began to transform Berlin's image: from defeated capital of Hitler's Third Reich to the bastion of a plucky set of survivors, determined to cling on to democracy. In contrast to the image of Germans in the 'rubble films', as pathetic but complicit perpetrators-turned-victims, people around the world began to see Berliners as heroic and determined. Their steadfastness in the face of adversity served, to some extent, to redeem all Germans in the eyes of the outside world. What now seems a somewhat strained and histrionic speech fitted with the mood of the time. Reuter, who had once campaigned for people to leave the churches, had some skills as a preacher. Historian Wilfried Rott argues that he had the force and will of an Old Testament prophet. Reuter reclaimed the word 'Volk', in reference to the Berliners, at the same time as internationalizing the dilemma they faced.[102] David Barclay emphasizes how electrifying Reuter's speech was, how he managed to strike exactly the right tone.[103] American journalist Drew Middleton contrasted the atmosphere of the crowd (containing no small number from the Soviet Sector) with the dull and regimented demonstrations, which were standard in East Berlin. By speaking truth to power, Reuter channelled the immense strength of anti-Communist feeling. For non-German observers, the experience was both 'tremendous and terrifying'.[104] Fired up by Reuter's words, some young men from the crowd pulled the red flag down from the nearby Brandenburg Gate. When the crowd threw stones at a Soviet jeep, the occupants fired back. Soviet soldiers from the nearby memorial came and tried to prevent the crowd from burning the Soviet flag. Nevertheless, the angry citizens ripped it to shreds before they could reach them.[105] As they were held back by British Military Policemen, the crowd shouted, 'Russian slaves, Markgraf pigs' at the officers they condemned as craven bloodhounds.[106] The Communist authorities claimed that one of the young men was a West Berlin policeman. A British Military Police officer intervened to hold the crowd back. In his view, the mob was so worked up that they wanted to invade the Soviet Sector and 'tear the Bolshies limb from limb'.[107]

Antipathy to the SED and its Soviet bosses was at a new peak. Despite British attempts to keep the youths out of the Soviet Sector, the Soviets retaliated and opened fire on the stone-throwers. They wounded six youths and killed a sixteen-year-old, called Wolfgang Scheunemann.[108] The British encouraged the Soviets to fall back, with guarantees of their safety. With a certain amount of cynicism, not to say blatant lies, the eastern press claimed that it was the demonstrators who had shot at their police. The crowd's actions were a clear demonstration of the effects of Reuter's demagogic 'pogrom speech'.[109] Typical of their cynical propaganda, the East Germans claimed that the youths were fascists, armed with American knuckledusters.[110] Although the British Military Government banned subsequent demonstrations near the border, the fact that they had only taken the decision after Reuter's speech was presented by eastern commentators as a calculated move.[111] The Soviets sentenced five youths involved in the flag incident to twenty-five years each. The SPD considered this shameful verdict the equivalent of a death sentence. The eastern justice system commuted one sentence, however, when it was discovered that the boy's father was an SED member.[112] Referring to the incidents, General Clay said that he disliked mass demonstrations because they could 'easily become disorderly' and out of control. Nevertheless, nobody could question the people of Berlin's determination to resist.[113]

Continued cross-border cooperation

Even after the split of the police, some administrative branches continued to function for the whole city until December 1948. In spite of the dramatic scenes of division and confrontation in August and September, certain continued cross-border, four-power cooperation was unavoidable. The Allies were stuck looking after seven German war criminals in an old and crumbling prison complex in the British Sector. Along with the (more important than ever) Berlin Air Safety Centre, Spandau Prison survived as a four-power operation. Housing the seven convicted war criminals was hugely expensive and entailed armed Soviet guards turning up in the British Sector one month in every four (and flying the red flag in the heart of West Berlin). This meant regular traffic of Soviet guards to and from the prison. Clashes could easily occur on any of the many journeys to and from the eastern sector. The handover ceremonies had become elaborate and spectacular. While the band played, the new guard unit saluted and presented arms to its predecessor.[114]

When the Federal Republic of Germany was formed, in May 1949, West Berlin was associated with, but not part of, it, because of Greater Berlin's continued special quadripartite occupation status. Were they to alter West Berlin's constitutional position in relation to the Federal Republic then the Allies risked undermining their continued right to be in Berlin. Unbroken occupation depended on the fiction of lingering four-power authority.[115] The Western Allies thereby persisted in exercising their rights and fulfilling their obligations, in accordance with quadripartite rule, while condemning unilateral actions by the Soviets.[116] Berlin specialist Wolfgang Ribbe argues that it was the French who were the chief opponents of Berlin's incorporation in the Federal Republic.[117] West Berlin's anomalous status meant that federal laws could come into force only if they were enacted as special Berlin cover laws.[118] To maintain legal parity and close links with the Federal Republic, the City Assembly (later the Senate) ensured that this was accomplished in nearly every case.[119] However, the rump Allied *Kommandatura* retained overall supervision of the Berlin police, because of the special circumstances and delicate security situation in Berlin.[120]

Conclusion

Although in some ways four-power government was a stopgap solution, all four powers had initially had their own ideas about how to improve German government, the economy, society and education. In the beginning, these goals had overlapped with a genuine concern to reform policing. The reformist endeavour was only reluctantly abandoned with the onset of the cold war. As the chapter showed, with increased tension, the police found themselves on the frontlines of a new and artificial geopolitical conflict. The juxtaposition and proximity of the sectors thwarted but did not erase attempts to establish separate political orders within the city. In the new situation of division, although both sides deployed police violence on people challenging their rule, neither side could fully claim that such violence was legitimate. Matters came to a head in the spring of 1948 with the issue of currency reform. The Americans presented this as a straightforward economic management matter. They blamed the Soviets for flooding Germany with occupation currency in 1945 and said that they refused to make the same mistake again. The Soviets did not understand why the Western Allies were ganging up against them or why they were refusing to address the matter in an equitable, four-power fashion. Nevertheless, their own aggressive actions alienated the three western powers and turned them away from any continued cooperation. The West pressed ahead with currency reform and the Soviets responded with the Blockade of Berlin. In the context of the onset of the cold war, unitary policing became impossible. The police force had drifted apart, caught between the irreconcilable claims of a Soviet-dominated Presidium and semi-autonomous western sector police chiefs.

The difficult political and public order situation at the border created fresh challenges for the recently divided police force. Both sides accused the other of orchestrating baying mobs to undermine unity, democracy and order. The Western Allies and their Soviet counterparts swung between encouraging and deploring certain transgressions. Following the split of city government, western democrats viewed the Communists as shameless totalitarians, while the latter argued that criminality was inherent in capitalism. Caught in such a stark dichotomy, an independent, neutral position was no longer possible. This chapter explains how ideological conflict enabled border-control guards to begin treating ordinary German border-crossers as if they were enemies, a good thirteen years before the Berlin Wall. Because of the eastern police's refusal to exercise authority around the Town Hall, the western powers feared an insurrection. Nevertheless, the violent conspiracy or insurgency, that the sporadic violence seemed to presage, did not materialize.

Although it quickly became the defining feature of relations, such a scenario had been unimaginable to contemporaries (Allied and German) only three years earlier. Nobody could have foreseen that a dangerous international frontier would run through the heart of the city. If the metropolis on the Spree had previously possessed one personality, it became increasingly split: previously united communities, families and friendship networks were rent asunder by an invisible, but potentially deadly, border. In coping with a much more fraught, but fluid, situation, the police in West Berlin increasingly turned to two-way radio technology. This greatly improved their response time and, with it, their ability to exert control over their scattered territory. Following the splitting of the police force, the 'interregnum period' of 'platonic' sector boundaries was definitively over.[121] The allegation that the Americans were mistreating and 'terrorizing' citizens in the western sectors of the city was clearly a counter-charge to the allegations of Soviet kidnappings.[122] The cold war was now in full swing. In the months following the division of the police, the border became the centre of focus for political provocations, but also for ongoing black-market activity. Unilateral attempts to police illegal trading seemed doomed to failure. The combination of large, angry crowds and Soviet-Sector gunfire created a very dangerous situation, with ordinary Berliners injured and killed. Only the bravery and cool headedness of individual Allied Military Policemen prevented the situation from degenerating and becoming much worse. The *Reichstag* demonstration of 9 September 1948 was a potent symbol of Berliners' inextinguishable desire for democracy. However, fears for security led the British Commandant to ban further demonstrations near the border.

Discursively, each side accused the other of holding the truncheon of authority in one hand and the cudgel of mob rule in the other. If Potsdamer Platz, the meeting point of three sectors, represented one hotspot, another was the City Assembly building in the Parochialstrasse. The Communists had no qualms about disrupting a local democracy weighted against them. Their interference continued for two months and ultimately destroyed the possibility of the *Magistrat* continuing to meet in East Berlin. Markgraf's police officers looked on, as the Soviets brought demonstrators to disrupt the work of the City Assembly and Executive. Between summer and autumn 1948, the security situation deteriorated substantially as both bodies continued to try and meet in East Berlin. Western policemen were at the forefront of attempts to preserve local democracy and found themselves arrested by the Soviets, while trying to defend the Town Hall from Communist mobs. From now on, Berlin had two separate governments that were inimical to each other. Physically attacking 'legislative members' inside the chamber showed a deep-seated contempt for democracy. Diminutive but feisty Jeanette Wolff refused to be beaten or kicked into submission: 'Those who summoned the mob to serve them today have lost their last bit of respect among Berlin's people. We shall not stumble, and we shall not fall. This is not Prague, this is Berlin.'[123]

To the straight-talking, sharp-shooting Howley, 'the Reds' were using 'goon squads' to intimidate and harass Social Democrats right on the steps of City Hall.[124] Mayor Friedensburg's ill-judged attempt to deploy western policemen outside their sectors was folly in the extreme. It could easily have had catastrophic consequences for those concerned. The Soviets had no hesitation about handing down twenty-five-year sentences for attacks on the symbols of their rule. Faced with overt intimidation and extra-parliamentary pressure, non-Communist politicians and council workers were henceforth forced to meet in the western sectors. Mayor Ernst Reuter managed to articulate the hopes and fears of hundreds of thousands of his fellow citizens, in a speech entitled 'Look at This City'. He argued that the handcuffs used to cart away the imprisoned police stewards, after Kotikov broke his word to Ganeval and arrested them, was a clear and unambiguous symbol of eastern tyranny.[125]

Notes

1 Steege stresses the unsettling violence of much of the liminality, as experienced on streets and squares near the border, especially during the UGO strike, against the *Reichsbahn* leadership, of May 1949. Paul Steege, *Black Market, Cold War: Everyday Life in Berlin, 1946-1949* (Cambridge: Cambridge University Press, 2007), 247. Cf. Mark Fenemore, *Fighting the Cold War in Post-Blockade, Pre-Wall Berlin: Behind Enemy Lines* (London: Routledge, 2019), 66-7.
2 'Head of Chancery: Draft Intel: Legal basis of occupation of Berlin', 21 January 1955, UK National Archives, FO 1008/327.
3 '"Black Guards" in US Sector: Armed Civilians', (1947–1948), UK National Archives, FO 1012/738.
4 'A Russian View of American Zone', *Manchester Guardian*, 27 December 1947.
5 'Thema des Tages', *Tägliche Rundschau*, 13 March 1948.
6 'Kotikow beschuldigt Westmächte. Vierstündige Angriffe des Sowjetvertreters in der Alliierten Kommandantur', *Telegraf*, 24 April 48.
7 'Extract from the Minutes of Deputy Commandants', Meeting, 4 June 1948: Armed German Civilian Detachments in the US Sector of Berlin', UK National Archives, FO 1012/738.
8 'Extract from Minutes of the Deputy Commandants' Meeting', 7 May 1948, UK National Archives, FO 1012/738.
9 'Public Safety Branch: Armed German Civilian Detachments in the US Sector of Berlin', 26 February 1948. US National Archives, RG260, box 893.
10 Jean Edward Smith (ed.), *The Papers of Lucius D. Clay: Germany, 1945-1949* (Bloomington, IN: Indiana University Press, 1974), 2: 698-9.
11 'Magistratsmehrheit wider alle Vernunft für Doppelwährung und Zollschranken in Berlin, für Chaos, Hunger und Arbeitslosigkeit', *Neues Deutschland*, 24 June 1948.
12 'Polizei, Wechselstuben, Kontensperre', *Der Abend*, 24 August 1948.
13 'Attempts to Solve Financial Muddle in Berlin', *Manchester Guardian*, 13 July 1948.
14 *Telegraf*, 24 June 1948.
15 'La Situation à Berlin', no date, ca. 1948, Archives Diplomatiques, GMFB 1/214.
16 'Berlin Tension Grows', *Times*, 8 September 1948.
17 'Political Report No. 2', 26 June 1948, US National Archives, RG260, 390/48/27/3, Box 903.
18 SPD leaflet: 'Die Banditen von Berlin', 23 June 1948.
19 'Vereinigung der Verfolgten des Naziregimes', *Neues Deutschland*, 24 November 1946.
20 Jael Geis, 'Jeanette Wolff', Jewish Women's Archive, https://jwa.org/encyclopedia/article/wolff-jeanette (accessed 31 March 2020).
21 'VVN-Kritik am Berliner Magistrat', *Neues Deutschland*, 17 June 1948.
22 'Das war Demokratie, Berliner! Ein Nachwort zu der vorgestrigen Kundgebung in der Parochialstraße', *Neues Deutschland*, 25 June 1948.
23 Steege, *Black Market*, 196–7, 200.
24 'Reds Again Invade Berlin City Hall; Regime May Move', *Stars and Stripes*, 28 August 1948.
25 Präsidium der Volkspolizei (ed.), *Zeittafel zur Geschichte der Volkspolizei Berlin 1945-1961* (East Berlin: Präsidium der Volkspolizei, 1985).
26 Stuart Hall et al., *Policing the Crisis: Mugging, the State and Law and Order*, 2nd edn. (Basingstoke: Palgrave Macmillan, 2013), 235, 206, 70.

27 In December 1948, its members voted to change the LDP's name to the Free Democratic Party (FDP) to distinguish itself more clearly from the party of the same name in the Soviet Zone.
28 'Das ist Demokratie! Die Werktätigen greifen ein', *Neues Deutschland*, 24 June 1948.
29 'Berlins Bevölkerung ist empört! Der Verlauf der gestrigen Stadtverordnetensitzung. Die Vernunft blieb in der Minderheit', *Neues Deutschland*, 24 June 1948.
30 'Der dokumentarische Beweis für die Spionagetätigkeit der SPD', *Neues Deutschland*, 29 June 1948.
31 'Berlins Bevölkerung ist empört!'
32 'Lange Gesichter am Schwarzen Markt', *Neues Deutschland*, 25 July 1948.
33 'Täglich 61 000 Hamsterer', *Tägliche Rundschau*, 8 October 1948.
34 'Immer wieder Razzien', *Neues Deutschland*, 12 August 1948.
35 'Menschen rennen, Hunde bellen. Sonntägliches Treiben an der Dreisektoren-Ecke', *Der Abend*, 24 August 1948.
36 'Schwarzmärkte fliegen auf. Ununterbrochener Einsatz der Polizei – Schieber retten sich in die Westsektoren', *Tägliche Rundschau*, 11 August 1948.
37 'Schwarze Märtyrer', *Neues Deutschland*, 14 August 1948.
38 'Schwarzmarkt aus der Vogelperspektive', *Neues Deutschland*, 14 August 1948.
39 'Auf der Jagd nach Preissündern und Schwarzhändlern', *Tribüne*, 18 August 1948.
40 'Stumm-Polizei sieht untätig zu. Schwarzmarkthyänen fühlen sich in guter Obhut', *Berliner Zeitung*, 22 August 1948.
41 'Folge der Polizeispaltung', *National-Zeitung*, 20 August 1948; 'Kriminelle Polizeiführer', *Tagesspiegel*, 21 August 1948.
42 'So kam es zu der Schießerei', *Der Abend*, 20 August 1948.
43 Steege, *Black market*, 193.
44 'Anschlag auf die Sicherheit Berlins. Schwarzhändler und Nazibanden überfallen Polizei. Zwölf Polizisten verletzt', *Berliner Zeitung*, 20 August 1948.
45 'Die Vorbereitungen', *Neues Deutschland*, 21 August 1948. 'Schwarze Garde organisiert Überfall: MP und Stumm-Abteilungen schützen Schwarzhändler und ehemalige SS', *Vorwärts*, 20 August 1948.
46 Ruth Andreas-Friedrich, *Battleground Berlin: Diaries 1945-1948*, trans. Anna Boerresen (New York: Paragon, 1990), 240.
47 Major Bond said that, prior to the incidents on Potsdamer Platz, Soviet Military Police had made an incursion into Kreuzberg. 'Reds "Invade" U.S. Berlin Sector Twice', *The Daily Illini*, 13 August 1948.
48 'Warnschüsse? – Warnschüsse!', *Der Abend*, 20 August 1948.
49 'Faschistische Provokation am Potsdamer Platz', *Neues Deutschland*, 20 August 1948.
50 'Losgelassene Markgraf-Polizei. Es wird scharf geschossen – "Faschistische Provokation"', *Der Kurier*, 20 August 1948.
51 'Dreiländer-Platz', *Der Tag*, 27 April 1948.
52 'Russian Pressure on Berlin', *Times*, 26 August 1948.
53 'Schwarze Garde'.
54 '"Kriminelle Polizeiführer". Howley über die Zwischenfälle am Potsdamer Platz', *Tagesspiegel*, 21 August 1948.
55 Steinborn and Krüger accuse Howley of defending the black marketeers as if they were political resisters. Norbert Steinborn and Hilmar Krüger, *Die Berliner Polizei 1945 bis 1992: von der Militärreserve im Kalten Krieg auf dem Weg zur bürgernahen Polizei?* (Berlin: Arno Spitz, 1993), 82.

56 'Polizei, Wechselstuben, Kontensperre. Der Magistrat zu Berliner Probleme', *Der Abend*, 24 August 1948.
57 'Ein neuer Zwischenfall', *Sozialdemokrat*, 24 August 1948; 'Neue Entführung am Potsdamer Platz', *Telegraf*, 24 August 1948.
58 'Westpolizisten freigelassen', *Tägliche Rundschau*, 27 August 1948.
59 'Stacheldraht am Potsdamer Platz – zum Schutz der Schieber und Schwarzhändler', *Nacht-Express*, 23 August 1948.
60 'Ruhe und Ordnung', *Telegraf*, 25 August 1948.
61 Murphy to the Secretary of State, 30 November 1948, United States Department of State, *Foreign Relations of the United States (FRUS), 1948*, vol. 2, *Germany and Austria* (Washington, DC: United States Government Printing Office, 1973), 1275.
62 'Berlin Councillors Challenge Reds', *Daily Mail*, 27 August 1948.
63 'Wilder Chauvinismus', *Neues Deutschland*, 7 September 1948.
64 Andreas-Friedrich, *Battleground Berlin*, 225.
65 'Red coup we can't stop in Berlin', *Daily Mail*, 30 August 1948.
66 'Intimidation in Berlin. Communist Mob's Tactics', *Times*, 28 August 1948.
67 'L'Assemblée Municipale se transportera-t-elle dans le secteur occidental?', *Le Monde*, 30 August 1948.
68 'Stadtstreich', *Der Spiegel*, 4 December 1948.
69 Major-General E. O. Herbert, 'The Cold War in Berlin', *Journal of the Royal United Service Insitution* XCIV, 574 (1949): 165–77, 171.
70 'Political Report No. 14', 5, 11 September 1948, US National Archives, RG260, 390/48/27/3, Box 903.
71 Ferdinand Friedensburg, *Es ging um Deutschlands Einheit: Rückschau eines Berliners auf die Jahre nach 1945* (West Berlin: Haude and Spenersche, 1971), 268.
72 'Illegal im Stadthaus', *Neues Deutschland*, 8 September 1948.
73 'Befohlene Stadthausprovokation', *Tägliche Rundschau*, 8 September 1948.
74 Gerhard Keiderling, *Berlin 1945-1986: Geschichte der Hauptstadt der DDR* (East Berlin: Dietz, 1987), 291. Here, Keiderling's view does not seem to have changed much in spite of the *Wende*. Although he has access to new sources, not least Friedenburg's papers, he persists with the argument that the stewards were violent members of the Black Guard. Gerhard Keiderling, *Um Deutschlands Einheit: Ferdinand Friedensburg und der Kalte Krieg in Berlin 1945-1952* (Cologne: Böhlau, 2009), 305.
75 'Dr Friedensburg plant Rollkommandos im Stadthaus', *Tägliche Rundschau*, 31 August 1948. 'Die "Rollkommandos" der Stadtverwaltung bereits ausgesucht', *Tägliche Rundschau*, 5 September 1948.
76 'Die Stadtverordneten hätten tagen können', *Neues Deutschland*, 7 September 1948.
77 'Berlin Police Kidnapping', *Stars and Stripes*, 9 September 1948.
78 Michael Derenburg, *Streifzüge durch vier RIAS-Jahrzehnte: Anfänge und Wandlungen eines Rundfunksenders* (Berlin: Presse- und Informationsamt des Landes Berlin, 1986), 30. Keiderling, *Um Deutschlands Einheit*, 307.
79 Friedensburg, *Es ging um Deutschlands Einheit*, 268.
80 Murphy to the Secretary of State, 7 September 1948, *FRUS, 1948*, 2: 1132–4, 1134.
81 'Berlin Tension Grows'.
82 Friedensburg, *Es ging um Deutschlands Einheit*, 269. 'Rüge für Dr. Friedensburg', *Berliner Zeitung*, 8 September 1948.
83 'Gefährliche Komödie im Stadthaus', *Der Kurier*, 8 September 1948.
84 Frank L. Howley, *Berlin Command* (New York: G. P. Putnam's Sons, 1950), 216–17.

85 Wilfried Rott, *Die Insel: Eine Geschichte West-Berlins 1948-1990* (Munich: C. H. Beck, 2009), 14.
86 Howley, *Berlin Command*, 216.
87 'Public Safety, July 1945 to 31 August 1949', 5, US National Archives, RG260, 390/48/27/2, Box 893.
88 'Zeitung im Visier der Stasi', *Tagesspiegel*, 18 March 2015.
89 Murphy to the Secretary of State, 7 September 1948, *FRUS, 1948*, 2: 1131.
90 Rott, *Die Insel*, 13–14.
91 *Telegraf* (10 September 1948). Even after these events, Friedensburg sought to avoid splitting Berlin's administration further and continued to attend *Magistrat* meetings until November.
92 Ernst Reuter, 'Schaut auf diese Stadt', 9 September 1948, http://archiv.spd-berlin.de/geschichte/personen/l-z/reuter-ernst/ernst-reuter-schaut-auf-diese-stadt/ (accessed 15 October 2013).
93 David E. Barclay, *Schaut auf diese Stadt: der unbekannte Ernst Reuter* (Berlin: Siedler, 2000), 65f.
94 Taylor Interview, 14 May 1981, Landesarchiv Berlin, B Rep. 037, Nr. 96.
95 Encyclopaedia Britannica.
96 Kees Van Hoek, 'Lord Mayor Reuter of Berlin', *The Contemporary Review* 181 (1952): 145–8, 146.
97 Michael Balfour and John Mair, *Four-Power Control in Germany and Austria, 1945-1946* (London: Oxford University Press, 1956), 209.
98 Encyclopaedia Britannica.
99 Anthony Read and David Fisher, *Berlin: The Biography of a City* (London: Pimlico, 1994), 259.
100 Richard Brett-Smith, *Berlin '45: The Grey City* (London: Macmillan, 1966), 81.
101 Taylor Interview, 5.
102 Rott, *Die Insel*, 16.
103 Barclay, *Schaut auf diese Stadt*, 194.
104 Drew Middleton, *The Struggle for Germany* (Indianapolis, IN: Bobbs-Merrill, 1949), 120.
105 'Blut in den Straßen Berlins. Zusammenstöße am Brandenburger Tor. Rote Fahne heruntergerissen', *Der Kurier*, 10 September 1948.
106 Zwischenbericht: 'Weitere Ermittlungen bezüglich der Vorkommnisse am Brandenburger Tor und nähere Umgebung in den Abendstunden des 9.9.1948', 13 September 1948, Landesarchiv Berlin, C Rep 303-09, Nr. 2, 122f.
107 Middleton, *The Struggle for Germany*, 120.
108 'Red Troops Open Fire. Germans seize Russian flag', *Daily Mail*, 10 September 1948.
109 'Verhetzte Demonstranten schießen auf Polizei', *Die Tribüne*, 10 September 1948. 'Faschistische Pogromreden der Reuter und Neumann', *Tägliche Rundschau*, 24 September 1948.
110 'Des soldats russes tirent sur la foule. Le drapeau soviétique est arraché de la porte de Brandenbourg', *Le Monde*, 11 September 1948.
111 'Faschistische Zusammenrottung an der Sektorengrenze', *Tägliche Rundschau*, 10 September 1948.
112 'Les Russes condamnent à vingt-cinq ans de travaux forcés cinq manifestants allemands', *Le Monde*, 15 September 1948. SPD: 'In den Tod geschickt', (leaflet, 9 September 1948).
113 Lucius D. Clay, *Decision in Germany* (Westport, CT: Greenwood, 1970), 377–8.

114 Neal Ascherson, 'The Media Did It', *London Review of Books* 29, no. 12 (21 June 2007). https://www.lrb.co.uk/the-paper/v29/n12/neal-ascherson/the-media-did-it.
115 'Declaration by the three Western powers, 26 May 1952' as cited by G. W. S. Robinson, 'West Berlin: The Geography of an Exclave', *Geographical Review* 43, no. 4 (1953): 542, note 5.
116 Walter Krumholz, *Berlin-ABC* (West Berlin: Verlag Documentation, 1969), 698. C. D. Lush, 'The Relationship between Berlin and the Federal Republic of Germany', *The International and Comparative Law Quarterly* 14, no. 3 (1965): 743.
117 Wolfgang Ribbe, *Berlin 1945-2000* (Berlin: Berliner Wissenschaftsverlag, 2002), 88.
118 Robert Spencer, 'The Berlin Dilemma', in *The Shaping of Postwar Germany*, ed. Edgar McInnis, Richard Hiscocks and Robert Spencer (New York: Frederick A. Praeger, 1960), 131.
119 Robinson, 'West Berlin', 543.
120 'Statement of Principles governing the relationship between the Allied *Kommandatura* and Greater Berlin', 14 May 1949.
121 Wolfgang Schivelbusch, *In a Cold Crater: Cultural and Intellectual Life in Berlin, 1945-1948*, trans. Kelly Barry (Berkeley, CA: University of California Press, 1998), 80, ix.
122 'Berlin Police Chief Flees Russians', *Stars and Stripes*, 28 April 1948.
123 Emmet Hughes, 'Berlin under Siege', *Life*, 19 July 1948.
124 Howley, *Berlin Command*, 150.
125 Ernst Reuters Rede am 9. September 1948 vor dem Reichstag', https://www.berlin.de/berlin-im-ueberblick/geschichte/historische-reden/ernstreuterrede.de.html (accessed 24 June 2015).

8

The Soviet Blockade and Allied Airlift

West Berlin's continued separate existence depended to a large extent on reliable supplies of food and fuel. However, the western occupiers' rights of access were limited by the agreements they had made with the Soviets in the first weeks and months of the occupation. They had never been free and unfettered but had functioned adequately in the two and a half years since joint occupation. Despite the increasing tensions, the Western Allies pressed ahead with the application of the new currency to the western sectors. On 24 June 1948, gambling that the Western Allies would be forced to abandon their sectors, the Soviets cut ground access to the city. The Blockade was in large part self-inflicted. What triggered Stalin's angry move was the Western Allies' decision to further the creation of a West German state by means of currency reform.[1] In the eyes of General Clay, such a move was long overdue. The failure to create a secure currency was causing overwhelming and ongoing economic chaos.[2] The western powers could neither allow the Soviets to control the economy of West Berlin nor permit them to undermine the economic recovery of the western zones. The political implications to any change in monetary policy were huge. As Mayor Ernst Reuter had argued, 'Whoever controls the currency wields the power.'[3]

With hindsight, both sides blamed the other for causing the division of Germany. While blaming the Western Allies for fostering a separate West German government, the Soviets pushed through with a Sovietization in their Zone. Although offering to consult with his Soviet Allies on four-power matters affecting Germany as a whole, General Clay continued to pursue both West German state formation and currency reform. Fearing that a resurgent West Germany could become part of an anti-Soviet Bloc, Stalin began to rattle his sabre.[4] Although blamed by traditionalist cold-war historiography, the Soviets saw their response as primarily defensive. For them, it was the currency reform that constituted an overtly hostile act, in breach of the Potsdam Agreement. Fearing that it would be the prelude to the creation of a disciplined, well-armed and effective West German army, the Soviets were desperate to prevent the creation of a separate West German state. While they could do little to alter developments in West Germany, they could use controls on access to West Berlin to put pressure on the British and Americans at this highly sensitive pinch point. Hitherto, shipping the tens of thousands of tons of supplies West Berlin needed every week had depended on Soviet cooperation. With hindsight, by not regulating access in sufficient detail early on, it seemed that the Western Allies had needlessly put their heads into a noose. In not having insisted upon specific means of ingress, the postwar

British and American negotiators had shown extraordinary negligence. Thinking that the occupation would be short-lived and nearing the end of his own life, President Roosevelt did not kick up an undue fuss about access to Berlin. US negotiator Philip E. Mosely later claimed that when asked about access, the Soviet representative, Fedor T. Gusev, had promised the other Allies that 'of course' they would have free transit to and from Berlin.[5]

A new currency was desperately needed because inflation was rampant, and the old money was worthless.[6] General Clay blamed the Soviets for having misused 'the military currency plates' granted to them immediately after World War Two. In his view, they had 'glutted the country' with worthless banknotes.[7] As the Anglo-Americans worked on a new currency behind the scenes, speculation about what might happen led to panic buying among the population. Prices went up, as black-market traders withdrew their commodities, in the expectation of soon getting hard currency for them.[8] When the other Allies pressed ahead with their currency preparations, in mid-June 1948, the Soviets tried to block the introduction of Westmarks to the area of Greater Berlin. Seeing capitalism as rapacious and invasive, in no way could they envisage allowing two competing currencies to exist in Berlin. They saw the introduction of a new currency as a systematic attempt to plunder the Soviet Zone of valuable resources. The Soviets feared that a unilateral currency reform by the western powers would lead Berliners to dump large quantities of their worthless old Reichsmarks in their Zone.[9] The Soviets now claimed that West Berlin lay within their Zone and that this gave them sole responsibility for introducing any new Berlin currency. Marshal Sokolovsky argued that currency arrangements had been agreed jointly by the four powers and could be altered or amended only by joint quadripartite action. Nevertheless, Soviet claims to be authorized to decide monetary matters for the whole of Greater Berlin were tenuous at best. On June 21, in a letter to Sokolovsky, General Clay admitted that the introduction of another currency into Berlin would cause serious 'economic problems'. Nevertheless, his offer to hold bilateral talks to settle the issue through negotiation was partly disingenuous.[10]

Neither side expressed a particular measure of good faith or understanding. While they held the other Allies up in fruitless negotiations, the Soviets moved to pre-empt their opponents by introducing their own new currency to their Zone and to the whole of Berlin.[11] Despite the increasingly unbridgeable ideological chasm developing within the city, the Soviets insisted that their currency reform applied to all four sectors of Berlin. Although the Soviets had had plenty of time to plan their currency reform, the actual result was slapdash. The new Eastmark was just the old Reichsmark with a coupon stuck onto it. Forged stickers, which transformed worthless paper into actual money, were soon selling like hot cakes on the black market.[12] Dismissing the Soviet currency reform as rushed and slipshod, the Western Allies refused to accept Eastmarks as the sole currency, arguing that this would have meant a tacit acknowledgement of Soviet claims to sovereignty over the whole of Berlin.[13] The French had been disinclined to take part in the creation of a single currency, uniting the western sectors with the western zones.[14] Nevertheless, at the last moment, they abandoned their opposition and joined the other Allies with only minimal reluctance.

Soviet Blockade of West Berlin

Immediately after the western currency reform was extended to the western sectors, on 24 June 1948, the Soviets thus imposed a Blockade on West Berlin, claiming that they had to protect the Soviet Zone economy against unilateral 'illegal' actions by the western powers.[15] As well as cutting off electricity to the western sectors, they blocked rail, road and canal traffic, arguing that this was necessitated by ill-defined 'technical difficulties'. Sokolovsky said that the technical difficulties would continue until the Western Allies abandoned their plans for a separate West German government.[16] The Blockade was the culmination of the pinprick warfare launched in the spring. The tit-for-tat battle led to a severing of infrastructural pipes, cables and lines at the border. West Berlin only had food and fuel for a month and a half. Without immediate funding, the city would have remained without power, and thereby fully at the mercy of the Soviets. As the US Political Adviser in Germany, Robert D. Murphy put it, the position of the Western Allies was 'delicate and difficult'. Any retreat or withdrawal would cause grave psychological shockwaves. Given how fragile the overall European situation was, events in Berlin could have a major knock-on effect.[17] In the view of democratic leaders, were the Allies to abandon Berlin then they risked losing the rest of Western Europe.[18] The British Commandant, Major-General Otway Herbert, viewed the Soviet goal as being to discredit the Western Allies, in the eyes of the Germans, by making them look 'weak and feeble'.[19] Stalin seemed convinced that he could provoke a major crisis and impasse for the capitalist system. Believing that Berlin was the point where, if he poked hard enough, he could tear the Western Alliance 'apart at the seams', he attacked western access routes.[20] He sought to squeeze further concessions from the Western Allies, by placing intolerable pressure on the population of West Berlin. Faced with such prevarication, Clay opted for intransigence and dug his heels in. Convinced that if Berlin fell the whole of Western Germany would be next, he now argued that saving Western Europe from communism meant refusing to budge in Berlin.[21] An unstoppable force met an immovable object. To his chagrin, 'Clay was the only four-star general in the US military who had never commanded a combat unit'.[22] In many ways, the Blockade was his blooding. Iron-willed and unequivocal, Clay was quite willing to risk censure if he felt that he was in the right. Having initially tried to work with his Soviet counterparts, he now became their implacable opponent. Together with his irascible junior, Howley, the West Point graduate found it easy to adopt the guise of a cold warrior.

There is evidence that the British and French governments were not entirely behind General Clay and his belligerent and provocative stance in June 1948. Despite losing their obstructive, neutralist position, the French were more worried about the impact of the developing cold-war rift on French interests overseas. They were already mired in the Indochina War against Ho Chi Minh. For his part, the British Military Governor, Sir Brian Robertson, had orders from London not to worsen relations with the Soviets. In his more intense moments of blustering rage, Clay had to be restrained from dispatching armed convoys to break through the Soviet Blockade.[23] His suggestion of probes by an armed advance party, with bridging equipment, greatly alarmed his own government in Washington, as well as those in Paris and London. Clay's resolute stance had the advantage of being unambiguously firm, but as Robertson pointed out to him in no uncertain terms, such a rash action would mean certain war.[24] In the end, Clay's personality made the Airlift possible; his understanding of logistics and ability to deploy efficient experts made it a tremendous success.

Realist historian Vojtech Mastny argues that it was the Soviets' lack of desire to negotiate which caused the rupture; they repeatedly aggravated the situation while ignoring the opportunities to reduce tension. Stalin was so confident that the Western Allies would be forced into a humiliating climb-down, that he neglected to include the air corridors in the Blockade.[25] His advisers in Germany supported his overly optimistic view, by arguing that an Airlift would prove far too expensive to carry out. The Soviets had already pre-emptively left the Allied *Kommandatura*; they were effectively abandoning the fiction of quadripartite government and leaving the West Berliners to fend for themselves. Although rupture had been in the air for months, when the Soviets took decisive action, the US government was manifestly ill-prepared. Both the Blockade and the Airlift were hastily improvised, without careful planning in advance. There is little documentary evidence of Soviet preparations. Everything suggests that the Blockade was cobbled together at short notice. Stalin was the driving force, and he appears to have taken his decision without careful forethought or planning.

New York Times columnist Arthur Krock was unsympathetic for the situation the Western Allies found themselves in. He suggested that they only had themselves to blame. They had painted themselves into a corner, by not ensuring adequate land corridors from their zones to West Berlin. He argued that Americans were expected to be naive (because of their long period of international isolation), but even the British and the French – who were supposedly highly adept at handling diplomatic negotiations with tricky Asian despotisms – had failed to see what the Soviets would do. Krock concluded that the Western Allies had tried to play 'sandlot baseball' against a team from the big league. Too much admiration for Soviet fortitude and sacrifices led them to neglect the need for precision. A lack of exactness left an open goal that led straight to the Soviet Blockade of Berlin.[26] As a result, they were now entirely cut off. It was easy, with hindsight, to criticize the Western Allies' lack of foresight and prevision. However, everyone – from Yalta through to Potsdam – had assumed that the Soviets would supply West Berlin with food, as usual, from the surrounding agricultural region. Marshal Georgy Zhukov had completely confounded his interlocutors, on 29 June 1945, by insisting that the Western Allies feed West Berlin, without granting them guaranteed access routes. As early as December 1945, the editors of *Cosmopolitan* argued that 'The Russian, like any good horse trader, asks for more than he expects to get. If you give it to him right off, it disconcerts him – and he secretly despises you for being too easy'.[27] Zhukov does seem to have been surprised that Clay caved so easily.

General Clay believed that he had negotiated a gentleman's agreement with Zhukov regarding Allied rights of access and transportation to Berlin, but frustratingly he had nothing in writing to show for his negotiations.[28] Revisionist historian Carolyn Eisenberg blames Clay for not having had the foresight to get Zhukov to agree to permanent and unequivocal rights of access.[29] With hindsight, it is easy to heap the blame on Clay, but failure to guarantee access was part of a wider failing on the part of the American and British political, diplomatic and military establishments, from the Prime Minister and President down.[30] Between 1944 and 1946 there had been several opportunities to discuss access to Berlin, but no written agreement was reached. It was not Clay's fault that the details of the occupation of Berlin were not discussed until the arrival of the Allies in Berlin was imminent.[31] Clay claimed that American diplomats had not pressed the issue or secured an agreement in writing because they feared hampering the creation of a cordial 'mutual understanding' with the Soviets.[32] In other words, in an effort not to antagonize the Soviets, the Allies had made access to Berlin dependent on maintaining goodwill on the part of their interlocutors. For his part, Clay did not want to reduce his options; he did not want to bind himself to anything less than the right of absolute and unfettered access. Preoccupied with feeding the starving city, as well as getting on with their Soviet Allies, the Western Allies did not want to limit themselves to a few, prescribed routes when, in theory, there were multiple routes to and from the former German capital.

With hindsight, President Truman did not think that it would have made much difference to the Soviet leadership whether his administration had obtained an 'agreement in writing' or not.[33] Ignoring the Yalta and Potsdam Agreements, in 1948 the Soviets now claimed that Berlin lay in the centre of the Soviet Zone and was an integral part of that Zone.[34] In long, drawn-out discussions with Stalin and his Foreign Minister, Vyacheslav Molotov, the three western powers insisted that their rights to be in Berlin were incontrovertible.[35] However, convinced that the Airlift would fail, Stalin and Molotov refused to compromise. They fully expected that the Western Allies would have to abandon Berlin. When the other Allies met with Marshal Sokolovsky in Berlin, he promptly ignored all the painstakingly detailed negotiations which had been undertaken in Moscow and gave every appearance of reneging on Stalin's tacit agreement to terminate the Blockade.[36]

The West Berlin press saw the Blockade as a systematic attempt to starve ordinary Berliners into submission. Naturally, western journalists put all the blame on the Soviet Union. For the British-licensed SPD newspaper *Der Telegraf*, freedom was at stake: in the face of terror, Berliners were demonstrating an 'exemplary attitude'. The whole city was 'fighting for its liberty'.[37] The French Commandant, Ganeval, esteemed that the population of Berlin's greatest wish was to 'live in freedom' and to be 'free from fear'. In desiring to 'exchange the fruits of their labour with the four zones', he presented the entire population of Berlin as freedom-loving and entrepreneurial economic liberals.[38] When his military authorities moved some of their personnel out of the city, the eastern press accused the French of wanting to flee Berlin. They presented the proud *Gallic Coq* as a cowardly chicken. Mayor Friedensburg, meanwhile, admired the French Commandant's openness and energy. Possessing the common touch, Ganeval single-handedly brought general affection for the French occupation regime, on the part of the Allies and the population of Berlin. When the situation in Berlin became extremely tense, the Buchenwald survivor retained his level-headed *sangfroid*. Compared to the Americans, he was extremely soft-spoken, careful and considered.[39] By contrast, Friedensburg found the British supposed objectivity and balance distant and opaque.[40]

The Airlift

Two days after the imposition of the Blockade, the Western Allies declared that they were staying in Berlin: come what may, they were sticking to their guns and defending their rights. In the House of Commons, British Foreign Minister Ernest Bevin refused to abandon 'those stout-hearted Berlin democrats'. There was no possibility of surrendering the city to its blackmailer.[41] In order to keep West Berlin alive, the Western Allies resorted to the untried and untested Airlift. They would bring in by air everything that a city of 2.5 million needed to survive. Historian Richard Reeves claims that the Airlift was a British idea.[42] Initially, many within the American air force feared that such an endeavour was 'doomed to failure'. The British Commandant, General Herbert, was pessimistic and predicted riots in West Berlin when people got sick of their basic rations.[43] Given what had happened from June to September, he and Robertson expected and prepared for widespread civil unrest. The Soviets could be expected to carry out abductions and sabotage in the western sectors. In Washington, the consensus of the military experts was that West Berlin's position was strategically indefensible.[44] Airlifts had not worked well during World War Two. Attempts to supply Leningrad and Stalingrad from the air had proved extremely difficult and dangerous.[45] The Airlift could easily have led to war. Clay began the undertaking 'on his own initiative, without clearance, without permission, without coordination' from Washington.[46] Truman, who was seeking re-election, decided unequivocally to remain in Berlin.

The combination of plucky resolve, technical ingenuity and a tremendous work ethic makes the Airlift a popular subject with historians in Britain and the United States as well as in Germany.[47] The slightly hokey name of 'Operation Vittles' concealed its enormous importance. It was a high-risk gamble – never having been attempted before – but in the end proved to be a tremendous logistical achievement. Transport planes were called in from all over the world. The British asked for help from Canada, Australia and New Zealand; the Americans took planes from as far away as Alaska, the Pacific and Panama.[48] The three 23-mile-wide air corridors between West Germany and Berlin were soon thick with aircraft. At first these were mainly C-47s, which by 1948 were often elderly rust buckets.[49] Even in concentrated form – like milk and egg powder or dried potato – West Berlin required 2,000 tons of food a day.[50] Although the population needed clothing, coal and medicines, precious cargo space was also given over to paper, without which West Berlin risked losing the propaganda war. Tempelhof airport demonstrated a military operation running with enormous precision. Unloading took only nine minutes; in less than twelve, planes could land, unload and take off again. The whole operation ran like clockwork in all weathers thanks to dedicated Allied pilots and relentlessly efficient German ground crew. The planes flew around the clock: journalist Egon Bahr got so used to the drone of planes flying low overhead that he only noticed it when it stopped.[51] Technically minded Germans, young and old, were impressed by the sheer scale of the operation, how it was planned down to the smallest detail, allowing it to act like an intricate, carefully oiled machine.

For William H. Tunner, the American expert in charge of improving the operation, planning and coordination were more important than dramatic gestures. The unglamorous reality was the steady erosion of water dripping relentlessly on stone. 'There's no frenzy, no flap, just the inexorable process of getting the job done.' He was more excited by graphs showing tonnage increasing and accidents going down, than by dramatic gestures popular with journalists.[52] By shaving minutes and seconds off the unloading time, they steadily increased the tonnage delivered day by day until they were operating at maximum efficiency. Tunner decided that if a plane missed its landing slot, then it would fly back to the western zones and make a second approach. This measure greatly improved safety: the chances of fully loaded, not very manoeuvrable aircraft colliding over densely populated urban areas were diminished. Nevertheless, the Airlift was still very costly in terms of lives. The RAF lost eighteen airmen; a further twenty-one civilian employees died. Thirty-one American pilots died, in addition to fifteen German civilians.[53] They gave their lives to defend West Berlin's freedom and to keep the fledgling democracy alive.

Difficulties faced by the population

The Blockade was designed to make things unpleasant for the Allies, but first and foremost it hit ordinary Berliners. They were by no means rich and had already been through several difficult winters with little food or fuel. According to Howley's account, 6,000 babies in the American Sector were immediately threatened with starvation. When Radio Berlin warned German mothers that the Americans would be unable to feed their babies, he 'fought back over the air'. Thanks to the Airlift's ability to provide formula, none of 'his' babies died.[54] This was a marked turnaround from his earlier statements. In 1945, when Allied-German relations had been more strained, he had loudly proclaimed that the only reason he was feeding Berliners was so that 'their rotten corpses' did not infect his troops.[55]

Hampered by fuel shortages, electricity was only available for four hours a day. However, it was particularly the lack of meat or oil that plagued Berliners.[56] They missed fat, as a food group, 'more than anything'. Food was tight and monotonous: people lived on 30g of tinned meat, 50g of cereal products and 5g of cheese a day. They made do with dried potatoes, eggs and milk.[57] At first, Berliners celebrated meagre mealtimes of tuna fish and dehydrated potatoes, by candlelight because of electricity blackouts. Then candles became difficult to come by and paraffin was rationed. Public transport was disrupted by the electricity shortages and shut early. In his diary, young Social Democratic politician Willy Brandt recorded the lack of heat, light and power.[58] Clay perceptively realized that the number of calories they received counted as much as concepts of democracy, in determining which side the population of Berlin would take (and, with it, which way the geopolitical domino would fall).[59] Shortages of heat and light particularly affected those from lower-income brackets with the least education.[60] The question of whether the population could hold out indefinitely on limited rations of food, fuel and electricity remained moot. Many thoughtful, responsible Germans viewed the psychological tipping point as being not far off. Further difficulties in supplying food and heat, plus growing unemployment, could cause despondency on a large scale, potentially blowing the lid off the rattling psychological pressure cooker.[61]

How long could they last without light, work or even fresh potatoes? Nevertheless, contemporary accounts emphasize a resurgence of community spirit and collective support: one family might use their allotted hour of electricity to boil the potatoes for several other households, while their neighbours cooked string beans, salvaged from an allotment.[62] Ironically, Stalin's pressure increased anti-Communist solidarity. After two months, the Airlift was such a success that General Clay was able to announce ration increases.

Diplomatic incidents

Stalin's ultimate goal seems to have been to bring the Western Allies back to the negotiating table. Offering to lift the traffic restrictions, in return for a withdrawal of western currency, the Soviet dictator stressed that the 'only real issue' he was concerned about was the formation of a separate West German government.[63] Nevertheless, as Eisenberg argues, if his goal was to halt 'the momentum toward partition', his plan spectacularly backfired.[64] Thanks to the success of the Airlift, Stalin possessed little leverage. With hindsight, Nikita Khrushchev remarked that his predecessor's attempt to prod 'the capitalist world with the tip of a bayonet' had been 'badly thought through'.[65] Stalin's aggressive move was an overt failure, and his critics needed to do little, to turn public opinion in the West against him. He had tested western mettle, and the Allies had called his bluff. If his aim had been to force them back to the negotiating table, then the Blockade only strengthened their resolve to resist him. Instead of halting the move towards the partition of Germany, Stalin's aggressive move speeded it up.

Even the insolent and audacious Soviet commanders came to experience the built-up hostility created by the Blockade. Clay ordered his Military Police officers to set up speed traps for Soviet vehicles. Their most significant scalp was Marshal Sokolovsky, who refused to stop for a jeep patrol. It radioed ahead, allowing an armoured car to intercept him. His bodyguards made the mistake of jumping out of the limousine with guns in hand. A Mexican standoff ensued, in which the Americans pointed their machine guns at Sokolovsky's stomach.[66] It was hard to mistake the six-foot-four person wearing Marshal's shoulder boards and a chest full of decorations. Nevertheless, feigning ignorance of who he was, the American Military Policemen approached the highest-ranking officer present and showed him a 'three-language card'. In Russian as well as in German, it instructed him to accompany them to the nearest control point.[67] After he had been held for an hour, an American officer deigned to identify and release him. Clay claims to have felt genuinely bad about the incident, though not enough to apologize for his men's actions.[68] Sokolovsky interpreted his rough and disrespectful treatment as a deliberate attempt to humiliate him; it was no way to treat an 'old friend'. Nevertheless, the needling continued. A mischievous Howley found out that Sokolovsky's house was supplied by a gasometer in the American Sector. Not only did he have the gas turned off, but when Sokolovsky tried to move his furniture to a new, less chilly abode, Howley's men stopped the removals truck, en route through the western sectors, and confiscated the contents.[69]

The French economy and air force were too weak for France to participate equally in the Airlift, but Ganeval announced that the French would support the joint endeavour by hastily beginning construction of Tegel airport within their Sector.[70] Constructed in autumn 1948, the facility was largely paid for by the Americans. Out-of-work Berliners, many of them women, undertook the spadework. Using crushed masonry, they constructed the much-needed runways largely by hand. Forty per cent of the construction crew was female; photographs show them barefoot in shorts. It only took them three months to build the airfield with the longest runway in Europe 'from scratch'. The Soviets refused to move their radio transmitting towers, which impeded the approach, so Ganeval had them blown up. When asked by his Soviet opposite number how he could possibly have done such a thing, Ganeval replied, tongue-in-cheek, 'With dynamite, *mon cher*'.[71] Typical for the behaviour of the Military Government, the French Commandant had taken the decision without consulting the *Magistrat* or the district mayors. In retaliation, the Soviets took back the village of Stolpe, which they had initially agreed to provide the French so they could build an airport. The villagers were naturally furious at being abandoned to the Soviet Zone.[72]

Economic consequences of the Blockade

At first, the Blockade seemed to threaten a catastrophic crash and widespread bankruptcy in the western sectors. Economically, the existence of two currencies represented an unequivocal economic disaster for West Berlin. Businesses hoarded Westmarks while using Eastmarks to pay their outgoings. The Airlift could prevent West Berliners from succumbing to starvation or frostbite, but it could not keep businesses open indefinitely, the only way to ensure workers remained employed. By summer 1949, West Berlin had built up an 800 million Westmark deficit. As many as a third of the working-age population was unemployed. There was only a limited possibility of bringing in raw materials by air, or of exporting finished goods to West Germany, so several West Berlin industries had to close. Nevertheless, the closures and layoffs were less dramatic than might have been expected.[73] In some cases, people kept their jobs, but their salaries were sharply reduced.[74] With trams and the underground not working, those West Berliners still in work faced an arduous four-hour commute on foot.

William Stivers argues that West Berlin firms tried to get round the Blockade, by exporting to the Soviet Zone. Ironically, given its presentation as a 'Hunger Blockade', both sides allowed trade between the Soviet Zone and West Berlin to continue until January 1949. Therefore, the initial counter-blockade inhibited trade between the western zones and the Soviet Zone but did not apply to West Berlin.[75] Some politicians in the West saw Berlin as a 'bottomless pit' or vortex; it sucked in resources but was unable to pay for them.[76] Workers paid with Westmarks proved more costly. Demand for the hard currency greatly outstripped supply. Those businesses still working paid only a quarter of their employees' wages in Westmarks, but increasingly service providers (chief among them cinemas and theatres) would only accept payment in the stable western currency.[77] Driven by a desire to protect cross-border commuters

(*Grenzgänger*) from ruin, the Western Allies initially insisted on 1:1 parity between the two currencies. This meant that, at first, West Berliners could use Eastmarks to pay for rent, utility bills, taxation, communication and transport.[78] However, over time, the dual currency in West Berlin had serious economic consequences. There were significant differences in the ability of different firms to pay their employees in Westmarks. Because most people paid their taxes and utility bills in Eastmarks, it was difficult to see how the Berlin local administration could afford to pay its employees in Westmarks.[79] People hoarded their Westmarks or used them to take capital out of the city. The dual currency allowance came to an end on 20 March 1949. Henceforth, the Westmark was 'sole legal tender' in the western sectors.[80]

Mayor Reuter had supported this move, seeing it as a way of tying the city closer to West Germany.[81] Ganeval agreed that banning payment in Eastmarks would bring West Berlin more into West Germany's orbit.[82] In the border areas, the separation between East and West became more visible, because of the currency differences. Shops began catering for people from one system or the other. Homogenous neighbourhoods began to cleave in two. The few remaining bus and tram lines which crossed the border had to change ticket collectors at the border, to cope with the currency difference.[83] Some black-market operators began to shift from trading in goods to trading in currencies. Zoo Station became their centre of operations. The western authorities feared that enforced indolence could undermine Berlin's precarious political stability. For their part, the East German authorities tried to undermine the sense of solidarity, by encouraging West Berliners to register for ration cards in East Berlin. This would enable them to shop in the prestigious, state-owned HO (Trading Organization) stores.[84] About 120,000 – or 5 per cent of the West Berlin population – accepted the offer. Howley condemned West Berliners who took the eastern shilling as spineless quislings and 'German backsliders'.[85] Taking Soviet bread was equated with supporting Soviet policies. For Ernst Reuter, it amounted to selling their 'birth right of freedom' for a few lousy 'days of lentil stew'.[86] Nevertheless, Steege suggests that even SED members in the western sectors were slow to sign up for eastern ration cards. Consequently, he denies that we can read into the decision to accept or reject Soviet ration cards a political outlook.[87]

Despite the real hardships they faced, the vast majority of West Berliners were very suspicious of Soviet offers to feed the entire city, fearing what this would entail. In surveys, 92 per cent of West Berliners said that the Airlift must be continued, whatever it took.[88] In the mythic, post-victory view of the Airlift, West Berliners preferred to eat dehydrated potatoes than to buy them fresh in the eastern sector. The few who did so were seen as disloyal, asocial consumers who did not deserve the rights and privileges of living in the free world. In reality, they were often poor pensioners or unemployed people.[89] Although most accounts paint the Soviets as the villains, Stivers insists that West Berliners were never really at risk of starvation. He estimates that West Berliners obtained a third of their food from the Soviet Zone during the supposed 'Hunger Blockade'.[90] One popular slogan during the Blockade was 'Rather Pom', American dehydrated potato, than '*Frau-komm*', the words Red Army rapists had used during the initial occupation of Berlin.[91] *Neues Deutschland* tried to reverse the formula by rhyming, 'Don't be lured by promises sweet. Think of all the dried potatoes you've had to eat', but they were clearly losing the propaganda war.[92] Nevertheless, West Berliners could not be expected to carry on subsisting on the bare minimum forever, without becoming resentful at their privations.

The civilian population showed tremendous bravery and fortitude. They preferred to live in the dark and in the cold rather than have the Soviets back again. They froze and went hungry in the name of democratic freedom. Generally, the Blockade increased anti-Soviet feelings rather than turning Berliners against the Western Allies.[93] The Soviets also failed to consider what damage the Allied counter-blockade (introduced on 24 June 1948) would do to the eastern-zone economy.[94] East German industries were heavily dependent on raw materials and spare parts from West Germany. Despite protests, Clay and his British colleagues blocked imports to the Soviet Zone from all Western Europe, reducing the Communist regime's capacity to remain afloat economically.[95] Separating infrastructural networks proved more difficult than abandoning four-power government. During the Blockade, the Soviets cut supplies of gas and electricity to the western sectors. Deprived of power, sewage treatment facilities could no longer function and discharged raw effluent into the rivers and lakes. This posed a major health hazard as well as upsetting the fragile balance of the ecosystem. Additionally, the Soviets could have deliberately cut off the water to and sewage from West Berlin, but chose not to, given the health implications.[96] For technical and economic as well as health reasons, separating the sewage system proved unfeasible. The methane it generated was a source of power and hard currency.

The Soviets made no attempt to block completely the transport of small quantities of food and fuel to the western sectors. Lorries were able to carry duplicate manifests. One version said that their destination was the Soviet Zone. In reality, they carried food and other goods to West Berlin.[97] Shots were fired when truck drivers tried to run the checkpoints.[98] Nevertheless, Berliners repeatedly found ways to get round the controls. They traversed ruins on the sector boundary on foot to avoid sentries. The Soviets could have made the Blockade much more stringent sooner but failed to do so because of the negative consequences. In the end, the Airlift proved to be a tremendous success. It came at great cost, but, at the height of operations, the Allies were able to transport 12,848 tonnes on a single day.[99] By its end, they had been able to build up a stockpile of five months' supplies.[100] The lifting of the Blockade provided the Western Allies with a sense of triumph. It was a small victory, and had come at great cost, but it was a victory nonetheless.

If currency reform had been the trigger, the real cause of the Blockade was progress towards the creation of a separate West German state.[101] In relation to the wider history of the cold war, Stalin's manoeuvre catastrophically backfired. Instead of bringing the West back to the negotiating table, the Blockade hastened the division of Germany. The Basic Law, the constitution of the Federal Republic adopted on 8 May 1949, allowed for a coalition government to take office in September of that year.[102] In part, the strength of West Berliners' resilience had made the Federal Republic possible. The Federal Republic's first President, Theodor Heuss, was quick to visit the 'brothers and sisters' in West Berlin, but it took Chancellor Konrad Adenauer much longer to visit the stricken city.[103] Adenauer instinctively disliked Berlin, with its outspoken Social Democratic Mayors and rival Christian Democratic politicians, and avoided visiting it if at all possible.¹⁰⁴ Nevertheless, it was the British, Americans and French who blocked Berlin's incorporation as twelfth Land of the Federal Republic. They insisted that the city remain separate, with different regulations – including those shaping defence and policing – holding sway.¹⁰⁵

The Western Allies succeeded in turning Stalin's Blockade into a propaganda triumph. The German public remembers the American pilots who bombed them no longer with explosives, but instead with candy. The shared suffering and sense of victory welded together the occupiers and the occupied. From being very ambivalent about the Germans because of their culpability and complicity in World War Two, the Western Allies came to see West Berlin as a bastion of freedom and democracy to be preserved at any cost. Once portrayed as the epicentre of evil, Berlin became a potent symbol of resistance and freedom. After the success of the Airlift, Allied withdrawal ceased to be conceivable. Convinced that any weakness would be humiliating and globally damaging for their interests, the Americans and their British and French Allies were determined to defend West Berlin. The city became the most powerful symbol of resolute defiance in the face of the Communist threat.

The end of the Blockade (May 1949)

Without consulting their officers in Berlin, US diplomats in New York negotiated an end to the Blockade.¹⁰⁶ Surprisingly, given how important the matter had been during the Blockade/Airlift, the diplomats in New York failed to set down regulations and agreements on rights of access to Berlin. On 12 May 1949, all counter-blockade restrictions placed on communications, transportation and trade were lifted.¹⁰⁷ The Soviets were not entirely to be trusted; every now and then they again threatened continued access to cross-border utilities, to flex their muscles.¹⁰⁸ But, once the Blockade was lifted, conditions returned more or less to normal (as much as cold war Berlin could ever be 'normal'). In certain areas – medical care, rubbish removal and parcel delivery – usual service was resumed.¹⁰⁹ Mayor Reuter called for West Berlin to be not just an example of freedom but also a 'show window' for prosperity. The West Berlin that emerged from the Blockade was still economically damaged. Thirty-seven per cent of the workforce were unemployed in 1950.¹¹⁰

Conclusion

The rivalry of the two German Marks provided the impetus and backdrop to the Soviet Blockade and Allied Airlift. The introduction of a new currency secured the economy of West Berlin (linking it more directly to the political and economic systems of the western zones) but upset the fragile balance of cooperation and exchange with the East. Currency reform was a crucial step towards the creation of a West German government, and, as such, it was a step that Stalin was desperate to prevent. From 24 June 1948, the ideological divide suddenly made a much more tangible and direct imposition on the lives of Berliners. Overnight, the introduction of the new currency eradicated the need for a black market and for western shopkeepers to hoard supplies. Due to the leakiness of the Blockade, with food available from both Soviet and private sources, West Berlin's population never truly faced starvation. Germany's huge military and economic potential pushed Stalin to act aggressively and to provoke the outcome he was desperate to avoid – German rearmament.[111] Ceasing cooperation with their Western Allies, the Soviets pressed forward with the political and economic integration of their Sector. Although technically a distinct political unit, East Berlin increasingly became merged with the rest of the Soviet-Occupied Zone.

The Soviets could not gain credence for their aim of achieving German unification while simultaneously strangling West Berlin. In the face of this Soviet attempt to starve them out, the Western Allies were forced to resort to the previously untried solution of an Airlift. Against all predictions, this proved to be a tremendous technological and logistical success, helping to transform relations between West Berliners and 'their' Allied occupiers (this is recognized in the German description of 'air bridge'). While developed by accident, on an ad hoc basis, the Airlift dramatically changed the balance of power in the West's favour. Allied resolve bent but crucially did not break. With hindsight, the air bridge came to symbolize the selflessness of the Western Allies. Despite occasional continued drunken attacks by their soldiers, overnight the occupiers had become full protectors. It was a supreme example of the Allies serving their own interests by selflessly catering to the needs of others. Over the chasm of the cold-war divide, the Airlift created an emotional bridge between the Western Allies and ordinary Berliners, to the detriment of four-power relations. With the Soviets in the role of despised others, the West Berliners seemed a lot more amenable to the Western Allies. At times, an impatient and restless General Clay had to be stopped from sending tanks along the motorway to break the Blockade. Nevertheless, Clay's stridency would not have been necessary if the Western Allies had insisted on explicit, watertight access rights in the beginning.

In the early cold war, West Germany's SPD leader, Kurt Schumacher, could fall back on his brave opposition to the Nazis and, from the start, made no secret of his hostility to the Western Allies. However, unlike his party leader, Mayor Reuter recognized the contribution of the Allies, particularly the Americans, in keeping West Berlin free. Historian Hélène Miard-Delacroix argues that West Berliners unquestionably saw the Americans as liberators after the Airlift.[112] Because of this international, humanitarian project, the hostility of the early days gave way to friendship and mutual respect. Whereas Mayor Friedensburg hoped it could still be a bridge to mutual understanding, Reuter unequivocally saw West Berlin as a 'bulwark' or an 'outpost'. In subsequent years, Reuter did his best to exploit West Berlin's position as a thorn in the Soviet flank.[113] CIA historian Donald Steury argues that 'the dramatic success' of the Airlift tends to obscure the extent to which Berlin's position was perilous during the summer of 1948.[114] Other historians agree that the margin for success was extremely slim.[115] The operation was successful because the technology of the time gave the Western Allies a narrow margin of advantage. Later advances in Soviet electronic warfare capabilities made another Airlift, on the same scale, much less feasible.[116] The determination and resolve shown by the Allies greatly improved Berliners' view of the continuing occupation. The Airlift made a major impact on German public opinion, in a way that a more cautious and expedient policy would not have done. After the Blockade, West Berliners could see themselves as genuine allies of the occupying powers. For RIAS reporter Gerhard Löwenthal, the Airlift represented a bridge of 'deep, humane understanding' between the Allies and their former enemy.[117] Instead of driving a wedge between the Germans and their Western Allies, the Blockade brought them together, strengthening both their emotional bonds and their sense of mutual dependency. Berliners may have been emaciated and ravaged compared to Germans in the Federal Republic, but for the first time they were fully behind the Americans. As a Soviet counter-intelligence officer was forced to admit, the Blockade had provided no strategic benefits to the Soviet side. Instead, it had done much to stir animosity among the German population.[118] With hindsight, Stalin's bullying gambit had proved to be a massive, irreparable blunder. The Soviet leader had chosen a particularly inopportune time to rattle his sabre, and thereby increase US military and Marshall Aid spending.

The consequences of the failed Blockade and the successful Airlift were far-reaching. The divided city became the overarching symbol of Germany representing the fault line of a divided continent. What began as a dual currency area ended with two separate German states. The fully psychologically weaponized cold war was now in full swing; despite the lessening of tension within the city, when the Soviets lifted their Blockade, the enmity remained palpable. In General Clay's view, hardly anyone in West Berlin dared openly to express support for communism after they had so demonstrably failed in their attempt at extortion.[119] The undaunted cold warrior claimed that it had been a ruthless and reckless attempt to use 'mass starvation' as a means of applying 'political coercion'. Henceforth, Berlin's stubborn resilience was equated with an innate love of freedom. Thanks to their shared suffering, West Berliners managed, partially, to atone for their complicity in Nazi crimes. Through sacrifice and suffering, they had managed to earn back the right to share in freedom.[120] Rather than unrepentant Nazis, the Berliners were now presented as 'heroic belt-tighteners', who had refused 'to knuckle under'.[121] Confounding Allied expectations, the Berliners had shown extraordinary tenacity and backbone. Exhausted but proud and relieved, they had refused to be bullied and cajoled by the Soviets. Psychologically, this was very important and had significant political implications. The moral courage they had demonstrated in 1948-9 had important implications for the decades to come.[122]

The Airlift allowed a reframing and reconceptualization of the relationship between occupiers and occupied. The technological and logistical feat – in defeating the Blockade and neutralizing the threat of hunger – became a very important symbol of international reconciliation. Where once capitalism had seemed rapacious and greedy, now it offered democratic salvation. The spectacle of the Allies joining together, to sacrifice themselves for their Berlin inhabitants, had an important 'redemptive power', recasting West Berliners as needy, but deserving, victims of Soviet encroachments. The Airlift (or bridge) helped to reframe ordinary Berliners as plucky, fearless democrats and the Allies as their noble, self-sacrificing liberators. The transformation of Berliners from craven former Nazis to victims of Stalinist totalitarianism was achieved by symbolically marrying 'German hunger' with 'American abundance'.[123] By choosing to go hungry, ordinary citizens became heroic foot soldiers in the new global struggle developing between East and West. By deciding which foods to eat, and which to ignore, Berliners defined their allegiance and sense of belonging. By suffering for democracy, they implicitly asked for forgiveness of their past sins. Colonel Howley felt that the Airlift taught not just the Germans and Soviets, but also the French, a useful lesson.[124] Despite a residue of stubborn Gallic pride, they finally and definitively realized that they could no longer go it alone.[125] The Blockade contributed to (and hastened) the signing of the North Atlantic Treaty in Washington on 4 April 1949. West Germany was not yet a signatory, but most of Western Europe was united in the conviction that solidarity was essential in countering Soviet aggression.

Notes

1. Roger G. Miller, *To Save a City: The Berlin Airlift 1948-1949* (Washington, DC: Air Force History and Museums Program, 1998), 18.
2. Irwin L. Collier and David H. Papell, 'About Two Marks: Refugees and the Exchange Rate Before the Berlin Wall', *American Economic Review* 78, no. 3 (1988): 531.
3. As cited by Lothar Kettenacker, *Germany Since 1945* (Oxford: Oxford University Press, 1997), 32.
4. Geoffrey Roberts, *Stalin's Wars: From World War to Cold War, 1939-1953* (New Haven, CT: Yale University Press 2006), 350, 26.
5. Neil Spitzer, 'Dividing a City', *Wilson Quarterly* 12, no. 3 (1988): 105.
6. Michael W. Wolff, *Die Währungsreform in Berlin: 1948/49* (Berlin: Walter de Gruyter, 1991), 58–9.
7. Richard D. McKinzie, 'Oral Interview with Lucius D. Clay', 16 July 1974, http://www.trumanlibrary.org/oralhist/clayl.htm (accessed 23 February 2014), 18–19.
8. 'Monatsbericht für das Amerikanische Hauptquartier für die Zeit vom 16.6. bis 15.7.1948', 22 July 1948, Landesarchiv Berlin, C Rep 303-09, Nr. 18, 436.
9. Charles E. Bohlen, *Witness to History, 1929-1969* (New York: Norton, 1973), 275.
10. Foreign Policy Studies Branch, Division of Historical Policy Research, US Department of State, 'The Berlin Crisis', no date, Truman Library, 4.
11. Murphy to the Secretary of State, 23 June 1948, United States Department of State, *Foreign Relations of the United States (FRUS), 1948*, vol. 2, *Germany and Austria* (Washington, DC: United States Government Printing Office, 1973), 913.
12. 'The Breakdown of Four-Power Rule in Berlin', *World Today*, 1 August 1948, 331.
13. Lucius D. Clay, *Decision in Germany* (Westport, CT: Greenwood, 1970), 364.
14. Erika M. Hoerning, *Zwischen den Fronten: Berliner Grenzgänger und Grenzhändler 1948-1961* (Cologne: Böhlau, 1992), 106.
15. Secretary of State to the Embassy in the United Kingdom, 9 July 1948, *FRUS, 1948*, 2: 954–956, 955, 1000.
16. Clay, *Decision in Germany*, 367.
17. Murphy to the Secretary of State, 1 April 1948, *FRUS, 1948*, 2: 885–6, 886. British Foreign Minister Ernest Bevin had a similar view. *FRUS, 1948*, 2: 925.
18. Ambassador in the United Kingdom (Douglas) to the Secretary of State, 17 July 1948, *FRUS, 1948*, 2: 967–70, 970.
19. Major-General E. O. Herbert, 'The Cold War in Berlin', *Journal of the Royal United Service Insitution* XCIV, no. 574 (1949): 168.

20 Donald P. Steury (ed.), *On the Front Lines of the Cold War: Documents on the Intelligence War in Berlin, 1946 to 1961* (Washington, DC: CIA History Staff, Center for the Study of Intelligence, 1999), 128.
21 Spitzer, 'Dividing a City', 112.
22 Wilfried Rott, *Die Insel: Eine Geschichte West-Berlins 1948-1990* (Munich: C. H. Beck, 2009), 35.
23 D. G. Williamson, *A Most Diplomatic General: the Life of General Lord Robertson of Oakridge* (London: Brassey's, 1996), 127. Clay, *Decision in Germany*, 374.
24 Bohlen, *Witness to History*, 277.
25 Vojtech Mastny, *The Cold War and Soviet Insecurity: the Stalin Years* (New York: Oxford University Press, 1996), 47-49.
26 Arthur Krock, 'The Man Who Painted Himself In', *New York Times*, 8 July 1948.
27 J. P. McEvoy, '4 Strange Bedfellows of Berlin', *Hearst's International Combined with Cosmopolitan* 119, no. 6 (1945): 28-9, 220-1, 225-6, 29.
28 Secretary of State (Marshall) to the Soviet Ambassador (Panyushkin), *FRUS*, 1948, 2: 950-953. Clay, *Decision in Germany*, 26, 358.
29 Carolyn Eisenberg, *Drawing the Line: The American Decision to Divide Germany, 1944-1949* (New York: Cambridge University Press, 1997), 79.
30 Eric Morris, *Blockade: Berlin and the Cold War* (London: Hamish Hamilton, 1973), 42-5.
31 Herbert, 'The Cold War in Berlin', 167.
32 Clay, *Decision in Germany*, 15.
33 Harry S. Truman, *Memoirs of Harry S. Truman: Years of Trial and Hope* (New York: De Capo Pres, 1987), 123.
34 Soviet Ambassador (Panyushkin) to the Secretary of State 14 July 1948, *FRUS, 1948*, 2: 960–964, 963.
35 Ambassador in the Soviet Union (Smith) to the Secretary of State, 17 August 1948, *FRUS, 1948*, 2: 1049–1053, 1050.
36 'Political Report No. 17', 2 October 1948, US National Archives, RG260, 390/48/27/3, Box 903.
37 'Von der Behinderung zur Blockade. Systematische Vorbereitung der Aushungerung und Eroberung Berlins durch die Sowjetunion', *Telegraf*, 1 October 1948.
38 'M. J. Tarbe de Saint-Hardouin, Ambassadeur de France, Conseiller Politique en Allemagne à son Excellence Monsieur Robert Schuman Ministre des Affaires Etrangères', no date, stamped 5 October 1948, Archives Diplomatiques, GMFB1/212.
39 Dorothea Führe, *Die Französische Besatzungspolitik in Berlin von 1945 bis 1949: Déprussianisation und Décentralisation* (Berlin: Weißensee-Verlag, 2001), 351, 349, 362.
40 Ferdinand Friedensburg, *Es ging um Deutschlands Einheit: Rückschau eines Berliners auf die Jahre nach 1945* (West Berlin: Haude and Spenersche, 1971), 262-3.
41 Robert Spencer, 'The Berlin Dilemma', in *The Shaping of Postwar Germany*, ed. Edgar McInnis, Richard Hiscocks and Robert Spencer (New York: Frederick A. Praeger, 1960), 123.
42 Richard Reeves, *Daring Young Men: The Heroism and Triumph of the Berlin Airlift, June 1948-May 1949* (New York: Simon and Schuster, 2010), 33. Rott also argues that Robertson got the idea from a trip he had made to China in 1943. Rott, *Die Insel*, 35. Keen dismisses the idea that the Airlift was the brainchild of any single individual. Richard Keen, 'Half a Million Tons and a Goat: A Study of British Participation in the Berlin Airlift, 25 June 1948–12 May 1949', PhD, University of Buckingham, 2013, 6.

43 Frank L. Howley, *Berlin Command* (New York: G. P. Putnam's Sons, 1950), 206.
44 William Stivers, 'The Incomplete Blockade: Soviet Zone Supply of West Berlin, 1948-49', *Diplomatic History* 21, no. 4 (1997): 601, 599.
45 Deborah Welch Larson, 'The Origins of Commitment', *Journal of Cold War Studies* 13, no. 1 (2011): 180–212, 183. This is why Stivers argues that it is perverse and wrong to compare the leaky Berlin blockade with the 'starvation siege' of Leningrad. Stivers, 'The Incomplete Blockade', 576.
46 Jean Edward Smith (ed.), *The Papers of General Lucius D. Clay: Germany 1945-1949* (Bloomington, IN: Indiana University Press, 1974), xxviii, xxxvi.
47 Kaete M. O'Connell, 'Weapon of War, Tool of Peace: U.S. Food Diplomacy in Postwar Germany', PhD, Temple University, 2019, 3, 21.
48 'L'Ambassadeur de France en Grande-Bretagne à Son Excellence Monsieur Georges Bidault, Ministre des Affaires Etrangères', 9 July 1948, Archives Diplomatiques, GMFB1/212. Cf. Clay, *Decision in Germany*, 381.
49 Miller, *To Save a City*, 22.
50 Murphy to the Secretary of State, 26 June 1948, *FRUS, 1948*, 2: 918–19, 919.
51 Egon Bahr, *Zu meiner Zeit* (Munich: K. Blessing, 1996), 48.
52 William H. Tunner, Lieutenant General, United States Air Force, *Over the Hump* (Washington, DC: Office of Air Force History, 1985), 162. For Tunner's first-hand account of the airlift, see *A Report on the Airlift, Berlin Mission: The Operational and Internal Aspects of the Advance Element* [no date], http://www.afhso.af.mil/shared/media/document/AFD-120627-031.pdf (accessed 4 April 2014).
53 Miller, *To Save a City*, 54. There was a certain amount of pilfering. About a hundred unloaders were sacked for stealing food. Ibid., 88, 157, 109.
54 Howley, *Berlin Command*, 3–4.
55 'Foreign News: New Commander', *Time Magazine*, 15 August 1949.
56 W. Phillips Davison, *The Berlin Blockade: A Study in Cold War Politics* (Princeton, NJ: Princeton University Press, 1958), 314.
57 'Berlin Krise', *Der Spiegel*, 9 October 1967, 42.
58 Hélène Miard-Delacroix, *Willy Brandt: Life of a Statesman*, trans. Isabelle Chaize (London: I.B. Tauris, 2016), 47.
59 Smith (ed.), *The Papers of General Lucius D. Clay*, xxix.
60 'Attitudes and Resources of Berliners as they look forward to a Blockaded Winter', 15 December 1948, Landesarchiv Berlin, F Rep. 037, Acc. 3971, Nr. 169.
61 'Political Report No. 8', 9, 31 July 1948, US National Archives, RG260, 390/48/27/3, Box 903.
62 Spitzer, 'Dividing a City', 111.
63 Larson, 'The Origins of Commitment', 206.
64 Eisenberg, *Drawing the Line*, 10.
65 Spitzer, 'Dividing a City', 111.
66 Clay, *Decision in Germany*, 372–3.
67 'Incident involving Soviet Marshal Sokolovsky in the American Sector', June 1948, US National Archives, RG260, box 899.
68 Clay, *Decision in Germany*, 373.
69 Howley, *Berlin Command*, 204.
70 M. J. Tarbe de Saint-Hardouin: 'Les travaux se poursuivent très activement sur le nouveau terrain de Tegel', 2 November 1948, Archives Diplomatiques, GMFB1/212.
71 'Gestorben: Jean Ganeval', *Der Spiegel*, 19 January 1981, 4.

72 'Das Dorf Stolpe und die Welpolitik. Verträge, machtlose Proteste und preisgegebene Menschen', *Die Zeit*, 30 December 1948.
73 Paul Steege, *Black Market, Cold War: Everyday Life in Berlin, 1946-1949* (Cambridge: Cambridge University Press, 2007), 253.
74 Frank Roggenbuch, *Das Berliner Grenzgängerproblem: Verflechtung und Systemkonkurrenz vor dem Mauerbau* (Berlin: Walter de Gruyter, 2008), 47.
75 Stivers, 'The Incomplete Blockade', 589, 595.
76 'Verbands-Nachrichten', *Die Berliner Polizei* 1, no. 1 (1949): 13. West Germany's first Economics Minister, Ludwig Erhard, had been opposed to having the same currency for West Berlin as for West Germany. Rott, *Die Insel*, 33.
77 'Berlin zwischen den zwei Währungen. Wandlungen im Straßenbild. Der Schwarzmarkt existiert weiter', *Handelsblatt*, 24 September 1948.
78 D. M. Giangreco and Robert E. Griffin, *Airbridge to Berlin: The Berlin Crisis of 1948: Its Origins and Aftermath* (Novato: Presidio, 1988), 88.
79 Roggenbuch, *Das Berliner Grenzgängerproblem*, 43–5.
80 Clay, *Decision in Germany*, 388.
81 Steege, *Black Market*, 263.
82 'Soviet Mark Illegal in West Berlin. Relieving Economic Muddle. Closer Link with the Three Zones', *Manchester Guardian*, 21 March 1949.
83 Hoerning, *Zwischen den Fronten*, 49, 24, 31.
84 Katherine Pence, 'Herr Schimpf und Frau Schande. Grenzgänger des Konsums im geteilten Berlin und die Politik des Kalten Krieges', in *Sterben für Berlin? Die Berliner Krisen 1948:1958*, ed. Burghard Ciesla, Michael Lemke and Thomas Lindenberger (Berlin: Metropol, 1999), 187.
85 Howley, *Berlin Command*, 259.
86 *Der Sozialdemokrat*, 28 July 1948.
87 Steege, *Black market*, 214, 218.
88 'Office of Military Government for Germany (U.S.), Public Information Office', 6 August 1948, Archives Diplomatiques, GMFB1/212.
89 Andreas Hallen and Thomas Lindenberger, 'Frontstadt mit Lücken. Ein Versuch über die Halbwahrheiten von Blockade und Luftbrücke', in *Der Wedding - hart an der Grenze*, ed. Berliner Geschichtswerkstatt (Berlin: Nishen, 1987), 182–204.
90 Stivers, 'The Incomplete Blockade', 580.
91 Pence, 'Herr Schimpf und Frau Schande', 186, 189, 193.
92 Davison, *The Berlin Blockade*, 224.
93 Steege, *Black Market*, 209.
94 Spencer, 'The Berlin Dilemma', 121.
95 Clay, *Decision in Germany*, 388–9.
96 'La tension à Berlin ce matin', *Le Monde*, 25 June 1948.
97 Morris, *Blockade*, 141.
98 'Driver Killed at Checkpoint By Soviet Sector Police', *Stars and Stripes*, 26 January 1949.
99 '12848 t an einem Luftbrücken-Tag. Howley: Blockade technisch überwunden', *Tagesspiegel*, 20 April 1949.
100 'Aufgabe der Luftbrücke erfüllt. Vorräte für fünf Monate. Allmähliche Einstellung der Lufttransporte', *Tagesspiegel*, 30 July 1949.
101 Steege disagrees, seeing the blockade as more an attempt to counter the black market in the Soviet Zone than an attempt to prevent the creation of a West German state. Steege, *Black Market*, 212.

102 Morris, *Blockade*, 135–7.
103 Anthony Read and David Fisher, *Berlin: The Biography of a City* (London: Pimlico, 1994), 266.
104 In the 5 December 1948 elections, the SPD gained a whopping 64.5 per cent with the CDU only getting 19.4 per cent. Rott, *Die Insel*, 28.
105 Mark Fenemore, *Fighting the Cold War in Post-Blockade, Pre-Wall Berlin: Behind Enemy Lines* (London: Routledge, 2019), 46.
106 Philip C. Jessup, 'Park Avenue Diplomacy – Ending the Berlin Blockade', *Political Science Quarterly* 87, no. 3 (1972): 377–400.
107 'Allied Kommandatura Berlin to the Oberbürgermeister of the City of Berlin: Cancellation of Counter-Blockade Orders', 10 May 1949, US National Archives, RG260, box 893.
108 'Coupures de l'eau et de l'electricité', July 1950, Archives Diplomatiques, GMFB 1/1068.
109 'Zusammenarbeit in Berlin ist möglich. Was lernen die Berliner aus der Aufklärung des Mordfalles Kusian?', *Berliner Zeitung*, 13 January 1950.
110 T. H. Elkins and B. Hofmeister, *Berlin: The Spatial Structure of a Divided City* (London: Methuen, 1988), 46–7. On the economic struggles, see Fenemore, *Fighting the Cold War*, 129–32.
111 Scott Parrish, 'The Marshall Plan, Soviet-American Relations and the Division of Europe', in *The Establishment of Communist Regimes in Eastern Europe, 1944-1949*, ed. Norman Naimark and Leonid Gibianskii (Boulder, CO: Westview Press, 1997), 272.
112 Miard-Delacroix, *Willy Brandt*, 48.
113 Fenemore, *Fighting the Cold War*, 11.
114 Steury (ed.), *On the Front Lines of the Cold War*, 131.
115 Davison, *The Berlin Blockade*, 378.
116 William Burr, 'Avoiding the Slippery Slope: The Eisenhower Administration and the Berlin Crisis, November 1958-January 1959', *Diplomatic History* 18, no. 2 (1994): 181.
117 Radio broadcast on the Airlift reproduced in the Allied Museum Berlin.
118 David E. Murphy, Sergei A. Kondrashev and George Bailey, *Battleground Berlin: CIA vs. KGB in the Cold War* (New Haven, CT: Yale University Press, 1997), 69.
119 Richard D. McKinzie, 'Oral Interview with Lucius D. Clay', 16 July 1974, http://www.trumanlibrary.org/oralhist/clayl.htm (accessed 23 February 2014), 37.
120 Clay, *Decision in Germany*, 365, 388.
121 Steege, *Black Market*, 4.
122 Drew Middleton, *Where Has Last July Gone? Memoirs* (New York: Quadrangle, 1973), 168–9.
123 Alice A. Weinreb, 'Matters of Taste: The Politics of Food and Hunger in Divided Germany 1945–1971', PhD, University of Michigan, 2009, 147, 151–2.
124 Howley, *Berlin Command*, 273.
125 Führe, *Die Französische Besatzungspolitik in Berlin*, 15.

Part III

Cases of continued cross-border crime amid divided policing. Stopping cross-border crime sprees in their tracks, despite limits on police cooperation

9

Cross-border capers

The Gladow Gang

Having outlined the issues that thwarted cooperation in four-power government, the book concludes with two case studies, demonstrating the continued threat posed by cross-border crime in spite of divided policing. Criminals displayed no more respect for geopolitical niceties than they did legal restrictions. The resulting politicization, orchestrated around a few high-profile criminal trials, showed that justice would not be immune to or separate from the cold war. This was the beginning of a process, in which the act of crossing the border became inexorably politicized and criminalized. The black market that the Allies failed to suppress, in the period 1945–8, had a major negative impact on young people, who were already damaged by Nazism and the horrors they had experienced during the Battle for Berlin. If anything, observers predicted, the psychological wounds that had been inflicted on the souls of the city's youth would persist longer than the physical ruins.[1] Meanwhile, the splitting of the police, in 1948, created tremendous opportunities for criminals to escape justice.[2] The two rival police forces continued to exchange information about murders, robberies, unidentified bodies and missing persons, but the division of the city created numerous 'hiding places' for criminals.[3] Previously, the only way to elude police pursuit was to flee overseas. Now the nearby sector boundary offered seemingly safe and secure asylum.[4] Numerous cases reinforced the truism that 'Death and crime know no sector boundaries'.[5] Forty-four criminal gangs were said to be operating in divided Berlin. Some were heavily armed; others were equally dangerous, if less obtrusive, trading in fake penicillin (Figure 4).[6]

While West Berlin was blockaded and the border between the sectors was on high alert, one particular gang of criminals managed to steal pistols and ammunition from a total of sixteen policemen in streets near to the border: four in Köpenicker Str. (November 1948), eight in Treptow (January 1949) and four in Reinickendorf (April 1949).[7] The gang brazenly committed the later hold-ups of policemen because they were running low on ammunition, having shot their way out of capture on several occasions. In the last case, the criminals used a stolen taxi to drive up to the border and then suddenly jumped out with pistols pointed at the border guards.[8] The hold-ups of policemen took place on both sides of the border and used it as a means of escape. The gang chose the border at Treptow because it offered so many escape opportunities. With so many weapons they could embark on a deadly, cross-border crime spree.[9]

Figure 4 A police chase over the sector boundary: 'Help, he's trying to kidnap me!' Kutz, *Frischer Wind*, 15.5.1948.

Investigators described the Gladow Gang as one of the most prolific and dangerous robber bands that stalked the postwar period.[10] The prosecution eventually listed a total of forty-five people, directly or indirectly involved in the crimes, including receiving of stolen goods and failure to report criminal activity.[11] The head of the criminal gang was the baby-faced would-be gangster Werner Gladow.[12] Born in May 1931, he lived with his parents in the Schreinerstrasse, in the working-class district of Friedrichshain (in the Soviet Sector).[13] He had begun his criminal career in 1945, at the tender age of fifteen, with *Kippergeschäften* on Alexanderplatz.[14] The main trade there was in cigarettes, but people also bartered with shoes and clothing. The situation of hunger and misery was such that tearful old women would trade their last good sheet for a few potatoes or a lousy piece of bread.[15] Gladow's skill was as a trickster: he would offer to exchange cash for an item, but as the dupe handed over his article for inspection an accomplice would shout 'Police! Razzia!' and they would run off, leaving only a worthless bundle of paper behind. Alexanderplatz policeman Günter Malitz describes the technique of disguising the wad with a few genuine Reichsmark notes.[16] Clueless provincials offered rich pickings for Gladow and his associates. The Alexanderplatz made infamous by Alfred Döblin and Heinrich Zille had a lasting magnetic effect on the teenager and his friends. With gaps in the crooked urban smile, the criminal '*Milljöh* (milieu)' flourished blithely in the absence of a countervailing Police Presidium building. While still at school, Gladow had got to know the boys who hung around there. Losing any desire to return to the classroom, he established a reputation as a *Kipper* as if it was a high-status occupation.[17] Alex was where Gladow met most of his criminal associates. In the late 1940s, the area was still infamous as a hotspot for crime. Not for nothing, the back alleys of the *Scheunenviertel* were known as 'the criminal quarter (*Verbrecher Viertel*)'.[18] It attracted people from all social strata and was serviced by black marketeers, big and small. Swiss writer Max Frisch described Alex as still populated with would-be gangsters and prostitutes. It was the 'Threepenny

Opera without the Songs'. Jewish regulars had mostly been deported and exterminated, but the criminals still peppered their jargon with Yiddish phrases.

Werner Gladow's criminal career

Thanks to the war, Gladow had attended no fewer than eleven schools in Germany as well as in annexed territory in Poland and Czechoslovakia. This kind of evacuation was disrupting and unsettling, but also liberating; it served to undermine an already tenuous parental authority. In sports, games and brawls, he was always the go-getting leader, weighing in to settle disputes and assign victory. His school friends spoke admiringly of him as a 'Master of the Mask'.[19] So good was he at masking his intentions that even his own parents could not see through his deceptions. Werner and several of his Hitler Youth associates had been called up by the *Volkssturm* in the last hours of the war. In the Nazis' desperate and suicidal attempt to stave off the Soviet seizure of Berlin, twelve-year-olds had been thrown into battle against tanks and artillery armed with rocket-propelled grenades. The experience of fighting with the SS against the Soviets was tremendously exciting as well as risky. Several of the boys, Werner foremost among them, developed a ruthless and reckless taste for adventure. Addicted to adrenaline, they dreamed of high-risk situations that would make the Battle of Berlin appear mere play fighting.[20] Gladow may have experienced Hitler's Germany as pressure and compulsion, but he found its aftermath thrilling. Not particularly fond of military drill, he had gone out to get food during the Soviet invasion and takeover of Berlin. Separated from his mother for twelve days, he had no choice but to become a man.

After 1945, the boys, who had been through this baptism of fire, found it difficult to find their way back to an ordered existence. The wartime horrors had left them jaded and blasé. In the aftermath of defeat, Gladow made up his mind to find a particularly dangerous job. From an early age, he was very interested in acquiring weapons.[21] *Neues Deutschland* later wrote that it was the Hitler Youth who taught Gladow to kill. Following such an experience, a human life meant nothing to him; the slightest, split-second pressure on the trigger could extinguish it. And young Werner was trigger-happy.[22] Asked what he wanted to be, Gladow saw himself as an 'international spy' or an expert in quenching oil-well fires. At a crucial stage in his adolescent development, a daredevil lust for adventure had gripped his soul. In May 1946, the fifteen-year-old left Berlin, with his friend Wilhelm M., to serve on North Sea minesweepers. Rejected by the British authorities because they were so young and inexperienced, the two friends spent two difficult months hiking right across Germany. Somehow, they managed to make it back to Berlin, mostly on foot.[23]

His parents wanted young Werner to return to school, but he missed the black market too much. Like the other 'wide boys', he obtained his vocational education through illicit trading rather than securing an apprenticeship. Police historian Hartmut Zander describes Gladow's father as an abusive and workshy drinker.[24] Released from American imprisonment in 1946, he became a member of the Watch Police in Treptow and remained with it until 30 June 1949 when it was wound up.[25] Brutal and easily angered, he routinely threatened his son with an axe.[26] Werner lost respect for his father because of his argumentativeness and domestic violence. When he returned from the British Zone, he was now strong and confident enough to keep his father physically in check, overpowering the choleric, but cowardly, progenitor. From this point on (1948), his father ceased to have any further influence on his conduct or upbringing. He remembered seeing eye-to-eye with his mother, but he hid his continued criminal activities from her.[27] Worshipping the ground he trod on, she encouraged Werner's aspirations and propensity to ostentation.[28]

Gladow tried his hand at bogus calling, by pretending to be a gas man and then robbing the victim. Despite his quick-wittedness, he was twice detained while still under the age of eighteen. He received a sentence for *Kipperei* at the end of 1947. By his own account, he was one of the 'best swindlers (*Kippern*)' on Alex. Although not apprehended for his bait-and-switch, he got caught up in a police razzia on 17 November 1947. He tried to resist the arrest by aiming blows at the policemen, who in return gave him a severe beating.[29] On this occasion, he received a four-month sentence in a juvenile prison for resisting arrest. He said that the later disarming of the policemen was in reprisal for the rough treatment he had received from the defenders of law and order.[30] Perceiving it as unjust, he was determined to get revenge. While in Plötzensee prison, he met Werner Papke ('Sohni'). At first, they thumped each other to establish who was top in the pecking order. However, when put in a cell together, Gladow managed to win Sohni over by giving him a piece of bread. His argument that they needed to stick together against the guards was convincing. Sohni appreciated Werner's matiness and willingness to sacrifice himself.[31] To pass the time, Gladow recounted the hundreds of crime stories that he had read.

Gladow hero-worshipped Al Capone and dreamed of achieving notoriety in Berlin with similarly audacious crimes. East German writer Erich Loest represented the American manipulation of young people via trash literature, Wild West and gangster films – designed to brutalize them ready for another war – as deliberate. Nevertheless, he suggested that Gladow was unaware of the nefarious effects of what he was absorbing. The view that the Americans used thrilling films, with high body counts, to distract people from political affairs reflects GDR propaganda about psychological warfare.[32] The SED regarded such brutalization as conscious and systematic.[33] Nevertheless, hundreds of thousands of eastern teenagers watched the same films and read the same true-crime stories without turning bad. For his part, Sohni boasted of his own offences and told Gladow that he possessed two pistols. The young wannabe gangster, who associated weapons with power, was deeply impressed.[34] He saw firearms as the way to acquire power not just over a gang of criminals, but over an entire city. Despite his youth, Gladow was a skilled manipulator with undoubtable charisma. Neither Sohni nor Werner came from stable homes. Nevertheless, Sohni's father later blamed Gladow's nefarious influence for leading his son astray.[35] Fifty years later, Sohni regretted not having seen that Gladow was deadly earnest about the comparison with Capone.

At this formative stage in his criminal career, Gladow came under the wing of a would-be mastermind. Until August 1948, Gustav Völpel acted as an assistant executioner for several Berlin occupation authorities. He boasted of having carried out nearly fifty executions and was well known for conspicuously carrying his own axe to work in a distinctive green case.[36] Whenever he had earned a thousand marks for an execution, he would come to boast about it in the pubs of Alexanderplatz. He would get drunk while telling his audience all the gory details of the beheading. The criminals admired Völpel's ruthless cold-bloodedness.[37] Richard Evans, who has studied capital punishment in Germany during this period in depth, argues that Völpel's assertions about his role as an executioner remain 'demonstrably false'.[38] According to Völpel's own account, the Allied authorities let him go as an executioner, in 1948, forcing him, unwillingly, to hang up his axe. Whatever the truth, 'Hangman-Hannes' saw considerable potential in the much younger Gladow. Völpel was impressed with his 'fantastic' ability, both physical and mental, to defend himself. Recruiting him for break-ins, he taught the eager youngster a few tricks of the trade. Proud to be an accomplice of such a notorious figure, the would-be gangster soaked up the lessons in how to evade capture by the police. In the event that he was arrested, Völpel offered him useful advice on how to behave and react.[39] The older malefactor used his connections with all sorts of criminal networks to propose jobs and to act as the gang's fence for stolen property. Having spent some time in a Concentration Camp, he was able to claim that he was a 'victim of fascism'.[40] When they arrested him, the police found a thirty-year-old prostitute living with him and his wife.[41] The latter was known as the blonde Martha. Also a prostitute, she hid weapons and passed on messages between members of the gang.[42] Martha evidenced a perversely incestuous, maternal interest in young Werner. Gladow's crime spree began with an attempted robbery on a photography shop in Rankestraße, near Zoo Station, in April 1948. He took what he thought was a camera, but it turned out to be a fake display model. When the shop owner gave chase, Gladow simply shot him in the leg. The robbers commandeered a car and drove to the Soviet Sector. When People's Policemen tried to surround the car, they shot their way free.[43] This was an early sign of the young career criminal's ambition and moxie, but also demonstrated his reckless dilettantism.

In October 1948, Gladow and Werner P. undertook another robbery, this time more successfully. As they attempted to steal money from the cashier of the 'Exer' fairground in Prenzlauer Berg, Gladow shot the fairground man in the arm, while Werner P. fired off several shots at their pursuers. They were able to escape into the nearby French Sector.[44] Analysing how the robbery had gone, Gladow felt that the pistol he had used had been too small to scare anyone. As a result, he and Werner P. decided to hold up policemen at the border a month later. He wanted heavy-calibre weaponry to make more of an impression. The fear-inducing effects (*Schreckwirkung*) would be greater if he could brandish a bigger pistol. Having the same type would also allow pooling and sharing of ammunition.

Seeing two policemen standing on the eastern side of the sector border, under a streetlight at around 10 pm, they went straight up to them, pulled out their pistols and shouted, 'Hand's up!' When one of them moved in an attempt to flee or to resist, Sohni shouted, 'Go on and shoot him, Fatty'. After they left with one pistol (one of the policemen was unarmed), they slipped back over the border as the policemen tried to signal for help by blowing their whistles. The brazen duo made it home without any trouble.[45] Ironically, the fact that the policemen were focused on watching the border made them easier to approach from behind. They carried out another hold-up the next night in the same manner, this time approaching the policemen from the opposite direction, walking past and then suddenly turning round and shouting, 'Hands up!' The policemen handed over their pistols but said that they were only trainees and had only been on duty for fourteen days. The gang went over the border to rob other policemen (*Stummpolizisten* this time). Within the space of a few minutes, they had their hands on a further two weapons. That the border guards could so easily be disarmed by criminals was deeply embarrassing. Unsurprisingly, many Berliners, in both East and West, found their mortification hilarious. Police President Markgraf tried to respond to the threat, by ordering the police patrols to have their pistols ready in their coat pockets.[46]

Gladow's family and several associates confirmed that he was fascinated by true-crime fiction. Titillating whodunits, in book or film form, were his main source of conversation.[47] He had started off reading Edgar Wallace and Jack Kelly at thirteen. Later, the would-be kingpin memorized crime stories as if they were instruction manuals, watching crime films as how-to guides.[48] The 'perfect murder' was particularly instructive.[49] In *Little Caesar*, the Al Capone figure states, 'When I get in a tight spot, I shoot my way out of it.'[50] Gladow dreamed of keeping a whole city in terrified anticipation and dread. He copied Capone's ruthlessness and determination to command others. Shooting first and arguing about it afterwards became Gladow's mantra. Gaining the respect of his fellow criminals was more important to him than accumulating money. In the spree he orchestrated, the gang's crimes ranged from bodily harm to murder.

Völpel introduced Gladow to several older, more experienced criminal associates. At its peak, the gang had over seventy members. Gerhard Rogasch and Kurt Gaebler were schoolfriends and 'career felons'. During the war, Rogasch had driven a tank; afterwards, he went straight back to black marketeering.[51] Rogasch was illegitimate; his rap sheet stated that he had been called up in 1942 but had escaped from Soviet imprisonment at the end of the war and had handed himself over to the Americans. Returning from Bavaria, he had lived with his mother in very cramped conditions. He had numerous convictions for horse theft and break-ins. Gaebler had served on U-Boats in Italy and impressed Gladow with his sharp Italian suit. Sentenced to four years for plundering, he was released back to the front. He met his Italian wife, a nightclub singer, while recovering from injuries in hospital. After the war, he accompanied her on singing tours to the western zones and described himself as an impresario. After the switch to the new currency, in the western sectors in June 1948, they had undertaken foraging trips to the Soviet Zone. Gaebler told Rogasch there was easy money to be made from break-ins. Through his wife Käte, Rogasch met Gladow in November 1948.

In his thirst for action, Gladow imposed tests of courage on new joiners. Morose Dietrich Bohla and his 'weasel-faced' friend Dieter W. had been preoccupied with scrap metal collection since August 1948.[52] When Bohla expressed an interest in joining the gang, Gladow challenged him to demonstrate that he could keep his nerve, while robbing a jeweller in the Tauentzienstraße. He carried out this 'test of courage (*Mutprobe*)' on 15 January 1949, in the middle of the Soviet Blockade. Bohla described witnessing manically laughing officers shooting deserters at the end of the war. The officer said that it should be a warning to the juvenile recruits.[53] He sought to gain the court's clemency by insisting that the psychological scarring, caused by such an experience, had added to the general Nazi poisoning of his soul. After the war, he had managed to rebuild his life. He had earned such good money as a lorry driver that he had even been able to buy a motorboat. Bohla claimed that Gladow's gratuitous acts of cruelty had brought back his nightmares of the Third Reich. He believed the young boss 'capable of anything'. At the trial, he claimed that Gladow had 'hypnotized' him and that he had been powerless to disobey. His 'every word and gesture betrayed brutality and callousness'. Living in fear, he tried to win Gladow's trust, but secretly hated him. Werner's cold-blooded hunger for power kept the large gang of older criminals in check.[54]

The police interrogations reveal all sorts of interesting characters, with colourful life stories, who tagged onto the gang. Another petty criminal, associated with the gang, had been an apprentice butcher for one and a half years before having to join the 'so-called *Volkssturm*' in the last days of the war. He survived the Battle of Berlin and wanted to go back to his old job, but the master had to close because he had been a member of the Nazi Party. So, in 1945, he found himself working for the Soviets as a butcher. He also helped them to build the memorial at the Brandenburg Gate. Following a period working for the Americans, in January 1948, he was caught during a break-in and was sentenced to a year in prison. After that, he was unable to find a job and began dealing cigarettes on the Alex.[55] Although he dabbled in crime, Charlie the Artist's true vocation was as a dancer and an acrobat. In this guise, he had travelled between East Prussia, Hamburg and Denmark in the 1930s. He was briefly a member of the *Schutzpolizei* before being called up in the *Wehrmacht*. He took part in the invasion of Poland and reported afterwards to the navy. He went as crew on a boat, disguised as a merchant ship, to Santos in Brazil and tried to desert there. Caught and interned, he was sent back to Bremen in disgrace.[56] After the war, his wife was forced to sell their remaining valuables in return for food. Their cash reserves had dwindled to nothing. Ironically, currency reform had created a personal and economic crisis for many of the black-market traders. Charlie and his wife wanted to develop an artistic routine for Barlay's Circus, but hunger had reduced their physical capacities as performers.[57] Another member of the gang had been sentenced by the Nazis to a Concentration Camp for repeatedly fighting with SA men. In the camp, he was given a black triangle for asocials rather than a red one for politicals. As a result, after the war he was not recognized as a victim of fascism.[58]

With their stylish Budapest shoes and white ties, the Gladow Gang saw themselves as 'gentlemen' thieves.[59] Nearly all Gladow's associates knew each other only by their first names or nicknames (Neese, Macky, Bomme, Frannek, Bubi, Doktorchen, one-armed Fred, Seppl and Langer). 'Neese' was so-called because of his conspicuously bulbous nose.[60] The boys burned their way through cash, with ever-lit cigarettes and a wardrobe of flashy clothes. Adopting a wide-striped, double-breasted suit, Gladow topped it off with a grey *Wehrmacht*-style mackintosh and a fedora.[61] In their free time, the gang boxed, went to the cinema or visited dance halls.[62] They amply rewarded the girls, who hung around with them, with stockings and expensive underwear.[63] Some of these paramours prostituted themselves or got involved in black-market trading in the nearby station complex.

Violent, cross-border crime spree

Despite his young age, Gladow was a vicious thug, completely lacking in scruples. From the beginning, he dreamed of making it big through the audaciousness and violence of his actions. However, despite leaving a trail of dead and wounded bodies in their wake, the gang never seemed to gain much booty from their crime spree. When they broke into a barter centre in Friedrichshain wearing masks, on 7 December 1948, Gladow threatened to cut the nose and ears off the owner, if he did not tell him where his money was hidden. The shop was a conspicuous beacon of prosperity amid a sea of poverty and despair. Gladow's neighbour, Gerhard Winter, said that, as an effeminate and unpleasant nouveau riche, the owner was unpopular in the neighbourhood, where he had been seen ostentatiously feeding chocolate to young women.[64] Gladow burnt the man's feet and repeatedly stabbed the manageress with a knife.[65] Disturbed by a night watchman, Gerhard Rogasch and Werner P. only managed to escape by shooting at their pursuers. All they got hold of was a small amount of money, a goose and some butter; however, when they returned to where they had hidden them, they could no longer find any trace of the loot. Mittmann argues that Gladow and Sohni tricked their associates out of the 6,000-Mark booty.[66]

As Gladow brought more and more people into the gang, their chances of getting caught increased considerably. In February 1949, Völpel introduced Gladow to Franz Redzinski ('Bomme'). Bomme was a career criminal who had begun stealing in 1931, at the tender age of sixteen. He had previously belonged to a gang in Moabit, renowned for using submachine guns.[67] Brought up by his grandmother until he was aged twelve, Bomme had only attended a Polish school sporadically. Returning to live with his parents in Berlin, his licence to do what he wanted had been sharply curtailed. His father, who had trained as a butcher, was a heavy drinker who hit him a lot. He left school unable to read or write German. He had to abandon an apprenticeship as a carpenter because he was caught stealing from his employer. He embarked on a career of petty crime, with only a brief interlude in 1933–4, when he took part in labour service and attended a *Stahlhelm* camp. Stupid, cruel and lacking anything resembling a conscience, Bomme had been involved in all sorts of crimes, including sexual offences, for which he served a sentence in Kiel. Following his call up to the *Wehrmacht* in 1938, he had served in various punishment battalions.[68] Gladow later told his interrogators that he viewed Bomme as a coward by nature. Nevertheless, his ruthlessness with weapons was appealing.[69]

A female acquaintance had given the gang a tip about the female boss of her father. The victim was an artist and the owner of a radiator factory, who lived alone in a villa in Dahlem.[70] Not put off by the fact that her neighbour was none other than Police President Dr Stumm, who had an armed guard, the gang planned on an audacious home invasion.[71] The drone of the planes coming in to land in Tempelhof, for the Airlift, provided them with cover. Breaking in through the cellar, they found the owner and her dog on the second floor. To silence them, Bomme beat both with a rubber cudgel, knocking them unconscious. Binding her hands and feet, Neese tried to stop Bomme from hitting her further. Furious, the career criminals began fighting. In the ensuing confusion, the gang failed to find the safe, which was hidden behind an undistinctive picture. The injuries caused to the villa owner were such that she lay at death's door in hospital for three months. Although she lived until 1972, she never recovered from her injuries and was paralysed down one side of her body. The eastern press presented the failure to apprehend the criminals as evidence of the laziness and incompetence of the western police. The Berlin underworld was amused by a story that the gang had brazenly stolen a ladder from Dr Stumm's property to carry out the daring home invasion.[72]

Under Gladow's leadership, the outlaws responded to their meagre hauls with spiralling rashness and violence. In a series of botched robberies, the gang proved both reckless and trigger-happy. On 9 April 1949, he smashed the window of a jewellery shop. When the unarmed employees chased after him, trying desperately to defend their property with their bare hands, he fired on them. One managed to grab his getaway bicycle so Gladow shot him several times at point-blank distance. Despite bystanders throwing stones and a car following him, he managed to escape into Friedrichshain Park. The shooting in the back (through the lung) of the jeweller was proof that, for Gladow, human life had no significance. From the beginning to the end of his criminal spree, he was ready to shoot his way out of trouble.[73] As a consequence, a man was permanently crippled by the gunshots. Nevertheless, despite the offer of a 50,000 Mark reward, the witnesses gave conflicting descriptions of the offender.

A couple of weeks later, on 22 April 1949, Gladow and accomplices held up the Grundmann Pub in the outlying district of Berlin-Kaulsdorf. When the 59-year-old, disabled, female owner resisted, they shot her in the shoulder.[74] Faced with an old woman armed with a walking stick, who was trying to remove his mask, Gaebler shouted, 'Shoot her! Get on with it!'[75] Other shootings were equally asymmetrical and unnecessary. Gladow claimed that he fired shots at a gang of youths who tried to steal his coat; he was always armed and dangerous.[76] Young Werner insisted that he had to use his gun to establish respect as gang leader. In this capacity, he had to set an example; he shot at anyone who got in his way.[77] With Gladow's trigger-happy recklessness, it was only a matter of time before he killed someone. On 11 May 1949, he shot the chauffeur Eduard Alte on *Unter den Linden*, in an attempted carjacking. Gladow had aimed for the upper arm; the bullet hitting the driver in the chest was just bad luck. Nevertheless, because it hit an artery, the bullet killed the 44-year-old father instantly. Gladow planned to use the stolen BMW to drive to the Berlin Gasworks Corporation (GASAG) headquarters, to rob their safe room, but a vigilant porter thwarted their entry. The brazen attempted robbery, right in the middle of the government quarter, succeeded in mobilizing the highest authorities in the GDR. Asked why they had not interfered, pedestrians said that they thought they were witnessing a secret-police arrest.

By the time they were arrested, the gang had stolen a total of twenty-one pistols, of which fifteen could be recovered. They even considered robbing the police training school in Oberschöneweide to get their hands on its submachine guns. In the end, Gladow seemed to have stolen guns from the police just for the fun of it. Gaebler said that during one hold-up, the teenage gangster had told the hapless policemen, 'Get going, forward march!' He ordered them to show him who could run the fastest. When they asked him where they should run to, he told them to run all the way home with their tails between their legs.⁷⁸ Their cowardice fired Gladow's arrogance, encouraging him to behave as if he was invincible. His associates grumbled about why he had such an impulse to disarm policemen. Towards the end, he was doing this unplanned on the spur of the moment. Beyond humiliation, it did not seem to serve any purpose. Deliberately emasculating the police was not a wise career move for a would-be gangster. Likewise, the number of shots fired during the botched robberies went against standard criminal operating behaviour.⁷⁹ One policeman pleaded with Bohla to give him his weapon back; he said that the policemen who had previously been disarmed were now rotting in prison.⁸⁰ Allowing someone to steal one's service revolver was a serious offence. The police hierarchy sought to punish every loss of a service pistol, regardless of how it occurred.⁸¹ Gladow claimed to have thrown six pistols in the Spree, keeping only the ammunition. He taunted the police, by phoning them up and telling them where to look for the missing weapons so that they would have a few firearms left.⁸² In a similar display of hubris in February 1949, he shot his own thumb off while practising marksmanship in the Grunewald.⁸³

The gang seemed to be operating in the divided city with impunity. However, without fanfare, the police were gradually joining up the dots and making sense of the apparently disparate crimes. Shell casings from the shootings proved that they were connected.⁸⁴ As early as April 1949, 'Hangman-Hannes' (Völpel) had been caught committing a crime in West Berlin.⁸⁵ Witnesses to the pub robbery remembered that one of the gang had a distinctive, waddling gait. Others provided details for sketches of the perpetrators. Overall, the robberies followed the same modus operandi. Despite the ongoing cold war, policemen from East and West met up on the sector boundary for informal discussions of the case. Thanks to this invaluable assistance, inexorably the net closed in on the gang.⁸⁶ Gladow was always ready to shoot, even if his accomplices preferred not to. He repeatedly told Dietrich B. that he should aim and fire at pursuers, rather than firing wildly into the air.⁸⁷ When they tried to warn him to be careful not to kill anyone, he told them that he was no beginner and knew where he had to shoot.⁸⁸ The accomplice, who had known him the longest, Werner P., said that Gladow often said that he wanted to be infamous; he wanted to carry out incredibly 'audacious hold-ups'. He genuinely wanted to emulate Al Capone by having the whole of the city trembling at his feet.⁸⁹ It is surprising that the older members of the gang never questioned Gladow's role as leader. Despite his baby face, he was ruthlessly in command.

Shoot-out, arrest and trial

The East Berlin police arrested Werner Gladow on 3 June 1949, a month after he turned eighteen. When told that the men outside were from the Job Centre, his father dutifully opened the apartment door. Hysterically screaming that the detectives were bandits and would-be murderers, his mother tried to block the policemen from entering the flat.⁹⁰ Her cries gave her son time to lock his bedroom door.⁹¹ As they tried to force their way in, he fired from a pistol in each hand.⁹² Mrs Gladow's little Werner then engaged in an hour-long firefight with police and received several bullet wounds (in the chin and thigh). For Gladow, his mother's hysterical determination to protect him during the shoot-out was comic. The press reported that she had directed his fire at the police officers, who were taking up position in the building opposite.[93] It even claimed that she reloaded his pistols for him.[94] Nevertheless, the court later found her not guilty of assisting an offender in resisting arrest.[95] In all, sixty shots were exchanged. Gladow had fired from three pistols; a fourth was found hidden in the rabbit hut in the flat.[96] He managed to wound three policemen in the shoot-out. The first detectives had come unprepared, with only eight bullets each and no backup. Although there was no escape, Gladow played to the gallery of spectators gathered below, saying that the police needed reinforcements.[97] Halfway through the firefight, he broke off to taunt his adversaries: 'I've killed this lot. Can you send up the next ones?'[98] Before her son was overpowered, his mother told him, 'You're hit boy, the tart is to blame for everything. She caused all this.'[99] Her son stopped firing only because he lost consciousness. Simultaneously, police reached the balcony with fire-engine ladders.

On 21 March 1950, Werner Gladow, Kurt Gaebler and Gerhard Rogasch appeared in court, accused jointly of two murders, nineteen attempted murders, multiple aggravated robberies and several serious hold-ups.[100] In all, the police accused the gang of 352 crimes, 127 of which were serious. In his interrogations with the police, Gladow cheerfully played the role of childish criminal-mastermind. The police noted that the interrogation was difficult because of the shot he had received in the jaw.[101] He emphasized what he had learned his trade from reading true-crime stories and talking to older criminals in prison. In court, he sought to impress the spectators with his offhand callousness, rather than making any pretence at appearing contrite or repentant. For Curt Riess, the contrast between his boyish blond curls and his Hitler-like tone was macabre. Gladow insisted that he alone had decided on the plans and ordered their precise execution.[102] From the start, the eastern authorities conceived of it as a show trial. Using all the tricks up their sleeves, they ensured that it took place under portraits of Stalin, Lenin and Wilhelm Pieck in the culture room of the *Reichsbahn* headquarters in East Berlin. 'In his elegant suit with a Schiller collar, Gladow looked like a well-mannered boy from a good family.'[103] Although the trial took place in the Soviet Sector, court observers were evidently amused by his tales of police incompetence. Gladow characterized Gaebler and Rogasch as particularly useful to him because they were intelligent as well as dangerous. He saw Bomme as being largely stupid and naïve, but he could nevertheless make use of his brutality and viciousness. One of the gang's associates, Ernst M., denied having possessed large quantities of ammunition or offering to sell it to them. He argued that the three live grenades, found by police in his orchard, probably came from children trying to knock the fruit down.[104] Four years after the war, he suggested, powerful explosives were simply lying around.

Although the trial took place in East Berlin, the court asked the divided city's foremost pathologist to offer his expert judgement, as a psychiatrist, on Gladow's behaviour. Dr Waldemar Weimann was a senior medical officer and head of the court-medical institute in Berlin.[105] In addition to autopsies and expert forensic assessments, he carried out psychiatric analyses. Weimann had begun his illustrious career – studying all manner of 'death, putrefaction, crime and vice' – in the 1920s. He was the expert who performed the post-mortem on Horst Wessel and had carried on working as a pathologist, conducting thousands of autopsies and crime-scene analyses, throughout the 1930s and 1940s. In their first encounter, the well-built boy bounded out of his cell naked but for a pair of trunks. As well as having the body of an Olympic swimmer, Weimann noticed that he had intelligent eyes. For the sinister boss of a criminal gang, he seemed blithe and guileless. Weimann was shocked to find that Gladow appeared unaware of the seriousness of the situation he found himself in. He viewed the psychiatrist's visit merely as 'a pleasant interruption' to his solitude. He saw the expert as an interesting conversation partner, and 'walking encyclopaedia', who could satisfy his unquenchable hunger for knowledge. Bombarding him with medical questions, he recounted that his gang called him 'little doctor' because he 'could throw around Latin technical terms'. He had managed to convince them that he had spent a 'few semesters in medical school'.[106]

The incongruously cheerful young man Weimann interviewed appeared fully sane, but psychologically and morally immature. He laughed happily as he recounted disarming the police. Intellectually, he was able to dominate the gang of older criminals; despite his lack of experience, he was able to play the role of experienced gangster convincingly. Gladow clung to his fictional idol, Al Capone, like a child who refused to accept that Winnetou was fictional. He was less interested in money, than 'the deeds themselves'. Sometimes he was so busy planning the next job that he forgot to eat. He wanted the world to talk about his criminal escapades and to tremble before him. Weimann suggests that it was Gladow's overeager amateurism that made him so dangerous. For someone like Gladow, possessing a pistol was like taking a powerful drug. In his expert assessment, Dr Weimann found that Gladow came from a family of psychopaths. Both his mother and father, as well as his paternal grandfather, possessed this trait. 'Besides work and beatings, my mother didn't get much out of life,' he confided. The twentieth child of a small farmer in Masuria, Gladow's mother married a womanizing bully. According to Werner, his father beat them just for the fun of it.[107] With a brutal loser of a father and a hysterical mother, who overly doted on him, Werner was poorly prepared for leading an honest life.

The fact that he could not see the consequence of his crimes was evidence, for Weimann, of Gladow's complete lack of maturity, even though technically he had reached the age of eighteen.[108] Weimann insisted that Gladow was too immature to be sentenced under adult law. He was a 'childish fantasist' rather than a mature, hardened criminal. As a young boy, Werner said as little as possible and buried himself in his books. He lied prodigiously to his parents, having no confidence in opening up to them or discussing personal issues with them. Even during his police interrogations, he maintained a friendly demeanour, always quick with his 'boyish smile'. He recounted his crimes as 'amusing and funny anecdotes'. Talking about how he had disarmed the police officers, he was quick to laugh. He seemed to have no grasp of the gravity of his actions or of the danger of the situation he was in. Disarming the policemen had been a hilarious game for Gladow. Despite possessing significant intelligence, Weimann judged him still very childlike. Gladow was basically stuck in the action and adventure outlook of the very young. During interrogations, he went red in the face as he gesticulated, while trying to reconstruct and illustrate his crimes.[109] Coupled with his juvenile desire for escapades, he had an underdeveloped sense of morality. The fact that he was going to be guillotined for his crimes does not seem to have troubled him too much.[110] The East Berlin court nevertheless found a way round this assessment, in large part because the political leadership desired it so.[111]

In his memoirs, Weimann was critical of what, from personal experience, he assessed as 'Zonenjustiz'. As soon as he entered the courtroom, he could sense the tense atmosphere. Robust young men in leather coats occupied the spectators' benches. The Minister of Justice of the Soviet Zone, Max Fechner, appeared, accompanied by the Attorney General and the Police President of East Berlin. In the light of his overly independent and objective report, Weimann's West Berlin place of residence was now held against him. Police Superintendent Schläwicke, who had coordinated the botched arrest, appeared as a witness. He argued that it was a disgrace for someone from West Berlin to claim that this or that criminal could not be tried as an adult. 'The so-called expert opinion given here this morning is idiotic.'[112] In vain, the psychiatrist argued that Gladow was driven by a desire to be completely free and not to be tied down. Already at the age of eleven, he thought only of accomplishing a 'dangerous job'. In his childish imagination, which he kept into his late teens, he wanted to be a professional boxer, an international spy or an oil-well firefighter. For Weimann, this sensation-seeking reflected an excessive yearning for admiration. He told the police that he wanted to be a surgeon, hence his nickname 'Little Doctor (*Doktorchen*)'. He said that he would have had no hesitation about taking the necessary actions to save someone's life, in the same way that he had no hesitation about taking one.[113] Throughout the trial, he endeavoured to appear relaxed, unemotional and thereby superior.

Gladow squandered considerable sums to look the part of the dashing gangster. Although boasting of being able to have sex eight times a night, he kept girls at arm's length. Although occasionally he went dancing, he preferred the company of men. He never took the time to enjoy the fruits of his crimes. Instead, he thought only of new, more daring robberies. Particularly in the last six months of the cross-border crime spree, he seemed to rush 'like a madman' from one crime to the next, with little care for the consequences. Sohni left the gang because he had not reckoned on doing robberies as a full-time job.[114] For Gladow, the proceeds of his crimes represented only a 'pleasant side effect' of the life of crime he had chosen. The thrill of armed robbery was far more important than the concrete gains. His fellow criminals did not share this outlook and reproached him for taking risks which were disproportionate to the rewards gained. Seemingly addicted to the adrenaline of armed robbery, Gladow fell victim to delusions of grandeur. The big haul was always just over the horizon. Increasingly, gang members wanted out; they were only held in check by Gladow's threats of violence.[115] In spite of his youthful appearance, Gladow was very cold and calculating; he obsessively thought up new criminal opportunities. He repeatedly encouraged his associates to shoot to kill if challenged. At the end of the spree, Gladow was shooting people in broad daylight. Never in Berlin's long history of crime was 'so much blood been spilled for so little booty'.[116]

In view of his lack of remorse, the prosecution demanded the death penalty. After shooting (and killing) the BMW chauffeur, outside the Café Kranzler on *Unter den*

Linden on 11 May 1949, Gladow had told Gaebler that the death would help to instil the necessary respect. Other drivers would think twice before resisting. His main preoccupation was getting ordinary Berliners to realize that they were not dealing with boys who were 'wet behind the ears (*Milchjungen*)'.[117] It was only when he was confronted by the driver's devastated eleven-year-old son in court that Gladow lost his insouciant composure. Unable to meet his gaze, he stated, 'I'm just beginning now to understand [the damage] that I actually caused.'[118] Far too late, he expressed an inkling of shame and remorse. For her part, the Dahlem victim earned disapproval from a coterie of eastern female spectators, for being so ready to forgive the youths she regarded as misguided and deluded.

Along with Gaebler and Rogasch, Werner Gladow was sentenced to death for his crimes.[119] Gladow had shot and killed the chauffeur Eduard Alte just three days after he turned eighteen, making him fully responsible according to the law.[120] Nevertheless, Weimann disputed that he was psychologically mature, and mentally developed enough, to stand trial as an adult. He diagnosed the eighteen-year-old as suffering from delayed, late-onset puberty.[121] Had he been successful in convincing the court to judge him as a criminally irresponsible minor, it might have saved the young criminal's life. The judge fell back on a Nazi law from 1939, Paragraph 20 of the Youth Penal Code, which allowed for serious young offenders to be tried as adults.[122] 'Healthy public sentiment' was enough to allow a juvenile to be tried as if he was an adult. Consequently, the court used a trick to sentence a 'pubertal criminal' to death as 'Public Enemy No. 1'.[123] Asked if he wished to be reprieved, reckless to the last, Gladow said that he preferred death, though it would be more fun to be executed by firing squad. He was executed in Frankfurt an der Oder on 10 November 1950. According to one account, the guillotine got stuck and severed his head only at the third attempt.[124] The experience of witnessing the executions converted the prosecutor Steltzer into a lifelong opponent of the death penalty, once he had fled to the West. *Neues Deutschland* hoped that the underworld would get the message that there was no place for Al Capones in Berlin.[125] Newsreels claimed that the arrests had once again demonstrated the population's gratitude, trust and respect for the People's Police.[126]

Conclusion

In a city wounded and scarred by conflict, Nazism and wartime disruption had poisoned countless teenagers. In the last days of the Third Reich, they had learned the power that holding weapons gave them. Rich pickings on the black market led them to become cynically dismissive about boring education and worthy 'normal jobs'. A generation of young people had been taught to see the widespread flouting of the law as everyday and normal. Gladow adapted to the difficult postwar economic situation by becoming a streetwise swindler. Older criminals took youngsters like him under their wing and taught them how to carry out more audacious crimes. Nevertheless, the East German authorities emphasized the impact of American media and trash literature in strengthening his criminal mindset. For East German propagandists, Gladow seemed to epitomize American psychological warfare by means of mass-cultural barbarization. The court psychiatrist, Dr Weimann, argued that it was his education in the Third Reich and the 'deep impressions' left by the Battle of Berlin that had prepared him for a life of crime.[127] The crime spree took place at the height of the cold war, with the Airlift planes and electricity blackouts giving cover. While newspapers kept their readers in a state of tension, the gang seemed to be profiting from the unusual geopolitical situation created by ideological tension.

In prison, the sixteen-year-old had made contacts with other criminals, young and old. Dreaming of becoming Berlin's answer to Al Capone, he recruited a motley gang of older career criminals, including an official executioner. Arming his gang, by stealing 08-pistols from the police at the border, Gladow orchestrated an unprecedented cross-border crime spree. Associating weapons with power, he was desperately hungry for both. The gang repeatedly used the border dividing the city as a means of escape. What he lacked in experience, the teenager made up for with a reckless lack of concern for his victims. As a result, he and his gang left behind a trail of people crippled and nearly killed by needless shoot-outs. The trial resulted in his execution at the tender age of nineteen. For Gladow, the thrill of the crimes and the power he had over his gang were more important to him than money. He was prepared to sacrifice lives for the adrenaline rush he craved. He made a fool out of the police in both East and West but allowed himself to be caught in the wrong sector. Had he been picked up in West Berlin, he would probably have been spared the death penalty. The cold-war division initially hampered the investigation of the cross-border crime spree, but gradually a pattern emerged. The gang could not hide their crimes indefinitely behind the East-West split. Their recklessness meant that capture was only a matter of time. The break-in, at the villa next to Police President Stumm's own home, was embarrassing as was the disarming of the policemen at the border.

Novelist Horst Bosetzky suggests that, because of his attempts to outwit the police in East and West, Gladow was revered as something of a hometown folk hero.[128] Despite his young age, Gladow managed to control a gang of older, deadly serious criminals. They brought their own violent excesses but were generally more cautious about provoking the police. Money may have been 'just a pleasant side effect' of crime, for him, but the other crooks grumbled that the risks greatly exceeded the rewards.[129] The advice of older criminals like Gustav Völpel and the stealing of police weapons allowed Gladow to plan more audacious crimes, but many of the robberies were botched because he embarked on them on the spur of the moment or to impress his underlings. Gladow was vicious and trigger-happy; according to his reckoning, human life in the divided city was extremely cheap. Only when he was on trial, and directly faced by their pain and reproach, could he begin to conceive what the murders meant to the families of the victims. He nevertheless continued to recount his devil-may-care deeds with childish relish and bravado. The shoot-out with the police proved Gladow's desire to win a reputation for himself even if it meant his own death. His immature desire for glory made him far more reckless and dangerous than if he had just pursued wealth. Crime had become his reason for existence. He failed in his endeavour to become Berlin's Al Capone, but he died trying.

Notes

1. Waldemar Weimann, *Diagnose Mord: Die Memoiren eines Gerichtsmediziners* (Bayreuth: Hestia, 1964), 275–6.
2. Wolfgang Mittmann, *Gladow-Bande: Die Revolverhelden von Berlin* (Berlin: Das Neue Berlin, 2003), 165. Hans Pollak, *Tatort Sektorengrenze: Berliner Kriminalfälle der Nachkriegszeit* (Berlin: Verlag Neues Leben, 1994). For his book, Klaus Schlesinger used court files as well as interviews with eyewitnesses. Klaus Schlesinger, *Die Sache mit Randow: Roman* (Berlin: Aufbau, 1996). Gunter Pirntke, *Der Al Capone von Berlin: Werner Gladow* (Dresden: Das elegante Buch, 2019). Regina Stürickow, *Verbrechen in Berlin: 32 historische Kriminalfälle 1890-1960* (Berlin: Elsengold, 2014).
3. Berliner Polizei, 'Jahresbericht 1959', Landesarchiv Berlin, E Rep 200-25, Nr. 173, III, 9.
4. Norbert Steinborn and Hilmar Krüger, *Die Berliner Polizei 1945 bis 1992: von der Militärreserve im Kalten Krieg auf dem Weg zur bürgernahen Polizei?* (Berlin: Arno Spitz, 1993), 80–1. Cf. 'Gespaltenes Berlin – günstig für Verbrecher', *Der Morgen*, 19 August 1948.
5. Weimann, *Diagnose Mord*, 8.
6. Mittmann, *Gladow-Bande*, 5.
7. Unless otherwise indicated, the interrogations and other reports are located in Landesarchiv Berlin, B Rep 058. In all, the Gladow Gang obtained twenty-one pistols from border hold-ups. Weimann, *Diagnose Mord*, 285.
8. 'Abschrift. Pol. Insp. Reinickendorf, Fr. S.: Überfall auf zwei Polizei-Angehörige der Fahrzeugkontrolle an der Sektorengrenze unweit des Bhfs. Berlin-Wilhelmsruh durch bewaffnete Banditen', 22 April 49, Landesarchiv Berlin, B Rep 058, Band E (Anzeigen).
9. '200 Gladow-Verbrechen', *Neues Deutschland*, 26 June 1949.
10. 'Schläwicke, Polizeirat (K) & Schwarz, Pol. Ob. Komm. (K): Vorführungsbericht', 8 June 1949, Landesarchiv Berlin, B Rep 058, Band 14, 531–3.
11. 'Der Generalstaatsanwalt bei dem Landesgericht Berlin: Anklageschrift Gladow', 1 Febuary 1950, Landesarchiv Berlin, B Rep 058, Band E (Anzeigen).
12. Rüdiger Strempel, 'Der Mörder mit dem Milchgesicht', *Spiegel*, 16 May 2019. Uta G. Poiger, *Jazz, Rock and Rebels: Cold War Politics and American Culture in a Divided Germany* (Berkeley, CA: University of California Press, 2000), 48f. David Meeres, 'Policing "Wayward" Youth: Law, Society and Youth Criminality in Berlin, 1939–1953', PhD, University of Limerick, 2014. A film was made of Gladow's exploits: *Engel aus Eisen*, directed by Thomas Brasch (West Germany, 1980). It recreates the chaotic atmosphere of the period, with fear and paranoia rampant.
13. *Die Gladow-Bande: Chicago in Berlin*, directed by Ute Bönnen and Gerald Endres (ARD, 2000). The documentary contains interviews with some of the surviving gang members, together with eyewitness accounts and newsreel footage.
14. 'Anklageschrift gegen Gladow und andere wegen Mordes', 6 January 1950, Landesarchiv Berlin, B Rep 058, Band 43.
15. Mittmann, *Gladow-Bande*, 46, 48–9.
16. Bönnen and Endres, *Die Gladow-Bande*.
17. 'Vernehmung des am heutigen Tage in das Polizeikrankenhaus Scharnhorststr. eingelieferten Werner Gladow', 3 June 1949, Landesarchiv Berlin, B Rep 058, Band 13.
18. Richard Brett-Smith, *Berlin '45: The Grey City* (London: Macmillan, 1966), 142.

19 Weimann, *Diagnose Mord*, 280.
20 'Sohni' interviewed for Bönnen and Endres, *Die Gladow-Bande*.
21 'Der Angeschuldigte über seine persönlichen Verhältnisse befragt, erklärte', 12 September 1949, Landesarchiv Berlin, B Rep 058, Band IV.
22 'Der Schüler Werner Gladow lass "Ein Mensch wurde Verbrecher . . ." Giftimport auf Leinewand und Papier. Erster Tag des Gladow-Prozesses', *Neues Deutschland*, 22 March 1950.
23 'Anklageschrift gegen Gladow und andere wegen Mordes'.
24 Hartmut Zander, 'Falldarstellung: Die Gladow-Bande', in *Festschrift: 75 Jahre Mordinspektion in Berlin, 1926–2001*, ed. Der Polizeipräsident in Berlin (Berlin: Polizeipräsident, 2001), 82–4, 82.
25 Interrogation of Ernst Gladow (born 8 June 2003), father of Werner. Landesarchiv Berlin, B Rep 058, Band 16, 734f.
26 'Ein Psychiater und ein Kommissar', *Berliner Zeitung*, 1 April 1950.
27 'Vernehmung des . . . eingelieferten Werner Gladow'.
28 Mittmann, *Gladow-Bande*, 11.
29 'Vernehmung des . . . Werner Gladow', Fortsetzung, 9 July 1949, Landesarchiv Berlin, B Rep 058, Band 13.
30 'Vernehmung des . . . Werner Gladow', Fortsetzung, 1 July 1949, Landesarchiv Berlin, B Rep 058, Band 13.
31 'Sohni' in Bönnen and Endres, *Die Gladow-Bande*.
32 Erich Loest, *Die Westmark fällt weiter* (Halle, Saale: Mitteldeutscher Verlag, 1952), 8, 31, 189–90. When I interviewed him in the 1990s, Loest said he retained his antipathy towards Gladow. Despite his youth, he possessed a marked brutality, desiring to be Al Capone of Berlin and shooting without warning. For the ex-Nazi, he suggested that people existed who were even worse criminals.
33 'Amerikanische Kulturbarbarei bedroht unsere Jugend', *Neues Deutschland*, 4 April 1950.
34 Mittmann, *Gladow-Bande*, 12.
35 'Familien zerschellten an Schundromanen. Zweiter Tag im Prozeß gegen die Gladow-Bande. Ein Vater rechnete ab', *Neues Deutschland*, 23 March 1950.
36 'Gladow-Bande hingerichtet. Henker in Haft', *B.Z.*, 25 September 2002. Keiderling confirms that Völpel carried out executions in both parts of Berlin between 1946 and 1948. Gerhard Keiderling, 'Der Al Capone vom Alexanderplatz', http://www.luise-berlin.de/bms/bmstxt99/9907prof.htm#seite34 (10 April 2018).
37 Interrogation of Artur J., blackmarket trader. Landesarchiv Berlin, B Rep 058, Band 16, 747. Cf. '"Doktorchen" und 17 Komplicen gefaßt. Volkspolizei machte gefährlichste Verbrecherbande unschädlich', *Neues Deutschland*, 9 June 1949.
38 Richard J. Evans, *Rituals of Retribution: Capital Punishment in Germany 1600-1987* (London: Penguin, 1996), 774.
39 'Vernehmung des . . . Werner Gladow', Fortsetzung, 9 June 1949.
40 Mittmann, *Gladow-Bande*, 241.
41 Interrogation of Käte T., Landesarchiv Berlin, B Rep 058, Band 16. It was Völpel's wife who eventually denounced Gladow.
42 'Schläwicke, Polizeirat . . .: Vorführungsbericht'.
43 Keiderling, 'Der Al Capone'.
44 Mittmann, *Gladow-Bande*, 83.
45 'Vernehmung des . . . eingelieferten Werner Gladow'.
46 *Telegraf*, 4 December 1948.

47 Interrogation of Ingrid U., Landesarchiv Berlin, B Rep 058, Band 16, 721–2.
48 'Gerichtsmedizinisches Untersuchungsamt: Zur Begutachtung der sittlichen Reife Gladows', 31 March 1950, B Rep 058, Kiste Nr. 411, Band 6.
49 'Vernehmung des ... Werner Gladow', Fortsetzung, 9 July 1949.
50 *Little Caesar*, directed by Mervyn LeRoy (Warner Bros., 1931).
51 Mittmann, *Gladow-Bande*, 40.
52 Ibid., 90, 121.
53 'Gnadengesuch für Dietrich B'. [no date, ca. 1955], Landesarchiv Berlin, B Rep 058, Band 43.
54 'Der dritte Tag des Gladow-Prozesses. Gangster von der traurigen Gestalt', *Neues Deutschland*, 24 March 1950.
55 Interrogation of Fritz S., Landesarchiv Berlin, B Rep 058, Band 16, 711–2.
56 Interrogation of Artisten Charlie, Landesarchiv Berlin, B Rep 058, Band 16, 761–2.
57 Landesarchiv Berlin, B Rep 058, Band 16, 763.
58 Interrogation of Herbert N., Landesarchiv Berlin, B Rep 058, Band 16.
59 Sohni in Bönnen and Endres, *Die Gladow-Bande*.
60 It was so distinctive that he could not join in with hold-ups and made his money largely by collecting lead. Mittmann, *Gladow-Bande*, 90.
61 Interrogation of Ernst Gladow.
62 Landesarchiv Berlin, B Rep 058, Band 14, 467.
63 Interrogation of Alma M., Landesarchiv Berlin, B Rep 058, Band 16.
64 Bönnen and Endres, *Die Gladow-Bande*.
65 It was entirely fitting that this scene was reproduced on the cover of a trashy true-crime story book, albeit one published in the East. Florian Brand, *Polizeifunk meldet: Gladow Bande zur Strecke gebracht* (Berlin: Vorwärts, 1949).
66 Mittmann, *Gladow-Bande*, 114.
67 He got the nickname 'Bomme' because he was in the habit of saying '*Auf die Bomme wichsen*'. 'Vernehmung des ... Werner Gladow', Fortsetzung, 9 July 1949.
68 Franz R. was eventually released in 1970 having served twenty years. 'Gnadenentscheid & Haftentlassung für Franz R', 1 Febuary 1970, Landesarchiv Berlin, B Rep 058, Band 43.
69 'Vernehmung des ... Werner Gladow', *Fortsetzung*, 14 June 1949.
70 Interrogation of Käte R., Landesarchiv Berlin, B Rep 058, Band 14, 498–501. Cf. Mittmann, *Gladow-Bande*, 160f.
71 'Vernehmung des ... eingelieferten Werner Gladow'.
72 'Der vierte Tag des Gladow-Prozesses', *Neues Deutschland*, 25 March 1950.
73 'Anklageschrift gegen Gladow und andere'. Cf. 'Schläwicke, Polizeirat ...: Vorführungsbericht'.
74 'Schläwicke, Polizeirat ...: Vorführungsbericht'. Cf. Mittmann, *Gladow-Bande*, 194.
75 'Der sechste Tag des Gladow-Prozesses. Gladow "filmte" nach bewährten Mustern', *Neues Deutschland*, 29 March 1950. Bönnen and Endres, *Die Gladow-Bande*.
76 'Vernehmung des ... eingelieferten Werner Gladow'.
77 'Vernehmung des ... Werner Gladow', *Fortsetzung*, 17 June 1949.
78 'Kurt G. Vernehmung', 10 June 1949, Landesarchiv Berlin, B Rep 058, Band 13.
79 Bönnen and Endres, *Die Gladow-Bande*.
80 'Vernehmung Dietrich B', 29 June 1949, Landesarchiv Berlin, B Rep 058, Band 13.
81 'Instructions for Checkpoints on the Sector border from the Kdo. d. Schupo', 3 March 1949, Landesarchiv Berlin, Rep. 26, Nr. 143, Bl. 63.

82 'Vernehmung des ... eingelieferten Werner Gladow', Fortsetzung, 23 June 1949. Mittmann thinks that this was a lie. Mittmann, *Gladow-Bande*, 283.
83 Dietrich B. later told the police that Gladow shot his thumb while trying to threaten him into staying in the gang. Mittmann, *Gladow-Bande*, 151. A photograph of the missing thumb was printed in *Quick* magazine. Police Museum, Gladow File.
84 Mittmann, *Gladow-Bande*, 145f., 198f., 226, 267.
85 Bönnen and Endres, *Die Gladow-Bande*.
86 Although cross-border cooperation had been important in capturing the gang, eastern news reports suggested that its apprehension was entirely down to the work of the People's Police. 'Berlin dankt der Volkspolizei. Vernichtung der Gladow-bande ist Verdienst ihrer erfolgreichen Arbeit', *Neues Deutschland*, 9 April 1950.
87 Interrogation of Dietrich B., 13 September 1949, Landesarchiv Berlin, B Rep 058, Band IV.
88 Interrogation of Gerhard R., 13 September 1949, Landesarchiv Berlin, B Rep 058, Band IV.
89 Interrogation of Werner P., 13 September 1949, Landesarchiv Berlin, B Rep 058, Band IV.
90 'Gangster: Feuer unter Kaufmannsfüße', *Spiegel*, 6 April 1950.
91 Mittmann, *Gladow-Bande*, 251.
92 'Vernehmung des ... eingelieferten Werner Gladow'.
93 Mittmann, *Gladow-Bande*, 255.
94 Bönnen and Endres, *Die Gladow-Bande*.
95 'Lucie Gladow freigesprochen', *Neues Deutschland*, 9 April 1950.
96 'Schläwicke, Polizeirat ...: Vorführungsbericht'.
97 Mittmann, *Gladow-Bande*, 250, 254.
98 Weimann, *Diagnose Mord*, 298.
99 Interrogation of Ernst Gladow. Cf. 'Berlins Al Capone ist scharf auf seine Mutti', *Die Welt*, 21 March 2013.
100 'Schläwicke, Polizeirat ...: Vorführungsbericht'. 'Der Schüler Werner Gladow lass "Ein Mensch wurde Verbrecher ..."', *Neues Deutschland*, 22 March 1950.
101 'Vernehmung des ... eingelieferten Werner Gladow'.
102 Curt Riess, *The Berlin Story* (London: Frederick Muller, 1953), 231.
103 Weimann, *Diagnose Mord*, 300.
104 Landesarchiv Berlin, B Rep 058, Band 14.
105 'Der Mörder ist noch unter uns', *Kurier*, 10 January 1950.
106 Weimann, *Diagnose Mord*, 278–9.
107 Ibid., 303, 299.
108 'Ein Psychiater und ein Kommissar'.
109 'Gerichtsmedizinisches Untersuchungsamt, Magistrat von Gross-Berlin: Gutachten über den Geisteszustand des Angeklagten Werner Gladow', 13 January 1950, Landesarchiv Berlin, B Rep 058, Kiste Nr. 411, Band 6.
110 Peter Maxwell, 'Todesstrafe in der DDR. Erich Mielkes ganz kurze Prozesse', *Spiegel-Online*, 17 July 2012.
111 Zander, 'Falldarstellung', 84.
112 Weimann, *Diagnose Mord*, 304.
113 'Hauptjugendamt, Magistrat von Gross-Berlin: Haftbericht über Werner Gladow', 30 January 1950, Landesarchiv Berlin, B Rep 058, Kiste Nr. 411, Band 6.
114 Bönnen and Endres, *Die Gladow-Bande*.

115 Mittmann, *Gladow-Bande*, 208, 150, 231. In all, the police estimated the gang had stolen 800,000 Marks. Ibid., 292.
116 Weimann, *Diagnose Mord*, 301.
117 'Gerichtsmedizinisches Untersuchungsamt: Gutachten'.
118 'Der siebente Tag des Gladow-Prozesses. Zu spät, Werner Gladow! Begegnung zweier Söhne. "Ich schäme mich so.." sagte Gladow', *Neues Deutschland*, 31 March 1950. The 44-year-old driver, Eduard A., was the father of three children. Mittmann, *Gladow-Bande*, 204.
119 'Todesurteil an Gladow vollstreckt. Im demokratischen Sektor Berlins kein Platz für Gangster', *Neues Deutschland*, 11 November 1950. To pass the time on remand in prison, the 'friendly, smiling youth' learned English and Russian. 'Prominente Häftlinge in Zelle Nr. 1', *Neue Zeit*, 15 February 1950.
120 'War der Bandenchef erwachsen?', *Der Tag*, 1 April 1950.
121 Weimann, *Diagnose Mord*, 291.
122 Mittmann, *Gladow-Bande*, 318.
123 Weimann, *Diagnose Mord*, 305.
124 'Gladow-Bande hingerichtet. Henker in Haft'. The policeman, Arno Krone, who witnessed the execution, did not make any such claim. Bönnen and Endres, *Die Gladow-Bande*.
125 'Das Urteil im Gladow-Prozeß. Berlin ist nicht Chikago. Todesurteil für Gladow, Gäbler und Rogasch', *Neues Deutschland*, 9 April 1950.
126 Bönnen and Endres, *Die Gladow-Bande*.
127 'Die Beweisnahme ist zu Ende', *Tägliche Rundschau*, 1 April 1950.
128 Horst Bosetzky, *Cold Angel: Murder in Berlin 1949*, transl. Catherine D. Miller (New York: Enigma, 2012), 46.
129 Weimann, *Diagnose Mord*, 289, 291.

10

The 'charming murderess'
Elisabeth Kusian

As the Gladow case showed, sectoral boundaries – based on administrative fiat but exacerbated by clashing ideologies – were artificial and unhelpful in solving crime. Their deployment in the 'cold' civil war in Berlin suggested that, in part, the policemen had begun to neglect their actual or original purpose of fighting crime. For some commentators, however, Berlin's postwar dismemberment was fitting punishment for the Berliners' complicity in Nazi crimes. The moral landscape, created by the 'wasteland of ruins', was one of poverty, everyday brutality and hunger. As the Gladow case demonstrated, poor economic conditions and the population's daily exposure to an immoral black market had acted as a catalyst for crime, in the period 1945–9. For the eastern propagandists, it was western currency manipulation that was the cause of continued high levels of unemployment, and with it, criminality. The ongoing sporadic violence seemed to presage another, even more gruesome form of conflict. For the eastern press, life in West Berlin was as cheap as in American thrillers and gangster films.[1] For both western and eastern newspapers, Berlin constituted a criminals' paradise. Hoodlums easily slipped through the cracks of the cold war, as waged every day in a city ripped in two. Suggesting that life in postwar Berlin was cheap, rumours spread that unscrupulous butchers were selling children's flesh as meat. Conditions in postwar Berlin were such that there was a good chance of ending up in tiny pieces, somewhere amid the ruins.[2] The murderer's motivation was either sexual gratification or greed.

Discovery of male and female body parts

Four and a half years after the war had ended, yuletide Berlin was hit by a diabolical, mini crime wave. On 9 December 1949, around 19.30, a Police Constable found a male torso amid the ruins in Charlottenburg. The policeman had been chasing scrap collectors when he stumbled on the body. Although it was dark, what was underneath his feet did not feel quite right. On immediately calling the murder squad, precipitin-level tests showed that these remains were human. In addition, the crime-scene analysis ascertained that the arms, legs and head had been expertly severed at the joints.[3] The crime-scene investigator opined that the precision of the incisions demonstrated that the dismemberment had to have been accomplished by an expert. Most headless/limbless bodies were crudely butchered. Dismemberers usually proceeded more hesitantly and left irregular, jagged incisions. In this case, the uniformity of the cuts suggested almost scientific exactness, suggesting considerable knowledge of anatomy. The murderer had dissected the limbs with scalpel-like proficiency, pointing to either a butcher, a medical student or someone with surgical expertise. In the words of Dr Weimann, again called as an expert, 'A surgeon could not have done a better job.'[4] The male genitals were still attached to the unclothed trunk and had not been mutilated.[5] The remains of the neck showed marks of strangulation.

The next day, on 10 December, detectives from the eastern sector appeared in West Berlin looking for 56-year-old travelling salesman Hermann Seidelmann, who had been reported missing by his brother. Variously described as a showman or pedlar, he had been staying at his sister's apartment but had gone missing. On the same day, the eastern press revealed that on 5 December, while playing, children had discovered other male body parts – two calves and a thigh – in the eastern sector. They were hidden in ruins opposite Stettiner Station (today Nordbahnhof).[6] Visiting Berlin to attend his mother's funeral, Seidelmann had sought to change money at Zoo Station.[7] Awkwardly belonging to the eastern transport police's jurisdiction, the station complex was the main locus of unofficial money changing in West Berlin. At first, the police suspected the unauthorized currency speculators as being responsible for the murder; they found one, who had cheated Seidelmann of 200 Westmarks on 2 December 1949. They estimated that the Saxon had roughly 1,800 Marks left. His relatives confirmed that it was his body, thanks to a plaster stuck over a freshly operated corn. The police offered a reward of 500 DM for information about what had happened.

The case created a peculiar post-mortem, East-West puzzle for the pathologists. The trunk, found in West Berlin, was taken to the Pathology Institute of Moabit hospital.[8] East Berlin pathologists examined the rest of the body at the forensic morgue, next to the *Charité* hospital in East Berlin. After some wrangling about jurisdiction and precedence, the eastern authorities sent their body parts (arms, legs and head) westwards. The western experts were then able to prove that they came from one and the same body. Loss of blood flow to the brain had resulted in unconsciousness. There was no sign of livor mortis (or pooling of the blood), suggesting that the body had been drained shortly after death. Given the cold weather, the pathologists estimated that the body had probably lain outside for a week. In all likelihood, he had been killed on 3 December.

On 4 January 1950, the West Berlin police received a telex from the Soviet Sector saying that, during the afternoon, children had found further body parts in a ruined house adjacent to Alexanderplatz Station. The killer had unwittingly chosen to dump the body parts in the ruins of the former police headquarters. It was clear that the discovery site was not the scene of the crime. Although their genders differed, the modus operandus for both bodies was the same. Like Seidelmann, the head and limbs had been separated from the trunk with relatively clean cuts. This time, the killer had made less strenuous efforts to hide the body parts and had also left some personal items with them. The eastern pathologists estimated that the body had been dead between ten and fourteen days.⁹ This time, the body parts belonged to a woman aged between thirty-five and forty-five years old. The murderer had throttled her from behind, then cleanly separated her head and limbs from her torso. The find was reported in the eastern and western press the next day. Given the yawning geopolitical chasm, separating the sectors, the murderer's chances of being caught initially seemed slim.

The woman's body matched a week-old, missing-person description. On 5 January, the owner of a typewriter shop learned that his manageress, Frau Merten, was missing. Having read about the discovery of a woman body's in the eastern sector, in the *Telegraf* (5 January 1950), he took himself to the East Berlin police headquarters in the Neue Königstraße, to see the body. He identified it indisputably as being that of his married employee, Doris Merten.¹⁰ Merten was forty-seven years old, nearly 5.5 feet tall and quite broad. She was identifiable thanks to her dyed auburn hair and one gold tooth in her upper jaw. She lived in an allotment (*Kolonie Hanseaten*) in Spandau. Her husband had reported her missing three days after she had failed to return home. It turned out that on the day of the murder Merten had been due to take a portable typewriter to a flat in Charlottenburg in the British Sector. The potential customer was a 35-year-old nurse called Elisabeth Kusian, who rented a room in an apartment on the fourth floor of Kantstraße 154.¹¹ Not having seen his wife, since her errand to Kusian's apartment, Merten's husband reported her missing. Kusian subsequently sent her a New Year's greeting card, stating that she had left her umbrella in her apartment. On 6 January, the eastern detectives learned from her landlady that Kusian was on her way to Friesenstrasse police headquarters, in the American Sector. Despite her being the last person to see Merten alive, the West Berlin police did not suspect Kusian at this point. Informed that was where Kusian was headed, the eastern detectives called the western missing-persons section and asked them to direct Kusian to their headquarters in East Berlin. Despite the cold war, the western police did as they were asked. They merely asked Kusian if she had any misgivings about going to the eastern sector. There, she feigned ignorance of the crime, but during questioning she got herself tangled up in inconsistencies. For the GDR's foremost court reporter, Cobra, Kusian's fatal mistake was to underestimate the People's Police.¹² While suggesting that the western police had been lax, in letting the nurse walk free, the People's Police strove feverishly to solve the case.

From her landlady, the eastern detectives had discovered that Kusian's boyfriend was a married West Berlin policeman (Detective Sergeant Kurt Muschan). He was a section head at a police station, working mainly on the night shift. When requested by telephone to do so, Kurt M. appeared at the Police HQ in East Berlin, to answer questions. His account failed to provide her with an alibi. In the eyes of contemporaries, the brutally 'dismembered corpse' reflected the unnatural dismemberment of their city.¹³ Reassembling the body initially seemed to be as difficult a task as reunifying Berlin. Seeking a solution to the gruesome 'meat jigsaw', detectives from East and West found sparks of residual unity. Merten constituted a West Berlin body left in the Soviet Sector. Officially, non-cooperation was the norm at this stage of the cold war.¹⁴ Nevertheless, for this exceptional case, the two police forces worked together, jointly searching Kusian's flat for evidence on 7 January. Bypassing Stumm's West Berlin police hierarchy, eastern-sector detectives had directly telephoned their colleagues in

Charlottenburg and arranged to meet them at the flat. Officially, criminal investigators from either side of the border only communicated with each other through telephone and telex from headquarter to headquarter. Unofficially, however, the *Ost-Kripo* carried out investigations in West Berlin any way it saw fit.[15] By dealing directly with their detective colleagues in the British Sector, they were implicitly refusing to recognize the authority of Stumm's Friesenstrasse Police Presidium. At this time, the People's Police rated the cooperation they received as highly professional and advantageous for the investigation.[16]

The cardinal questions of any crime-scene analysis, or forensics investigation, are: 'What, when, where, with what, how and why'. Answering them would eventually lead to the murderer.[17] Both sets of investigators found a substance resembling blood in the cracks between the floorboards. They confirmed the presence of blood with benzidine. The investigators also found traces of blood on a breadknife, women's clothing and blankets. A 'rubber glove with a few pubic hairs' suggested that the room had been the site of the dismemberment.[18] Armed with this incontrovertible evidence, the interrogators put renewed pressure on Kusian. She continued to lie and, in the process, accused several other people of her crime. But 'under the weight of the extensive incriminating evidence', on 10 January 1950, she finally confessed. Unbeknown to their western colleagues, the East Berlin police had already found a woman's umbrella and wristwatch in an unauthorized search of her flat the previous evening. Showing disregard for jurisdiction and legal niceties, they had let themselves in with a skeleton key. They also found Seidelmann's distinctive red and yellow striped tie. These personal possessions, found in her room, confirmed that the victims had been there and that, in all probability, she was the last person to see them alive. In subsequent days, both police forces managed to trace items of Seidelmann's clothing that Kusian had sold to acquaintances.[19] Realizing the seriousness of the offences his mistress had committed, Kurt M. helped the eastern investigators fully with their enquiries: he did not try to cover up what his girlfriend had done, even if it made him look bad. Telling her that she was incriminating him pushed her over the edge psychologically. Breaking down on seeing her boyfriend in handcuffs, she admitted that she was responsible for both murders and had carried them out alone.[20] From his vantage point, as an independent expert, Dr Weimann saw this technique as 'highly dubious', close to the psychological 'third degree'.[21]

There followed nearly four weeks of limbo, in which the eastern police had Kusian while the western police retained the evidence from her room. Using what her interrogators interpreted as delaying tactics, Kusian only revealed details reluctantly.[22] In holding her to account, they were hampered by the reluctance of the western police to share physical evidence from the crime scene. This consisted of a bloody suitcase and a rucksack, found in the flat, that had clearly been used to transport the body parts. Her interrogators argued that, had they had these items, they could have provoked a complete confession sooner.[23] Because of her propensity to lie, she admitted the truth only after considerable prevarication and stalling. Nevertheless, she eventually confessed that she alone was responsible for the murders. Nurse Kusian appeared to those interviewing her to be 'completely callous'. To the surprise of her interrogators, she suddenly expressed the desire to see the murdered woman's body. While looking at the corpse, she murmured 'Terrible, terrible, it's not possible at all. . . . How can human beings do such terrible things?'[24] In part, Kusian confessed to deflect suspicions from Kurt M. Although up to this point, it had been his kindness she had appreciated, he now helped the eastern police to destroy her resistance. By allowing her to give him presents, taken from the murder victims, he had unconsciously made himself complicit in her crimes. In eliciting her confession, her policeman boyfriend could not discern any noticeable emotion in her face. The hard People's Police interrogation had clearly worn her down, but she remained detached from reality. She later attempted to commit suicide by slitting her wrists in her cell.[25] Kurt M. told his superiors about the arrest of his girlfriend. Although they did not charge him with an offence, his career was over, and they unceremoniously removed him from his position.[26]

Private life of a double murderess

Much about the case resembled a bad detective novel. Many people associated the nursing profession with selflessness. However, Kusian had been wantonly pursuing an affair with a married man. The couple had planned to spend Christmas together in her room. They had been looking forward to giving each other presents. She had decorated the room with a tree and candles. Kurt M. had often said how much he would like to have a travel typewriter. It would speed up his work and give him more time for their extramarital dalliance. Shortly before Christmas, Kusian had dropped hints that she planned to surprise him with the travel typewriter he had set his heart on. Having finally found a man who was 'honest, clean, and respectful of women', she was determined not to lose him. His gifts were paltry by comparison.[27] Overcome with emotion, M. was monosyllabic. 'You're crazy,' he grumbled.[28] Fearful of losing him, she desperately gave him ever more valuable gifts. If anything, the extravagance irritated and annoyed him, because he could not reciprocate. 'I could not return the favour, by responding in kind, with my salary.'[29]

Kurt M. gave a detailed description of the portable typewriter that she had given him; it was an 'Erika' brand. She told him that she had bought it in Potsdamer Strasse. Although it was used, he was very pleased with it. As far as he was concerned, it looked faultless, and he looked forward to typing his police reports on it. She had also given him a hat, braces and a watch; these turned out to have belonged to Seidelmann. Kurt M. had last seen his girlfriend on the evening of 26 December 1949. She had met him on the stairs and told him to wait for her in a pub because she had visitors. She later told him that she had had to look after a sick relative. When he reached her room, he saw an unfamiliar woman's coat together with a lady's hat hanging behind the door but did not think anything of it. Addicted and in debt, Kusian played the married detective like the typewriter she killed to give him. Despite his position as a Detective Sergeant (*Kriminal-Sekretär*), Kurt M. seemed to be a better judge of things than of people. During his interrogation, he revealed that he often had the feeling that Kusian was telling him stories. Over time, he realized that most of her tales about her family situation were entirely fictitious. 'She has a volatile nature.' She often suffered what he took to be heart attacks; she would suddenly fall to the ground and lie there for several minutes without any movement. He only found it possible to bring her round by splashing water on her face.[30] She did not smoke or drink, though she was particularly fond of what he called a 'respectable cup of coffee' (something which was not that easy to find in postwar Berlin). What he had not noticed was that she was in the habit of injecting herself with morphine and then taking amphetamines to perk herself up.

While being treated for a shrapnel injury acquired during the Battle for Berlin, she had been given morphine for the first time. When her husband returned from captivity as a POW, their relationship had been very strained, so she had begun stealing morphine. The opiates had a soporific, calming effect, helping her to forget about her worries and to go to sleep. When she changed hospitals, it became more difficult for her to steal the narcotics, so she began to buy them from dealers in Zoo Station. She was also able to get hold of Pervitin (an amphetamine) if she wanted 'to be fresh'. She could buy this from street dealers or from pharmacies, if she told them that she was a nurse on night duty.[31] The Matron of the Robert Koch hospital said that Kusian had been dismissed for bringing the nursing profession into disrepute. Sullying the hospital's reputation, she had repeatedly borrowed money from her patients and then failed to repay them. She described Kusian as a 'habitual liar', who had misused her uniform and brought the profession into ignominy.[32] To the eastern police, Nurse Kusian demonstrated an expert mendacity, marked by a compulsive need for status. Over the border, her psychiatric examination, conducted by none other than Dr Weimann, suggested someone desperate for admiration and attention, with a con artist's lack of scruples. Her neighbours recounted an assortment of fairy tales that she had told them, referring to her aristocratic lineage and artistic abilities. She seemed to fit the description of a 'pathological liar', her head filled with the most bizarre notions and inventions. Kurt M. had met Kusian in the summer of 1948, during an interview in relation to a theft. At the time, she had been a witness rather than a suspect. During his questioning, she had offered to get him medicine for a sore, arthritic toe. When he visited her flat to pick up the medicine, they got to know each other better and began what he called a 'friendly relationship'.[33]

The eastern police tracked Kusian's three offspring to a children's home in Teltow (in the eastern sector). They told of trips to the Zoo with 'Uncle Kurt'. Their mummy had told them about his important job with the police. Although they were disappointed that he did not wear a uniform, during the excursion, '"Uncle Kurt" had been very kind to them.'[34] A medical orderly, the children's father – Kusian's former husband, Walter – had been a member of the NSDAP in Berlin from as early as 1926.[35] He was also a Sergeant in the storm troopers. Kusian tricked him into marrying her, to escape her abusive situation in Thuringia. Damaged by her misrepresentations and their thirteen-year age gap, the marriage became more and more strained. She bridled at the fact that they rarely went out to the cinema, the theatre or even for a walk in the fresh air. She would have preferred him to spend his time at the SA-pub. She subsequently described their marriage as a form of torture. When her several suicide attempts failed, she developed what Weimann dubbed 'hysterical behaviour'.[36] To outmanoeuvre her husband, she began to lie instinctively and routinely pretended to faint.

At her hearing, it was revealed that she too had been a member of the Nazi movement.[37] She did not deny her husband's accusations of having had lovers while he was a soldier during the war. Going to dances, she forgot the restrictions of life with Walter. Reversing her former doormat status, she began spending his savings. She had had one lover, but he had died in a bomb raid. To cheer her up, the other nurses brought along other soldiers to meet her.[38] At the end of the war, Walter's gold party badge suddenly became deleterious. Although divorced, she told people that she was widowed. After her boyfriend at the time was arrested, she discovered that she was pregnant and got herself an abortion. Despite being injured from the grenade splinter, she tried to keep the family together. She was evicted from the family home, with her children, because in 1945 Walter was deemed a 'war criminal'. To get a job, she lied, in saying that he had gone missing as a surgeon on the Eastern Front. She printed a fake obituary notice, claiming medical credentials for her and her ex-husband. There was a suggestion that she had also performed back-street abortions at this time.

The murders

Although nurses had been involved in some of the Nazis' worst crimes, people still associated the uniform with respectability, selfless care and devotion.[39] Berliners commonly dubbed the wearers angels of mercy. Contemporaries associated the white pinafore, in particular, with motherliness and nurturing care. In the case of Kusian, the unremarkable, benign exterior concealed a real monster. She was the first nurse to rob and murder without scruple while wearing the uniform. Contemporaries expressed astonishment that a woman could be capable of such crimes.[40] But, at the time of the killings, she was unemployed and heavily in debt. Even for such a driven and perspicacious observer as Dr Weimann, psychologically assessing her was difficult. She was clearly pragmatic, egotistical and forceful but wholly lacking in empathy. She possessed a unique combination of greed and anatomical expertise.

In her diary entry of 20 June 1949, she recorded a determination to use all the means at her disposal to extricate herself from her situation.[41] She met her first victim at Zoo Station, a louche milieu frequented by black marketeers, vagrants and prostitutes. Against the backdrop of money changers, standing near the entrance calling out 'East for West, East for West', they exchanged a few words. Amid the flotsam and jetsam of Zoo Station, Kusian's nurse's uniform inspired confidence. She needed Eastern Marks for her children; Seidelmann wanted to swap them for several hundred Deutschmarks. Neither having enough cash on them, he asked her where she lived and said he would call round later. The police later found a cigarette packet on which he had written 'the beautiful woman from Zoo station'.[42] Seidelmann had a wife and children in Plauen, Saxony. The police suggested that he often came to Berlin, where he could make money and seek sex.[43] He turned up at her flat as arranged, and she entertained him with a RIAS musical programme. As he was sitting on the couch, reading a western magazine, she approached him from behind with a thin piece of washing line. 'I came up behind him and threw the noose over his head. S. immediately jumped to his feet.' He tried desperately to turn towards her, but within seconds he was unconscious.[44]

Although she told the interrogators several lies, Kusian did, eventually, give them details about the murder and dismemberment that only the killer could know. After she was sure that he was unconscious, she said that she tied the rope around his neck and waited for him to die.[45] His hands and neck exhibited a lack of defensive wounds. Using the breadknife from her shared flat, she then began cutting up the body.[46] It was surprising that none of the four other subtenants heard the murder take place or noticed the dismemberment going on in the next room.[47] She collected the blood in a bucket and dumped it in the shared toilet. A macabre detail was that she was wearing her uniform when she killed him.[48] Kusian did not express having any moral qualms about the murder. For her, it seemed just to be a practical matter of how to kill him and then how to dispose of the body. As a surgical nurse, Kusian had assisted operations in the Virchow hospital and retained a scalpel. She only had a small suitcase and a rucksack, in which to transport the body parts, so she had to cut them small enough to fit. Beginning with the arms, she proceeded to cut off the legs. Her decision to sever the legs at the knee joint stemmed from the size of the bags.[49]

Kusian left her parcels of misery right across the ruined landscape of the divided city. In the interrogation, she suggested that someone, who was taking morphine and amphetamine together, was capable of anything. When she heard that the S-Bahn was running, she took her luggage first to Zoo Station. The city might have been ideologically divided, with two antagonistic police forces and a cold war going on, but for this murdering drug addict, the small matter of where she dumped the body parts was apparently unimportant. 'It was immaterial to me which direction I travelled in.' She took the first train and got out at Friedrichstraße station, where there were plenty of ruins. Asked why she had dumped the body parts in two different locations, she said that the suitcase was heavy, and she did not have the energy to take it deeper into the ruins. No personal possessions accompanied Seidelmann's body parts.

The killing of Frau Merten took place in much the same way, though with more premeditation. Kusian gave her guest coffee, containing sleeping pills. To lull her victim into dropping her guard, she was again wearing her nurse's uniform. It was possible to throttle her from behind as she sat on the couch. Although several residents reported being awakened by a scream, this does not fit with the time frame of the murder. Kurt M. stayed the night with Kusian; in the morning, before she went to the bathroom, she expressly told him not to get out of their couch-bed. Something about her tone unsettled him. Once she was arrested, he accepted that she had probably hidden the body of the murdered Doris Merten underneath that couch.[50] Kusian later admitted that she had indeed made love to Kurt M. while the body lay inches beneath them.[51] The busy Christmas period meant that she could not dismember the body as rapidly. She left the window open while the cadaver lay in her room. Once she had got rid of her overly trusting and incurious boyfriend, it took her three, cross-border trips to dispose of Merten's body parts.[52] This time, the dismemberment was more laborious, leaving her with less energy and imagination for disposal. Rigor mortis had set in before she could undress Merten. Livor mortis (or hypostasis) had also occurred before she could begin sectioning the body. While she had left Seidelmann's body in several sites, she did not bother with Merten. Unlike Seidelmann, Kusian left underwear on the trunk and a pair of pyjamas next to the body. The police suspected that this was with the intention of deceiving them. She hoped that the presence of underwear would make them think that men, who had lured her to an apartment, had killed the victim.[53] She wanted it to appear as a sex crime rather than a murder-robbery. In her mind, their lives had been cheap; she gained little more than 300 DM from each of the killings.

Sensational trial

The method of murder and disposal was particularly perfidious. While Kusian cited convenience as her primary motivation in choosing locations to deposit the body parts, the eastern police also suspected a desire to exploit the unnatural, cold-war divide. The killer had banked on the police forces not communicating or cooperating with each other. She had reasoned that, on finding the body parts in their sector, the eastern police would look for the perpetrator there. Whether or not the killer intended it as such, the case had major political implications. Some eastern policemen also saw the depositing of the body parts in their sector as a taunt, designed to blacken the GDR's good name. At the very least, the discovery would stain the reputation of the eastern police. Eastern propagandists argued that the subsequent western, tabloid headline – 'Dismembered corpse in eastern sector' – was designed to defame the 'democratic' (that is to say Communist) authorities.[54]

From beginning to end, the geopolitical divide threatened to complicate the solving of the crime. Kusian had banked on Berlin's police being too divided to find the truth. However, their cooperation ended her mini crime wave. On 8 February 1950, the eastern police handed her over, along with several volumes of written evidence, to their western counterparts at the border.[55] The policemen formally raised their hats in the neutral space, in the middle of the *Sandkrugbrücke*, near *Lehrter Bahnhof* (today the Central Station). After exchanging the prisoner and the dossiers, they drove off in opposite directions.[56] People wanted for non-political crimes were routinely handed over in this way; both sides were happy to demonstrate their efficiency.[57] The Kusian case seemed to illustrate that cross-border assistance and teamwork were still possible. The case demonstrated the potential benefits to Berlin's population, if the two sides could work together. Cross-border collaboration may not have been important to the 'politicians', but it greatly affected the lives of the millions of ordinary workers, who had to live with the daily detriments of division.[58] While she had been held in the eastern sector, Kusian had confessed to both of the murders, but once she was in custody in West Berlin, she refused to repeat her confession. 'She stressed that she had already made her statements in the eastern sector and was not willing to repeat them.'[59] She maintained her innocence for months, before making a full and frank statement, admitting her guilt to the western interrogators. Citing drug addiction and financial problems, she confirmed that she alone had carried out the murders and the disposal of the body parts.

On meeting Kusian, Dr Weimann was convinced that he had seen her 'full, sensuous mouth' before. Despite the unflattering prison uniform, her feminine allure and charisma made a deep impression on him.[60] It turned out that she had attended his lectures on unnatural deaths at the Robert Koch hospital. The authorities intended them as training for the officers of the police training school in Spandau, but they also attracted curious onlookers among the medical personnel. During these lectures, the stellar scientist had provided forensic pictures of different modes of killing. In grim, postwar Berlin, nurses in search of entertainment eagerly attended the graphic depictions of true crimes. Weimann showed forensic pictures in a grisly 'Murder 101'. To his gripped audience, he stressed the differences between hanging, strangling and garrotting. His audience learned that throttling killed by blocking blood to the brain, rather than through asphyxiation. Kusian was one of his more attentive ghoulish spectators. Dr Weimann had pointed to this method as a way for a wily, female perpetrator to overpower a stronger male victim. In retrospect, the talks seemed like a 'how-to guide' on killing; he had managed to help train a murderer. As a newspaper report put it, she managed to turn the theory of murder 'into ghastly practice'.[61] In her hands, the mundane washing line became a lethal weapon. It was paradoxical that the man responsible for establishing Kusian's responsibility and guilt had also taught her how to kill. Painstakingly dissecting the layers of her depravity, Dr Weimann crops up with surprising frequency in the Kusian case. Four days and 4 kilometres separated the autopsy in East Berlin from that in West Berlin. It had been Weimann who had carried out the autopsy on the male remains, in both sectors, and who had subsequently been able to match the body parts, proving that they belonged to the same person. The relationship between the expert witness and the defendant was a strange one. She accused him, in a letter from 2 December 1950, of undermining her, by ripping elements of her life out of context. Citing emotional pain, she initially refused to repeat what she had said to the eastern police. Weimann wondered if she was feigning a breakdown to avoid answering difficult questions, particularly those that revealed her premeditation. While some memories gushed out of her, others had to be prized out with great effort. The rare nuggets of truth were always mixed with lies.

Reinforcing their odd pupil-teacher relationship, Weimann was allowed by the police to ask Kusian questions, during her month-long interrogations in West Berlin.[62] He not only examined the bodies, but assisted with police interviews and offered the detectives his psychiatric expertise: 'Because I had dissected both victims, and because the forensic problems would play a decisive role in the questioning of Kusian, I was called in as an expert advisor.' He felt qualified to match the profile of the crime to that of the alleged criminal.[63] Seeking the 'psychological key' that would 'open her soul', he won her confidence by telling her how impressed he was by the skill with which she had severed the limbs from the torso.[64] When he expressed admiration for her skill in exemplary dismemberment, 'K. kept quiet, sank her head and shook it to and fro'. She agreed with him that she had needed to inject a lot of morphine to take on the gruesome task of cutting up the bodies with the breadknife.[65] He had earlier told the *Kurier* that the skill she had demonstrated, acquired as a nurse assisting in operations, put Berlin's amateur dissectors to shame.[66] He suggested that his 'intimate tone' of professional admiration gradually overcame her resistance. Grotesque as the situation she found herself in was, she positively bloomed at his praise. They developed a strange, mutual fascination and macabre rapport. While she hero-worshipped him, he was fascinated and intrigued by her cold-bloodedness. In framing his memoirs, he described her as his 'most mysterious and enigmatic murderess'.[67] He had several one-on-one meetings and continued to exchange letters with the suspect. His detailed assessment involved giving her a physical exam. It was no wonder that she complained that he was needlessly rummaging around in her soul.

During the interviews, Kusian repeatedly assured Weimann that she had committed the crimes alone and without assistance. He argued that only a direct participant could be so precise about all the gory details.[68] At the trial, he was called as an expert witness, not just on the pathology of the victims, but also on the psychology of the murderess. The odd enthralment and mutual admiration persisted during the court case. Despite his role in getting her conviction, Weimann rated their connection as exceptionally good. Nevertheless, for onlookers, it took on grotesque forms.[69] Stranger still, Waldemar's brother, Dr Arno Weimann, defended Kusian.[70] When the case came to trial in Moabit, a year after her first arrest, there was a huge and rather morbid public interest in the 'charming' 36-year-old murderess.[71] She was dubbed the 'Sister of Death' by the tabloids. The case had everything: drugs, sex, a nurse's uniform, a married policeman and assorted body parts.[72] The media interest was such that there was a scrum for the few, precious tickets to the public gallery. Scuffles broke out as people jostled for their ringside seat to the Kusian Circus. The morbidly obsessed audience, of ghouls and assorted riffraff, were ready to camp overnight and pay as much as 100 DM for a seat in court.

The media on both sides fully exploited the spectacle, while accusing the other side of hypocrisy. Some saw the Kusian entertainment show as an artificially induced collective psychosis, or 'Kusianitis', centred on her profession and disguise.[73] On the first day of the trial, photographers struggled with the police to get shots of the defendant. The *Berliner Zeitung* newspaper argued that the spectators were only behaving as American gangster films had taught them to: by taking pleasure in the pain and suffering of other people.[74] Propagandist Cobra suggested that the murder stories were like a type of opiate. They served the purpose of 'distracting the masses like a drug, so that the imperialists could carry out their plans undisturbed'.[75] Over the week of coverage, the reason given for the West Berlin government's need for a diversion varied. What was consistent was the claim that, due to their evil machinations, the diabolical western powers required a distraction. The sensationalist ballyhoo was all about masking the truth and blinding the public. West Berlin's puppet masters were trying to deflect people from their real problems and worries, by providing them with sensational and gory details of gruesome crimes so that they would forget their troubles.[76] A would-be representative worker condemned the fascination with a murderess: 'We know these women, who seem so refined, but who chased SA-men then and the Yanks now.'[77] The trial attracted cranks, notably including an astrologist, who pretended to be a witness in order to gain entry.[78] She claimed her evidence was based on a 'purely scientific' study of the stars. Harping on about sinister and insidious western psychological warfare, eastern propagandists suggested that this charlatan fully reflected the fairground-nature of the proceedings. With her red headscarf, the fortune teller was worthy of Hollywood giant Metro-Goldwyn-Mayer.[79]

The line taken by the eastern press was that the case was so embarrassing to the western authorities that they had orchestrated the spectacle of the trial to distract people from the cold war. Over the course of the five-day trial, the repeated sensations

– that Kusian's lover was a married policeman and that Merten's body had lain under the couch – kept interest bubbling away. Kusian may have exploited the 'unfortunate division of the city', for her own macabre ends.[80] Nevertheless, as the *Berliner Zeitung* insisted, it was thanks to the eastern police that the city had been freed of a gruesome murderess. The newspaper stressed that she had learned how to commit her crimes through the schooling provided by Nazism. There was no question that this West Berlin citizen had learned utter moral corruption thanks to her experiences of Hitler's war and of the black market.[81] The eastern press juxtaposed the fiendish rubbernecking of the court in Moabit with the heroic actions of the People's Police. It stressed that Kusian's arrest had taken place in the eastern sector. East Berlin detectives had learned from her landlady that she had gone to the missing people's office in the West Berlin police headquarters in the Friesenstrasse. There, officers did not notice anything amiss as she enquired after Merten. It was more of a friendly chat than an interrogation. Nevertheless, responding to a request from East Berlin, the officers told her that she should go to the East Berlin Police HQ. The eastern press condemned the western response as patchy and superficial, when compared to the exemplary and faultless work of the People's Police.[82]

> What is scandalous about the affair is not only that the Stumm police apparatus totally failed to solve the crime – the Berlin public are used to that – much more aggravating was the attempt by the Stumm police to [try and] delay the successful investigation by the People's Police.[83]

Arguing that, throughout, the Stumm police had tried to undermine the work of the People's Police to resolve the case, the *Tägliche Rundschau* newspaper linked this to the embarrassing situation that one of their detectives was Kusian's lover.

The eastern press tried to argue that their police were solely responsible for bringing Kusian to justice. The West Berlin police had patently failed.[84] The arrest was a triumph for the People's Police and a testament to the painstaking thoroughness of their investigators. Unlike the Stumm police, they were not preoccupied with hunting down freedom fighters. Thanks to their skills and efforts, a sinister crime wave was over, and the city could breathe again.[85] They blamed the investigative failings of the West Berlin police on the fact that so many seasoned police specialists had been dismissed, merely because they had progressive views. Competence and democratic notions of justice were supposedly at odds with the new, cold-war climate of lockstep intransigence and brutal authoritarianism. For his part, the head judge, Dr Korsch, praised the work of the eastern and western police equally. They had shown extreme judiciousness and care in their investigations. 'But', asked the *Kurier*, 'who could see through a woman who sacrificed a human life only so she could use the loot to brighten up Christmas night in the arms of her lover?'[86] The eastern press wantonly named and shamed Kurt M., the married *Stummpolizist* boyfriend, and mocked his lack of detective skills. That one of West Berlin's finest – a Detective Sergeant no less – had been so closely connected to the murderess and yet had failed to spot the fact that there was a dead body, under the couch where he was bedding his mistress, was 'painfully embarrassing'.[87] Although Kurt M. was forced to admit that he had received property, belonging to the victims, from Kusian, he claimed to have had no knowledge whatsoever about her crimes.[88] The defence nevertheless suggested that Kusian had only confessed in order to remove suspicion from her boyfriend.[89]

Kusian span such a labyrinthine tissue of lies that the lawyers had to dissect her confessions, claim by claim, falsehood by falsehood. She was such a fantasist that journalists wondered whether she still knew that she was lying or whether she had come to consider her lies as the truth. She tried to argue that a cut on her hand meant that she could not have carried out the dismemberments. The court's medical expert argued that this was untrue. She had a plaster on her hand, not a splint. Seidelmann's widow confirmed that the clothing Kusian had sold had belonged to her husband. At one point, the case seemed to hinge on whether there was enough room for a body under the 20-centimetre-high sofa. It was brought into the court room. A defence attorney tried to demonstrate its too small height, but instead lent weight to Kusian's original confession.[90] For Cobra, the presence of the couch, on which the couple had made love, put the spectators in a state of delighted, macabre anticipation.[91] The numerous defence ploys were simply designed to obscure the truth. The many twists and turns of the trial were difficult to follow. After first pleading guilty, on the second day of the trial, Kusian suddenly changed her story. Dramatically withdrawing her confession, she now claimed that it was her ex-husband Walter who had carried out the murders.[92] This would have provided a convincing explanation for the skill with which the bodies had been dissected. She said that he was driven first by jealousy of Seidelmann and then by greed in relation to Merten. 'Clearly shocked, Walter Kusian disputed any involvement in the deed.' He was arrested while his alibis were checked.[93] 'When reproached by the judge, Kusian claimed that she had arranged to take the blame', on behalf of her husband, in order not to put the care of their three children in jeopardy.[94] Although it created a sensation, the argument was quite clearly flimsy. Although Walter Kusian could possibly have helped his ex-wife to dispose of the body parts, the killings and dismemberment unquestionably took place at her apartment, one she shared with four other people. Walter's jealousy could explain the murder of Seidelmann but not that of Merten. Why would Walter kill Merten to get a typewriter for Kurt M.? While Kusian continually lied in her confessions, she knew details about the murders, dismemberment and body disposal that only the killer could know. There was no contradiction between the autopsy reports and Kusian's first confession. Walter lacked means and motive for the murders. Although some knowledge or involvement in her crimes was difficult to rule out, it was farfetched to suggest that he could have committed them without her approval. When no evidence of his involvement could be found and the court had heard sufficient evidence to exculpate him, Walter Kusian was quietly released.

Kusian now claimed that her confession in the eastern sector had been forced. She clearly believed that the fact that she had first confessed to the anti-democratic People's Police could invalidate her confession in a West Berlin court.[95] *Berliner Zeitung* used the chaotic scenes to suggest that Dr Korsch had lost control of the proceedings. *Neues Deutschland* contrasted his fatherly concern for Kusian with the high-handed and authoritarian treatment he usually applied to Communist demonstrators in his court.[96] Compared to how he normally shouted down witnesses and the accused, his leisurely, gentle treatment of the murderess was disconcerting.[97] Nevertheless, at the end of the 'sensational trial', Elisabeth Kusian was found guilty and given two life sentences.[98] Unidentified items in her apartment raised the possibility of more victims.

In retrospect, Weimann called her the 'most mysterious murderer of my career'.[99] The rapport between the killer and the medical examiner/psychiatric expert was remarkable. Although recognizing that she was a compulsive liar, he nevertheless found her compelling, intriguing and in part persuasive. Although she pledged to tell him the truth about the killings once the trial was over, this proved to be another lie. By confirming that her confession to the People's Police remained the most accurate depiction of the course of events, Dr Weimann implicitly commended the work of the eastern police authorities.[100] The *Berliner Zeitung* concluded that the Kusian case showed that cross-border cooperation was still possible. Without it, it would not have been possible to find the murderess so quickly or to establish her guilt so convincingly. Without this crucial cooperation, her killing spree might have continued to haunt the inhabitants of the divided, prostrate city.[101] In an interview, Weimann revealed that Seidelmann and Merten were not the only two bodies to be found in the ruins of divided Berlin. Since the collapse of the Third Reich, he had dissected about forty to fifty other headless, dismembered bodies. They were usually buried in rubble or thrown into water. Most were found near Zoo Station, but some had been deposited as far afield as Neukölln. Twenty to thirty cases had not been resolved; the dead were nearly all old women. Mostly, they had been crudely decapitated with an axe or had their heads roughly sawn away from the body.[102] What had stood out in the Kusian case was the adroitness of the cuts, suggesting someone with more than an elementary knowledge of anatomy.

Conclusion

Kusian banked on lack of cooperation or communication between the police forces in East and West. Despite the recent splitting of the police, in the spring of 1950, eastern detectives had cooperated with their western colleagues in reassembling the bodies and identifying the victims. The two forces managed to cooperate sufficiently to bring Berlin's cold-blooded angel of death to justice. Kusian was the most high-profile person to be handed over at the border in the early 1950s. Despite cold-war tensions, her case demonstrated the need for some residual cooperation between criminal investigators. She nevertheless tried to use the political differences as a way of discrediting her confession in the East and avoiding confirming her guilt in the West. Thanks to the impact of the cold war, detectives from one city police precinct had to fear the consequences of cooperating with the investigations of those from another. Kusian was going out with a married West Berlin detective and had attended lectures on murder methodology by Berlin's foremost autopsy expert, Dr Waldemar Weimann. She accidentally gave meaning to the deepening cold-war division of the city by depositing the body parts (that she had carefully dismembered in her shared flat) in both the East and West of the city. She was caught when the police cooperated across the border and reunited the scattered body parts (in a gruesome exercise in matching up the 'meat jigsaw'). She had given her detective boyfriend a typewriter stolen from her second victim. He had not noticed he was sleeping and wooing on a couch lying over a day-old corpse.

Weimann felt a certain responsibility and guilt for having given instructions to a murderer. The Kusian case again demonstrates the harmful effects of the war in encouraging such desperate acts. People had learnt to become ruthless in the aftermath of defeat. Mentally and physically scarred by the fighting, Kusian was a nurse who had come through the Battle for Berlin with an addiction to morphine. The Kusians' marriage had broken down and their children languished in an orphanage in the Soviet Sector. Unable to support her children, she lived alone with a landlady and three fellow pensioners in Charlottenburg. *Neues Deutschland* suggested that the crime would have been unthinkable in a city with a united police force and seamless justice systems.[103] By expressing rival claims to hegemony, the cold war politicized crime solving and the exercise of justice. Demonstrating police and judicial competency was a way of exercising one's state's claim to legitimate authority and sovereignty. For Cobra, it was thanks to the men and women of the People's Police that Berlin could free itself from a 'cruel murderess', who had learned her sinister craft through exposure to national socialism, Hitler's war and the omnipresent black market.[104]

Stealing from her patients to pay for her fix, Kusian struggled to hold down a nursing job. Amid postwar deprivation, she had attended Dr Weimann's lectures as a form of macabre divertissement. There, she had learnt the most effective way for a woman to kill a man, by sneaking up behind him with a length of rope. Kusian seemed to see herself as an angel of death, dispensing with worthless victims. The innocent offer of a cup of coffee was the prelude to murder. Despite sharing her flat with others, Kusian took the bread knife from the shared kitchen and used it to dissect the bodies of her victims. She showed a remarkable degree of skill and dexterity, in spite of her drug addiction. While it is not that surprising that she was ready to throw her ex-husband under the bus, in an effort to exculpate herself, it is remarkable that to express her love and appreciation for her new lover, Kusian was prepared to commit murder. Pleasing him was the chief motivation for her crimes. With hindsight, his readiness to accept her gifts, without questioning how she could pay for them, seemed suspect.[105]

Cobra presented the case as an unparalleled furore.[106] Exploiting the cold-war division of the city, she decided to leave the body parts in separate areas of the city. Seeking to use the fact of division to her advantage, by scattering of the body parts half in the East and half in the West, Kusian had attempted to confuse the police investigation.[107] The fact that her married policeman boyfriend had not detected the crime, despite having sex on top of the crime scene, was painfully embarrassing. Stashing the bodies under the couch on which they made love was too piquant a detail not to fascinate the tabloid press. In retrospect, too unlikely or farfetched to form the plot of a dime novel, even a hardboiled *noir* writer would have blanched at such a scenario. The case is interesting in what it reveals about the continued degree of police interaction and cooperation. Dr Weimann not only played an important role in providing a blueprint for the crime and a profile for the killer. He also questioned the murderess and provided a psychiatric report at the trial. He noted the macabre chemistry that developed between them once he had praised her skill in dissection.

Kusian's crimes destroyed four families: her victims', her own and her lover's. She died of cancer in 1958. It must have been awful for her children to grow up without a mother in an eastern orphanage. Leaving a trail of broken bodies in their wake, both Gladow and Kusian exhibited a lack of impulse control. The artificial division of the city failed to improve the dire postwar economic situation or psychological scars left behind by the Nazism and the war. Only residual East-West cooperation, in spite of the cold war, could bring their cross-border sprees to an end.

Notes

1. Cobra, 'Mordprozeß Elisabeth Kusian. Sensation um Jeden Preis. Herr M. macht von sich reden', *Berliner Zeitung*, 16 January 1951.
2. Horst Bosetzky, *Cold Angel: Murder in Berlin 1949*, trans. Catherine D. Miller (New York: Enigma, 2012), 40. Written by a sociologist, this is fiction 'backed up with' contemporary documentary material.
3. The gruesome autopsy photographs show that the body had been 'cleanly sectioned' with an 'expert release of the bone head'. Police Museum, Elizabeth Kusian File.
4. Waldemar Weimann, *Diagnose Mord: Die Memoiren eines Gerichtsmediziners* (Bayreuth: Hestia, 1964), 7.
5. 'Schlußbericht', 27 February 1950. Files unless otherwise stated from Landesarchiv Berlin, B Rep 058, Nr. 7030, Box 121. Cf. Ingo Wirth and Andreas Schmeling, *Kriminelle Leichenzerstückelung: Phänomenologie und Untersuchungsmethodik* (Baden-Baden: Nomos, 2017).
6. They were found in the ruins near Borsigstrasse. 'Schlußbericht', 23 January 1950, Landesarchiv Berlin, B Rep 058, 7030/1, Box 120.
7. While neither side condoned criminality, they did turn a blind eye to certain (minor) offences in certain areas.
8. Implausibly, Kusian turned out to have been working a few hundred yards away from the autopsy room, in the same hospital. Weimann, *Diagnose Mord*, 12.
9. Landesarchiv Berlin, B Rep 058, Nr. 7030, Box 121.
10. 'Vermerk', 6 January 1950.
11. The police report shows photographs of the flat and her room. Police Museum. Kusian was born Elisabeth Richter in Thuringia in May 1914.
12. Cobra, 'Berlins Volkspolizei meldet: Doppelmörderin Kusian legt Geständnis ab. Erfolge unserer Volkspolizei Tagesgespräch von Berlin. Unfaßbare Bluttaten einer Frau', *Neues Deutschland*, 11 January 1950.
13. Bosetzky, *Cold Angel*, 67.
14. Cobra juxtaposed the People's Police's help in solving the Kusian case with the Stumm police's supposed obstruction of the trial of the Gladow Gang. Cobra, 'Mordprozeß Elisabeth Kusian. Walter Kusian haftentlassen. Fauler Astrologen-Zauber', *Berliner Zeitung*, 20 January 1951.
15. Weimann, *Diagnose Mord*, 8.
16. Cobra, 'Berlins Volkspolizei meldet'.
17. Weimann, *Diagnose Mord*, 8.
18. Bosetzky, *Cold Angel*, 169.

19 'Mordserie einer Krankenschwester? Erfreuliche Zusammenarbeit der Polizei in Ost- und Westberlin', *Neue Zeit*, 10 January 1950.
20 'Schlußbericht', 23 January 1950.
21 Weimann, *Diagnose Mord*, 20. Berlin's foremost pathologist and head of the Institute for Forensic Medicine was a rare *Ostgänger*, a West Berliner who worked in East Berlin. While many of the forensic experts had fled to the West, Weimann persisted in carrying out dissections in both East and West Berlin. As in the Gladow case, he also provided the police with forensic expertise.
22 'Geständnis der Mörderin Kusian. Beim Anblick der Krawatte des Opfers zusammengebrochen', *Tagesspiegel*, 11 January 1950.
23 'Zusammenarbeit in Berlin ist möglich. Was lernen die Berliner aus der Aufklärung des Mordfalles Kusian?', *Berliner Zeitung*, 13 January 1950.
24 Interrogation of Krim.-Sekretär Kurt M. [no date, ca. January 1950]. Cf. Weimann, *Diagnose Mord*, 20.
25 'Schlußbericht', 23 January 1950.
26 'Der Geliebte der Doppelmörderin', *Neues Deutschland*, 17 January 1950.
27 Interrogation of Krim.-Sekretär Kurt M.
28 Weimann, *Diagnose Mord*, 36, 41.
29 Ibid., 17.
30 Interrogation of Krim.-Sekretär Kurt M.
31 'Verhandelt', 13 February 1950.
32 'Schlußbericht', 23 January 1950.
33 'Verhandelt', 10 January 1950.
34 'Bericht', 10 January 1950.
35 In Bosetzky's account, the ambitious Nazi metamorphoses into a war criminal. Bosetzky, *Cold Angel*, 111.
36 Weimann, *Diagnose Mord*, 32.
37 'Ein für die Stumm-Polizei peinlicher Prozeß', *Tägliche Rundschau*, 16 January 1951.
38 'Verhandelt', 13 February 1950.
39 Wendy Lower, *Hitler's Furies: German Women in the Nazi Killing Fields* (London: Vintage, 2014). Amy L. Zroka, 'Serving the Volksgemeinschaft: German Red Cross Nurses in the Second World War', PhD, University of California, San Diego, 2015.
40 Cobra, 'Berlins Volkspolizei meldet'.
41 *Telegraf*, 14 January 1951, as cited by Bosetzky, *Cold Angel*, 209.
42 '"Die schöne Frau vom Zoo . . ." stand auf der Zigarettenschachtel des ermordeten Seidelmann', *Der Abend*, 11 January 1951.
43 'Verhandelt', 13 February 1950.
44 'Verhandelt', 15 February 1950.
45 'Verhandelt', 16 February 1950.
46 The knife was very ordinary looking with a straight blade. Police Museum, Elizabeth Kusian File.
47 'Doppelmörderin Kusian legt Geständnis ab. Erfolge unserer Volkspolizei Tagesgespräch von Berlin. Unfaßbare Bluttaten einer Frau', *Neues Deutschland*, 11 January 1950.
48 'Die Gutachter haben das Wort. Die Kusian ist für ihre Taten voll verantwortlich – Schiffbruch der Verteidigung', *Neue Zeit*, 18 January 1951.
49 'Verhandelt', 15 February 1950.
50 'Verhandelt', 10 January 50.
51 'Verhandelt', 16 February 1950.

52 'Vermerk', 10 February 1950.
53 Interrogation, 21 February 1950.
54 Cobra, 'Berlins Volkspolizei meldet'.
55 'Die Kusian kam über die Sektorengrenze. Ostberlin lieferte die Doppelmörderin an Westberlin aus – Übergabe an der Sandkrugbrücke', *Neue Zeitung*, 9 February 1950; 'Eine Mörderin wird ausgeliefert', *Neues Deutschland*, 9 February 1950.
56 Kube, 'Uns ist aufgefallen: Eine Mörderin wird ausgeliefert', *Neues Deutschland*, 9 February 1950.
57 'Die Kusian kam über die Sektorengrenze', *Kurier*, 9 February 1950.
58 'Zusammenarbeit in Berlin ist möglich'.
59 'Übernahme der Kusian von der Kriminalpolizei des Ostsektors am 8.2.1950', Landesarchiv Berlin, B Rep 058, Nr. 7030, Box 121.
60 Weimann, *Diagnose Mord*, 21.
61 '"Das gemeinste Weib, das ich kenne". Was eine Untersuchungsgefangene über die Kusian sagte – Der Gerichtspsychiater als Zeuge', *Telegraf*, 24 January 1951.
62 Together with medical officer Dr Rolf Niedenthal, Weimann wrote an official 71-page report on the murders. Based on their observations of police interviews and their own questioning, they judged Kusian a hysterical psychopath who clearly lacked empathy. Nevertheless, the two experts judged her neither 'mentally ill nor feeble minded', thereby fully responsible for her criminal acts. Gunther Geserick, Klaus Vendura and Ingo Wirth, *Zeitzeuge Tod: spektakuläre Fälle der Berliner Gerichtsmedizin* (Leipzig: Militzke, 2001), 81, 83.
63 'Das gemeinste Weib, das ich kenne'. Strangely, they only asked for him to assist the interrogations relating to Seidelmann's death.
64 Weimann, *Diagnose Mord*, 22.
65 'Verhandelt', 13 February 1950.
66 'Der Mörder ist noch unter uns', *Kurier*, 10 January 1950.
67 Weimann, *Diagnose Mord*, 20, 5.
68 'Der Neujahrsglückwunsch der Mörderin', *Neue Zeit*, 24 January 1951.
69 'Das gemeinste Weib, das ich kenne'.
70 Bosetzky has the eloquent defence attorney criticizing his brother's qualifications. Bosetzky, *Cold Angel*, 253.
71 'Das gemeinste Weib, das ich kenne'. Bosetzky stresses Kusian's sexpertise. In his imagination, she really knew how to drive men crazy. 'No man can resist me usually, it works every time'. Bosetzky, *Cold Angel*, 102, 107.
72 'Lügen, Morphium, Liebe, Mord . . . Das Leben der Elisabeth Kusian – Über ihre Verbrechen schweigt sie – Erste Zeugenaussagen', *Telegraf*, 16 January 1951. Cf. Walter Stumm, 'Les Meurtres d'Elisabeth Kusian', *Revue Internationale de Police Criminelle* 62, no. 7 (1952): 278–88.
73 Cobra, 'Mordprozeß Elisabeth Kusian. Das dicke "Geständnis" der Mörderin. Ehemann schwer belastet', *Berliner Zeitung*, 17 January 1951. Cf. 'Kusianitis', *Neues Deutschland*, 20 January 1951.
74 Cobra, 'Mordprozeß Elisabeth Kusian. Sensation'.
75 Bosetzky, *Cold Angel*, 216.
76 'Rummel um den Kusian-Prozeß. Ablenkung von der Remilitarisierung. Welche Rolle spielte Kurt M.?', *Neues Deutschland*, 16 January 1951. Nevertheless, the eastern press also provided juicy details about her life in prison. Kiebitz, 'Kakao gemixt mit Leidenschaft. Die Zellengenossin der Frau Kusian', *Berliner Zeitung*, 26 December 1950.

77 'Eine Mörderin interessiert sie mehr', *Berliner Zeitung*, 20 January 1951.
78 'Hatte die Angeklagte Helfer?', *Tagesspiegel*, 20 January 1951.
79 Cobra, 'Mordprozeß Elisabeth Kusian. Walter Kusian haftentlassen'. 'Kopflosigkeit im Westberliner Kusian-Prozeß. Unzulängliche Prozeßführung – Ehemann Kusian wieder frei', *Neue Zeit*, 20 January 1951.
80 Cobra, 'Mordprozeß Elisabeth Kusian. Sensation'.
81 Cobra, 'Justitia tanzte Boogie-Woogie. Hinter den Kulissen des Kusian-Theaters in Moabit', *Berliner Zeitung*, 26 January 1951.
82 Kusian supposedly smiled when she remembered the cluelessness of the West Berlin police. Cobra, 'Mordprozeß Elisabeth Kusian. Walter Kusian haftentlassen'.
83 'Ein für die Stumm-Polizei peinlicher Prozeß'.
84 Cobra, 'Mordprozeß Elisabeth Kusian. Vorbildliche Arbeit der Volkspolizei – einzig verläßliche Unterlage', *Berliner Zeitung*, 18 January 1951.
85 Cobra, 'Berlins Volkspolizei meldet'.
86 'Höchststrafe für Frau Kusian. Es bleiben Rätsel – aber keine Zweifel!', *Kurier*, 25 January 1951.
87 Cobra, 'Mordprozeß Elisabeth Kusian. Sensation'.
88 'Die Westjustiz wird mit dem Fall Kusian nicht fertig', *Tägliche Rundschau*, 17 January 1951. Kusian's defence team did try to throw suspicion on Kurt M.
89 'Rummel um den Kusian-Prozeß'.
90 'Verteidiger unter der Mord-Couch', *Telegraf*, 18 January 1951.
91 Cobra, 'Mordprozeß Elisabeth Kusian. Vorbildliche'.
92 'Das gemeinste Weib, das ich kenne'.
93 Presenting Walter as a cold-blooded killer, who had joined the NSDAP in 1926, Bosetzky takes the possibility that he was involved in his ex-wife's murders as the basis for his novel. Bosetzky, *Cold Angel*, 8.
94 'Volkspolizei hat vorbildlich gearbeitet. Der zweite Tag des Kusian-Prozesses. Neue "Geständnisse"', *Neues Deutschland*, 17 January 1951.
95 'Kusian-Prozeß auf dem toten Punkt', *Tägliche Rundschau*, 18 January 1951.
96 'Umgangsformen mit einer Mörderin: Friedenskämpfer sind für die Westberliner Justiz "gefährlicher"', *Neues Deutschland*, 18 January 1951.
97 Cobra, 'Mordprozeß Elisabeth Kusian. Vorbildliche'.
98 'Zweimal lebenslänglich für Kusian. "Sensationsprozeß" konnte das Westberliner Elend nicht verschleiern', *Neues Deutschland*, 25 January 1951.
99 Bosetzky, *Cold Angel*, 256.
100 'Die Gutachter haben das Wort'. Cf. Cobra, 'Mordprozeß Elisabeth Kusian. Abschluß der Beweisaufnahme', *Berliner Zeitung*, 24 January 1951.
101 'Zusammenarbeit in Berlin ist möglich. Was lernen die Berliner aus der Aufklärung des Mordfalles Kusian?', *Berliner Zeitung*, 13 January 1950.
102 'Der Mörder ist noch unter uns'.
103 'Was die West-Justiz nicht wahrhaben wollte. Nur das erste Kusian-Geständnis bei der Volkspolizei ist wahr', *Neues Deutschland*, 24 January 1951.
104 Cobra, 'Justitia tanzte Boogie-Woogie'.
105 'Die Westjustiz wird mit dem Fall Kusian nicht fertig'.
106 Cobra, 'Mordprozeß Elisabeth Kusian. Sensation'.
107 Kusian insisted that she did not think anything – 'I wasn't thinking at all' – when she dumped the body parts. Under the influence of the drugs, she just found the suitcase heavy and cumbersome. Weimann, *Diagnose Mord*, 29.

Conclusion

Each post-conflict city acts as a laboratory for studying outside attempts to achieve societal change by means of reformed policing. Realistic foreign policing advisers admit that it will probably take a generation to implement their reforms effectively.[1] Western, liberal commentators and donors tend to assume that their way is the best way. Their attempts to reform policing structures often fail because they do not sufficiently take local cultures, customs and norms into account. They seek to apply a model based on democratic and community-policing objectives to societies that have very little or no intrinsic democracy and starkly hierarchical social structures. Alice Hills is an expert on post-conflict policing. She is sharply critical of western assumptions, seeing attempts to create multi-ethnic forces, with a high proportion of female officers, as nothing less than ethnocentric and deluded (pie-in-the-sky) impositions. This lesson has been repeated around the world in cities as varied as Basra, Baghdad, Freetown, Grozny, Juba, Kabul, Kaduna, Kigali, Kinshasa, Mogadishu, Monrovia and Sarajevo. Again and again, she found that outside ideas simply bounced off resilient police structures, without making any discernible long-term impact or dent.

Upending engrained police values was difficult: the only universal trait policemen seem to possess is a reluctance to follow outside calls to reform themselves. Even in a society that is not recovering from conflict, or beset by foreign occupation, changing a police culture is easier said than done. The prevailing informal 'cop culture' proves highly resistant to change.[2] When outside authorities and donors are split, it becomes even more difficult to formulate and implement coherent reform policies. Sporadic and ill-coordinated reforms are easier to frustrate and repel.[3] The case of postwar Berlin suggests that the concrete impact of international attempts to reform indigenous German policing was similarly muted. However well-meaning and enlightened, the reforms were piecemeal and contested rather than sweeping. Although the Allies ended up staying in Berlin for forty-nine years (from 1945 to 1994), policing had their undivided attention for only two. They were simply not united or cohesive enough to provide sustained engagement. Consequently, much of the organization's pre-existing structure, outlook and approach survived intact. Despite the attempts at reform, a distinctly local 'police culture' or identity persisted. Self-conceptions, ethos and psychology were only partially influenced by reforms and changes to basic training. In the long run, the impact of outside reforms on everyday policing was minor. If, compared to other post-conflict cities, the Berlin police were more protectors than predators, they nevertheless tended to ignore foreign interference or guidance.

Street-level policing tends to reveal the true nature of power and the hierarchical relationships on which it is based.[4] Citizens, law abiding or not, gain their impressions of the police through their everyday encounters with ordinary, rank-and-file, patrol officers. They are generally unaware of the overarching strategy or reform agenda supposedly guiding their conduct. As a manifestation of the power of the state, at the level of the street corner, the police officer represents the 'relations of power' within his or her society. Their rule (*Herrschaft*) is blatant, but how it is carried out reflects subterranean mechanisms and processes of discrimination in the exercise of power.[5]

This book has explored the power imbalance and sense of upended hierarchy that existed between the occupiers and occupied, or rulers and ruled, in damaged, scarred Berlin. Virtue rubbed shoulders with everyday squalor and iniquity, with structural asymmetries favouring the latter. The occupation was an exercise in blatantly imbalanced power. From the beginning, the positions were intentionally unequal. With the Allies meting out rewards and punishments, they tarred the civilian population of Berlin with all-encompassing guilt.[6] One of the policemen, who served in 1945, was tasked with preventing children from rummaging for scraps in the bins, while the British Military Government sat down to full banquets inside their headquarters.[7] This amply illustrates the aloof lack of empathy of the occupiers. It would be easy to present the occupiers as simply exploiting the Germans as if they were inferior colonial subjects.[8]

Life could be cheap in a city still heavily marked (psychologically as well as physically) by the recent conflict. Within days of taking over their Sector, the Americans had shot and killed marauding Soviet soldiers. Well-nourished, rambunctious American children could, if the situation required it, shoot and kill German intruders, without concern for the consequences. Foreign whippersnappers were higher in the pecking order than ordinary German policemen. The gulf separating the occupation officers from the occupied comes close to a caste system. American officers were dismissive of the idea that they had created anything like such a system in Germany. As Susan Carruthers argues, to the beneficiaries of such a system, entitlement is often invisible.[9] As they had previously done in Shanghai, the British, French and Americans demonstrated that they could single-mindedly pursue their own interests, with scant regard for a defeated nation's sovereignty. General Sir Brian Robertson believed that the British occupation was benevolent and enlightened. Nevertheless, he recognized that a protracted, colonial-style tutelage would inevitably delay democratic recovery.[10]

The Allies self-consciously arrived as conquerors rather than as liberators.[11] Their initial preoccupation was with controlling vanquished German civilians rather than rebuilding the devastated city. Only a rare set of exceptional individuals straddled both worlds, capable of seeing how what was envisaged as 'justice' in one could mutate into 'injustice' in the other.[12] There was not just one rule for the rich; the Allies had their own legal system and could not be pursued or prosecuted by German courts. The policemen tasked with restoring law and order had no right to arrest Allied servicemen however improper or dangerous their behaviour. In West as well as in East Berlin, the Berliners had no right of legal redress against any of their foreign occupiers.[13] It took a long time for Berliners to see the Western Allies as genuine providers of security and democracy, focused on indigenous wellbeing. Journalist and broadcaster Egon Bahr felt neither defeated nor liberated in 1945. Instead, he and other Berliners merely found themselves the objects and playthings of the victors.[14] Unexpectedly, it was the

Airlift that helped to build an emotional bridge between the Berliners and their onetime enemies (allowing Allied flyers to be recast as newfound saviours).

The prevalence of poverty and crime considerably complicated attempts to reimagine policing. A gulf separated the worldview of the new rulers and the desperation of the emaciated survivors. Long after the victory, hunger was an aching, nagging pain that never went away.[15] It is difficult for the well-fed to imagine the distress and agony caused by this inescapable craving for sustenance. The sole concern of the anonymous journalist, in April–May 1945, was for appeasing her stomach. All her thoughts and feelings, all her wishes and hopes, began and ended with food.[16] This book seeks to understand the specific reality of Berlin as a living, breathing, but scarred city. By assessing the actions and behaviours of its plucky, ducking and diving inhabitants, we can seek to assess their mentalities. Of those dwelling within its municipal boundaries between 1945 and 1950, most were German, considerably more than half were women, while an important minority were foreign. Multiple Berliners had been injured or scarred, physically or mentally, by the recent conflict. As well as the four victors, multiple nations, ranging from Brazil to Australia, had Military Missions in the ex-capital. Of the soldiery, a few were black, possessors of a much-sought-after culture as well as objects of racial prejudice. Without always speaking the language, the occupiers lived alongside the occupied. In West Berlin, the Americans enjoyed the most distance and aloofness; the French, by contrast, endured considerable familiarity-driven contempt.

The context for what eventually became a cold-war conflict was a city in ruins, the capital of a defeated, divided, occupied country. The audience the would-be moral re-educators were playing to was a population deeply scarred by Nazism, total war, cold, hunger and mass rape. The experience of living in a dictatorship increasingly overtly marked by murderous racism had already done much to erode traditional notions of morality. Ending the Nazi vision of a racial New Order, the epic nature of the Battle for Berlin led to a further catastrophic collapse of boundaries. This was, after all, a combat in which fourteen-year-old boys were thrown into battle against Soviet tanks. There followed what historian Ralf Dahrendorf called a 'supreme, horrible moment of utter lawlessness'. Amid the chaos of destruction and defeat, stealing was the first notion to lose its meaning.[17]

Imbalanced occupier-occupied relations were most starkly expressed in the black market and in the adjunct everyday economy of sex. The murky tawdriness of the ex-Nazi capital both astounded and allured outsiders. As contemporaries (foreign and German) recounted, the derelict landscape provided secluded spaces for all sorts of illicit trading. In the eyes of the haughty victors, the natives, young and old, were equally disposable: the Allies found love and hate, but above all sex, among the ruins.[18] The chief interface between occupiers and occupied, in the first eighteen months after the occupation began, was oral-genital; tinned meat bought hanky-panky and vice versa. If occupation was designed to 're-educate' Berliners in an almost Skinnerist way – with clear incentives and disincentives to particular behaviours – the equation of 'sex = cigarettes = survival' created its own perverse and irrefutable logic.[19] By linking sustenance with sex, they characterized and tainted the occupation for years to come. Postwar Berlin was a strange city where cigarettes had monetary value but could not be bought with banknotes. Tremendous, corrosive misery lay alongside undreamed-of luxury.[20] A chasm separated the haves from the desperate have-nots.

If power corrupts, absolute power corrupts absolutely. Charity and concern could not disguise the starkly asymmetrical relations of power. As British poet and essayist T. S. Eliot implored, 'O Lord, deliver me from the man of excellent intention and impure heart: for the heart is deceitful above all things, and desperately wicked.'[21] Was the 'good occupation', fondly remembered by veterans and popular culture, really a sordid, debased one?[22] Coloured by the previous mass rapes, committed by the victorious Soviet troops, the postwar shenanigans were part of what had wounded the city.[23] The saviours rode in, tried ineffectually to 'reform' a dysfunctional police system, and then rode out again, having liberally sexually exploited the local population. In already hopelessly damaged and bereft societies, knights in shining armour – although claiming to bring the ethos and values of the gleaming 'city on the hill' – can quickly turn into villains. In *A Foreign Affair*, the Austrian-born Hollywood director (and ex-Berlin cultural officer) Billy Wilder managed to capture the juxtaposition of poverty and plenty in a city mired in corruption and vice.[24] Exposés of sexual violence and exploitation, perpetrated by peacekeepers and supposedly humanitarian aid workers, suggest that the Allies were not alone in mixing the 'business' of occupation with their own, sordid versions of pleasure.[25] Partying in the ruins of a deeply wounded city, the sex tourism had a mawkish quality. If anything, these intimate, personal-political (or biopolitical) entanglements are more revealing of mentalities than their geopolitical variant.

Allied and German Berlin were overlapping, but separate (political, economic and emotional) worlds. Most Berliners never came within spitting distance of an Allied officer, but they keenly felt the impact of the latter's policy decisions. For most British and American occupation personnel, the only Germans they really 'knew' were their gardeners, nursemaids, drivers or cooks; in other words: servants. Relaxing at home during a meal, 'one of our star-studded military men' unconsciously happened to rest his foot on the buzzer connected to the kitchen. A furious German cook ensured that he never made that mistake again.[26] General Clay could rule his Sector and Zone as if he were a Roman emperor, dictating laws on the hoof, but he did so without caring to learn any (even broken) German. Nevertheless, postwar Allied 'engineers of the soul', like Clay, proved to be sensitive and perspicacious administrators. Without speaking their lingo, he felt that he nevertheless intrinsically understood the Berliners and was able to get on their wavelength.

In the introduction, I asked whether Berlin was sui generis or if it behaved similarly to other cities emerging from the violence of war? For Hills, Berlin and Vienna in the 1940s were as notorious, as hotbeds of crime and disorder, as Mogadishu and Belgrade were in the 1990s.[27] One way to present the crucial post-conflict years in the ex-Nazi capital would be in terms of pluck. The noble victors enabled the spirited and resolute Berliners – foremost among them female police recruits – to put their beloved, but wounded, city back on its feet. There is certainly evidence to support this contention: alongside the very real sacrifices of the 'rubble women', we can see glimpses of potential equality in female involvement in policing. Yet, even at the precise moment when they were putting their lives on the line, their male superiors went out of their way to dismiss them, aided and abetted by would-be objective journalists, who openly patronized the brave recruits. So, do these faint whiffs of freedom really matter if the system and the prevailing mentalities (both Allied and German) remained patriarchal and overtly clientelist in their everyday transactions? Men in authority show an incredible ability to dismiss, ignore and then rapidly forget female (and non-white) contributions. Berlin from 1945 to 1949 was no exception. Pace Hills, German society may not have got the policing it deserved, but it got the form, expression and culture (or modus operandus) that those in power wanted.

In fighting the lawlessness and topsy-turvy disorganization of postwar Berlin, the city's policemen and policewomen showed exemplary courage and resourcefulness. But law and order did not exist separately to issues of governance just as mentalities did not exist independently of gender. The disconcerting limbo and savage lawlessness of sole Soviet rule cast a long shadow, poisoning even ardent German Communists against such an occupation. Physical destruction to police infrastructure together with the psychological impact of decisive defeat eroded traditional forms of social control to cause a spike in crime. The decisions taken (and not taken) by the governing authorities improved or worsened this situation. Occupation historian Donnison reflected the fears of many of his contemporaries when he argued that, without a swift re-establishment of order and sufficient food, the occupation governments could have lapsed into anarchy, chaos and bloodshed.[28] At times, the veneer separating order from chaos seemed wafer thin. If the economic-supply situation remained chaotic and fundamentally unequal, how could they hope to stamp out the black market and the various adjunct forms of corruption and criminality? Withholding food from a hungry population is, in itself, a form of violence. As General Clay perceptively remarked, it would prove impossible to try to rebuild democracy on top of a heap of ruins and a 'starvation diet'.[29]

This book takes governance – good and bad – seriously, seeing how it impacted on order and policing at different levels, sometimes creating perverse incentives for illegality. In part, the crimes of violence that occurred did so because of the poverty and hunger imposed on the population for years following the Armistice. Germany's defeat fostered theft and the black market, bringing large numbers of people into crime (and contact with criminals) for the first time.[30] Even without a legacy of ethnic cleansing and genocide, healing the scars and divisions of a city wracked by violence could be daunting. Five years after the Armistice, much scar tissue remained. Like other post-conflict cities, Berlin suffered from a surfeit of poverty, hunger and crime together with depleted mechanisms of social control.[31] A subsection of Berliners had been corrupted by the black market and seemed unwilling or unable to unlearn criminal behaviour. If surviving in cold-war Berlin was a tightrope act, remaining on the straight and narrow path to redemption seemed almost impossible for many. Criminals with experience of the '*Milljöh*' (as artist Heinrich Zille dubbed the pre–World War One criminal milieu) are the foremost practitioners of '*Berliner Schnauze*' (the inimitable brand of coarse, outspoken, garrulous humour). Threatened with the death penalty, for example, one of Gladow's gang suggested they lay his headless corpse on its front so that the prosecutor could better lick his dead arse.[32]

What was the point of pursuing 'reform' – denazification and professionalization of the police via major recruitment initiatives and training endeavours – if, because of low pay and poor conditions, those recruits only stayed for a few months? Attempts to reform policing were important for the long term, but in the short term, threatened to undermine attempts to control crime in the city. The Allies went into Berlin convinced that the only way to reform policing was to impose their own ideas on the nascent, re-emergent police force. They could not trust Germans, even anti-Nazis, to provide the necessary oversight and guidance.[33] We can ask whether reforms made that much difference to the policing of the ex-capital in the three years between defeat and division. For the Berlin police, social and national continuities in mentality often had a greater impact than the novel (geo-)political boundaries. Despite a genuine desire to reform on the part of the Allies, language, tradition, custom, expressions of masculinity, psychology and, not least, the law saw policing revert to its familiar form and function. 'Reformers forget at their peril the social realities of policing, the multiplicity of ways in which order is reproduced, and the multidimensional nature of security.'[34] Berlin in the 1940s supports Hills's argument about the nous and wherewithal police officers can manifest, in warding off and manipulating external pressures for change. As in other post-conflict cities, reform initiatives, in the period 1945–7, proved temporary and sporadic, allowing policing standards and procedures to 'drift back' to the supposedly superseded norm.[35] What the Allies were unable to change was as important as what they could. Only with great difficulty could these foreign advisers infect German beat policemen with an ethos or a set of values that were unfamiliar or alien to them. Greater familiarity with local conditions, customs and mentalities – not least being able to speak the lingo – tended to trump even urgent and insistent foreign interventions.

If anything, having four separate, foreign stakeholders reduced their shared capacity to influence the implementation of policy. Even before the onset of the cold war, and routine use of the veto to stymie progress, there was little shared vision or common ground, especially on a topic as sensitive, and as nationally and ideologically divergent, as policing. Having four armies in one city, each with its own bureaucratic machinery (let alone differences of language and culture), was always going to be a recipe for chaos. It was easy for the Berliners to exploit contrasting positions and outlooks and to play divide and rule with the victors. Berlin politicians were able to use the developing cold war to bolster their position vis-à-vis the foreign occupiers.[36] The one language not spoken in the *Kommandatura* was German. This speaks volumes about that *Gremium*'s capacity to enact change. If the Allies could not manage to speak with a single, authoritative voice, why should the German police chiefs listen to them?

With the rank-and-file thick as thieves, strategies for change are slow to filter through intact. The policy implemented at the lowest level, on the street, can be very different from how it was envisaged in the high command.[37] With the onset of cold-war tension, the Allies became increasingly watchful of each other, and this tended to take their eyes off both the German governors and the governed. Although more sustained than in the subsequent decade, much of their intervention was consequently discursive rather than pragmatic. Outside advisers, especially ones who disagree about their remit, tend not to make much of an impact. With such radically different outlooks, ideals and values, within the *Kommandatura* and its Public Safety Committee, it was easy for discussion of policing reform to become stymied and kicked into the weeds. There is a gulf between Public Safety Committee horse trading and what mattered to recruits:

uniforms, equipment, notably footwear and weapons, pay and conditions (not least rations). Nobody wanted a police force exhibiting corruption or brutality and yet there were important obstacles to cooperation and realism. As the war receded, Berliners began to ask why 'their' police force should adopt the values of Britain, France, the United States or the USSR.[38] In some ways, Berlin's police coped with the crime wave so admirably because it proved so impervious to change. Whatever the foreign designs, it stayed connected to, and on the same wavelength as, the local culture and society. The understanding of their role – shared by both the police and the policed – never wavered. Policing was like a 'Stretch Armstrong' toy: it could be pulled and poked, stretched and twisted, but it unerringly reverted to its original shape.

Political scientist Mark Neocleous argues that order and security, together with the related concepts of policing and law enforcement, are 'fetishized concepts' that reflect the self-understandings of bourgeois society. Whether in Communist East or capitalist West Berlin, ordinary citizens would have regarded such a statement with incredulity.[39] The police played a crucial role in re-establishing and enforcing public order, whether reflective of state-socialist or of bourgeois rule. If anything, the East German Communists were more inclined to fetishize order than their 'hopelessly bourgeois' democratic rivals. Despite some populist features, there was a strong sense that the police in the eastern sector served the state rather than the people. If the initial goal of policing was, broadly speaking, conflict prevention, then the goalposts radically shifted. In Berlin, order could be a naked and brutal expression of power. In part, from 1948 onwards, the rival police forces became proxies in a symbolic battle for control of the streets. Nevertheless, it is important to note that a major *bavure* like the Ohnesorg killing came in 1967 and not in 1947. The shots fired during the 1949 *Reichsbahn* strike represented the most out-of-control situation of the postwar period.[40] It was not an experience that either side wanted to repeat.

Whatever the cartoonists may have thought, West Berlin was never policed by bobbies, *gendarmes* or sheriffs. Even in female form, the uniformed patrol officers bore a strong resemblance to their German predecessors. Despite the all-too-real Nazi excesses, the Berlin police had a tradition of civilized policing that they could both be proud of and fall back on.[41] In this sense, the police force did not just pursue law and order; it also acted as a political force, with constitutional aims and implications in terms of legitimacy, hegemony and *Herrschaft*. When the Western Allies eventually disengaged from four-power governance, they became more unified, and of one mind, in pursuing the cold war. Nevertheless, even here differences persisted. The Stumm police came to represent a fundamental component of West Berlin's separate, sovereign existence. The only overtly military forces allowed in the city belonged to the four victorious Allies. So, in the absence of a West Berlin army, the police (including from 1950 its paramilitary *Bepo* element) carried the burden of protecting and defending the polity.[42]

Hills ends up concluding that 'societies get the policing they deserve.'[43] Despite the visible legacy of World War Two and knowledge of the Holocaust, Berliners struggled to understand what they had done to deserve their fate, especially in relation to policing. The security void of the weeks immediately after the Armistice was replaced by a different kind of insecurity. The visible employment of women officers was the most blatant incidence of the Allies using policing in pursuit of social change. Nevertheless, because of the persistence of the macho 'canteen culture', it is not clear that their presence tempered the militancy or outlook of the force. The cold war complicated the 'exit strategies' possessed and pursued by the victors. None of the four powers could now afford a humiliating withdrawal. This strengthened the hands of conservatives in the (West Berlin) police hierarchy like Dr Stumm. The goals of the force he presided over were, in important ways, different from the original rationale of the Public Safety Committee in 1945. During early 1948, the splitting of the Berlin police into antagonistic, rival entities became a major goal of the rulers in Washington and Moscow. The cold war created a certain amount of legal plurality within the city, with overlapping and entangled jurisdictions. English-language histories of postwar German policing represent an underdeveloped area.[44] The role of policing in accelerating the onset of the cold war in Berlin is particularly under-researched.[45]

Visitors to postwar Berlin interpreted it according to their own preoccupations and obsessions. For some African Americans, it was Shangri-La, for ex-bomber Sir Arthur Tedder it was Carthage and for those fearing its lawlessness, kidnapping and espionage activities, it was a new Shanghai. For Berliners, unitary policing was the norm; when it came, the rupture on 28 July 1948 was sudden and catastrophic. Dividing a city is like severing its limbs; the remaining trunk was incapacitated, but retained feelings for the phantom, dismembered appendages. The cold war cannot be understood without assessing the paradoxical, conflicting, but also intertwined, histories of the two conjoined twins, East and West Berlin.

We commonly look to the state to provide us with protection. In 1940s Berlin, that protection was not guaranteed to all citizens. With the onset of the cold war, it became completely impossible to reconcile the conflicting positions. The logic of this displaced, proxy warfare encouraged both sides to pursue dissensus. One of the four occupying powers had begun to renege on its contract with its own and the neighbouring citizens, with grave implications for the security of the local population. Cold-war enmity increasingly hijacked policing within local power relations. The parallel, hostile police forces were the most blatant symbol of the city's division. A divided police force complicated the question of who possessed legitimate violence. Hannah Arendt insisted that if the state exercising it was not legitimate, then the violence it exerted could not be legitimate. 'Violence can be justifiable, but it never will be legitimate.'[46] At times, notably during the summer of 1948, shootings occurred which threatened to degenerate into a wider conflict. This new form of hostility, the war of a thousand pinpricks, required men with great inner strength and unflappability. A very thin line, made up of human beings, prevented everyday brinkmanship in Berlin from erupting into World War Three. At moments of extreme tension, continued peace depended on the presence of mind and cool judgement of junior officers. A solitary British Deputy Provost Marshal could calmly walk over to the armed Soviets and, 'with his swagger stick', gently nudge them away from the riled-up German demonstrators.[47] Armed with little more than a conducting baton and a sense of purpose, a lone figure could pull the divided city back from the brink.

The psychological wounds produced by the disorder of defeat took a long time to heal. Berlin was still very much a 'wounded city' in 1961 as well as 1951; the open, but disputed, border was a lasting legacy of sustained 'urban trauma'.[48] Germans have a reputation for loving order, but defeated Berlin suffered a catastrophic collapse of organization and authority. Both the Gladow and the Kusian cases show that the very difficult situation and conditions at the end of the war cast a long shadow. Kusian's cosy furnished room offered the incongruity of 'soft music' and brutal murder. As microhistorians, we can find meaning in such criminals' extraordinary misbehaviour as well as in the banal and the mundane.[49] A combination of Nazism and postwar confusion had shattered 'pre-existing conceptions of morality'. That nurse Kusian chose to dump her grim collection of body parts in both East and West Berlin was 'probably an attempt to confuse the police investigators, but it also represented an unconscious metaphor for the dismembered, ripped apart, severed city. Nevertheless, despite the urge for competition and factionalism within the police as a profession, a residue of cooperation persisted. As the Kusian case showed, in spite of the division, the police authorities occasionally continued to cooperate and hand over wanted criminals at the border.

Viewed through the lens of everyday microhistory, or the history of mentalities, what do the 'true crime' case studies say about agency, legitimacy, hegemony or *Herrschaft*? Were the perpetrators more than mere passive objects of the history they lived through? It is difficult to describe either Kusian or Gladow as possessing agency. In the defeated, dismembered city, any such agency was tainted by illegality or complicity. To some extent, the binary is an expression of human nature, of pessimism vs. optimism. In committing murder, Kusian and Gladow exhibited a tremendous criminal energy not fitting either category. Maybe we need a new conceptual palette. As social historians of cold war and of crime, we can focus on what makes humans warm and interesting or cold and calculating. Both conjure up the intimate feelings of people in the past, but the latter characteristics better reflect the asymmetrical relations of power. In their desperate urge to escape their circumstances, Gladow and Kusian briefly took leave of their senses. Their violent pursuit of wealth and autonomy briefly seemed liberating before the 'iron cage of structure' (and justice) resoundingly clanged shut. What meaning did their serious and serial transgressions have? Systemic limits do not get much more real – demonstrating the imbalance between and gulf separating the weak and the powerful – than prison bars or capital punishment. The attempt of this book is to rescue criminals like Kusian and Gladow not from the condescension of posterity, but from empty sensationalism. They cannot easily be celebrated as 'heroes, proto-feminists or freedom fighters'.[50] Rather, they (and some of their victims) were charlatans – illusionists, barkers and roguish hucksters, determined to trick people out of their money – rather than intellectuals or dissidents.[51] They were human and fallible petty criminals, with ideas above their station. Nevertheless, in committing their crimes, they produced meaningful acts.

The Berliners' '*Uns kann keener*' ('Nobody can outsmart us') mentality was infectious.[52] How does it impact on notions of *Herrschaft* and hegemony? The regime that the forces of order were defending and protecting differed markedly between East and West from spring 1948 onwards. Driven by the onset of the cold war, the split of 1948 left both police forces suffering from a deficit in legitimacy. However, it was more keenly felt by the population ruled by the *Volkspolizei*-controlling East Berlin 'Pankow' regime. There was a clear hypocrisy in senior policemen claiming that public order was sacrosanct at one point on the border and then going out of their way to undermine it at another. The eastern authorities reduced their capital of hegemony and legitimacy by allowing insurrectionary gymnastics, in the form of orchestrated street violence, when it suited their immediate, short-term goals. In supporting the most extreme and violent minority, against what remained of their shared, four-power goals, they abandoned attempts to convince and win over the mass of Berliners. There was no question, well into the 1950s, that the citizens of the 'free' western sectors enjoyed greater liberty together with a good measure of order. Consequently, West Berlin functioned as an exemplary and shining symbol of the benefits of liberal democracy.

If Stalin had planned to use the Blockade to prevent the creation of a West German state, then his stratagem dramatically backfired. Against all predictions, the Airlift proved to be a technological miracle and a tremendous political success. West Berliners proved that they were ready to go hungry and to endure continued privations to defend their freedom. When the Airlift allowed the Western Allies to recast their occupation as humanitarian aid and defence of democracy, one of the few sources of hegemony left to the Communist government in East Berlin was to stress their crime-fighting capabilities. Criminalization helped the eastern authorities to stigmatize and scapegoat anybody who continued to oppose them or their rule. Throughout the cold war (from the 1940s to the 1980s, but especially in 1961), the Soviets presented their western counterparts (and their local-government supporters) as soft on crime. There was more stress on order than on liberty or law in the eastern system, but more energetic and draconian law enforcement (locking up and executing dangerous criminals) did provide the regime with a way to appear legitimate and valid. Capturing and 'dealing with' criminals, including through execution, satisfied a widespread thirst for no-nonsense punishment and retribution. Oppressing lawbreakers was permissible and laudable because, as people, they represented nefarious oppressors who deserved their comeuppance. The freedoms enjoyed by lawbreakers in the western sectors could be presented as anarchy rather than as democracy. After the difficult postwar years, there was some mileage in condemning the other side as 'soft on crime' and overly tolerant of criminals.[53] However, Berliners in both East and West embraced the slogan '*Lieber Pom als Frau komm*', suggesting that they had impeccable memories of which of their occupiers had been most involved in perpetrating crimes against them.

Eschewing a glib and overly schematic tale of 'us' versus 'them', this book reveals the true complexity of the entangled, embittered relations of power (or domination), whether seen as sovereignty or hegemony. In the unscrupulous landscape (or borderscape) of defeated, postwar Berlin, no side was pristine or free from the taint of duplicity. Studying inter-Allied and occupier-occupied power relations, at the onset of the cold war, reveals much about both mentalities (as expressed through concrete actions and behaviour) and the exercise of *Herrschaft*. It was not just the Soviets who expected Berliners to comply with their ideologically based exigencies. All four occupiers could hurt and humiliate as well as protect and preserve. Relations of power were often slippery, asymmetrical and calculating as well as messy and confused. Up to and beyond the onset of the cold war, the Allies wanted vassals and playthings as well as partners and collaborators.

Notes

1. Alice Hills, *Policing Post-conflict Cities* (London: Zed, 2009), 211.
2. Janet Chan, 'Changing Police Culture', *British Journal of Criminology* 36, no. 1 (1996): 109–34.
3. Hills, *Policing Post-conflict Cities*, 20, 23–4, 211.
4. *The Monopoly of Violence*, directed by David Dufresne (France 2020).
5. Michel Foucault, *Discipline and Punish: The Birth of the Prison*, trans. Alan Sheridan (New York: Vintage, 1977).
6. Susan L. Carruthers, *The Good Occupation: American Soldiers and the Hazards of Peace* (Cambridge, MA: Harvard University Press, 2016), 12.
7. Willi Neumann cited by Hans-Werner Hamacher, *Polizei 1945 – Ein neuer Anfang*, 2nd edn. (Hilden: Verlag Deutsche Polizeiliteratur, 1989), 217, 270.
8. Giles MacDonogh, *After the Reich: The Brutal History of the Allied Occupation* (New York: Basic Books, 2007).
9. Carruthers, *The Good Occupation*, 219.
10. Kurt Jürgensen, 'British Occupation Policy After 1945 and the Problem of "Re-Educating Germany"', *History* 68, no. 223 (1983): 243.
11. General Dwight Eisenhower had stressed that although the Allies definitely came 'as conquerors', they would not take on the role of oppressors. 'As Conquerors not Oppressors: Eisenhower Proclamation to Germany', *Manchester Guardian*, 29 September 1944.
12. See, for example, Major General John J. Maginnis, *Military Government Journal: Normandy to Berlin* (Amherst, MA: University of Massachusetts Press, 1971), 264–5, 319, 259.
13. Wolfgang Heidelmeyer, 'Immunität und Rechtsschutz gegen Akte der Besatzungshoheit in Berlin', *Zeitschrift für ausländisches öffentliches Recht und Völkerrecht* 46 (1986): 521.
14. *Die Frontstadt: Berlin im Kalten Krieg*, directed by Andreas Hacke (ZDF, 2017).
15. Gerhard Keiderling, *Berlin 1945-1986* (East Berlin: Dietz, 1987), 110.
16. Anonyma, *A Woman in Berlin*, trans. Philip Boehm (London: Virago, 2005), 5.
17. Ralf Dahrendorf, *Law and Order* (London: Stevens, 1985), 3, 2.
18. Jennifer V. Evans, 'Protection from the Protector: Court-Martial Cases and the Lawlessness of Occupation in American-Controlled Berlin, 1945-1948', in *GIs and Germans: The Social, Economic, Cultural and Political History of the American Military Presence*, ed. Detlef Junker and Thomas W. Maulucci (New York: Cambridge University Press, 2013), 212–34.
19. When not conditioning lab rats, Skinner imagined a future society without sexual hang-ups. B. F. Skinner, *Walden Two* (New York: Macmillan, 1948), 140.
20. Curt Riess, *The Berlin Story* (London: Frederick Muller, 1953), 86.
21. T. S. Eliot, *The Rock* (London: Faber and Faber, 1934), 38.
22. Carruthers, *The Good Occupation*, 116.
23. Karen E. Till, 'Wounded Cities: Memory-work and a Place-based Ethics of Care', *Political Geography* 31, no. 1 (2012): 3–14.
24. In Wilder's version, the hero-villains could take straight-laced, cornfed, female, Iowan form. *A Foreign Affair* directed by Billy Wilder (Paramount, 1948).
25. If, as Hills argues, it is only foreign donors who consider women and girls to have any significance in urban environments like Baghdad, Freetown or Gaza City, the

reports on Haiti suggest that there too the focus can be sporadic and self-serving, rather than committed or sustained. Hills, *Policing Post-conflict Cities*, 23, 225. 'When Charity Workers Turn Predatory', *New York Times*, 24 February 2018; Justin W. Moyer, 'Report: U.N. Peacekeepers in Haiti had "Transactional Sex" with Hundreds of Poor Women', *Washington Post*, 11 June 2015.

26 *Operation Vittles Cookbook, Compiled by the American Women in Blockaded Berlin in January 1949* (Berlin: Deutscher Verlag, 1949), 51.
27 Hills, *Policing Post-conflict Cities*, 33.
28 Frank S. V. Donnison, *Civil Affairs and Military Government* (London: HMSO, 1966), 128, 341.
29 Lucius D. Clay, *Decision in Germany* (Westport, CT: Greenwood, 1970), 265–6.
30 Paul Steege, *Black Market, Cold War: Everyday Life in Berlin, 1946-1949* (Cambridge: Cambridge University Press, 2007), 58. Laura J. Hilton, 'The Black Market in History and Memory: German Perceptions of Victimhood from 1945 to 1948', *German History* 28, no. 4 (2010): 479–97.
31 Hills, *Policing Post-conflict Cities*, 7.
32 *Tatort Berlin: Werner G., der Kopf der Gladowbande*, directed by Gabi Schlag and Benno Wenz (Phoenix, 2015).
33 Cf. Lindsay K. MacNeill, 'Professionalism and Brutality: The Viennese Police and the Public in Extraordinary Times, 1918-1955', PhD, American University, Washington DC, 2020, 352, 356, 359, 363.
34 Hills, *Policing Post-conflict Cities*, 222–3.
35 In terms of denazification, this reversion was particularly apparent in the early 1950s. See Mark Fenemore, *Fighting the Cold War in Post-blockade, Pre-wall Berlin: Behind Enemy Lines* (New York: Routledge, 2020), ch. 4.
36 Steege, *Black Market*, 4, 198.
37 Chan, 'Changing Police Culture', 110, 122.
38 Hills, *Policing Post-conflict Cities*, 76.
39 Mark Neocleous, *The Fabrication of Social Order: A Critical Theory of Police Power* (London: Pluto, 2000), xii, 43.
40 Fenemore, *Fighting the Cold War*, 243, 65–7.
41 Cf. MacNeill, 'Professionalism and Brutality', 342.
42 Fenemore, *Fighting the Cold War*, ch. 4.
43 Alice Hills, 'Policing in Post-Conflict Societies', IIEA, 9 November 2016, https://www.youtube.com/watch?v=yA-TkdX2o8M (accessed 18 January 2022). Cf. 'How can Donors Best Support Police Reform in Non-Western Contexts?', https://howtoreformthepolice.com/2021/06/14/how-can-donors-best-support-police-reform-in-non-western-contexts/ (accessed 18 January 2022).
44 Richard Bessel, 'Policing in East Germany in the wake of the Second World War', Crime, History and Societies 7, no. 2 (2003). Cf. Norbert Steinborn and Hilmar Krüger, *Die Berliner Polizei 1945 bis 1992: von der Militärreserve im Kalten Krieg auf dem Weg zur bürgernahen Polizei?* (Berlin: A. Spitz, 1993).
45 A notable exception here is Eugene Gilbert Jones, 'The Allied Reconstruction of the Berlin Police, 1945-1948', PhD, University of California, San Diego, 1986.
46 Hannah Arendt, *On Violence* (San Diego: Harcourt, 1970), 52.
47 Frank L. Howley, *Berlin Command* (New York: G. P. Putnam's Sons, 1950), 217–18.
48 Till, 'Wounded Cities'. Cf. Fenemore, *Fighting the Cold War*, ch. 1.
49 Brad S. Gregory, 'Is Small Beautiful? Microhistory and the History of Everyday Life', *History and Theory* 38, no. 1 (1999): 100.

50 Andrew I. Port, 'History from Below, the History of Everyday Life, and Microhistory', in *International Encyclopedia of the Social and Behavioral Sciences*, ed. James D. Wright, 2nd edn. (Amsterdam: Elsevier, 2015), 111.
51 Guy Debord, *Comments on the Society of the Spectacle*, trans. Malcom Imrie (London: Verso, 1998), 41, 92.
52 Wilfried Rott, *Die Insel: Eine Geschichte West-Berlins 1948-1990* (Munich: C. H. Beck, 2009), 28.
53 Stuart Hall et al., *Policing the Crisis: Mugging, the State and Law and Order*, 2nd edn. (Basingstoke: Palgrave Macmillan, 2013), 223.

Bibliography

Adler, K. H. 'Selling France to the French: The French Zone of Occupation in Western Germany, 1945–1955'. *Contemporary European History* 21, no. 4 (2012): 575–95.
Andreas-Friedrich, Ruth. *Battleground Berlin: Diaries 1945–1948*, translated by Anna Boerresen. New York: Paragon, 1990.
Anonyma. *A Woman in Berlin*, translated by James Stern. New York: Harcourt Brace, 1954.
Anonyma. *A Woman in Berlin*, translated by Philip Boehm. London: Virago, 2005.
Arendt, Hannah. *On Violence*. San Diego, CA: Harcourt, 1970.
Bahr, Egon. *Zu meiner Zeit*. Munich: K. Blessing, 1996.
Balfour, Michael. *West Germany: A Contemporary History*. London: Croom Helm, 1982.
Balfour, Michael and John Mair. *Four-Power Control in Germany and Austria, 1945–1946*. London: Oxford University Press, 1956.
Banton, Michael P. *The Policeman in the Community*. London: Tavistock, 1964.
Barclay, David E. *Schaut auf diese Stadt: der unbekannte Ernst Reuter*. Berlin: Siedler, 2000.
Barclay, David E. 'Division of the Spoils: Berlin as Symbol and as Prize'. In *Cold War Berlin: Confrontations, Cultures, and Identities*, edited by Scott H. Krause, Stefanie Eisenhuth and Konrad H. Jarausch, 31–40. London: Bloomsbury, 2021.
Barden, Judy. 'Candy Bar Romance – Women of Germany'. In *This is Germany: A Report on Post War Germany by 21 Newspaper Correspondents*, edited by Arthur Settel, 161–76. New York: William Sloane, 1950.
Bédarida, Renée. 'Une Française à Berlin en 1945'. In *France-Allemagne 1944–1947*, edited by Klaus Manfrass and Jean-Pierre Rioux, 149–52. Paris: Institut d'histoire du temps present, 1990.
Beevor, Antony. *Berlin: The Downfall 1945*. London: Penguin, 2002.
Beevor, Antony. 'Introduction' to Anonyma, *A Woman in Berlin*, translated by Philip Boehm. London: Virago, 2005.
Berdahl, Daphne. *Where the World Ended: Re-unification and Identity in the German Borderland*. Berkeley, CA: University of California Press, 1999.
Bessel, Richard. 'Policing in East Germany in the Wake of the Second World War'. *Crime, History and Societies* 7, no. 2 (2003): 5–21.
Bessel, Richard. *Germany 1945: From War to Peace*. London: Harper Collins, 2009.
Bessel, Richard. 'Establishing Order in Post-war Eastern Germany'. *Past and Present* 210, Supplement 6 (2011): 139–57.
Boelcke, Willi. *Kriegspropaganda 1939–1941*. Stuttgart: Deutsche Verlags Anstalt, 1966.
Bohlen, Charles E. *Witness to History, 1929–1969*. New York: Norton, 1973.
Die Gladow-Bande: Chicago in Berlin, directed by Ute Bönnen and Gerald Endres. ARD, 2000.
Bosetzky, Horst. *Cold Angel: Murder in Berlin 1949*, translated by Catherine D. Miller. New York: Enigma, 2012.
Boveri, Margret. *Tage des Überlebens: Berlin 1945*. Munich: R. Piper, 1968.

Brand, Florian. *Polizeifunk meldet: Gladow Bande zur Strecke gebracht*. Berlin: Vorwärts, 1949.
Engel aus Eisen, directed by Thomas Brasch. West Germany, 1980.
Brett-Smith, Richard. *Berlin '45: The Grey City*. London: Macmillan, 1966.
Burr, William. 'Avoiding the Slippery Slope: The Eisenhower Administration and the Berlin Crisis, November 1958–January 1959'. *Diplomatic History* 18, no. 2 (1994): 177–205.
Buruma, Ian. *Year Zero: A History of 1945*. New York: Penguin Press, 2013.
Byford-Jones, Lieutenant-Colonel W. *Berlin Twilight*. London: Hutchinson, 1947.
Cairncross, Alec. *A Country to Play With*. Gerrards Cross: Colin Smythe, 1987.
Carruthers, Susan L. *The Good Occupation: American Soldiers and the Hazards of Peace*. Cambridge, MA: Harvard University Press, 2016.
Chan, Janet. 'Changing Police Culture'. *British Journal of Criminology* 36, no. 1 (1996): 109–34.
Churchill, Winston S. *The Second World War, Vol. 6, Triumph and Tragedy*. London: Cassell, 1954.
Ciesla, Burghard, Michael Lemke and Thomas Lindenberger (eds), *Sterben für Berlin? Die Berliner Krisen 1948:1958*. Berlin: Metropol, 1999.
Clay, Lucius D. *Decision in Germany*. Westport, CT: Greenwood, 1970.
Collier, Irwin L. and David H. Papell. 'About Two Marks: Refugees and the Exchange Rate Before the Berlin Wall'. *American Economic Review* 78, no. 3 (1988): 531–42.
Conradt, Sylvia und Kirsten Heckmann-Janz. *Reichstrümmerstadt: Leben in Berlin 1945–1961*. Darmstadt: Luchterhand, 1987.
Dahrendorf, Ralf. *Law and Order*. London: Stevens, 1985.
Dalfiume, Richard M. *Desegregation of the U.S. Armed Forces: Fighting on Two Fronts, 1939–1953*. Columbia, MO: University of Missouri Press, 1969.
Darnton, Robert. *The Great Cat Massacre*. London: Penguin, 1991.
Davis, David Brion. 'The Americanized Mannheim of 1945–46'. In *American Places: Encounters with History*, edited by William Leuchtenburg, 79–91. Oxford: Oxford University Press, 2000.
Davis, Franklin M. *Came as a Conqueror: The United States Army's Occupation of Germany, 1945–1949*. New York: Macmillan, 1967.
Davison, W. Phillips. *The Berlin Blockade: A Study in Cold War Politics*. Princeton, NJ: Princeton University Press, 1958.
Debord, Guy. *Comments on the Society of the Spectacle*, translated by Malcom Imrie. London: Verso, 1998.
Derenburg, Michael. *Streifzüge durch vier RIAS-Jahrzehnte: Anfänge und Wandlungen eines Rundfunksenders*. Berlin: Presse- und Informationsamt des Landes Berlin, 1986.
Dobler, Jens. 'Die Berliner Polizei und die Nachkriegsdelinquenz'. In *Großstadtkriminalität: Berliner Kriminalpolizei und Verbrechensbekämpfung 1930 bis 1950*, edited by Jens Dobler, 247–57. Berlin: Metropol, 2013.
Donnison, Frank S. V. *Civil Affairs and Military Government*. London: HMSO, 1966.
The Monopoly of Violence, directed by David Dufresne. France, 2020.
Eisenberg, Carolyn. *Drawing the Line: The American Decision to Divide Germany, 1944–1949*. Cambridge: Cambridge University Press, 1996.
Eliot, T. S. *The Rock*. London: Faber and Faber, 1934.
Elkin, Henry. 'Aggressive and Erotic Tendencies in Army Life'. *American Journal of Sociology* 51, no. 5 (1946): 408–13.

Elkins, T. H. and B. Hofmeister. *Berlin: The Spatial Structure of a Divided City*. London: Methuen, 1988.
Evans, Jennifer V. 'Life Among the Ruins. Sex, Space and Subculture in Zero Hour Berlin'. In *Berlin Divided City, 1945–1989*, edited by Philip Broadbent and Sabine Hake, 11–22. New York: Berghahn 2010.
Evans, Jennifer V. *Life Among the Ruins: Cityscape and Sexuality in Cold War Berlin*. Basingstoke: Palgrave Macmillan, 2011.
Evans, Jennifer V. 'Protection from the Protector: Court-Martial Cases and the Lawlessness of Occupation in American-Controlled Berlin, 1945–1948'. In *GIs and Germans: The Social, Economic, Cultural and Political History of the American Military Presence*, edited by Detlef Junker and Thomas W. Maulucci, 212–34. New York: Cambridge University Press, 2013.
Evans, Richard J. *Rituals of Retribution: Capital Punishment in Germany 1600–1987*. London: Penguin, 1996.
Fay, Jennifer. 'Germany is a Boy in Trouble'. *Cultural Critique* 64 (2006): 196–234.
Fehrenbach, Heide. *Race After Hitler: Black Occupation Children in Postwar Germany and America*. Princeton, NJ: Princeton University Press, 2005.
Fenemore, Mark. *Fighting the Cold War in Post-Blockade, Pre-Wall Berlin: Behind Enemy Lines*. London: Routledge, 2019.
Foucault, Michel. *Discipline and Punish: The Birth of the Prison*, translated by Alan Sheridan. New York: Vintage, 1977.
Foucault, Michel. *The Birth of Bipolitics: Lectures at the Collège de France, 1978–79*, edited by Michel Senellart. Basingstoke: Palgrave Macmillan, 2008.
Friedensburg, Ferdinand. *Es ging um Deutschlands Einheit: Rückschau eines Berliners auf die Jahre nach 1945*. West Berlin: Haude and Spenersche, 1971.
Fritzsche, Peter. *The Turbulent World of Franz Göll: An Ordinary Berliner Writes the Twentieth Century*. Cambridge, MA: Harvard University Press, 2011.
Führe, Dorothea. 'Der Vergessene Sektor. Die französische Besatzungsmacht in Reinickendorf und im Wedding'. In *Sterben für Berlin? Die Berliner Krisen 1948:1958*, edited by Burghard Ciesla, Michael Lemke and Thomas Lindenberger, 79–100. Berlin: Metropol, 1999.
Führe, Dorothea. *Die Französische Besatzungspolitik in Berlin von 1945 bis 1949: Déprussianisation und Décentralisation*. Berlin: Weißensee-Verlag, 2001.
Fürmetz, Gerhard, Herbert Reinke and Klaus Weinhauer. 'Nachkriegspolizei in Deutschland. Doppelte Polizeigeschichte 1945–1969'. In *Nachkriegspolizei: Sicherheit und Ordnung in Ost- und Westdeutschland, 1945–1969*, edited by Gerhard Fürmetz, Herbert Reinke and Klaus Weinhauer, 7–33. Hamburg: Ergebnisse Verlag, 2001.
Gebhardt, Miriam. *Als die Soldaten kamen: die Vergewaltigung deutscher Frauen am Ende des Zweiten Weltkriegs*. Munich: Deutsche Verlags-Anstalt, 2015.
Geertz, Clifford. *The Interpretation of Cultures*. New York: Basic Books, 1973.
Geis, Margaret L. and George J. Gray. *The Relations of Occupation Personnel with the Civil Population, 1946–1948*. Karlsruhe: Historical Division, European Command, 1951.
Geis, Margaret L., Dorothy Russell and W. H. Maehl. *Morale and Discipline in the European Command, 1945–1949*. Karlsruhe: Historical Division, 1951.
Geserick, Gunther, Klaus Vendura and Ingo Wirth. *Zeitzeuge Tod: spektakuläre Fälle der Berliner Gerichtsmedizin*. Leipzig: Militzke, 2001.
Giangreco, D. M. and Robert E. Griffin. *Airbridge to Berlin: The Berlin Crisis of 1948: Its Origins and Aftermath*. Novato, CA: Presidio, 1988.

Giese, Fritz. *Girlkultur: Vergleiche zwischen Amerikanischem und Europäischem Rhythmus und Lebensgefühl*. Munich: Delphin, 1925.
Ginzburg, Carlo. *The Judge and the Historian*, translated by Antony Shugaar. London: Verso, 1999.
Goedde, Petra. *GIs and Germans: Culture, Gender, and Foreign Relations, 1945–49*. New Haven, CT: Yale University Press, 2003.
Gregory, Brad S. 'Is Small Beautiful? Microhistory and the History of Everyday Life'. *History and Theory* 38, no. 1 (1999): 100–10.
Grossmann, Atina. 'A Question of Silence: The Rape of German Women by Occupation Soldiers'. In *West Germany Under Construction: Politics, Society and Culture in the Adenauer Era*, edited by Robert G. Moeller, 33–52. Ann Arbor, MI: University of Michigan Press, 1997.
Grossmann, Atina. 'Home and Displacement in a City of Bordercrossers. Jews in Berlin 1945–1948'. In *Unlikely History: The Changing German-Jewish Symbiosis, 1945–2000*, edited by Leslie Morris and Jack Zipes, 65–99. New York: Palgrave, 2002.
Grossmann, Atina. *Jews, Germans and Allies: Close Encounters in Occupied Germany*. Princeton, NJ: Princeton University Press, 2009.
Grossmann, Atina. 'Grams, Calories, and Food: Languages of Victimization, Entitlement and Human Rights in Occupied Germany, 1945–1949'. *Central European History* 44, no. 1 (2011): 118–48.
Gunnarsson, Robert L. *American Military Police in Europe*. Jefferson: McFarland, 2011.
Die Frontstadt: Berlin im Kalten Krieg, directed by Andreas Hacke, ZDF, 2017.
Hall, E. T. 'Race Prejudice and Negro-White Relations in the Army'. *American Journal of Sociology* 52, no. 5 (1947): 401–9.
Hall, Stuart et al., *Policing the Crisis: Mugging, the State and Law and Order*, 2nd edn. Basingstoke: Palgrave Macmillan, 2013.
Hallen, Andreas and Thomas Lindenberger. 'Frontstadt mit Lücken. Ein Versuch über die Halbwahrheiten von Blockade und Luftbrücke'. In *Der Wedding - hart an der Grenze*, edited by Berliner Geschichtswerkstatt, 182–204. Berlin: Nishen, 1987.
Hamacher, Hans-Werner. *Polizei 1945 – ein neuer Anfang*, 2nd edn. Hilden: Verlag Deutsche Polizeiliteratur, 1989.
Hanauske, Dieter (ed.). *Die Sitzungsprotokolle des Magistrats der Stadt Berlin 1945/46*. Berlin: Arno Spitz, 1995.
Harris, William R. 'March Crisis 1948, Act II'. *CIA Studies in Intelligence* 11 (1967): 9–35.
Harrison, Hope. 'Berlin and the Cold War Struggle over Germany'. In *The Routledge Handbook of the Cold War*, edited by Artemy M. Kalinovsky and Craig Daigle, 56–73. London: Routledge, 2014.
I Was A Male War Bride, directed by Howard Hawks. USA, 1949.
Healey, Dan. 'Comrades, Queers, and "Oddballs": Sodomy, Masculinity, and Gendered Violence in Leningrad Province of the 1950s'. *Journal of the History of Sexuality* 21, no. 3 (2012): 496–522.
Heidelmeyer, Wolfgang. 'Immunität und Rechtsschutz gegen Akte der Besatzungshoheit in Berlin'. *Zeitschrift für ausländisches öffentliches Recht und Völkerrecht* 46 (1986): 519–38.
Herbert, Major-General E. O. 'The Cold War in Berlin'. *Journal of the Royal United Service Institution* XCIV, no. 574 (1949): 165–77.
Hills, Alice. *Policing Post-Conflict Cities*. London: Zed, 2009.
Hilton, Laura J. 'The Black Market in History and Memory: German Perceptions of Victimhood from 1945 to 1948'. *German History* 28, no. 4 (2010): 479–97.

Hitler, Adolf. *Mein Kampf*. Munich: Zentralverlag der NSDAP, 1940.
Höhn, Maria. *GIs and Fräuleins: The German-American Encounter in 1950s West Germany*. Chapel Hill, NC: University of North Carolina Press, 2003.
Höhn, Maria. '"We Will Never Go Back to the Old Way Again": Germany in the African-American Debate on Civil Rights'. *Central European History* 41, no. 4 (2008): 605–37.
Höhn, Maria and Martin Klimke. *A Breath of Freedom: The Civil Rights Struggle, African American GIs and Germany*. New York: Palgrave Macmillan, 2010.
Hoerning, Erika M. *Zwischen den Fronten: Berliner Grenzgänger und Grenzhändler 1948–1961*. Cologne: Böhlau, 1992.
Howley, Frank L. *Berlin Command*. New York: G. P. Putnam's Sons, 1950.
Hübner, Klaus. *Einsatz: Erinnerungen des Berliner Polizeipräsidenten 1969–1987*. Berlin: Jaron, 1997.
Hutton, Patrick H. 'The History of Mentalities: The New Map of Cultural History'. *History and Theory* 20, no. 3 (1981): 237–59.
Janis, Irving L. 'Group Identification Under Conditions of External Danger'. In *Group Dynamics: Research and Theory*, edited by Dorwin Cartwright and Alvin Zander, 3rd edn., 80–90. New York: Harper and Row, 1968.
Jessup, Philip C. 'Park Avenue Diplomacy – Ending the Berlin Blockade'. *Political Science Quarterly* 87, no. 3 (1972): 377–400.
Jones, Eugene Gilbert. 'The Allied Reconstruction of the Berlin Police, 1945–1948'. PhD, University of California, San Diego, 1986.
Jürgensen, Kurt. 'British Occupation Policy After 1945 and the Problem of "Re-Educating Germany"'. *History* 68, no. 223 (1983): 225–44.
Kahn, Arthur D. *Betrayal: Our Occupation of Germany*. Brooklyn: Beacon, 1950.
Keen, Richard. 'Half a Million Tons and a Goat: A Study of British Participation in the Berlin Airlift, 25 June 1948 –12 May 1949'. PhD, University of Buckingham, 2013.
Keiderling, Gerhard. *Berlin 1945–1986: Geschichte der Hauptstadt der DDR*. East Berlin: Dietz, 1987.
Keiderling, Gerhard. '"Als Befreier unsere Herzen zerbrachen". Zu den Übergriffe der Sowjetarmee in Berlin 1945'. *Deutschland Archiv* 28, no. 1 (1995): 234–43.
Keiderling, Gerhard. *Um Deutschlands Einheit: Ferdinand Friedensburg und der Kalte Krieg in Berlin 1945–1952*. Cologne: Böhlau, 2009.
Kennan, George F. *Memoirs 1925–1950*. Boston, MA: Little Brown, 1967.
Kennedy-Pipe, Caroline. *Stalin's Cold War: Soviet Strategies in Europe, 1943 to 1956*. Manchester: Manchester University Press, 1995.
Kettenacker, Lothar. *Germany Since 1945*. Oxford: Oxford University Press, 1997.
Kjellén, Rudolf. *Die politischen Probleme des Weltkrieges*. Leipzig: B.G. Teubner, 1916.
Knowles, Christopher. 'Winning the Peace: The British in Occupied Germany, 1945–1948'. PhD, Kings College, London, 2014.
Kopelev, Lev. *To Be Preserved Forever*. Philadelphia, PA: Lippincott, 1977.
Krumholz, Walter. *Berlin-ABC*. West Berlin: Verlag Documentation, 1969.
Kuby, Erich. *The Russians and Berlin, 1945*, translated by Arnold J. Pomerans. London: Heinemann 1968.
Larson, Deborah Welch. 'The Origins of Commitment'. *Journal of Cold War Studies* 13, no. 1 (2011): 180–212.
Leffler, Melvyn. 'The Cold War: What Do "We Now Know"? '. *American Historical Review* 104, no. 2 (April 1999): 501–24.
Leonhard, Wolfgang. *Child of the Revolution*, translated by C. M. Woodhouse. Cologne: Kiepenhauer and Witsch, 1979.

Little Caesar, directed by Mervyn LeRoy. Warner Bros, 1931.
Lindenberger, Thomas. *Volkspolizei: Herrschaftspraxis und öffentliche Ordnung im SED-Staat, 1952–1968*. Cologne: Böhlau, 2003.
Four in a Jeep, directed by Leopold Lindtberg and Elizabeth Montagu, Switzerland, 1951.
Loest, Erich. *Die Westmark fällt weiter*. Halle, Saale: Mitteldeutscher Verlag, 1952.
Lord Robertson of Oakridge. 'A Miracle? Potsdam – Western Germany 1965'. *International Affairs* 41, no. 3 (1965): 401–10.
Loth, Wilfried. 'Die französische Deutschlandspolitik und die Anfänge des Ost-West-Konflikts'. In *France-Allemagne 1944–1947*, edited by Klaus Manfrass and Jean-Pierre Rioux, 83–96. Paris: Institut d'histoire du temps present, 1990.
Lower, Wendy. *Hitler's Furies: German Women in the Nazi Killing Fields*. London: Vintage, 2014.
Lubin, Alex. *Romance and Rights: The Politics of Interracial Intimacy 1945–1954*. Jackson, MS: University of Mississippi, 2005.
Lüdtke, Alf. *The History of Everyday Life: Reconstructing Historical Experiences and Ways of Life*. Princeton, NJ: Princeton University Press, 1995.
Lush, C. D. 'The Relationship Between Berlin and the Federal Republic of Germany'. *The International and Comparative Law Quarterly* 14, no. 3 (1965): 742–87.
MacDonogh, Giles. *After the Reich: The Brutal History of the Allied Occupation*. New York: Basic Books, 2007.
MacGregor, Morris J. *Integration of the Armed Forces 1940–1965*. Washington, DC: Center of Military History, U.S. Army, 1981.
MacNeill, Lindsay K. 'Professionalism and Brutality: The Viennese Police and the Public in Extraordinary Times, 1918–1955'. PhD, American University, Washington, DC, 2020.
Maginnis, Major General John J. *Military Government Journal: Normandy to Berlin*. Amherst, MA: University of Massachusetts Press, 1971.
Major, Patrick. *Behind the Berlin Wall: East Germany and the Frontiers of Power*. Oxford: Oxford University Press, 2010.
Mastny, Vojtech. *The Cold War and Soviet Insecurity: The Stalin Years*. New York: Oxford University Press, 1996.
Meeres, David. 'Policing "Wayward" Youth: Law, Society and Youth Criminality in Berlin, 1939–1953'. PhD, University of Limerick, 2014.
Merridale, Catherine. 'Culture, Ideology and Combat in the Red Army, 1939–45'. *Journal of Contemporary History* 41, no. 2 (2006): 305–24.
Miard-Delacroix, Hélène. *Willy Brandt: Life of a Statesman*, translated by Isabelle Chaize. London: I.B. Tauris, 2016.
Middleton, Drew. *The Struggle for Germany*. Indianapolis, IN: Bobbs-Merrill, 1949.
Middleton, Drew. *Where Has Last July Gone? Memoirs*. New York: Quadrangle, 1973.
Miller, Francis P. *Man from the Valley: Memoirs of a 20th-Century Virginian*. Chapel Hill, NC: University of North Carolina Press, 1971.
Miller, Roger G. *To Save a City: The Berlin Airlift 1948–1949*. Washington, DC: Air Force History and Museums Program, 1998.
Mittmann, Wolfgang. *Gladow-Bande: Die Revolverhelden von Berlin*. Berlin: Das Neue Berlin, 2003.
Moore, Lyford. 'The Man in the Goldfish Bowl'. In *This is Germany: A Report on Post War Germany by 21 Newspaper Correspondents*, edited by Arthur Settel, 23–39. New York: William Sloane, 1950.
Morris, Eric. *Blockade: Berlin and the Cold War*. London: Hamish Hamilton, 1973.

Murphy, David E., Sergei A. Kondrashev and George Bailey. *Battleground Berlin: CIA vs: KGB in the Cold War*. New Haven, CT: Yale University Press, 1997.
Murray, William. *Germany Today*. Pathe, 1947.
Naimark, Norman. *Russians in Germany: A History of the Soviet Zone of Occupation, 1945–1949*. Cambridge, MA: Belknap Press of Harvard University Press, 1995.
Neocleous, Mark. *The Fabrication of Social Order: A Critical Theory of Police Power*. London: Pluto, 2000.
Nienhaus, Ursula. '"Für strenge Dienstzucht ungeeignete Objekte..." Weibliche Polizei in Berlin 1945–1952'. In *Nachkriegspolizei: Sicherheit und Ordnung in Ost- und Westdeutschland, 1945–1969*, edited by Gerhard Fürmetz, Herbert Reinke and Klaus Weinhauer, 129–53. Hamburg: Ergebnisse Verlag, 2001.
Niethammer, Lutz. *Ego-Histoire? Und andere Erinnerungs-Versuche*. Vienna: Böhlau, 2002.
O'Connell, Kaete M. 'Weapon of War, Tool of Peace: U.S. Food Diplomacy in Postwar Germany'. PhD, Temple University, 2019.
Operation Vittles Cookbook, compiled by the American Women in Blockaded Berlin in January 1949. Berlin: Deutscher Verlag, 1949.
Osmond, T. E. 'Venereal Diseases in Peace and War with Some Reminiscences of the Last Forty Years'. *British Journal of Venereal Diseases* 25, no. 3 (1949): 101–14.
Overy, Richard. 'Interwar, War, Postwar: Was there a Zero Hour in 1945?' In *The Oxford Handbook of Postwar European History*, edited by Dan Stone, 60–78. Oxford: Oxford University Press, 2012.
Parrish, Scott. 'The Marshall Plan, Soviet-American Relations and the Division of Europe'. In *The Establishment of Communist Regimes in Eastern Europe, 1944–1949*, edited by Norman Naimark and Leonid Gibianskii, 267–90. Boulder, CO: Westview, 1997.
Pence, Katherine. 'Herr Schimpf und Frau Schande. Grenzgänger des Konsums im geteilten Berlin und die Politik des Kalten Krieges'. In *Sterben für Berlin? Die Berliner Krisen 1948:1958*, edited by Burghard Ciesla, Michael Lemke, and Thomas Lindenberger, 185–202. Berlin: Metropol, 1999.
Pirntke, Gunter. *Der Al Capone von Berlin: Werner Gladow*. Dresden: Das elegante Buch, 2019.
Podewin, Norbert. *Otto Ostrowski - der gelöschte Oberbürgermeister: ein Schicksal im Berlin des Kalten Krieges*. Berlin: Luisenstädtischer Bildungsverein, 2004.
Poiger, Uta G. *Jazz, Rock and Rebels: Cold War Politics and American Culture in a Divided Germany*. Berkeley, CA: University of California Press, 2000.
Pollak, Hans. *Tatort Sektorengrenze: Berliner Kriminalfälle der Nachkriegszeit*. Berlin: Verlag Neues Leben, 1994.
Port, Andrew I. 'History from Below, the History of Everyday Life, and Microhistory'. In *International Encyclopedia of the Social and Behavioral Sciences*, edited by James D. Wright, 2nd edn., 108–13. Amsterdam: Elsevier, 2015.
Präsidium, der Volkspolizei (ed.). *Zeittafel zur Geschichte der Volkspolizei Berlin 1945–1961*. East Berlin: Präsidium der Volkspolizei, 1985.
Read, Anthony and David Fisher. *Berlin: The Biography of a City*. London: Pimlico, 1994.
Reeves, Richard. *Daring Young Men: The Heroism and Triumph of the Berlin Airlift, June 1948–May 1949*. New York: Simon and Schuster, 2010.
Reiner, Robert. *The Politics of the Police*. Brighton: Wheatsheaf, 1985.
Ribbe, Wolfgang. *Berlin 1945–2000*. Berlin: Berliner Wissenschaftsverlag, 2002.
Riess, Curt. *The Berlin Story*. London: Frederick Muller, 1953.
Roberts, Geoffrey. *Stalin's Wars: From World War to Cold War, 1939–1953*. New Haven, CT: Yale University Press, 2006.

Roberts, Geoffrey. 'Stalin at the Tehran, Yalta, and Potsdam Conferences'. *Journal of Cold War Studies* 9, no. 4 (2007): 6–40.
Roberts, Mary Louise. *What Soldiers Do: Sex and the American GI in World War II France*. Chicago, IL: University of Chicago Press, 2013.
Robinson, G. W. S. 'West Berlin: The Geography of an Exclave'. *Geographical Review* 43, no. 4 (1953): 540–57.
Roggenbuch, Frank. *Das Berliner Grenzgängerproblem: Verflechtung und Systemkonkurrenz vor dem Mauerbau*. Berlin: Walter de Gruyter, 2008.
Germany, Year Zero, directed by Roberto Rossellini. Italy, 1948.
Rott, Wilfried. *Die Insel: Eine Geschichte West-Berlins 1948–1990*. Munich: C. H. Beck, 2009.
Ruffner, Kevin C. 'The Black Market in Postwar Berlin. Colonel Miller and an Army Scandal'. *Prologue: Quarterly of the National Archives and Records Administration* 34, no. 3 (2002): 171–85.
Ryan, Brigadier C. E. 'The Kommandatura's Debut'. *Journal of the Royal United Service Institution* 96, no. 582 (1951): 267–70.
Ryan, Cornelius. *The Last Battle*. London: Collins, 1966.
Ryle, Gilbert. *The Thinking of Thoughts*. Saskatoon: University of Saskatchewan, 1968.
Saupe, Achim. *Der Historiker as Detektiv – der Detektiv als Historiker: Historik, Kriminalistik und der Nationalsozialismus als Kriminalroman*. Bielefeld: transcript, 2009.
Schivelbusch, Wolfgang. *In a Cold Crater: Cultural and Intellectual Life in Berlin, 1945–1948*, translated by Kelly Barry. Berkeley, CA: University of California Press, 1998.
Tatort Berlin: Werner G., der Kopf der Gladowbande, directed by Gabi Schlag and Benno Wenz. Phoenix, 2015.
Schlesinger, Klaus. *Die Sache mit Randow: Roman*. Berlin: Aufbau, 1996.
SHAEF. *Handbook for Military Government in Germany: Prior to Defeat or Surrender*. December, 1944.
Skinner, B. F. *Walden Two*. New York: Macmillan, 1948.
Smith, Jean Edward (ed.). *The Papers of Lucius D. Clay. Germany, 1945–1949*. Bloomington, IN: Indiana University Press, 1974.
Smith, Jean Edward. *Lucius D. Clay: An American Life*. New York: H. Holt, 1990.
Smith, William Gardner. *Last of the Conquerors*. London: Victor Gollancz, 1949.
Spencer, Robert. 'The Berlin Dilemma'. In *The Shaping of Postwar Germany*, edited by Edgar McInnis, Richard Hiscocks and Robert Spencer, 90–149. New York: Frederick A. Praeger, 1960.
Spitzer, Neil. 'Dividing a City'. *Wilson Quarterly* 12, no. 3 (1988): 100–22.
Staadt, Jochen. 'Die Berliner Polizei in der "Stunde Null"'. In *Feindwärts der Mauer: Das Ministerium für Staatssicherheit und die West-Berliner Polizei*, edited by Klaus Schroeder and Jochen Staadt, 18–87. Frankfurt am Main: Peter Lang, 2014.
Steege, Paul. *Black Market, Cold War: Everyday Life in Berlin, 1946–1949*. Cambridge: Cambridge University Press, 2007.
Steege, Paul. 'Ordinary Violence on an Extraordinary Stage: Incidents on the Sector Border in Postwar Berlin'. In *Performances of Violence*, edited by Austin Sarat, Carleen Basler and Thomas L. Dumm, 140–61. Amherst, MA: University of Massachusetts Press, 2011.
Steinborn, Norbert and Hilmar Krüger. *Die Berliner Polizei 1945 bis 1992: von der Militärreserve im Kalten Krieg auf dem Weg zur bürgernahen Polizei?* Berlin: Arno Spitz, 1993.

Steury, Donald P. (ed.). *On the Front Lines of the Cold War: Documents on the Intelligence War in Berlin, 1946 to 1961*. Washington, DC: CIA History Staff, Center for the Study of Intelligence, 1999.

Stirk, Peter M. R. 'Benign Occupations: The Allied Occupation of Germany and the International Law of Occupation'. In *Transforming Occupation in the Western Zones of Germany: Politics, Everyday Life and Social Interactions, 1945-55*, edited by Camilo Erlichman and Christopher Knowles, 43-59. London: Bloomsbury Academic, 2018.

Stivers, William. 'The Incomplete Blockade: Soviet Zone Supply of West Berlin, 1948-49'. *Diplomatic History* 21, no. 4 (1997): 569-602.

Stivers, William. 'Victors and Vanquished: Americans as Occupiers in Berlin, 1945-1949'. In *Armed Diplomacy: Two Centuries of American Campaigning*, edited by US Army Training and Doctrine Command and Combat Studies Institute, 157-76. Fort Leavenworth, KS: Combat Studies Institute Press, 2003.

Stivers, William and Donald A. Carter. *The City Becomes a Symbol: The U.S. Army in the Occupation of Berlin, 1945-1949*. Washington, DC: Center of Military History, United States Army, 2017.

Stumm, Walter. 'Les Meurtres d'Elisabeth Kusian'. *Revue Internationale de Police Criminelle* 62, no. 7 (1952): 278-88.

Stürickow, Regina. *Verbrechen in Berlin: 32 historische Kriminalfälle 1890-1960*. Berlin: Elsengold, 2014.

Teo, Hsu-Ming. 'The Continuum of Sexual Violence in Occupied Germany, 1945-49'. *Women's History Review* 5, no. 2 (1996): 191-218.

Thompson, Stewart and Robert Bialek. *The Bialek Affair*. London: Allan Wingate, 1955.

Till, Karen E. 'Wounded Cities: Memory-work and a Place-based Ethics of Care'. *Political Geography* 31, no. 1 (2012): 3-14.

Truman, Harry S. *Memoirs of Harry S. Truman: Years of Trial and Hope*. New York: De Capo Press, 1987.

Tunner, William H., Lieutenant General. *Over the Hump*. Washington, DC: Office of Air Force History, 1985.

United States Department of State. *Foreign Relations of the United States (FRUS), 1948, Vol. 2, Germany and Austria*. Washington, DC: United States Government Printing Office, 1973.

Usborne, Cornelie. *The Politics of the Body in Weimar Germany: Women's Reproductive Rights and Duties*. Ann Arbor, MI: University of Michigan Press, 1992.

Wagner, Patrick. *Hitlers Kriminalisten: die deutsche Kriminalpolizei und der Nationalsozialismus zwischen 1920 und 1960*. Munich: C. H. Beck, 2002.

Weber, Max. *Geistige Arbeit als Beruf: Vier Vorträge vor dem Freistudentischen Bund*. Munich: Duncker and Humblot, 1919.

Weimann, Waldemar. *Diagnose Mord: Die Memoiren eines Gerichtsmediziners*. Bayreuth: Hestia, 1964.

Weinhauer, Klaus. *Schutzpolizei in der Bundesrepublik: zwischen Bürgerkrieg und innerer Sicherheit: Die turbulenten sechziger Jahre*. Paderborn: Ferdinand Schöningh, 2003.

Weinreb, Alice A. 'Matters of Taste: The Politics of Food and Hunger in Divided Germany 1945-1971'. PhD, University of Michigan, 2009.

Werth, Alexander. *Russia at War*. New York: Dutton, 1964.

Whyte, Anne. 'Quadripartite Rule in Berlin: An Interim Report of the First Year of the Allied Control Authority'. *International Affairs* 23, no. 1 (1947): 30-41.

A Foreign Affair, directed by Billy Wilder. Paramount, 1948.

Williamson, D. G. *A Most Diplomatic General: The Life of General Lord Robertson of Oakridge*. London: Brassey's, 1996.

Willoughby, John. 'The Sexual Behavior of American GIs During the Early Years of the Occupation of Germany'. *The Journal of Military History* 62, no. 1 (1998): 155–74.

Winckler, Stefan. 'Ein Markgraf als williger Vollstrecker des Totalitarismus. Die Biographie des deutschen Berufsoldaten Paul H. Markgraf (SED) unter besonderer Berücksichtigung seiner Amtszeit als Berliner Polizeipräsident 1945–48/49'. In *Die DDR – Analysen eines aufgegebenen Staates*, edited by Heiner Timmermann, 343–56. Berlin: Duncker and Humblot, 2001.

Wirth, Ingo and Andreas Schmeling. *Kriminelle Leichenzerstuckelung: Phänomenologie und Untersuchungsmethodik*. Baden-Baden: Nomos, 2017.

Wolff, Michael W. *Die Währungsreform in Berlin: 1948/49*. Berlin: Walter de Gruyter, 1991.

Zander, Hartmut. 'Falldarstellung: Die Gladow-Bande'. In *Festschrift: 75 Jahre Mordinspektion in Berlin, 1926–2001*, edited by Der Polizeipräsident in Berlin, 82–4. Berlin: Polizeipräsident, 2001.

Ziemke, Earl F. *The U.S. Army in the Occupation of Germany, 1944–1946*. Washington, DC: Center of Military History, United States Army, 1975.

Zierenberg, Malte. *Berlin's Black Market, 1939–1950*. New York: Palgrave Macmillan, 2015.

Zink, Harold. *The United States in Germany, 1944–1955*. Princeton, NJ: D. Van Nostrand, 1957.

Zroka, Amy L. 'Serving the Volksgemeinschaft: German Red Cross Nurses in the Second World War'. PhD, University of California, San Diego, 2015.

Index

abortion   24, 44, 55, 211
access
  agreements   27–8, 104, 124–5, 150, 164–8, 175–6
  air   167
  ground   125, 164
  unfettered   164, 168
accidents   33, 44, 52, 84
  air   126, 170
Adenauer, Konrad (1876–1967), first Chancellor of the Federal Republic (1949–63)   174
African Americans   70, 103–22, 226, 231
Airlift, Allied   126, 164–82, 192, 199, 226, 233
airplanes   126–7, 169–70
airports   105, 156, 169, 172
Alexanderplatz   21, 47, 186, 189, 206
  police headquarters   21, 47, 206
allied
  bombing   8, 21–2, 24, 34, 40, 46, 211
  collaboration, cooperation
    breakdown   2, 110–18, 133–4, 136, 157, 185, 233
    model   5, 10, 27, 103–10
    Soviet/East German   34–5, 150, 164, 175–6
    sticking points   9–10, 132–3
  Control Council   33, 104–5, 107–9, 114, 124–5, 127
  encounters with Germans
    alliance/protection   170, 176–7, 233
    sex   62, 64, 82–99
    stereotypes/hostility   4, 8, 227
  expectations   8, 22, 88, 177
  Kommandatura
    cooperation   35, 48, 54, 75, 105–9, 116, 229
    lofty ideals   3, 5, 13
    oversight of policing   13, 106, 112, 137, 142, 229

  Soviet walkout   142, 156, 167
  tensions/breakdown   35, 114–16, 124, 127–34, 142–3, 167, 229
  veto   114–16, 136
  observers   9, 29, 31, 86, 114, 155, 185
  occupation law   42, 46, 107, 110, 225
  pilots   126, 169–70, 175, 226
  plans
    for 4-power governance   9, 106
    for police reform   128, 136
    for possession of western sectors   29, 31
    for postwar intelligence   71, 130
    for a separate West German governnment   116, 125, 166
  plenty   75, 87, 123, 177, 227
  resolve   169, 171, 176
  soldiers
    desire   52, 61–99
    hostility to Germans   25, 28, 61–81
    immunity   46, 54–5, 61
    interactions   4, 7–9, 61, 110
    protection of civilians   32, 153
    unity   106, 109, 113, 123, 127, 130
    withdrawal   28, 104, 126, 166, 175, 231
Alltagsgeschichte (the history of everyday life)   9–13, 35, 49, 232
American Sector
  arrival   28, 30–4
  lawlessness   133, 142–3
  policing   42–3, 46, 48, 51, 53, 62, 111–12, 127–8, 131, 207
  sovereignty   125–6, 170–1, 225, 227
Andreas-Friedrich, Ruth (1901–77)   25, 61, 88, 150
Anglo-Americans   30, 48, 105–6, 112, 127, 132, 165
anti-fraternization ban   8, 63–4, 66, 69, 75, 83, 89, 91, 93

arbitrary arrests   110, 128–31, 135, 152–3, 193
Ashworth, Ray (1905–60), Head of the US Public Safety Branch (1945–9)   109, 131, 136
asocials   44, 173, 191
asylum   149, 185

bad faith   9, 28, 112, 132, 165
Bahr, Egon (1922–2015)   33, 134, 169, 225
Balfour, Michael (1908–95)   7, 154
barter
  economy   68, 75
  mart   71–2, 192
behaviour
  bad   7, 23, 25, 30, 61, 66, 69, 73–4, 76, 84–7, 91, 111, 225
  civilized   25, 108
  criminal   3, 10, 47, 194–5, 210, 228
  symbolic   3–4, 12, 147, 233
Berlin
  Battle of   8, 187, 191, 199
  Constitution of   129, 134
  Schnauze   228
  stubborn resilience   174, 177
  underworld   53, 193, 198
Berliner Zeitung   27, 43, 150, 215–18
Berzarin, Nikolai (1904–45), Soviet Governor of Berlin (1945)   27, 40, 43
Bevin, Ernest, Foreign Secretary (1945–51)   169
biopolitics   3–4, 11, 227
Bizone   113, 123–4, 132
black
  Guards   142–3, 150–2
  identity (*see* African Americans)
  market
    Allied involvement   4, 8, 44, 61, 66–73, 75–6, 89, 117
    currency reform   148–51, 158, 165, 173, 176, 226
    DP involvement   8, 53–5
    German involvement   22, 45, 51–3, 185, 187, 190–1, 198, 205, 216, 219, 228
    police involvement   47, 55, 125, 131
  marketeers   45–6, 53–4, 72, 165, 173, 186–7, 190–1, 211

Blockade
  counter-blockade   172, 174–5
  hunger   172–3
  Soviet   11, 145, 148, 151–3, 157, 164–82, 190, 233
Bond, Captain Charles C.   32, 127, 150
border
  clashes   142–63
  warning signs   31, 151
borderscape   11, 233
Bourne, General (Baron) Geoffrey (1902–82), British Commandant (1949–51)   108
Brandenburg Gate   5, 29–30, 155, 191
Brandt, Willy (1913–92)   134, 170
bravery   40, 54, 62, 158, 174
Brett-Smith, Richard (1923–)   33, 155
British Sector
  historiographically neglected   1, 5
  policing   48, 50, 128, 207–8
  sovereignty   30, 42, 150
  Soviet interactions   10, 26, 30, 126, 153, 156
Buchenwald   112, 168
Byrnes, James F. (1882–1972), US Secretary of State (1945–7)   113

capitalism   11, 112–13, 124, 157, 165–6, 171, 177, 230
Capone, Al (1899–1947)   188, 190, 194, 196, 198–9
Carlucci, Orazio R. (1910–85), Director Criminal Investigation Division US Army (1946–9)   63, 73, 85
chaos
  economic   147, 164
  exploitation of   71, 117–18
  lawlessness of defeat   8, 21–2, 30, 32–3, 40–1, 44–7, 54–5, 226
  overcoming   55, 228–9
Charlottenburg   10, 42, 44, 133, 205, 207–8, 219
children
  American arming of   73
  crimes against   44, 55, 205
  crimes by   45, 48, 50–2, 195–6, 225
  dead, lost, traumatized   1, 21, 23, 206, 211, 217, 219–20
  'wild oats'   63, 82, 91–2, 94

Churchill, (Sir) Winston S. (1874–1965), Prime Minister (1940–5, 1951–5)   9, 28, 34, 103, 114, 117, 124, 126
cigarette economy
  combatting   109, 148–9
  exchanged for food   8, 47, 53, 75–6, 186, 191, 226
  exchanged for sex   50, 63–4, 67–9, 75–6, 90
City
  Assembly   115, 142, 144–7, 151–4, 156, 158
  Executive (*Magistrat*)
    in the power structure   13, 109, 172
    Soviet disruption   142, 144–7, 153, 158
    Soviet influence on   26, 106, 114–15
    western dominated   115, 129–30, 132, 134, 151
Clay, Lucius D. (1898–1978), US Military Governor (1947–9)
  decisions   5–6, 64, 66, 71–3, 75, 93, 103–7, 114, 117, 123–6, 170–1, 228
  Mark   148, 151
  perceptions   61–2, 107, 116–17, 129, 156, 170, 227–8
  relations with Howley   33, 106, 111, 133
  relations with Soviets   31, 70–1, 104–5, 107, 110–14, 124–6, 144, 164–71, 174, 176–7
coffee   53, 66–7, 75, 90, 148, 210, 212, 219
cold war
  French role in   5, 166
  height   135–7, 142, 146, 148, 151, 154–5, 158, 174–7, 199
  hiatus   51, 127
  historiography   5, 10, 113, 116, 123, 164
  logic   131, 215–16, 218–20
  onset   9–13, 94, 116, 118, 131, 157, 226, 228–33
  perceptions/outlooks   2–3, 116
colonial attitudes   6, 145, 166, 225

Communist Party of Germany (KPD)   9, 27, 44, 114, 154
Communists, German
  elections   113–15, 128
  involvement in local government   26–7, 35, 41–2
  involvement in policing   109, 130–1, 134–6
  pre-1945 outlook   43–4, 146–7
  public order   111, 144, 146–7, 151–2, 157–8, 230
  and Soviet capture of Berlin   25, 228
community   49, 52, 65, 171
  black   91
  policing   2, 49–50, 224
complicity   3, 25, 132, 175, 177, 205, 232
Concentration Camps   8, 43–4, 53, 62, 112, 125, 146–7, 154, 189, 191
crime
  cross-border   4, 11, 13, 185–204, 212, 220
  waves   13, 24, 55, 61, 205, 213, 216, 230
Criminal Investigation Division (CID)   63, 71, 73, 85
cruelty   2, 4, 25, 34, 44, 62, 72, 88, 94, 191, 219
currency reform   66, 123–5, 144, 148, 157, 164–6, 174–5, 191

Dahlem   192, 198
danger
  to Allies   61, 118, 169
  to German civilians   7, 22, 54, 66, 73, 75, 92, 129, 158, 193, 225
  to police   50–2, 153, 185–7, 193, 195–7, 199
  to public order   110, 151, 157–8
death penalty   83, 197–9, 228
defeat
  German
    Allied role in   7–10, 26, 28, 61–3, 73, 75, 82–3, 88, 93–4, 111, 116–18, 225–6
    consequences of   1–2, 4, 21, 33–5, 53–4, 187, 219, 228–9, 231–3
    overcoming   155
    policing   12–13, 41, 44

SED   114
    of the Soviet Blockade   177
De Gaulle, General Charles
        (1890–1970)   108
democracy
    American notions of   3, 34, 76, 85–6,
        91–3, 143, 170, 228
    different Allied notions   108
    as a form of 'reeducation'   3, 8, 71, 73,
        113–14, 118
    local, strength of   10, 43, 137, 152,
        154–5, 158, 170, 175, 178,
        224–5, 233
    in the police   135
    Polish   28
    Soviet contempt for   124, 146–7, 152,
        157–8
democratization   5, 40, 109, 113, 134, 198
denazification   5, 41, 47, 71, 103, 146,
        228
detective(s)
    carrying pistols   46
    female   51–2
    fiction   12–13
    phony   47
    private   85
    squads   41, 47–8, 194–5, 206–8, 216,
        218
    training   42
Deutschmark (DM)   144, 148, 165,
        172–3, 206, 211
dictatorship   9, 22, 26, 42, 111, 127–8,
        146, 171, 226
disappearances   41–3, 47, 110, 129–30
discipline
    Allied   7, 23, 61, 64, 66–7, 70, 83–5,
        93
    Communist   109
    female   50
    German notions of   35, 45, 54, 164
disease   7, 34–5, 105
    contagious   33, 107
    venereal   24, 44–5, 62, 65, 84, 90, 94
dismantling of industry   26, 31, 113, 123,
        136
Displaced Persons (DPs)   1, 8, 34, 46,
        53–4
drinking, drunkenness   22–3, 29–30, 63,
        66, 69, 74–5, 176, 210

East German
    Communists   230
    newsreel   136
    state   114, 124, 144, 173–4, 198
    writer(s)   188
Eastmark (*Ostmark*)   165, 172–3
East-West
    negotiations   28, 104–5, 144, 152, 165,
        167–8
    relations   6, 31, 71, 166, 176
        collapse   51, 110, 112, 114, 118,
        129, 131, 136–7
economy
    cigarette (*see* cigarette economy)
    collapse   109, 144, 147–8, 164–5,
        172–3
    recovery, revival   9, 113, 115–16, 123,
        144, 164
Eisenhower, General Dwight D. (1890–
        1969), Supreme Commander
        (1943–5), US Military Governor
        (1945)   9, 31, 73, 87, 91, 104
equality   82, 89, 91, 227
equipment, police   2, 40, 45, 54, 109, 127,
        230
espionage   2, 43, 71, 129, 152, 231
execution(s)   22, 42, 83–4, 188–9, 198–9,
        233

firearms   22
    Allied   32, 61, 87
    Gladow Gang   185, 187–90, 192, 194,
        198–9
    police   45–6, 230
flags
    American   31
    French tricolour   29
    Soviet red   30, 134, 155–6
food
    provisioning
        by all Allies   107, 144
        by Western Allies   9, 26, 31, 33,
        103, 130, 164–82, 228
    scarcity   8, 22, 26, 35, 45–7, 55, 61,
        63–4, 66, 148, 226
    swapped for sex   8, 24, 68–9, 75, 87,
        90, 227
forced labourers   21–2, 53
forgery   43, 52, 152, 165

four-power government
  experiment   1, 9, 13, 103–22, 125, 132
  stymying   5, 118, 132, 137, 142, 157, 174, 185
France
  German occupation of   66, 82–3, 109, 123
  and other Allies   5, 29, 104, 125, 172, 230
Fräuleins (*Veronikas*)   64, 66–7, 71, 74, 92
freedom
  fighters   113, 154, 216, 232
  gender   8, 228
  racial   3, 85, 88, 92
  West Berlin   143–4, 168, 170, 173–5, 177, 233
French Sector
  historiographical neglect of   1, 5, 123
  interactions with Soviets   105, 112, 172
  policing   46, 48, 130, 189
Friedensburg, Ferdinand (1886–1972), Interim Mayor of Berlin (1948)
  actions   134, 144, 152–4, 158
  causing suspicions   129, 147, 150, 176
  perceptions   24, 168

Ganeval, Brigadier General Jean (1894–1981), French Commandant (1946–50)
  actions as Commandant   112, 132–3, 153, 158, 168, 172–3
  biography   6, 112
gender   3–4, 93, 206, 228
genocide   3, 44, 53, 82, 146, 228, 230
geopolitics, geopolitical
  biopolitics   11, 227
  border   27, 157, 185, 199
  chasm   3–4, 207, 213
  implications   62, 144, 148, 170
German
  civilians
    crimes against   23–4, 31, 33–4, 62, 67, 69, 93, 143, 151
    fraternization with   64, 72, 87–9
    manipulation of   126–7, 225
    sacrifices of   170
  division   103, 113–14, 124, 164, 174
  economy   103–4, 113, 123, 144, 157

Federal Republic   6, 10, 44, 156, 174–5, 177
  'instinct to obey'   2, 129
  militarism   29, 123, 135
  punishing   24, 64, 113, 123, 205
  state(s)   30, 45, 177
    East German (*see* German Democratic Republic (GDR))
    West German   123, 125, 164, 174, 233
German Democratic Republic (GDR)   188, 193
Gestapo   40, 43–4, 71, 111, 133, 135, 143, 146, 154
GIs   62–4, 68–9, 75, 83–4, 87–90, 92, 94
Goebbels, Joseph (1897–1945)   4, 43, 88, 135, 155
governance
  correct   26
  cross-border   156, 213, 218
  four-power 'civico-military'   1–2, 103, 117, 228, 230
Greater Berlin
  boundaries of   105
  division of
    geopolitical   4, 10–12, 27, 103, 116, 228–9
    implications   13, 127, 142–63, 185, 199, 213, 216, 218–20, 231–2
    governance   40, 105, 116
    special quadripartite status   156, 165
Grunewald   29, 194
guilt   43, 47, 54, 69, 84, 146, 195, 213–14, 217–19, 225

hegemony   3, 34, 219, 230, 232–3
Heinrich, Karl (1890–1945), Head of the *Schutzpolizei* (1945)   42–4, 47, 130–1
Herbert, Major General E. Otway (1901–84) British Commandant (1947–9)   26, 108, 130, 153, 166, 169
Herrschaft (domination)   2–3, 146, 225, 230, 232–3
holocaust. *See* genocide
hostility
  to black soldiers   85, 88

cold war 9–10, 109, 115, 136, 171, 176, 231
  to Germans 8, 33, 63–4, 69
  from Soviets 34
Howley, Colonel Frank L. (1903–93), US Deputy Commandant (1945–7), Commandant (1947–9)
  arrival of US troops in Berlin 28–9, 31
  'Beast of Berlin' 29, 33, 173
  black market 67–8, 151
  hostility to Soviets 6, 32, 34, 108–9, 118, 158, 171, 178
  influence on policing 42, 73, 109, 111, 132–3, 151, 153
  and *Kommandatura* 133
  relations with Clay 106, 111, 166
humanitarianism 176, 227, 233
humiliation 5, 61, 108, 114, 167, 175, 231
hunger
  Blockade 172–3, 177
  as a cause of crime 12–13, 51, 55, 75, 186, 205, 228
  inescapable 8, 24, 33, 35, 45, 108, 177, 191, 226

illegal
  arms 61
  arrests 31, 128–9, 134
  police actions 144, 166
  trading 66–8, 70, 148, 151, 158
incidents
  border 126, 137, 151, 156
  diplomatic 32, 126, 130, 171
  involving black troops 83–4, 93
  involving French 67
  involving Russians 44
indiscipline 23, 64, 66, 84, 93
injury 22, 25, 52, 86, 108, 210
interference
  foreign 224
  French 67
  Magistrat 129
  Soviet 34, 43, 124–5, 158

Jews 8, 53–4, 82, 135, 146, 187
justice
  application 24, 42, 225
  eastern 156, 185, 197, 216, 218–19, 232
  racial 82–4
  summary 48, 83, 110
juvenile offenders 48, 188, 198

Kanig, Hans, Head of the *Schutzpolizei* (1945–8) 50, 112, 130–1, 134
Khrushchev, Nikita (1894–1971) 171
kidnapping(s) 55, 128–30, 132, 142, 158, 186, 231
Kotikov, Major General Aleksandr G. (1902–81), Soviet Commandant (1946–50) 132–3, 143, 152–3, 158
Kreuzberg 31, 111, 134, 143

law
  Allied occupation 1–2, 107, 127, 227
  British 42
  Federal German 156, 174
  German 42, 107, 110–11
  martial 42, 61, 107, 111
  Nazi 198
  and order
    collapse 1–3, 8, 13, 22, 85, 110
    concept 10, 27
    eroded by the black market 52, 76, 188
    maintaining 61–2, 67, 107, 112, 127, 144
    restoration 31–2, 34–5, 49, 54–5, 225–6, 228, 230–1, 233
lawlessness 8, 13, 52, 61, 85, 226, 228, 231
legal
  limbo 110, 129, 208, 228
  texts 48
Lenin, Vladimir (1870–1924), Head of the Soviet Government (1917–24) 154, 195
London 10, 166–7
looting 22, 26, 31–2, 62, 66
love
  Allied-German 63–4, 69, 75, 90–4, 226
  defending 23
  promiscuous 210–12, 216–17, 219–20

Magistrat. See City, Executive
market, black
   Allies   8, 22, 61, 185
   DPs   53–4
   immoral   4, 47, 52, 205, 216, 228
   necessitating currency reform   125, 148, 165, 176
   police and   55, 131
   sex and   44, 66–7, 71, 89, 226
   Soviets   67–8
marketeers, black
   Allied   68
   Allied wives   72
   child/adolescent   45
   currency reform   148–51, 165, 173
   foreign   53–4
   gangs   46, 186, 190–1, 211
Markgraf, Colonel Paul (1910–93), Police President (1945–9)
   biography   40–1
   deputy (*see* Stumm, Johannes (1897–1978), Police President of West Berlin (1948–62))
   Magistrat   109, 129, 144–5
   police   130, 134–5, 149–51, 154–5, 158
   as Police President   40–4, 46, 109, 112, 128, 131, 134, 137, 143, 153, 190, 197
   Public Safety Committee   109, 129, 131, 133
   supine attitude to the Soviets   41, 43, 112, 116, 127–9, 131
Marshall, George C. (1880–1959), US Secretary of State (1947–9)   107, 115–16, 177
Meader, George (1907–94)   84, 89, 93
media   112, 129, 142, 148, 198, 215
mentalities, history   1–4, 6, 10–12, 226–9, 232–3
military
   Government
      Allied   7, 61, 76, 107–8, 110–12, 129
      American   29, 31–2, 69–73, 92, 106, 111, 117, 125, 127
      British   30, 156, 225
      French   66, 130, 172
      Governors   5–6, 30–1, 64, 67, 73, 86, 107, 116, 124, 166

Policemen
   American   29, 46, 83, 149, 171
   British   42, 62, 150, 155
   French   67
   responsibilities   53, 61, 158
Miller, Colonel Francis P. (1895–1978)   63, 70–4, 82–5, 87
monetary   144, 164–5, 226
money
   exchange of   148, 206, 211
   gained from black market   68, 70
   ill-gotten gains   189–92, 196, 199, 210, 232
Montgomery, Field Marshal Bernard (1887–1976) British Military Governor (1945–6)   64, 104, 109
morale   64, 66, 76, 85, 87, 93
morality   68, 154, 197, 226, 232
Moscow   9, 28, 104, 117, 123, 132, 154, 168, 231
   Conference   103
   Radio   40
murder
   actors   1, 22, 30–1, 47, 91, 190, 194–5, 199, 205–23, 232
   attempts to combat   24, 42, 44, 135, 185
Murphy, Robert D. (1894–1978) US Political Adviser in Germany (1948)   153, 166
mutual suspicion   30, 106, 112, 117–18, 123–4, 129, 136–7

National Association for the Advancement of Colored People (NAACP)   83–4, 86, 90, 94
Nazism
   consequences of   52, 63
   resurgence   135, 154
   victims   23, 146, 185, 198, 216, 220, 226, 232
   victory over   44
Neues Deutschland
   opinion   48, 150, 187, 219
   propaganda   129, 146–7, 152, 173, 198, 217
Neukölln   31, 43, 51, 143, 146, 218

newspapers
  American 33
  black 87, 92
  German 50, 130, 199, 205
  West Berlin 115, 129, 131
NKVD 9, 31, 43, 110, 128
nurses, nursing 48, 207–12, 214, 219, 232

occupation, occupiers
  expectations 5, 8, 22, 104–5, 109
  guarantee of democracy 118, 136, 155, 175, 229, 233
  law 42, 107, 110, 112, 225
  nature 1–3, 5, 9, 61, 68, 72–6, 156, 224–5
  relations with Germans 3, 8, 29–30, 33, 46, 54, 61–2, 64, 67, 73, 115, 176–7, 225–6
  relations with Soviets 10, 28, 31–2, 35, 106, 130, 164–82, 226–8
  sexual politics 4, 8, 25, 62–4, 66, 69, 82–99, 226–7, 233
offspring, mixed-race. *See* children, 'wild oats'
operation
  'Talk Back' 117
  'Unthinkable' 28
  'Vittles' 169
Ostmark. See Eastmark

parasites 52, 54, 151
Paris 5, 10, 104, 106, 167
parties
  Antifascist 9, 27, 40, 114
  political 34, 106, 128, 131, 147
patrolling 42, 45–9, 143, 190
  Allied 27, 32, 171
  officers 49, 51, 55, 130, 224, 230
People's Police (*Volkspolizei*)
  dealing with Gladow 189, 198
  dealing with Kusian 207–9, 216–19
  post-split 11, 147–51, 153, 232
  pre-split 47
pistols
  in the hands of Allies 61, 73, 153
  in the hands of criminals 185, 188–90, 193–6, 199
  in the hands of police 27, 43, 46, 51, 135, 150–1

Poland 28, 135, 187, 191
police, policing
  activism 128
  canteen culture 49–50, 231
  criminal activity 130
  culture, values 3, 49, 224, 229–30
  English bobby as model 127, 230
  expertise 3, 41, 44–5, 47–8, 54, 127–8, 134, 136
  files 47, 83, 134, 136
  'flying squads' 53, 110
  mug-shots 134, 136
  People's (*see* People's Police (*Volkspolizei*))
  photographic lab 130
  post-conflict reform 2, 13, 107, 198, 224, 228–9
  precincts 49, 130, 151, 218
  President (*see* Markgraf, Colonel Paul (1910–93), Police President (1945–9); Stumm, Johannes (1897–1978), Police President of West Berlin (1948–62))
  Presidium 21, 40–1, 43, 128, 131, 157, 186, 208
  professionalization 44–5, 134, 228
  radio cars 130, 157
  reform
    hopes 2, 13, 40–1, 109, 157
    reality 49, 112, 127, 136, 157, 224–5, 227–9
  separation, splitting 123–43, 146, 148–51, 156, 158, 185, 218, 231–2
  structure 40–1, 224, 228
  unity 127, 130, 207
  women 2, 35, 48–52, 54, 228
politicians, non-Communist 115, 118, 136, 144–5, 147, 152–3, 158, 172, 174, 213, 229
Potsdam 29, 126
  Conference 5, 28, 46, 103, 108, 117, 123–5, 164, 167–8
Potsdamer Platz 54, 148, 150–1, 158
poverty 35, 75, 192, 205, 226–8
power
  Allied 127–8, 136
  asymmetrical imbalance 2–3, 50, 52, 66, 69, 73, 75, 92, 107, 111, 214, 224–5, 227, 230, 232–3

behind the throne   27, 116, 144, 155, 164, 175
local balance of   118, 124
powerless   5, 70, 191
Soviet   10, 43
of the street/crowd   147
vacuum   26
of weapons   188, 196, 198–9
prison
  Brandenburg   43–4
  Gladow   191, 194–5, 199
  Plötzensee   188
  sentences   23, 42–3, 52, 129, 153–4, 158, 232
  Spandau   10, 156
  transport   47, 213
Prisoners of War (POWs)   1, 22, 52
propaganda
  anti-Soviet   25–6, 93, 131, 175
  anti-Western   94, 112, 115, 117, 128, 132, 146, 149, 152, 155–6, 188
  Nazi   4, 24–5, 82, 88
  oral   8, 31
  Soviet   30, 40, 43
  war   3, 116–17, 142–4, 169, 174
prostitution   8, 44, 51, 53, 68–9, 75, 90, 92, 186, 211
protectors
  Allied   24, 29, 61–3, 76, 126, 153, 172–3, 233
  German   23
  state   47, 231
Prussian drill/militarism   5, 29, 45
psychological
  recovery   47
  warfare   41, 106, 131, 166, 170, 188, 199, 215
  wounds   11, 33, 70, 185, 191, 208, 214, 220, 228, 231
Public Safety
  Branch   47, 61, 85, 109, 128, 131
  Committee   13, 48, 106, 110, 127, 129–30, 229, 231

quadripartite government
  attempts to foster   32, 106–8, 114
  fiction   116, 130, 133, 167
  residue   117–18, 156, 165

racial
  defilement   82
  mixing   92
  problems   93
  superiority, supremacy   4, 7, 69, 74, 82, 86–7, 89, 91–4
  utopia   92
Radio in the American Sector (RIAS)   117, 130, 134, 152–3, 177, 211
rape   22, 29–30, 32, 42, 44, 61–3, 75, 83, 85
  'Frau komm'   23, 114, 173, 233
  gang, mass   10, 23–6, 226–7
razzias   51, 53, 107, 148, 150–1, 186, 188
Red Army   4, 7, 10, 24–7, 31–2, 34, 44, 68, 118, 143, 146, 173
refugees   1, 22, 33, 52, 107
Reichsbahn   126, 195, 230
Reichstag   152–3
  demonstration   154–6, 158
Reinickendorf   5, 67, 185
reparations   9, 25–6, 31, 103–4, 113, 115, 117, 123
reporting crime   22, 24, 186
respect
  to black soldiers   88–90
  criminal   185, 188, 190, 193, 198
  to victors   10, 30, 67, 118, 146, 158, 171, 176
  to women   209
  to women police   48
Reuter, Ernst (1889–1953), Mayor of West Berlin (1948–53)
  currency reform   144, 164, 173, 175–6
  local SPD leader   115
  Reichstag speech   153–6, 158
  Stumm and   136
  vetoed Mayor   115–16, 118
revenge   22–3, 25, 34–5, 67, 188
Riess, Curt (1902–93)   41, 76, 106, 195
robbery   22, 31, 42, 189, 193–4, 197, 213
Robertson, (Sir) Brian (1896–1974), British Deputy Military Governor (1945–8), Military Governor (1948–9)   6, 67, 116, 124, 166–7, 169, 225
Roosevelt, Franklin D. (1882–1945), President (1933–45)   28, 34, 165

rubble, ruins
  films 155
  moral landscape 185, 226–8
  prize 29, 72, 76, 148, 226
  stinking cemetery 12, 21, 33–5, 41, 218
  warren 7, 51–2, 68, 150, 174, 205–6, 212
  women (*Trümmerfrauen*) 172, 227

sacrifice 34, 50, 54, 94, 146, 177, 188, 199
sadism 23, 44, 75, 133
saluting 29, 32, 46, 156
Saxony 29, 206, 211
S-Bahn 26, 137, 212
scapegoats 146, 233
Scheunenviertel 186
Schöneberg 32, 147
Schroeder, Louise (1887–1957), Deputy Mayor of Berlin (1947–8) 116, 152
Schupos (*Schutzpolizei*) 29, 43, 50–1, 130, 150, 191
Schutzstaffel (SS) 21, 44, 143, 187
sector border, boundary
  commandants 4, 13, 31, 112, 115, 125
  four-sectory city 8, 67, 110, 156
  liminality as a source of crime 11, 13, 46, 66, 110, 174, 185–6, 189–90, 192, 212–13
  police (non-)cooperation 142, 148–51, 153, 157–8, 194, 199, 208, 218
  police permission to pass 135, 137
security
  Allies as a source 27, 30, 61, 64, 225
  French concerns 109, 114
  policing as a source 2, 46
  vacuum of 35, 73, 156, 158, 229–31
self-government 113, 142, 145
Senate, United States 70, 83–4, 89, 93
sexism 49, 51, 55
sexual
  gratification 205
  transmitted diseases 24, 44, 64–5, 90–1
  violence (*see* rape)
Shanghai 2, 110–11, 117, 225, 231

shootings, shoot-outs
  by Americans 9, 31–2, 73, 85, 133, 225
  by criminals 22, 155, 185, 189–90, 192–5, 197–8
  by French 67
  by police 53, 150, 158, 231
shop windows 12, 144, 175, 193
Smith, William Gardner (1927–74) 7, 89, 92
Social Democratic Party of Germany (SPD)
  forced merger 9, 113–15, 118
  leaders 67, 154, 176
  members in the police 41, 131, 136
  newspapers 144, 151, 168
  as a spearhead for opposition 146–7, 152, 156
Socialist Unity Party (SED)
  defeat 110, 114–15
  harassment 135
  infiltration 130–1
  members 41, 156, 173
  merger 9, 108, 114
  organ 146
  protests 116, 143–7, 188
  unpopularity 155
Sokolovsky, Marshal Vasily (1897–1968), Supreme Head of Soviet Military Administration German (1946–9) 6, 25, 107, 110, 124–6, 153, 165–6, 168, 171
sovereignty 3, 123, 144, 147, 165, 219, 225, 233
Soviet
  Memorial 10, 155, 191
  radio station 10, 30, 75, 144, 170, 172
  Sector
    comparison with other sectors 89
    lawlessness 46, 186, 189, 195, 206–7, 213
    policing 48, 53, 110–11, 130–1, 135–6, 150
    pre-emptive calculated actions 9, 26, 105–6, 114–15, 144–5, 152–3
    role in cold war 126–33, 155–6, 158
  walkout 125, 132–4, 142

Stalin, Joseph (1878–1953), General Secretary of the Communist Party of the Soviet Union (1922–52)
　Blockade　166–8, 171, 174–5, 177
　calculations, intentions　26, 28, 30, 34, 72, 104, 110, 113–14, 116–17
　Ernst Reuter　154–5
　fear of German resurgence　123–4, 164, 175–6, 233
Stalingrad　40, 127, 169
Stalinism　42, 124, 143, 146, 177, 195
Stasi (*Staatssicherheit*)　41–2, 135–6
station(s)
　Alexanderplatz　191, 206
　Friedrichstrasse　53, 212
　Lehrter　213
　Stettiner　206
　Zoo　173, 189, 206, 210–12, 218
street
　demonstrations　41, 111, 142, 146, 152, 155–6, 158
　fighting　191, 233
Stumm, Johannes (1897–1978), Police President of West Berlin (1948–62)
　biography　135–6
　as Police President　134–6, 149–52, 192–3, 199, 207–8, 231
　as Vice-President　41, 43–4, 50
Stumm Police　134, 136, 149, 151, 190, 216, 230
suffering, collective　23–6, 33, 35, 46, 69, 154, 175, 177–8
survival strategies　24, 63, 226

Taylor, General Maxwell D. (1901–87), US Commandant (1949–51)　6, 93, 155
terrorism　23, 85, 91, 130–1, 142–3, 146, 148, 152, 168
Thuringia　29, 210
Tiergarten　61
totalitarians　114, 146, 177
training, police　42, 45–6, 48, 49, 51, 127, 193, 214, 224, 228
trains　26, 33, 212
　military　124–6

Truman, Harry S. (1884–1972), US President (1945–53)　28, 34, 72–3, 85, 103, 115, 117, 124, 168–9
Trümmerfrauen. *See* rubble, ruins, women
truncheons　43, 45–6, 51, 149–50, 152, 158

Ulbricht, Walter (1893–1973), First Secretary of the SED (1950–71)　9, 26–7, 40, 127
uniform(s)　21
　American　46, 66, 83, 86–90, 94, 143
　nurse's　210–12, 215
　police　3, 41, 45, 48–50, 55, 133, 135, 210, 230
　Soviet　4, 46
uniformed police. *See Schupos*
United Nations (UN)　5, 53, 108
unity, German　104, 113–14, 124, 134, 146, 151, 157, 207
US intelligence　63, 66, 70–1, 73–4, 85, 117, 126

vice　8, 44, 52, 63, 66, 72, 196, 226–7
victors
　divisions　25, 30, 229, 231
　initial consensus　75, 103, 109, 111, 115, 227
　overbearing　225–6
　respect for Soviets　10, 118
　second-class　5
Vienna　2, 27, 47, 227
violence
　in and as a consequence of war　2–3, 7, 12, 52, 62, 227–8
　criminal　192–3, 197, 205
　legitimate　2, 34, 67, 231
　mob　114, 142–63
　sexual (*see* rape)
Volkspolizei. *See* People's Police (*Volkspolizei*)
Volkssturm　21, 187, 191
Völpel, Gustav (1901–59)　188–90, 192, 194, 199

Wagner, Rudolf　131, 150, 152
war of nerves　9, 116, 126, 133, 136–7

Washington, District of Columbia
  alarm in   124, 126, 153, 167, 169
  comparable crime rates   62
  orders from   9–10, 106, 169, 231
wedding   5, 67, 130
Wehrmacht   21, 40, 44–5, 50, 82, 143, 191–2
Weimann, Waldemar (1893–1965)   1, 195–9, 206, 208, 210–11, 213–15, 218–19
Weimar Republic   8, 41, 43, 128, 135, 152
Western Allies
  anti-Communism   104, 113–15
  changing views of Soviets   7, 25–7, 30–2, 34, 67, 109, 123, 143
  as conquerors   6, 29, 40, 46, 62, 74–5, 82, 118
  desire to cooperate with Soviets   8, 10, 105–7, 112, 117
  maintaining fiction of quadripartite government   115, 125, 127, 156
  as protectors/nurturers   1, 26, 42, 225, 233
  rupture   131–6, 144, 152–4, 157, 164–82, 230
western sectors
  differences from the East   29–30, 49, 51, 112, 135, 142
  lawlessness   61, 63, 110–11, 128, 158, 169
  open border   13, 125, 149, 231–2
  politics   114, 142, 144, 150, 157, 164–6, 171–4, 190
  safety   149, 151, 153, 233
  Soviet occupation of   26, 31, 136

Westmark. *See Deutschmark*
Wild West scenes   31–2, 34, 188
wives   8, 23, 63, 72–3, 92
Wolff, Jeanette (1888–1976)   146, 152, 158
Women. *See also* rubble, ruins, women police (*see* police, women)
  victims of crime   1, 22–5, 32, 34, 44, 62–3, 75, 83, 133, 147, 186
wounded city   198, 227, 231

Yalta Conference   9, 28, 103, 107–8, 117, 167–8

Zehlendorf   31
Zhukov, Marshal Georgy (1896–1974), Soviet Military Governor (1945–6)   28, 104, 107, 110, 167
zone (s)
  American   3, 9, 104, 126, 227
  British   6, 9, 188
  four   27, 107, 112, 125, 168
  French   123, 125
  Soviet
    justice   197
    politics   9, 111, 114–17, 125, 148, 190
    relations with West   113, 124, 164–6, 168, 174
    reparations   104
    territory   28, 172, 176
  western   103–4, 113, 123–5, 164–5, 167, 170, 175, 190

www.ingramcontent.com/pod-product-compliance
Lightning Source LLC
Chambersburg PA
CBHW062126300426
44115CB00012BA/1829